First World War
and Army of Occupation
War Diary
France, Belgium and Germany

23 DIVISION
Divisional Troops
Royal Army Service Corps
Divisional Train (190, 191, 192, 193 Companies A.S.C.)
1 September 1915 - 31 October 1917

WO95/2180/4

The Naval & Military Press Ltd
www.nmarchive.com
Published in association with The National Archives

Published by

The Naval & Military Press Ltd

Unit 10 Ridgewood Industrial Park,

Uckfield, East Sussex,

TN22 5QE England

Tel: +44 (0) 1825 749494

www.naval-military-press.com

www.nmarchive.com

This diary has been reprinted in facsimile from the original. Any imperfections are inevitably reproduced and the quality may fall short of modern type and cartographic standards.

© Crown Copyright
Images reproduced by permission of The National Archives, London, England, 2015.

Contents

Document type	Place/Title	Date From	Date To
Heading	WO90/2180/4 23 Division-Divisional Troops Divisional Train 1915 Sept-1917 Oct.		
Heading	23rd Division 23rd Divl Train A.S.C. Sep 1915-1917 Oct To Italy 190 To 193 Coys Asc.		
Heading	23rd Divn 23rd Divl: Train Vol. I Sept 15		
Heading	War Diary of Lieut: Col: A. Northen Commanding 23rd Divisional Train from 1st 9/15 to 30th 9		
War Diary	Tilques Nord 3 Miles from St Omer.	01/09/1915	02/09/1915
War Diary	Tilques.	03/09/1915	06/09/1915
War Diary	On March.	07/09/1915	07/09/1915
War Diary	Merris.	08/09/1915	16/09/1915
War Diary	Croix Du Bac.	17/09/1915	30/09/1915
Operation(al) Order(s)	23rd Division Operation Order No. 1. Appendix I.	05/09/1915	05/09/1915
Miscellaneous	March Table For 6th September. Appendix IA.		
Miscellaneous	Correction. Reference March Table For 6 September.	05/09/1915	05/09/1915
Operation(al) Order(s)	23rd Division Order No. 2. Appendix2	06/09/1915	06/09/1915
Miscellaneous	March Table 7th September. Appendix.2A.	07/09/1915	07/09/1915
Miscellaneous	To. OC Train. Appendix.3	11/09/1915	11/09/1915
Miscellaneous			
Operation(al) Order(s)	23rd Division Operation Order No. 3. Appendix.4	12/09/1915	12/09/1915
Miscellaneous	O.C., 97 Company, A.S.C., 27th Divisional Train. Appendix.5	15/09/1915	15/09/1915
Heading	War Diary of Lieut: Col: A. Northen Commanding 23rd Divisional Train From 1st October 1915. to 31st October 1915. Vol.2		
War Diary	Croix Du Bac.	01/10/1915	31/10/1915
Heading	23rd Div I. Train Vol.3. 121/7624. Nov.15		
Heading	War Diary Of. O.C. 23rd Div Train From 1-11-15 To 30-11-15 B.E.F. France Lieut-Colonel A-Northen A.S.C. Commanding 23rd Div. Train.		
War Diary	Croix Du Bac.	01/11/1915	30/11/1915
Heading	23rd Div I. Train Vol.4 121/7909		
Heading	War Diary. By Lt. Colonel. A. Northen Commanding XXIIIrd Divisional Train A.S.C. December 1915 To D.A.G. 3rd Echelon.		
War Diary	Croix-Du-Bac.	01/12/1915	31/12/1915
Operation(al) Order(s)	23rd Division Operation Order No. 22. Appendix (1).	01/12/1915	01/12/1915
Operation(al) Order(s)	23rd Division Operation Order No. 23. Appendix (2).	10/12/1915	10/12/1915
Operation(al) Order(s)	23rd Division Operation Order No. 24. Appendix (3).	18/12/1915	18/12/1915
Operation(al) Order(s)	23rd Division Operation Order No. 25. Appendix. (4).	25/12/1915	25/12/1915
Heading	23rd Div. Train Vol:5 Jan.		
Heading	War Diary of Lt. Colonel A. Northen. Commanding 23rd Divisional Train A.S.C. from 1st to 31st January 1916		
War Diary	Croix Du Bac.	01/01/1916	31/01/1916
Operation(al) Order(s)	23rd Division Operation Order No. 26. Appendix (1).	04/01/1916	04/01/1916
Operation(al) Order(s)	23rd Division Operation Order No. 28. Appendix. (2).	11/01/1916	11/01/1916
Operation(al) Order(s)	23rd Division Operation Order No. 29. Appendix (3).	18/01/1916	18/01/1916
Operation(al) Order(s)	23rd Division Operation Order No. 31. Appendix (4).	26/01/1916	26/01/1916
Heading	23rd Div Train Vol.6		

War Diary	Croix Du Bac.	01/02/1916	24/02/1916
War Diary	Estaire.	25/02/1916	26/02/1916
War Diary	Blaringhem.	27/02/1916	18/03/1916
Operation(al) Order(s)	23rd Division Operation Order No. 32. Appendix 1	04/02/1916	04/02/1916
Operation(al) Order(s)	23rd Division Operation Order No. 34. Appendix (2).	09/02/1916	09/02/1916
Miscellaneous	Table "A".		
Miscellaneous	To D.M.P. 35th Mobile Vet. Section. "Q". Train. 34th Division. 3rd Corps. Appendix.3	15/02/1916	15/02/1916
Miscellaneous	Reference Divl. Operation Order No. 33. (Table B.) Appendix (4).	16/02/1916	16/02/1916
Operation(al) Order(s)	23rd Division Operation Order No. 35. Appendix 5	16/02/1916	16/02/1916
Miscellaneous	Preliminary Order. Appendix (6).	23/02/1916	23/02/1916
Operation(al) Order(s)	23rd Division Operation Order No. 36. Appendix (7).		
Miscellaneous			
Miscellaneous	Entraining Tables.		
Miscellaneous			
Heading	War Diary By Lt. Colonel A. Northen Commanding 23rd Divisional Train A.S.C. from 1st to 31 March 1916 The D.A.G. 3rd Echelon. 23 Div. Train Vol.7		
War Diary	Bruay-Pas De Calais.	01/03/1916	04/03/1916
War Diary	Bruay.	05/03/1916	08/03/1916
War Diary	Maisnil Bouche.	09/03/1916	16/03/1916
War Diary	Bruay.	17/03/1916	22/03/1916
War Diary	Barlin.	23/03/1916	31/03/1916
Operation(al) Order(s)	23rd Division Operation Order No. 37. Appendix (1).	03/03/1916	03/03/1916
Operation(al) Order(s)	Operation Order 37. Copy No. 7 3.3.16	03/03/1916	03/03/1916
Miscellaneous	Appendix II. Moves On 8th And 9th.		
Operation(al) Order(s)	23rd Division Operation Order No. 39. Appendix (2).	12/03/1916	12/03/1916
Operation(al) Order(s)	23rd Division Operation Order No. 40. Appendix (3).	14/03/1916	14/03/1916
Heading	War Diary of Lt. Colonel A. Northen Comdg. 23rd Div Train A.S.C. from 1st to 30th April 1916. The D.A.G. 3rd Echelon. Vol.8		
War Diary	Barlin.	01/04/1916	19/04/1916
War Diary	Bruay.	20/04/1916	30/04/1916
Operation(al) Order(s)	23rd Division Operation Order No. 42. Appendix (1).	12/04/1916	12/04/1916
Miscellaneous	March Table issued with 23rd Division Operation Order.		
Miscellaneous	With reference to 23rd Division "Training Programme" issued on 13th April the following moves will take place on the 26th:- Appendix (2).	21/04/1916	21/04/1916
Heading	War Diary By. Lieut. Colonel. A. Northen D.S.O. Commanding 23rd Divisional Train A.S.C. 6th June 1916 in the field the D.A.G. 3rd Echelon. Vol.9		
War Diary	Bruay.	01/05/1916	13/05/1916
War Diary	Barlin.	14/05/1916	31/05/1916
Heading	War Diary By Lt. Colonel A. Northen D.S.O. Commanding 23rd Divisional Train A.S.C. B.E.F. France. from 1st to 30th June 1916 In the Field The D.A.G. 3rd Echelon Base. Vol.10		
War Diary	Barlin.	01/06/1916	13/06/1916
War Diary	Bruay.	14/06/1916	15/06/1916
War Diary	Bruay.	16/06/1916	24/06/1916
War Diary	Vaux En Amienois.	25/06/1916	30/06/1916
Operation(al) Order(s)	23rd Division Order No. 48. Appendix I.	13/06/1916	13/06/1916
Miscellaneous	March Table To Accompany 23rd Division Order No. 48		

Type	Description	Date From	Date To
Miscellaneous			
Miscellaneous	Reference 23rd Division Order No. 48, of to-day's date, following alterations are made in March Table:-	13/06/1916	13/06/1916
Miscellaneous	Officers for duty at entraining stations will be detailed as follows:- Appendix.II.		
Miscellaneous	Following Amendments Will Be Made to 23rd Division Instructions No. 2. Dated 20th April, 1916	16/06/1916	16/06/1916
Miscellaneous	Entraining Routes.	16/06/1916	16/06/1916
Miscellaneous	23rd Division Instructions No. 2	20/04/1916	20/04/1916
Operation(al) Order(s)	23rd Division Order No. 50. Appendix III.	30/06/1916	30/06/1916
Miscellaneous	March Table To Accompany 23rd Division Order No. 50		
Heading	War Diary By. Lt. Colonel. A. Northen. D.S.O. Commanding 23rd Divisional Train A.S.C. From 1st to 31 July 1916. Vol.11		
War Diary	Vavx.	01/07/1916	01/07/1916
War Diary	Baizieux.	02/07/1916	04/07/1916
War Diary	Dernancourt.	05/07/1916	11/07/1916
War Diary	St. Gratien.	12/07/1916	21/07/1916
War Diary	Henencourt.	22/07/1916	26/07/1916
War Diary	Albert.	26/07/1916	31/07/1916
Operation(al) Order(s)	23rd Division Order No. 31. Appendix No. I.	03/07/1916	03/07/1916
Operation(al) Order(s)	23rd Division Order No. 54. Appendix No. 4cb.	24/07/1916	24/07/1916
Heading	War Diary By. Lt. Colonel. A. Northen D.S.O. Commanding 23rd Divisional Train A.S.C. 1st to 31st August 1916 D.A.G. 3rd Echelon. Vol.12		
War Diary	Albert.	01/08/1916	08/08/1916
War Diary	Baizieux.	09/08/1916	10/08/1916
War Diary	St. Sauveur.	11/08/1916	11/08/1916
War Diary	Ailly Le Haut Clocher.	12/08/1916	13/08/1916
War Diary	Fletre.	14/08/1916	17/08/1916
War Diary	Steenwerck.	18/08/1916	29/08/1916
War Diary	Bailleul.	30/08/1916	31/08/1916
Operation(al) Order(s)	23rd Division Order No. 59. Appendix No. I.	03/08/1916	03/08/1916
Miscellaneous	A Form Messages And Signals.		
Miscellaneous	Move To Xth Corps Area. Appendix II.	08/08/1916	08/08/1916
Operation(al) Order(s)	23rd Division Order No. 60. Appendix III.	08/08/1916	08/08/1916
Miscellaneous	Table "A".		
Miscellaneous	Move By Rail On 11th-Dismounted Personnel Only, No Vehicles, Baggage Or Horses. Table "B".		
Operation(al) Order(s)	R.A. 23rd Division Order No. 58. Appendix IV.	12/08/1916	12/08/1916
Operation(al) Order(s)	R.A. 23rd Division Order No. 59. Appendix V.	15/08/1916	15/08/1916
Miscellaneous	Entrainment Table. 23rd Divl. R.A.		
Miscellaneous		10/08/1916	10/08/1916
Heading	War Diary By. Lt. Colonel. A. Northen D.S.O. Commanding 23rd Divisional Train A.S.C. from 1st to 30th Sept 16 The D.A.G. 3rd Echelon Base. Vol.13		
War Diary	Bailleul.	01/09/1916	06/09/1916
War Diary	Tilques.	07/09/1916	10/09/1916
War Diary	Allonville.	11/09/1916	12/09/1916
War Diary	Baizieux.	13/09/1916	19/09/1916
War Diary	Nr Albert.	20/09/1916	30/09/1916
Operation(al) Order(s)	23rd Division Order No. 66. Appendix.I.	02/09/1916	02/09/1916
Miscellaneous	March Table To Accompany Divisional Order No. 66		
Miscellaneous	A Form Messages And Signals.		
Operation(al) Order(s)	23rd Division Order No. 67. Appendix.II.	11/09/1916	11/09/1916

Miscellaneous	23rd Division No. A/2790/13	04/09/1916	04/09/1916
Miscellaneous	Arrival of 23rd Division. Administrative Instructions No. 21 dated 9/9/1916	09/09/1916	09/09/1916
Miscellaneous	March Table To Accompany Divisional Order No. 67		
Operation(al) Order(s)	23rd Division Order No. 68. Appendix III.	17/09/1916	17/09/1916
Miscellaneous	March Table To Accompany Divisional Order No. 68		
War Diary	Albert.	01/10/1916	10/10/1916
War Diary	Argoeuves.	11/10/1916	11/10/1916
War Diary	Ailly Le Haut. Clocher.	12/10/1916	12/10/1916
War Diary	St. Ricqier.	13/10/1916	15/10/1916
War Diary	Poperinghe.	16/10/1916	20/10/1916
War Diary	Busseboom.	21/10/1916	31/10/1916
Operation(al) Order(s)	23rd Division Operation Order No. 73. Appendix (1).	07/10/1916	07/10/1916
Operation(al) Order(s)	23rd Division Operation Order No. 74. Appendix (2).	10/10/1916	10/10/1916
Operation(al) Order(s)	23rd Division Operation Order No. 75. Appendix (3).	11/10/1916	11/10/1916
Operation(al) Order(s)	23rd Divisional Operation Order No. 76. Appendix (4).	15/10/1916	15/10/1916
Heading	War Diary By. Lt. Colonel A. Northen Commanding 23rd Divisional Train A.S.C. from 1st to 30th Nov 1916 The D.A.G. 3rd Echelon Base. Vol.15		
War Diary	Busseboom.	01/11/1916	30/11/1916
Operation(al) Order(s)	23rd Division Order No. 80. Appendix 1	07/11/1916	07/11/1916
Operation(al) Order(s)	23rd Division Order No. 81. Appendix II.	13/11/1916	13/11/1916
Operation(al) Order(s)	23rd Division Order No. 82. Appendix III.	19/11/1916	19/11/1916
Operation(al) Order(s)	23rd Division Order No. 83. Appendix IV.	26/11/1916	26/11/1916
War Diary	Busseboom.	01/12/1916	31/12/1916
Operation(al) Order(s)	23rd Division Order No. 84. Appendix I.	05/12/1916	05/12/1916
Miscellaneous	G.H.Q. O.A.212. Second Army G.900. X. Corps G.1/40/2. 23rd Division, No. A/4147. Appendix. II.	27/11/1916	27/11/1916
Operation(al) Order(s)	23rd Division Order No. 85. Appendix III.	14/12/1916	14/12/1916
Operation(al) Order(s)	23rd Division Order No. 86. Appendix IV.	20/12/1916	20/12/1916
Operation(al) Order(s)	23rd Division Order No. 88. Appendix. V.	28/12/1916	28/12/1916
Heading	War Diary By. Lt. Col. A. Northen D.S.O. Commanding 23rd Divisional Train A.S.C. from 1st to 31st Jan 1917. The D.A.G. 3rd Echelon Base. Vol.17		
War Diary	Busseboom.	01/01/1917	31/01/1917
Operation(al) Order(s)	23rd Division Order No. 89. Appendix I.	05/01/1917	05/01/1917
Operation(al) Order(s)	23rd Division Order No. 91. Appendix.II.	12/01/1917	12/01/1917
Operation(al) Order(s)	23rd Division Order No. 92. Appendix III.	20/01/1917	20/01/1917
Heading	War Diary By. Lt. Col. A. Northen D.S.O. Commanding 23rd Div Train A.S.O. 1st to 28 Feby 1917. Vol.18		
War Diary	Busseboom.	01/02/1917	27/02/1917
War Diary	St. Omer.	28/02/1917	28/02/1917
Operation(al) Order(s)	23rd Division Order No. 93. Appendix I.	28/01/1917	28/01/1917
Operation(al) Order(s)	23rd Division Order No. 95. Appendix II.	07/02/1917	07/02/1917
Operation(al) Order(s)	23rd Division Order No. 96. Appendix III.	14/02/1917	14/02/1917
Operation(al) Order(s)	23rd Division Order No. 97. Appendix IV.	19/02/1917	19/02/1917
Miscellaneous	March Table.		
Operation(al) Order(s)	23rd Division Order No. 99. Appendix V.	22/02/1917	22/02/1917
Heading	War Diary By Lt. Col. A. Northen D.S.O. Commanding 23rd Divisional Train A.S.C. from 1st to 31 March 1917 The D.A.G. 3rd Echelon Base. Vol.19		
War Diary	St Omer.	01/03/1917	20/03/1917
War Diary	Esquelbecq.	21/03/1917	31/03/1917
Operation(al) Order(s)	23rd Division Operation Order No. 101. Appendix I.	16/03/1917	16/03/1917
Miscellaneous	March Table.		

Type	Description	Date From	Date To
War Diary	Esquelbecq.	01/04/1917	07/04/1917
War Diary	Proven.	08/04/1917	11/04/1917
War Diary	Busseboom.	11/04/1917	30/04/1917
Operation(al) Order(s)	23rd Division Operation Order No:102. Appendix I.	04/04/1917	04/04/1917
Miscellaneous	March Table.		
Operation(al) Order(s)	Continuation of 23rd Division Order No. 102 dated 4th April, 1917. Appendix.II.	04/04/1917	04/04/1917
Operation(al) Order(s)	23rd Division Operation Order No:103. Appendix III.	12/04/1917	12/04/1917
Operation(al) Order(s)	23rd Division Operation Order No:104. Appendix IV.	12/04/1917	12/04/1917
Operation(al) Order(s)	23rd Division Operation Order No:105. Appendix V.	21/04/1917	21/04/1917
Miscellaneous	A Form Messages And Signals.		
Operation(al) Order(s)	23rd Division Operation Order No. 107. Appendix VI.	29/04/1917	29/04/1917
Miscellaneous	D.A.G. G.H.Q. Herewith Copy of April War Diary as Requested in Your Letter at 23-6-17, Please. July 10th 1917	10/07/1916	10/07/1916
War Diary	Esquelbecq.	01/04/1917	07/04/1917
War Diary	Proven.	08/04/1917	13/04/1917
War Diary	Busseboom.	13/04/1917	01/05/1917
War Diary	Steenvoorde.	02/05/1917	11/05/1917
War Diary	Busseboom.	12/05/1917	31/05/1917
Operation(al) Order(s)	23rd Division Operation Order No. 108. Appendix I (a).	08/05/1917	08/05/1917
Miscellaneous	Table of Relief of 19th Division By 23rd Division. Appendix I (b).		
Operation(al) Order(s)	23rd Division Operation Order No. 109. Appendix II (a).	12/05/1917	12/05/1917
Miscellaneous Diagram etc	Table Of Movements. Appendix II (b).		
Miscellaneous	23rd Division No. Q.S.96. Appendix II (C).	12/05/1917	12/05/1917
Miscellaneous	23rd Division No. Q.S. 97. Appendix II (d).	13/05/1917	13/05/1917
Operation(al) Order(s)	23rd Division Order No. 112. Appendix III.	22/05/1917	22/05/1917
War Diary	Busseboom.	01/06/1917	13/06/1917
War Diary	Meteren.	13/06/1917	30/06/1917
War Diary	Millekruisse.	30/06/1917	30/06/1917
Operation(al) Order(s)	23rd Division Operation Order No. 123	24/06/1917	24/06/1917
Miscellaneous			
Miscellaneous	Headquarters 23rd Division. Herewith War Diary for the month of July 1917	04/08/1917	04/08/1917
War Diary	Millekruisse.	01/07/1917	02/07/1917
War Diary	Zevecoten.	03/07/1917	22/07/1917
War Diary	Meteren.	23/07/1917	31/07/1917
Operation(al) Order(s)	To All Recipients Of 23rd Divisional Order No:132	20/07/1917	20/07/1917
Operation(al) Order(s)	23rd Division Operation Order No. 125. Appendix I.	01/07/1917	01/07/1917
Miscellaneous	Divisional Administrative Instructions No. 125. Appendix II.	03/07/1917	03/07/1917
Miscellaneous	Visit Of H.M. The King-Wednesday, 4th July, 1917- Appendix III.	01/07/1917	01/07/1917
Operation(al) Order(s)	23rd Divisional Order No. 126. Appendix IV.	01/07/1917	01/07/1917
Miscellaneous	23rd. Division No. S.G. 471/7/9. Appendix V.	17/07/1917	17/07/1917
Operation(al) Order(s)	23rd Divisional Order No. 132. Appendix VI.	19/07/1917	19/07/1917
Miscellaneous	March Table To Accompany 23rd Divisional Order No:132. Table "A".		
Operation(al) Order(s)	To All Recipients Of 23rd Divisional Order No:132	19/07/1917	19/07/1917
Miscellaneous	23rd Div. G.104/1/4. Appendix VII.	27/07/1917	27/07/1917
War Diary	Meteren.	01/08/1917	06/08/1917
War Diary	Gordardenne.	07/08/1917	07/08/1917
War Diary	Eperlecques.	09/08/1917	24/08/1917

Type	Description	Date From	Date To
War Diary	Esquelbecq.	24/08/1917	24/08/1917
War Diary	Reninghelst.	25/08/1917	25/08/1917
War Diary	Dickebusch.	26/08/1917	31/08/1917
Operation(al) Order(s)	23rd Divisional Order No:134. Appendix I.	05/08/1917	05/08/1917
Miscellaneous	March Time Table To Accompany 23rd Division Order 134. Appendix. Ia.		
Operation(al) Order(s)	23rd Divisional Order No. 133. Appendix II.	05/08/1917	05/08/1917
Operation(al) Order(s)	23rd Divisional Order No:135. Appendix III.	08/08/1917	08/08/1917
Operation(al) Order(s)	23rd Divisional Order No:136. Appendix IV.	09/08/1917	09/08/1917
Operation(al) Order(s)	23rd Divisional Order No:138. Appendix V.	22/08/1917	22/08/1917
Miscellaneous	March Table To Accompany 23rd Divisional Order No:138		
Miscellaneous	March Table To Accompany 23rd Divisional Order No:138. Appendix Va.		
Operation(al) Order(s)	23rd Divisional Order No:139. Appendix VI.	25/08/1917	25/08/1917
Miscellaneous	23rd Divn. No. S.G.116/7/4. Appendix VI a.	25/08/1917	25/08/1917
Operation(al) Order(s)	23rd Division Order No. 141. Appendix VII.	29/08/1917	29/08/1917
War Diary	Dickebusch.	01/09/1917	02/09/1917
War Diary	Steenworde.	03/09/1917	04/09/1917
War Diary	Lederzeele.	05/09/1917	14/09/1917
War Diary	Zevecoten.	15/09/1917	26/09/1917
War Diary	Westoutre.	27/09/1917	28/09/1917
War Diary	La Clytte.	29/09/1917	30/09/1917
Operation(al) Order(s)	23rd Division Order No. 143. Appendix No. 1	02/09/1917	02/09/1917
Miscellaneous	March Table Issued With 23rd Division Order No. 143. Appendix No. 1a.		
Miscellaneous	23rd Divisional Administrative Instructions No. 133 issued with reference to Divisional Order No. 143. 2nd September 1917. Appendix No. 1b.	02/09/1917	02/09/1917
Operation(al) Order(s)	23rd Division Order No. 144. Appendix 2	03/09/1917	03/09/1917
Operation(al) Order(s)	23rd Divisional Engineers Operation Order No. 31. Appendix 3	09/09/1917	09/09/1917
Operation(al) Order(s)	23rd Division Order No. 145. Appendix 4	11/04/1917	11/04/1917
Miscellaneous			
Miscellaneous	23rd Divisional Administrative Instructions No. 134 issued with reference to Divisional Order No. 145 dated 11th September, 1917. Appendix 4b.	11/09/1917	11/09/1917
Miscellaneous	Billeting Areas.		
Operation(al) Order(s)	To all recipients of 23rd Divisional Order No. 143. Appendix 5	15/09/1917	15/09/1917
Miscellaneous	Supply Arrangements for Operations. Appendix 6	08/09/1917	08/09/1917
Miscellaneous	Appendix B. The following shows detailed Supply arrangements:- Appendix 7		
Miscellaneous	Water. Appendix "E". Appendix 8	19/09/1917	19/09/1917
Miscellaneous	List of Casualties 21st Sept 1917. Appendix 9		
Miscellaneous	Special Order Of The Day. September 23rd 1917. Appendix 10	23/09/1917	23/09/1917
Operation(al) Order(s)	23rd Division Order No. 151. Appendix 11	22/09/1917	22/09/1917
Miscellaneous	March Table To Accompany 23rd Divisional Order No:151. Appendix 11a.		
Miscellaneous	69th Bde Co. 37 Coy No. 6. Area.		
Miscellaneous	23rd Divisional Administrative Instructions No. 135 issued with reference to Divisional Order No. 151 dated 22nd September, 1917. Appendix 11b.	22/09/1917	22/09/1917
Operation(al) Order(s)	23rd Division Order No. 152. Appendix 12	00/09/1917	00/09/1917

Type	Description	Date 1	Date 2
Operation(al) Order(s)	To all recipients of 23rd Div. Order No. 152. Appendix 12 A.	27/09/1917	27/09/1917
War Diary	La Clytte.	01/10/1917	02/10/1917
War Diary	Meteren.	03/10/1917	11/10/1917
War Diary	Dickebusch.	12/10/1917	23/10/1917
War Diary	Wizernes.	24/10/1917	31/10/1917
Operation(al) Order(s)	23rd Division Order No. 153. Appendix No. 1	30/09/1917	30/09/1917
Miscellaneous	March Table to accompany 23rd Div. Order No. 153. Appendix 1 A.		
Miscellaneous	23rd Divisional Administrative Instructions No. 136 Issued With Reference To Divisional Order No. 153 dated 30th September, 1917. Appendix 1B.	30/09/1917	30/09/1917
Miscellaneous	Supply Arrangements. Appendix 1C.		
Operation(al) Order(s)	23rd Division Order No. 154. Appendix 2	09/10/1917	09/10/1917
Operation(al) Order(s)	23rd Division Order No. 156. Appendix 3	18/10/1917	18/10/1917
Miscellaneous	March Table To Accompany 23rd Division Order No. 156. 20th September. Appendix 3A.	20/09/1917	20/09/1917
Miscellaneous	21st September.		
Miscellaneous	22nd/23rd September. Appendix 3B.		
Miscellaneous	Transport March Table. 70th Composite Brigade. Appendix 3D.		
Miscellaneous	Transport March Table. 68th Composite Brigade. Appendix 3E.		
Miscellaneous	Transport March Table. 69th Composite Brigade. Appendix 3F.		

WO 90 2150/4

23 Division - Divisional Troops

DIVISIONAL TRAIN

1915 SEPT - 1917 OCT

23RD DIVISION

23RD DIVL TRAIN A.S.C.
SEP 1915 – ~~MAR 1919~~
1917 OCT

TO ITALY

190 TO 193 Coys HSR

121/798

23rd Kasm

23rd Srits rain
Vol I
Sept 15
Nov 19

– Confidential –

War Diary

of

Lieut: Col: A. Northen

Commanding 23rd Divisional Train

From. 1st 9/15.   To. 30th 9/15.

WAR DIARY
or
INTELLIGENCE SUMMARY.

(Erase heading not required.)

Army Form C. 2118

Instructions regarding War Diaries and Intelligence Summaries are contained in F. S. Regs., Part II. and the Staff Manual respectively. Title pages will be prepared in manuscript.

Place	Date	Hour	Summary of Events and Information	Remarks and references to Appendices
TILQUES NORD 3 miles from ST OMER	1914 1st Sept	9 pm	Went to all Refilling Points in Corps Area. Saw Railhead, ST OMER. All Units Supply wagons withdrawn pending fresh Supply Columns found at Rail-head Company 2 Lt WALTON sent to BASE HT Depot HAVRE. By order of D.W.Q., being Surplus to establishment.	
		am	Inspected H.Q. G. details TILQUES and No 2 Co. SIEBEL - MOULE Fine but showery. Roads greasy	
"	2nd	am	Visited all Refilling Points, no difficulties. Inspected hair shelter of Nos. 3 & 4 Companys at MORDELINGHEM and LOISTRAT.	
		pm	To bleet H.A.Co. re arrangements for trying up new clothes. By army bargain etc. Warm but showery, harness & beds getting very boggy.	

Army Form C. 2118

WAR DIARY
or
INTELLIGENCE SUMMARY.
(Erase heading not required.)

Instructions regarding War Diaries and Intelligence Summaries are contained in F. S. Regs., Part II. and the Staff Manual respectively. Title pages will be prepared in manuscript.

Place	Date	Hour	Summary of Events and Information	Remarks and references to Appendices
TILQUES	3 Sept	am	Inspect Visited Refilling Points.	
			Visited Nos 2, 3 & 4 in arrangements for laying of main clothing.	
			Inducted for 6 horses on Dep R. Boulogne 3 ans 3 C., 2 ans 4 C., 1 No 2 C.	
"	4th Sept	am	Mr. Genl R. Cond. D.A. & M.G. 11th Corps came will Col N.O. Browne. A.A. & M.G. 2nd Div.	Maxisein I & IA 23rd Div Officers arr. W.O.I.
			Visited all Refilling Points & Railhead	
			Went to Offices D.of T. & D. of S. G.H.Q., in connection with T. & S. arrangements	
			Orders to indent for 3 G.S., & 2 G.S. limbered wagons as spares.	
			No Tn. wet	
"	5 Sept		Order to move Comms. to Lieu SLONE R - HAZEBROUCK	
			To Nos 2, 3, 4 Co. with orders for march	
			Baggage section to march with Groups.	
			Supply Section cancelled.	
			Lt Col Young A.D.T. G.H.Q. came to inspect billets of wagons, comment on report from W.O.	
			Fine.	

Army Form C. 2118

WAR DIARY
or
INTELLIGENCE SUMMARY.
(Erase heading not required.)

Instructions regarding War Diaries and Intelligence Summaries are contained in F. S. Regs., Part II. and the Staff Manual respectively. Title pages will be prepared in manuscript.

Place	Date	Hour	Summary of Events and Information	Remarks and references to Appendices
THIEVES	1915 6 Sep	am	Baggage section of Train marched with group under orders of Group Commander.	
		pm	Supply section all loaded at THIEVES after Divisional Supply Column arrived 5.15 pm. Train billetted for night:-	Appendix 2.2A 23rd Div. Operation Order No. 2.
			H.Q.C. LYNDE 10 miles	
			No. 2 C. HAZEBROUCK 14 miles	
			" 3 C. WALLON CAPPEL 14 miles	
			" 4 C. CAMPAGNE 14 miles	
			Very hot tiring march, road choking, no trouble in Train	
On march	7 Sep	am	Baggage section under group commander marched to:-	
			H.Q.C. MERRIS 14 miles	
			No. 2 C. MONTE BOON 10 miles	
			No. 3 C. BLEU 13 miles	
			No. 4 C. OUTERSTEEN 18 miles	
			All R.A. baggage wagon to billets south of STRAZEELE.	
			Rabbles HAZEBROUCK GARAGE.	
			Refilling Point, new Group Area. Group to Cappelli road, Supply Column did not complete dumping until 6 to 8 pm. Refilling 70 1304 Northwest to following morning - R.A. refilling completed 2 am 8 Sept.	

Army Form C. 2118

WAR DIARY
or
INTELLIGENCE SUMMARY.
(Erase heading not required.)

Instructions regarding War Diaries and Intelligence Summaries are contained in F. S. Regs., Part II. and the Staff Manual respectively. Title pages will be prepared in manuscript.

Place	Date	Hour	Summary of Events and Information	Remarks and references to Appendices
MERRIS	1915 8th Sept		Railhead HAZEBROUCK GARAGE	
			Refilling Point: Group areas	
			Following detachts to 20 D.Div. ESTAIRES:-	
			101st R.E., C.194, 106 R.F.A., Div. Bac. & D.A.C.	
			Supply wagon of above supplies until 20 D.Div. at ESTAIRES acting S.O. 2 Lt HOLMES	
			Following detachts to 27 D.Div:-	
			2 Bdgs, 102nd R.F.A. ⎫	
			" 104 " " ⎬ Supply wagons with 2 th PHEYSEY to LA MENEGATE, R.P. 27 D.Div.	
			" 105 " " ⎭	
			102nd R.E. Supply Officer (acting):- 2 Lt SHINGLETON	
			Supply wagon bivouacked in fields at x roads running S. from LA MENEGATE.	
			Fini	
"	9th Sept		Following to 20 D.Div:-	
			6 A.C. Hq. 13m 2 Co. D.Supp.Byt.	
			Train wagons for above marches to ESTAIRES under Lt McINTYRE.	
			B.A. Supply Officer Lt. NORTHEN Lt ESTAIRES 2 Lt. HOLMES returned.	
			Following to 27 D.Div:- 2 Bm, 69 R.Bde, 2 Bm, 70 R.Bde	
			Supply wagon of above to LA MENEGATE under 2 Lt FRANCIS. Baggage wagon with details.	
			Units Railed Supply Column lette owing to congested road.	

WAR DIARY
or
INTELLIGENCE SUMMARY.
(Erase heading not required.)

Army Form C. 2118

Place	Date	Hour	Summary of Events and Information	Remarks and references to Appendices
MERRIS	10 Sept	am	To Railhead. Met DAD S+T 1st Army, suffered difficulties in reason of Railway delay. Railway again delayed owing to failure of 27th Divn. R.P. at MENEGATE to apportion of train.	Appendices 3 23rd Divn Orders by 11-9-15
"	11 "	6 am	To 2nd & 3rd Bde Area on relief. BEF/BM reported not turned up, found all had been issued by 10.30 am From	
"		am	To Railhead and Refilling Point. Arrangements for further issues tomorrow. Refilling Point LA MENEGATE moved to adjacent road. Sent S.S.M. McGeorge to LA MENEGATE bivouac for duty. From	
"	12 "	am	Relieving the 27th Divn. H.Q. & 2 Bns. 69 C Bde, H.A. & 2 Bns. 70 Bde, 126 F.R.E. and ½ 186 & 102 & 103 & 104 Bns R.E.A. Reliefs from 27th Divn. 2 Bns. 69 C Bde, 102nd R.E. 15 wagons of ????? to LA MENEGATE under Capt. Kellah, 5 wagons returned. Visited 27th Divn. Area re Reliefs for train, and arrangements for T. & S. sources. 2/Lt. Watson to LA MENEGATE for duty.	

Ivry Ref

WAR DIARY
or
INTELLIGENCE SUMMARY.
(Erase heading not required.)

Army Form C. 2118
6

Place	Date	Hour	Summary of Events and Information	Remarks and references to Appendices
MERRIS	13 Sept.	am	Railhead LESTREM	
			Following to 27th Divn: 3½ Batteries R.F.A.	
			Supply wagons for same to LA MENEGATE north of 2½ Ritchell	Map 36 - A.22.c.
			No. 2 Gp marches to MEH Area near STEENWERCK (S.E.of) will attack 69 C/Bn *	s.4.
		pm	Inspected 1st Echelon Parks. 27th Divn Area But DARNG 22nd Divn well within T.3. & Train Supply Echelon Horses	Appendices 4 & 4A
			First	22nd Divn Operation Order No. 3 =
	14.	am	7th Bde. & No. 4 Co. Li. Horse Arr., billets near STEENWERCK	Map 36 - A.23.d. 3-8-
			Visited Supply Dump at LA MENEGATE	
			27th Train H.Q. re billeting area billets.	
			First	
	15th	am	69th Bde & No. 3 Co. Li. Horse arr., billets near STEENWERCK *	Map 36 A.22. d. 10-5-
			Visited R.P. La MENEGATE.	
		"	Supply Column Parks billets STEENWERCK	
		"	To LA GORGUE Railway Hd. and S.S.O. 20th Divn re S.P.T. arrangements for troops attached to 20th Divn	
			First	

WAR DIARY
or
INTELLIGENCE SUMMARY.
(Erase heading not required.)

Army Form C. 2118

Place	Date	Hour	Summary of Events and Information	Remarks and references to Appendices
MERRIS	1914 16 Sep	a.m	H.Q. Div & H.Q. Train to CROIX du BAC. H.Q.C. to Bau Bec near STEENWERCK *	* Appx 36 A2 E 3 & 5
			To Refilling Point LA MENGATE " our Railhead BAC ST MAUR	
		pm	Inspected H.Q.C. billets, New Area near STEENWERCK	* Appendix 5 27 E Train Orders Nov. 4 - 15 - 9 - 14
			23rd Div Train left before attacks H.Q.C. 10 wagon supplies for 13th R.F.A.	
			Train left Pellrant Day.	
			From	
CROIX du BAC	17 "	a.m	All Baggage wagons ordered to be continued by Units.	
			Train took over 27th Div Refilling Point at LA MENGATE	
		a.m	Reconnoitring roads for Supply Column from Refilling Point to Railhead & return to billets	
		pm	Inspected Nos. 2 3 & 4 Co. billets	
			From 9 wagon supplies for R.E. work, utilized Baggage wagons	
	18 "	a.m	Supply Column ordered to return from Railhead, utilized Baggage wagons	
			H.Q. Unit allows to retain Baggage wagons, Junior Officers to return to H.Q.C.	
		pm	Visited all our Companies	
			From 15 wagons for R.E. work	
	19 "	9.30 a.m	Church Parade at H.Q.C. lines	
			Visited all Lines Companies	
			From 13 wagons for R.E. work	

Army Form C. 2118.

WAR DIARY
or
INTELLIGENCE SUMMARY.
(Erase heading not required.)

Instructions regarding War Diaries and Intelligence Summaries are contained in F.S. Regs., Part II. and the Staff Manual respectively. Title pages will be prepared in manuscript.

Place	Date	Hour	Summary of Events and Information	Remarks and references to Appendices
Choque Au – 13AC	20 Sept	am	To Pipeling Point & Railhead	
		pm	To ESTAIRS re supplies for Troops attached 20th Div	
			Envoi + Cost Trugons for R.E.	
"	21st		To Pipeling Point & Railhead	
			Return to H.Q.C. & No. 4 C. Sect.	
			2 Lt. Osborne joined from England, posted to No. 3 C. "	
			Envoi + Cost. Reinforcements consisted Clerk by	
			10. wagons for R.E. etc.	
"	22nd		Transferred 2 Lt. SINGLETON to No. 2 Coy as S.O. via Lt MATTHEW to embark permanently & S.S.O	
			Appointed 2 Lt. OSBORNE R.O. 69 Siding Siding vice 2 Lt. SINGLETON	
			To STEENBECQUE with S.S.O to see O.C. 6th Reserve Park re return of petrol will be attached to 23rd Div	
			Envoi + Cost 7 wagons for R.E.	
"	23rd		Visited H.Q.C, Nos. 3 & 4 Cos.	
			" To 1st Army H.Q. for conference re use of Reserve Parks	
			Received from Personnel 14 H.D. Drivers & 1 extra	
			Sent in for promotion 2 Lt. MORTIMER to Capt., 2 Lt. SINGLETON, FRANCIS, THEVESEY to Lieut.	
			21 wagons for R.E. etc; and S.S.O sent blanks 6 & 8 Plan from 1st Res Park to STEENWERCK for troops	

Army Form C. 2118

WAR DIARY
or
INTELLIGENCE SUMMARY.
(Erase heading not required.)

Place	Date	Hour	Summary of Events and Information	Remarks and references to Appendices
CROIX-du-BAC	19/15 24 Sep		Supply Column stampeded at 3 am under Uhlan raid, rifles et Rifles et Rolleles at 6.10 crippled 7.15	
			Return ERQUINGHEM Bridge 7.45 am	
			To Refilling Point 9 am	
			Baggage wagon 6.P.13M sent to 1st Line Park to be beaded up	
			wet + close. 6 wagon RE work	
	25.		Supply Column on jobbing	
			15 wagon RE work	
			wet Battle began 1st Army taken 220 prisoners - LOOS - PUITS 14; HULLUCH -	
			French hush gained here on front 25 miles	
	26.		Church Parade H.A.C. Band	
			6.05 PM + No. 2 C. to 2nd F. Div	
			Wagon fr RE at 27	
			Reconnaissance Capt SCHUTE Conveys 23-24 Supply Col. fr Thumeries to Rega	
			1st Army: 2,800 prisoners. 8 guns. 22 MGs	
			wet. French 7,000 prisoners	

WAR DIARY
INTELLIGENCE SUMMARY

Army Form C. 2118

Place	Date	Hour	Summary of Events and Information	Remarks and references to Appendices
CROIX-du-BAC	1915 27 Sept	am	To Refilling Point	
		pm	66.F. Bde + No 2 Co. retained from 20.F Divn. waggons for R.E. ett. 24	
			List French 3 m Officers 31 gunners 20 gunners mch	
	28"		Received orders to retain all trans L.E. refs to Divn. Ammunition Shops	
			" " " all G.S. waggons until further notice	
			C Bty. 106 Bde R.F.A retained from 20.F Divn	
			6F.F Bde L. 20.F Divn. also received orders which amounted to following L.9.0.1-10.17 R.E 103rd R.F.A. 7.F F Amb S. B.AC + D.A.C Upwards Cancelled. S.S. Bates to A Divn. HQ vice Capt. Taylor	
			Lost 31 waggons for R.E.	
	29.5	9 am	Conference Divn. HQ Ein.	
			To H.Q.Co. + No. 2 Co. as starts for horses	
			To Divn. Supply Col. in charge of reinforcement	
			Sent in report re. Return of blankets waggon no reply to H.Q. letter	
			First 1st waggon R.E. French 2300m furnished 121 gunners	

Army Form C. 2118

WAR DIARY
or
INTELLIGENCE SUMMARY.
(Erase heading not required.)

Place	Date	Hour	Summary of Events and Information	Remarks and references to Appendices
Croix-du-Bac	1915 30 Sept	a.m. p.m.	To all Coys. as empowered to loan for men & horses. Being worked. Horse shelters being completed & reveille room. 2 s. wagons for R.E. work etc. Fins.	

Croix-du-Bac

A. Northen
Lt. Col. ASC
Comdg. 23rd Divl. Train

Confidential

O.C.
Train

Copy No. 8.

Ref. 1/100,000
HAZEBROUCK 5A.

23rd Division Operation Order No 1.

TILQUES.
Sept 5th 1915.

1. The Division will march to-morrow via St MARTIN au LAERT and ARQUES passing to the South of ST OMER to the area ARQUES - HAZEBROUCK. A further march will take place on the 7th Sept.

2. March Table is attached.

3. The 105th Bde R.F.A. is attached to 70th Bde Group until further orders.

4. The baggage Sections of Train will march with Brigade Groups. The remainder of Train as per March Table.

5. Refilling point - Main Road between TILQUES & ST MARTIN AU LAERT.

6. Reports to Divisional Headquarters TILQUES up to 9 a.m. after that hour to Chateau RENESCURE.

A. Blair
Lt. Col.
Gen. Staff 23rd Division.

Appendix I

Appendix I A

MARCH TABLE FOR 6TH SEPTEMBER.

Unit.	Starting Point.	Time	Billeting Area	Remarks.
D.M.T.	Church at ST MARTINS AU LAERT.	7. a.m.	RENESCURE.	
68th Bde Group. (under Br Gen. Serocold)	ditto.	7.8 a.m.	HAZEBROUCK.	Baggage Section of the Train will march with their Bde Groups.
69th Bde. Group. (under Br Gen. Derham)	ditto.	8.30 a.m.	WALLON CAPPEL	
H.Q. Group (less D.M.T.) (under Col. Thruston)	ditto.	9.50 a.m.	RENESCURE.	
70th Bde Group. (under Sir D.A. Kinloch C.B. M.V.O.)	DITTO.	10.10 a.m.	CAMPAGNE	
Divl. Amm Col. (Col. Drury)		11.50 a.m.		
Div. Train. less Supply Sect. Amm Sub Park. Div Supply Col.	Under their own arrangements.			

CORRECTION.

REFERENCE MARCH TABLE FOR 6 SEPTEMBER.

DIV. TRAIN (less Supply Section) should read DIV. TRAIN
       (less Baggage Section).

H. Q. 23rd Division,
5 September, 1915.

                              Lt. Colonel,
General Staff 23rd Division.

Appendix 2

Ref. 1/100,000
HAZEBROUCK 5A.

Copy No. 19

23rd DIVISION ORDER No. 2

6 Sept, 1915.

1. The Division will march to-morrow via HAZEBROUCK to the area HAZEBROUCK — BAILLEUL — STEENWERCK — NEUF BERGUI (exclusive of these places). Brigade areas will be allotted to Staff Captains this evening.

2. All Artillery units will march under orders G.O.C. R.A.

3. March Table is attached.

4. Reports to Div. H.Q. up to 10 a.m, after that hour to MERRIS.

5. Refilling points at Headquarters Brigade Groups.

Issued at
    p.m

A Blair Lt. Colonel,
G.S. 23rd Div.

Appendix 2A

March Table 4th September

UNIT.	STARTING POINT.	HOUR.	ROUTE	REMARKS.
68th Bde Group. (less R.A. Units) (under Brigr Serocold).	HAZEBROUCK Station.	9 a.m.	BORRE-STRAZEELE BAILLEUL (excl)	1. No artillery is to use the CAMPAGNE-RENESCURE-WALLON CAPPEL-HAZEBROUCK-BORRE-STRAZEELE road until the 70th Bde Group has passed. 2. Companies of the Train will march complete with their Groups.
69th Bde Group. (less R.A. Units) (under Br Genl. Derham)	ditto	10 a.m.	BORRE-STRAZEELE VIEUX BERQUIN	
H.Q. Group. (under Col Thruston)	RENESCURE	8.30 a.m.	HAZEBROUCK BORRE STRAZEELE to MERRIS.	
70th Bde Group. (less R.A.) (under Br Genl. Sir D. Kinloch C.B. M.V.O.)	RENESCURE	9.10 a.m.	HAZEBROUCK BORRE STRAZEELE MOOLENACHER.	

Secret   Appendix 3

SG 17

To. OC Train

1. Two Battalions of 69th Brigade and two Battalions of
70th Brigade, the 102nd [128th] Fd Co. R.E. and the personnel
of 70th [69th] Field Ambulance will proceed to-morrow to
the 27th Division for Training.

2. The two Battalions of 69th Brigade will be attached to
the 81st Infantry Brigade and will march so as to
reach BAC ST MAUR Bridge at 12 noon on the 12th inst.

3. The two Battalions of the 70th Infantry Brigade will
be attached to the 82nd Brigade and will march so as to
reach ERQUINGHEM Bridge at 12 noon on the 12th inst.

4. The 128th Fd. Co. R.E. will march so as to reach
ERQUINGHEM bridge at 10 a.m. on the 12th inst.
    The 102nd Fd. Co. R.E. will return to the 23rd Divisional
Area on the 12th inst under arrangements to be made by
the C.R.E. 27th Division.

5. Arrangements for the attachments of further
personnel of the Fd. Ambulances and Train of the 23rd Division
will be made between the A.D.M.S. & O.C. Train of the
two Divisions. Similarly the C.R.A.S. of the two
Divisions will arrange for attachments of Artillery Units

6. The Battalions of the 69th & 70th Brigades and the 128th Fd
Co. R.E. must move complete.

Please acknowledge

                            Signed   A. Blair, Lt. Col.
H.Q. 23rd Division.   General Staff 23rd Division.
   September 11th 1915.

~~Companies of visiting Boers who are actually in the trenches on the evening of 13th inst will be withdrawn and will march to bivouacs N. of Rundlys.~~

68 do not move

2 Bns. 69 will return to the Billets they left

2 Bns. 70 to ~~Steinbek~~ Steenwake

Train   *Appendix 4*

SECRET.   Copy....15......

Ref. $\frac{1}{40,000}$ H. Q. 23rd Division,
                                                 September 12th, 1915.

23rd DIVISION OPERATION ORDER NO 3.

1. The left sector of the 27th Division Area will be taken over by the 70th Bde., from the 82nd Bde. on the night 14/15 September, under orders to be issued by G. O. C. 27th Div.
   The 128th Fd. Co. R. E. is attached to the 70th Bde. and will go into the billets occupied by the 17th Fd. Co. R. E. on night 14/15 September.
   The 70th Fd. Ambulance will be attached to the 70th Bde. and will move to its position in the 70th Bde. Area on the night 14/15 September, under orders to be issued by A.D.M.S. 23rd Div.

2. The right sector of the 27th Division Area will be taken over by the 69th Bde. on the night of 15/16 September, under orders to be issued by G. O. C. 27th Division.
   The 102nd Fd. Co. R.E. is attached to the 69th Bde. and will go into the billets occupied by the 1st Wessex Fd. Co. R. E. on night 15/16 September.
   The 69th Fd. Ambulance will be attached to the 69th Bde. and will move to its position in the 69th Bde. Area on the night of 15/16 September under orders to be issued by A.D.M.S. 23rd Division.

3. The 68th Bde. will march to the 27th Divisional Reserve Area to billets N and N. W. of ERQUINGHEM - LYS on the night of 16/17 September under orders to be issued by the G.O.C. 20th Division.
   The 101st Fd. Co. R.E. *will be attached to 68th Bde. and* will march to ERQUINGHEM - LYS on the night of 16/17 September, and go into billets occupied by the 2nd Wessex Fd. Co. R. E. under orders to be issued by G.O.C. 20th Division.
   The 71st Field Ambulance will be attached to the 68th Bde. and will move to its position in STEENWERCK on the night of 16/17 September, under orders to be issued by A.D.M.S. 23rd Division.

4. The G. O. C. 23rd Division takes over the 27th Divisional Area at 10 a.m. on the 16th inst.

5. The move of the Artillery 23rd Division will be arranged by the C.R.A.'s 23rd and 27th Divisions. Reliefs to be completed by 6 a.m. on the 15th inst, with the exception of the Div. Amm. Col.

6. The Train will move to the 27th Divisional Area under orders of the Officer Commanding Divisional Train.

7. The 9th S. Staffords (Pioneer Bn) will march with the 68th Bde. to billets near FORT ROMPU (H 8 C) on night 16/17 September under orders by G.O.C. 20th Division.

8. Divisional H. Q., H.Q.R.A., H.Q.R.E., the Divisional Mounted Troops, the 35th Mobile Vet. Section and the Sanitary Section will march to CROIX DU BAC starting at 8 a.m. on the 16th inst under orders of LT. COL. TILNEY.

Appendix 4 A

9. The 69th and 70th Bdes. will take over all trench stores from the 27th Division including periscopes, bombs, etc.

10. All cable now laid out in the 27th Div. Area, both Divisional and Artillery, will be handed over to the 23rd Division and no paying back of cable will take place between units.
    If there is any of the 10 miles of D 5 cable which was recently allotted for the Artillery of the 27th Div. not laid out it will be handed over to the 23rd Div. Artillery.

11. Acknowledge.

Issued at 3 p.m.

N Blair.
Lt. Col.
General Staff, 23rd Div.

Copy No. 5   Appendix 5

O.C., 97 Company, A.S.C.,
  27th Divisional Train.

  The undermentioned wagons as complete turnouts, will, after delivering their supplies to their units tomorrow morning 16th September, proceed to the wagon lines of 97 Company, A.S.C.,

  At 2.30 p.m. in the afternoon, they will be handed over by the O.C., 97 Company, A.S.C., to the Officer Commanding the A.S.C., Company of the 23rd Divisional Train at A 22 d 2.6 (billet previously occupied by 96 Company, A.S.C.,) The men and horses should be in possession of the current days rations and rations for consumption on September 17th.

  These wagons will remain until further instructions are received, in this area, and will for all purposes come under the Officer Commanding the 23rd Divisional Train.

  Divisional Train wagons allotted to :-

   19th Brigade R.F.A., (including Head Quarters, and
    Brigade Ammunition Column.
    4 Wagons G.S., for Supplies.
    4 Wagons G.S., for Hay.
    8 pairs Heavy Draught Horses.
    8 Drivers of 27th Divisional Train.
    Escort and Loading Party as detailed by
     19th Brigade, R.F.A.,

 N O T E :- Wagons G.S., for baggage, and horses (8 complete turn outs) are already with the Artillery Brigade concerned.

         A.P. Liddell
          Lieut. Colonel.
15th September, 1915. Commanding 27th Divisional Train.

Copy No. 1 filed.
ditto 2 to O.C., 97 Company, A.S.C., 27th Divisional Train.
ditto 3 to C.R.A., 27th Division. (for information.)
ditto 4 to C.R.A., 23rd Division. (for information.)
ditto 5 to O.C., 23rd Divisional Train. (for information.)
ditto 6 to O.C., 98 Company, A.S.C., 27th Divisional Train.
      (for information).

23rd Division

12/7517

Original

Confidential

War Diary

of

Lieut: Col: A. Northen

Commanding 23rd Divisional Train

Vol 2

From 1st October 1915. To 31st October 1915.

WAR DIARY
or
INTELLIGENCE SUMMARY.
(Erase heading not required.)

Army Form C. 2118

Instructions regarding War Diaries and Intelligence Summaries are contained in F.S. Regs., Part II and the Staff Manual respectively. Title pages will be prepared in manuscript.

Place	Date	Hour	Summary of Events and Information	Remarks and references to Appendices
CROIX du BAC	1915 1st Oct	10 am	Self on Gen. Court Martial at Div. H.Q.²	
		"	101st Field Co. R.E. left 23rd Div. on temporary duty & took supply wagon with them.	
		"	Two Temporary 1st Line Transport Infantry Battalions assembled following men to Div. H.Q. for Batteries :- Capt. C. LANGFORD D.S.O. Applied J. Train, and No. T2/SR/1915 1st Class S.S.M. McGONAGIL E.T. 190 C. ASC. 21 wagons on R.E. work etc. weather - wet -	
"	2nd Oct	am	Two Battalions 66 F.Ly. Bde. returned to Division from 20 Div. ESTAIRES, their baggage wagons returned to Train. Visited H.Q.G. & M.G.G. in tents for horses etc.	
		"	Sgt. M.S.G. inspected returned Transport by S. Lt. Bryant. 25 wagons on R.E. work etc. weather - fine	

Army Form C. 2118.

WAR DIARY
or
INTELLIGENCE SUMMARY.
(Erase heading not required.)

Place	Date	Hour	Summary of Events and Information	Remarks and references to Appendices
CROIX du BAC	1915 3rd Oct	am	Sunday, no Church Parade.	
			Two Battalions 69 F. Inf. Brigade left Divisions h.q. join 20 F. Div. ESTAIRES, & took their baggage wagons & 2 F. Ambs.	
			18 wagons on R.E. work	
			Weather fine	
	4 Oct	am	Two Battalions 66 F. Inf. Brigade reported Division from 20 F. Div. ESTAIRES, & their baggage wagons rejoined Train	
			Headquarters 69 F. Inf. Bde. joined 20 F. Div. ESTAIRES taking baggage wagons with them.	
			Visited M.A.C. & No. 3. C.	
			24 wagons on R.E. work etc.	
			Weather showery	
	5 Oct	am	Visited No. 2 C. + No. 3 C.	
			No. 79/- 029692 A/Sergt. HESKETH T. No. 2 Co. shot himself with his rifle	
		pm	13 wagons R.E. work	
			Weather wet.	

Army Form C. 2118
3

WAR DIARY
or
INTELLIGENCE SUMMARY.
(Erase heading not required.)

Instructions regarding War Diaries and Intelligence Summaries are contained in F. S. Regs., Part II. and the Staff Manual respectively. Title pages will be prepared in manuscript.

Place	Date	Hour	Summary of Events and Information	Remarks and references to Appendices
CROIX du BAC	1914 6 Oct	9 am	Weekly Conference at Div. H.Q. Irs.	
			Appointed to act as Billeting Officer of Division under orders of "Q" staff.	
			14 wagons R.E. tools.	
			2 Lt. BARRY guarded train of stones to 13 F. unit.	
			Reinforcement of 5 men from Base H.T. Depot.	
			Weather dull.	
"	7 Oct	10 am	Court of Enquiry on Sergt HESKETH.	
		am	2 Lt. F. SHINGLETON admitted to Hospital BAILLEUL	
			Returned from Funerals, 2 officers clergy + 2 H.D. horses.	
			4 wagons on coal	
			Weather - fine.	
"	8 Oct		2 Lt. R.V. HOLMES appointed Supply Officer 6 Inf. Bde Group vice 2 Lt SHINGLETON	
			2 Lt. E.H. MITCHELL appointed R.D. 68 Inf. Bde Group vice 2 Lt. R.V. HOLMES	
			Inspected 1st Divn Transport 1st S. Stafford Regt. by Regiment of Town	
			On trekking only.	
			23 wagons R.E. work and coal	
			Weather - dull	

2353 Wt. W2544/1454 700,000 5/15 D. D. & L. A.D.S.S./Forms/C. 2118.

WAR DIARY or INTELLIGENCE SUMMARY

Army Form C. 2118

(Erase heading not required.)

Instructions regarding War Diaries and Intelligence Summaries are contained in F. S. Regs., Part II. and the Staff Manual respectively. Title pages will be prepared in manuscript.

Place	Date	Hour	Summary of Events and Information	Remarks and references to Appendices
Croix du Bac	1915 9 Oct.	am	Billeting duty.	
		pm	Inspection 1st Line Transport S. Stafford Regt.	
			18 wagons R.E. tools & coal	
			Weather dull.	
"	10 Oct.	9. am	Church Parade	
			2 R.A. SINGLETON invalided HOME	
			Two Battalions 69 F. Inf. Bde. rejoined Division from 20th Divn. ESTAIRES, & their baggage wagons rejoined Train	
		pm	Inspection 1st Line Transport S. Stafford Regt. with A.A. & Q.M.G.	
			Billeting duties.	
			26 wagons. H.E. tools & coal. Fuel	
"	11 Oct.	am	Two Battalions 70 F. Bde. to 20th Divn. ESTAIRES, included baggage wagons of same to 20th Divn. Train	
			Visits to Farm Carpenters.	
		pm	Inspection by G.O.C. Division of Train and 1st Line Transport Parties.	
			Weather very fine	
			25 farm carts + 1 dg. R.E. tools + baggage.	

Army Form C. 2118

WAR DIARY
or
INTELLIGENCE SUMMARY.
(Erase heading not required.)

Instructions regarding War Diaries and Intelligence Summaries are contained in F. S. Regs., Part II. and the Staff Manual respectively. Title pages will be prepared in manuscript.

Place	Date	Hour	Summary of Events and Information	Remarks and references to Appendices
Croix du Bac	1915 12 Oct	night	All vehicles to be marked with new Divisional mark, a white cross on white circle.	
			Billeting duties.	
			2.6 from R.E. work & coal	
			Weather, very fine.	
"	13.5	9 am	Conference showing how often in place of short after shoot often extend by rate of Division HQrs to commence hip	
			hardly conference Div Hospital	
		pm	Accompanied G.O.C. round R.A. wagon lines	
			24 from R.E. work & coal	
			Weather - Showery	
"	14.5		Lieut C.E. McIntyre admitted to Hospital - Bailleul	
		am	Visit A.A. & Q.M.G. concerning 2nd line Transport Parks & repairs of Billeting Area	
			18 from R.E. work	
			Weather, windy then very fine	
	15.5		D.A. and A.M.G. 3rd Corps visited Farm Lines	
			31 from R.E. coal & blankets	
			Weather - Dull	

2353 Wt. W2544/1454 700,000 5/15 D. D. & L. A.D.S.S./Forms/C. 2118.

Army Form C. 2118

WAR DIARY
or
INTELLIGENCE SUMMARY.
(Erase heading not required.)

Place	Date	Hour	Summary of Events and Information	Remarks and references to Appendices
Croix du Bac	15/15 16 Oct	am	Inspection of Equipment as a holding area for 1 Battalion.	
		pm	Withdrew R.A. baggage wagon for handing with Divisional train. 2/4 hours on R.E. work road week E. Dull.	
	17 Oct	9 am	Sunday. Church Parade for Town at R.A.C. billet. 2/4 T.V. Barry attended Field Protestant Service. Inspected Equipment and not A.A + R.M.G. 23rd Division. 2½ hours on R.E. work road weather fine.	
	18 Oct		R.A. Pol. Lt. Payne + 7 o.R. left Brigade Hqs. 23rd Division to join 8th Division at Smiley R.R. 2/4 O.R. 4/24 Inf. Bn. 8th Division joins 23rd Division. Only attached baggage wagons of Units remaining with Units after move was completed. Owing to Units 24 Div/Bn having one S.A.A. limbered wagon, they were allowed to keep their baggage wagon to carry extra + stores to trenches. 1½ hours on R.E. work road - 16 hour snow 70 Inf. Bn. weather cold + fine	

Army Form C. 2118

WAR DIARY
or
INTELLIGENCE SUMMARY.
(Erase heading not required.)

Instructions regarding War Diaries and Intelligence Summaries are contained in F.S. Regs., Part II. and the Staff Manual respectively. Title pages will be prepared in manuscript.

Place	Date	Hour	Summary of Events and Information	Remarks and references to Appendices
CROIX du BAC	1914 19th Oct	am	Inspected billets, found area - RUE MIRAGE and LA ROUMDERIE	7
		pm	Moved all men for Capturing Town	
		1½ pm	a R.E. work + rest.	
			thanks, pm	
	20"		101st Field Coy R.E. arrived to 2nd Division	
		9 am	Captures Dowland Photographed	
			27 prov R.E. tools & blankets	
			Weather, fine	
	21st Oct	10.a.m.	W. Riding Regt. 69 F/ROH to 20th Divn at ESTAIRES, rec 2nd Northampton Regt 24 Sep 1914	
			Visits LA ROUMDERIE and all R.E. Offrs in shelters & equipment	
		pm	To No. 2 Co. no shelter for horses —	
			22 prov R.E. work, 12 prov cart, 8 blanket etc.	
			Weather, fine	
	22"	am	Billeting orders, LE ROUMDERIE and FORT ROMPU area.	
		pm	On return Guntley H.Q.C. found Divnal 36 P.S. wagons - not fit for use of Divnal	
			Col. M. John Parker D.D.S.T. 12 army arrived Train	
			3-prov R.E. work	
			Weather fine	

2353 Wt. W2544/1454 700,000 5/15 D. D. & L. A.D.S.S./Forms/C. 2118.

Army Form C. 2118
8

WAR DIARY
or
INTELLIGENCE SUMMARY.
(Erase heading not required.)

Instructions regarding War Diaries and Intelligence Summaries are contained in F. S. Regs., Part II. and the Staff Manual respectively. Title pages will be prepared in manuscript.

Place	Date	Hour	Summary of Events and Information	Remarks and references to Appendices
CROIX du BAC	1915 23rd Feb.	am	Visited Camp of Auxiliary Transport Company.	
		pm	To N.B. 63 F.13 Bc. ROE MARRE and LA ROLANDERIE areas	
		pm	Visited No. 4 G's lines	
			3 8/hour R.E. work and coal.	
			Weather - showery.	
"	24th Oct	am 9.15	Sunday Church Parade	
			2 9/hour R.E. work	
			Weather fine	
"	25th "	am & pm	Battalion orders	
			30/hour R.E. work	
			Weather - wet.	
"	26th "	am 4pm	Battalion orders	
			Visited R.E.C. & No. 3 G. lines	
			29/hour R.E. work & coal.	
			Weather dull & cold.	
"	27th "	am 9 am	Battalion orders	
			Corporal Drummond Westgarten - Transportation 17/hours R.E. work & coal.	
			Weather wet & cold.	

Army Form C. 2118

WAR DIARY
or
INTELLIGENCE SUMMARY.
(Erase heading not required.)

Instructions regarding War Diaries and Intelligence Summaries are contained in F. S. Regs., Part II. and the Staff Manual respectively. Title pages will be prepared in manuscript.

Place	Date	Hour	Summary of Events and Information	Remarks and references to Appendices
CROIX du BAC	1915 28th Feb	6 am	4 wagon with team under an N.C.O. with a farrier & cook to LA MOTTE in detachment, to draw wood in front, for making stables.	
		10 am	Court of Inquiry on injuries Dr. Dackie 190 Co. A.S.C. Supply wagon to 6 W Riding Regt and 2nd Worcester Regt sent to 20th Div. Train ESTAIRES, there Batteries being attacked for action to 20th Div. for this date. 23rd Div. Supply Column attacks 2 horses to 20th Div. Supply Column for same purpose. Transport: 20 horse R.E work, 12 horse coal. Weather dull.	
"	29.5	9 am	Board of Officer to test rifles, etc of farriers. Detachment at LA MOTTE consist of 6: team of 6 horses, owing to they roads in front. Lieut R.C. Eden to LA MOTTE in charge of Detachment. Transport: R.E work 23 horse, coal 6. Weather fair.	
	30.5	am	13.C. leaving BUTEN, LA ROLANDERIE area Transport R.E work 24 horse Weather fair	

Army Form C. 2118

10

WAR DIARY
or
INTELLIGENCE SUMMARY.
(Erase heading not required.)

Instructions regarding War Diaries and Intelligence Summaries are contained in F.S. Regs., Part II. and the Staff Manual respectively. Title pages will be prepared in manuscript.

Place	Date	Hour	Summary of Events and Information	Remarks and references to Appendices
CROIX du BAC	1915 Oct 31		Sunday no Church Parade. Aeroplane rich. 2Lt W.G. LACY A.S.C. joined Train posted to 191 Co ASC. Transfer 34 pair R.E. boots. Weather wet. Drivers commenced drawing coal for 3rd Corps Coal Dump, GHQ 32 MMG.	

October 31/10/15

A. Noster
Lt Col ASC
Comg. 23rd Divl Train

23rd Div L: Train
Vol. 3

121/7694

Aug 6

Nov 15

Confidential

War Diary
Of. O.C. 23rd Div Train
From. 1-11-15 To. 30-11-15

Lieut-Colonel A. Northen
A.S.C.
Commanding 23rd Div. Train

B.E.F. France.

WAR DIARY
or
INTELLIGENCE SUMMARY.

(Erase heading not required.)

Army Form C. 2118

Instructions regarding War Diaries and Intelligence Summaries are contained in F.S. Regs., Part II. and the Staff Manual respectively. Title pages will be prepared in manuscript.

Place	Date	Hour	Summary of Events and Information	Remarks and references to Appendices
CROIX du BAC	1915 1st Nov.	am	Inspected 68th Inf. Brigade 1st Field Park re accommodation.	
			2 Lt E.H. MITCHELL took over duties of Reconnoitring Officer W.A. Group.	68th Bde Group
			2 Lt L.C. OSBOURNE Do.	
			2 Lt D.M. Webb Do.	69th Bde Group
		5.15 pm	Administrative Conference Divl. Headquarters	
			Transport 35 horses R.E. etc.	
			Weather wet.	
"	2nd Nov.	am	Inspected 24th S Inf Brigade 1st Field Park re accommodation	
			2 Lt GUPPY att 2nd Northants Regt handed over to team for cyclists while awaiting Continental Pass	
			Transport 20 horses R.E., 10 S.S.O., 12 for moving blankets of 6 Battalions	
			Weather - wet.	
			Conference Divl. Headquarters	
"	3rd Nov.	9 am	Inspected 69th Inf. Bde 1st Field Park re accommodation	
			Transport 29 horses R.E. etc.	
			Weather. Showery	

WAR DIARY
or
INTELLIGENCE SUMMARY.
(Erase heading not required.)

Army Form C. 2118

Place	Date	Hour	Summary of Events and Information	Remarks and references to Appendices
CROIX de BAC	1915 4th Nov	am	Inspected forward billetting area with O.C. 26th F.C. R.E. Major C.D.E. Upton acting D.A.A.M.G. of Div. from the eve: had H Northen acting S.S.O.	
			4 H.D. horses received from Remounts. 2 to 190 Co, 1 each to 191 & 192 Co.	
		pm	Transport 24 hour R.E. & S.S.O.	
			To H.Q.C. & No 3 Co.	
			Weather - fine - cold	
"	5th Nov	am	To 66th Bde Headquarters re accumulation & transport of 1st line.	
		pm	To all 4 Companies	
			Transport 16 hours R.E.	
			Weather - fine	
"	6th Nov	am	Visited all 1st line Parks re overhead cover for stabling	
			To No. 4 Co.	
		pm	Transport 16 wagons R.E., 12 wagons or blankets for 6 battalions	
			Weather fine	

WAR DIARY
or
INTELLIGENCE SUMMARY.
(Erase heading not required.)

Army Form C. 2118

Place	Date	Hour	Summary of Events and Information	Remarks and references to Appendices
CROIX du BAC.	1915 7 Nov.	9.15 am	Church Parade H.Q.C.	
			Transport 28 wagons RE & SSO, 6 wagons attached for 3 F.F. trains	
			Weather fine	
"	8 Nov.	am	Detachment 1 Offr 1 NCO 14 Gunners 26 horses & 4 wagons returned from July at LA NIEPPE	
		am	Visited forward billeting area with AA & QMG and GSO (3) 23rd Div	
		5.14 pm	Administrative Conference Div. Headquarters.	
			Transport 34 horses RE & SSO.	
			Weather fine	
	9 Nov.		Dvr. ELLIS and SCARROTT N.&C. died from Coal gas poisoning	
		am	Court of Inquiry on same	
		am	To Rouches BAC ST MAUR with O.C. 20th F.G. RE with regard to building stands for army rations	
			Medical inspection 19.C.	
			Transport 27 horses RE & SSO.	
			Weather - dull	

Army Form C. 2118

WAR DIARY
or
INTELLIGENCE SUMMARY.
(Erase heading not required.)

Instructions regarding War Diaries and Intelligence Summaries are contained in F. S. Regs., Part II. and the Staff Manual respectively. Title pages will be prepared in manuscript.

Place	Date	Hour	Summary of Events and Information	Remarks and references to Appendices
CROIX du BAC	1915 10 Nov	9 am	23rd Bde. R.G.A. Lift Division. Copies to Div. Headquarters	
		2.30pm	Funeral Drs. ELLIS and SCARROTT in ERQUINGHEM CEMETERY. Medical inspection 194 C. Transport 10.30 am R.E., 10 S.S.O., 8 r. Blankets. Weather dull & cold	
	11. Nov		To BETHUNE to see Chief R.T.O. re moving 13AC ST MAUR as Railhead Point. Commenced moving "moving Motors" from LA MEUGATE road. Medical inspection 192 C. Transport 25 R.E. Weather fine & cold.	
	12 Nov		1 Sqy 2. 6 Divn. to LA MIEPPE. Railhead Point at Railhead 13AC ST MAUR for consumption on 13th. Supply Column loaded out Supplies and Forage for 1 day now laid up at STEENWERCK. Medical inspection 193 C. Transport 24 R.E. Weather - Showery.	Found 2 Cadish Officers - 4 wagon with mules.

WAR DIARY or INTELLIGENCE SUMMARY

Army Form C. 2118

Place	Date	Hour	Summary of Events and Information	Remarks and references to Appendices
Croix du Bac	1915 13th Nov		Commenced erecting marquee tents at BAC ST MAUR station. 2nd Worcester Regt. rejoined 24th Bde. from 2nd Division ESTAIRES. Transport: 27 pairs R.E. 8 pairs blankets. Weather wet.	
"	14th "		Sunday – 10.0 Church Parade. 10 W Riding Regt. rejoined Division from 2nd Div. ESTAIRES. Transport 6 pairs R.E. 4 pairs blankets & baggage to Rising Pyjm. Weather fair, frost.	
"	15th "		Work on marquee tents at BAC-ST-MAUR station. Visited No.3 & 2 Coyfusion. Females refused on stretchers instead of Protos cars – we commuted 3 plants be returned while function of practice continued only, others felt influence necessary. Transport 16 pairs R.E. 4 pairs blankets. Weather fine.	
"	16th "		To ARMENTIERES AMBERG in Coit. Work on tents at BAC ST MAUR station. Transport: 22 R.E. 16 blankets. Weather cold – frost.	

WAR DIARY
or
INTELLIGENCE SUMMARY.
(Erase heading not required.)

Army Form C. 2118

Instructions regarding War Diaries and Intelligence Summaries are contained in F.S. Regs., Part II. and the Staff Manual respectively. Title pages will be prepared in manuscript.

Place	Date	Hour	Summary of Events and Information	Remarks and references to Appendices
Croix du Bac	1915			
	17th Nov	9am	Conference - Div. Head quarters - no horse casualties. Supply & Transport.	
			Visits R.A.C. & No.4 C.	
			To Armentieres no cal.	
			Transport 18 from R.E. 8 from Cal.	
			Weather - showery.	
	18th Nov	am	Meeting of Copey Commissions re accessory buildings to be used in them Corps + report for same forwarded P.S.	
			To Reffeling Point	
			Transport: 12 from R.E. La Motte, 17 from R.E. 10 from SSO Cal.	
			Weather - dull & cold.	
	19th Nov	am	Inspect'd wet bedding. also visit O.C. 2.ᵈ Army Tranp C. R.E. as to disposal of repairs.	
			Transport 8 from R.E. 20 from Cal. & mech.	
			Weather fine and cold.	
	20 "	am	Visits et from Cofermas	
			Transp 16 from R.E. 8 the Auto.	
			Weather - dull	
	21 "	am	Sunday. No Church Parade.	
			To Reffeling Point	
			Transport - 16 from R.E. 6 from C. La Motte. A.D.S.S. for Inspecting Motor.	
			Weather - fine.	

Army Form C. 2118

WAR DIARY
or
INTELLIGENCE SUMMARY.
(Erase heading not required.)

Instructions regarding War Diaries and Intelligence Summaries are contained in F.S. Regs., Part II. and the Staff Manual respectively. Title pages will be prepared in manuscript.

Place	Date	Hour	Summary of Events and Information	Remarks and references to Appendices
CROIX du BAC	1915 22nd Mar		24th F.Hardy Bryant having joined the Division permanently from 8 E. Div via 70 & 97 Brigades B99 92 wagons of 8 E Div Train were returned to them, and 23 wTrain baggage wagons received back. 9 G.S. wagons & 1 Limbered G.S. wagon. Transferred 14 horses R.E. 6 from LA MOTTE. Weather fine - frost.	
	23rd	5.15pm	Administrative Conference - Question about supply of stuff rations.	
		am	To Hqrs Rifle Brigade Pond, H.Q. & No.2 Companies. Transferred 16 wagons R.E. Weather - heavy frost.	
	24th	9 am	Conference in Divl Headquarters - No funds. Capt Langford D.S.O. commenced attendance at Divl Headquarters being absence of A.D.M.S. Transferred 14 horses R.E. 22 from or thereabouts. Weather fine, cold.	
	25th	am	Major UPTON, CAPTn HADDEN and KESSACK, Lieuts BERRYMAN and LLOYD DAVIS left on 7 days leave to ENGLAND. To all four Companies. Transferred 16 horses to LA MOTTE for horses. Weather cold & damp.	

2353 Wt. W2544/1454 700,000 5/15 D.D.&L. A.D.S.S./Forms/C. 2118.

Army Form C. 2118

WAR DIARY
or
INTELLIGENCE SUMMARY.
(Erase heading not required.)

Instructions regarding War Diaries and Intelligence Summaries are contained in F. S. Regs., Part II. and the Staff Manual respectively. Title pages will be prepared in manuscript.

Place	Date	Hour	Summary of Events and Information	Remarks and references to Appendices
CROIX du BAC	1915 26 Nov.	am	To ct for Corporate	
	27 Nov.	am	Transport 8 from R.E. 6 from Flaubaix. 16 from LA MOTTE. Weather fine & cold.	
		pm	Ripping Point and HERENTIGHES Reco'd No. 4 G.	
			Transport 12 from R.E. 6 from road, whom blankets. Weather frost.	
	28 Nov.	am	Sunday no Church Parade. Turned out by & on Supply Column.	
		pm	Visited Ruches & reported there arival by 2 O.C. Div. & 2 Capt Twiss leaving them Supply Column. 2nd Div' started 2 pm. completed 4.30 pm. Capt Twiss completed 6.15 pm.	
			Transport 8 from R.E. 12 from road, 10 from blankets. Weather heavy frost.	
	29 "	10 am	Bears on strong Saul at M.A.C.	
			Worked all am for Corporate.	
			Transport 8 from R.E. 9 from road, 16 from LA MOTTE. Weather wet.	
	30 "		To Ruches 13th ST MAUR, as are emport to Ripping.	
			Transport 12 from R.E. - 6 from huches, 5 from LA MOTTE. Weather fine.	

A. North
Lieut. Col.
Cmdg 23rd D.S. Staves
1-12-15

23rd Int. Sham.
Vol. 4

IC/7909

9 June

CONFIDENTIAL

WAR DIARY.

By Lt. Colonel. A. Northen

Commanding XXIIIrd Divisional Train A.S.C.

To D.A.G. 3rd Echelon

December 1915

WAR DIARY
or
INTELLIGENCE SUMMARY.
(Erase heading not required.)

Army Form C. 2118

Instructions regarding War Diaries and Intelligence Summaries are contained in F. S. Regs., Part II. and the Staff Manual respectively. Title pages will be prepared in manuscript.

Place	Date	Hour	Summary of Events and Information	Remarks and references to Appendices
CROIX-du-BAC	1915 1st Dec.	a.m.	Lieuts. J.S. MATTERSON, A.G. EDEN, 2 hund. D.M. WATSON, 1st Class S.S.M. C.F. McGONAGIL and 1 N.C.O. proceeded on 7 days leave to ENGLAND.	
		9 a.m.	Conference at Divisional Headquarters. Question of supply of certain vegetables, and ration of coal. The latter reduced to 1½ lbs. owing to short supply from ENGLAND.	
			For details No. 2 Company; Nunc. Transport 16 pairs R.E. Weather fine.	
	2nd Dec.	a.m.	Three motored lorries joined from Base M.T. Depot. 3 lorries transferred to Base M.T. Depot. To railhead APPEST. MAUR enough to convey drawing supplies at 7.45 a.m., & to supplied by 11 a.m. to allow 3rd Corps Troops to draw on the morning of the 2nd Division officers. * Transport 14 pairs R.E. 16 pairs for Blankets and Baggage. * Weather fine Day, wet night. Sergt. A.T. EMBLETON appointed A/S.S.M. for duty with 7th Field Ambulance, vice Sergt. J.B. Foster.	
	3rd Dec.	a.m.	Lt.Col A. MATTHEW proceeded on 7 days leave to ENGLAND. Transport 16 pairs R.E. 11 pairs 1/A MOTTS for two horsed C.T. for Mashing, 2 pairs blankets. Weather wet all day.	

Army Form C. 2118

WAR DIARY
or
INTELLIGENCE SUMMARY.
(Erase heading not required.)

Place	Date	Hour	Summary of Events and Information	Remarks and references to Appendices
CROIX du BAC	1915 4th Dec	—	Transport 8 pairs R.E. 16 pairs LA MOTTE for truckwork, 3 pairs bricks. Weather wet and rough.	
	5th Dec		Three entrained divisions joined from Base H.T. Depot. Transport 18 pairs R.E. Weather dull and wet.	
	6th Dec		Three diseased drivers transferred to Base H.T. Depot. Transport 22 pairs blankets, 10 pairs LA MOTTE for truckwork etc., 6 pairs R.E., 4 pairs S.S.O. Weather wet, cold. 3 H.D. horses received from Remount Depot. Capt. T. H. MONTGOMERY, J. W. C. AGATE, Lieut. H. NORTHEN, C.W.G. LODGE, A.W. HOOLEY proceeded on 7 days leave to ENGLAND.	(1) # Dec Junction from No. 22
	7th Dec		Transport 6 pairs LA MOTTE for truckwork etc., 8 pairs R.E., 2 pairs bricks. Weather mild showery. 3 H.D. horses received from Remount Depot.	
	8th Dec		1st Class S.S.M. C.J. McGONAGIL transferred to KENSINGTON Barracks LONDON. Reinforcement of nine drivers joined from Base H.T. Depot. Transport 14 pairs LA MOTTE, 8 pairs R.E. Weather dull.	A.G.13416 No.57/B276 of 5·12·15

Army Form C. 2118.

WAR DIARY
or
INTELLIGENCE SUMMARY.
(Erase heading not required.)

Instructions regarding War Diaries and Intelligence Summaries are contained in F. S. Regs., Part II. and the Staff Manual respectively. Title pages will be prepared in manuscript.

Place	Date	Hour	Summary of Events and Information	Remarks and references to Appendices
CROIX du BAC	1915 9th Dec		No. 7/1/1. Dr. T. HERN 193C. attached H.Q. 24th Bgde seriously wounded by shrapnel, admitted 7/1/2 Field Ambulance, died same day. ERAVINGHEM first shells. No. 7/4 SHO681 Dr. W. FERGUSON 191C. attacks H.R. 26C Bgade wounded by shrapnel admitted 7/1/F Ambulance.	
	10th Dec		Transport 12 horses LAMOTTE, 6 horses R.E. Weather very wet.	
	11th Dec		Transport 10 horses LAMOTTE, 6 horses R.E. Weather very wet. Capt. C. LANGFORD, DSO, Lieuts. E.A. SOUTHEE, E.H. MITCHELL, N.A. ELLIOTT and one NCO proceeded on 7 days leave to ENGLAND. Visits all from Companies. C.Q.M.S. JARRETT admitted to Hospital BAILLEUL on shock of shell fire from 4 cwt. Pte. A.G. EDEN on leave in ENGLAND granted extra leave until 20th 13 inst. Transport 14 horses R.E. Weather very wet.	
	12th Dec	a.m.	ERAVINGHEM Bridge about enough to floor, at depth about 30 ms. RAC 1st MAUR Bridge. Visits RAILWAY. Transport 6 horses R.E., 2 horses Baggage. Weather wet.	

Army Form C. 2118

WAR DIARY
or
INTELLIGENCE SUMMARY.
(Erase heading not required.)

Instructions regarding War Diaries and Intelligence Summaries are contained in F. S. Regs., Part II. and the Staff Manual respectively. Title pages will be prepared in manuscript.

Place	Date	Hour	Summary of Events and Information	Remarks and references to Appendices
CROIX du BAC	1915 13 Dec		Copy of New Defence Scheme (S.G. 12) received. Details by Hd/qrtrs to thoroughly inspect and report on all billets of the Division as to their accommodation arrangements for additional training, etc. Inspected RUE MARLÉ area.— Transport 16 horses LA MOTTE, 4 pair R.E. Weather – fine.	
	14 Dec		Inspected LA ROLANDERIE area. Transport 8 pair LA MOTTE, 4 pair R.E., 8 pair S.S.O., 16 pair Flanders etc. Weather – fine.	* (2) Div. Operation Order No. 23
	15 Dec	9 a.m.	Conference Divisional Headquarters, no particular points raised. Lieut. J.T. MATTERSON and 12 N.C.O.s and others Rhine for promotion of a V.C. No. 12946 A/Serjt H. PAYNE appointed A/CSMS 19ºC vice A/CSMS TARRETT. Transport: 14 horses LA MOTTE, 4 pair R.E. Weather – fine. Letter from W.O. London, stating Lieut. A.G. EDEN still on Furlough.	

Army Form C. 21

WAR DIARY
or
INTELLIGENCE SUMMARY.
(Erase heading not required.)

Instructions regarding War Diaries and Intelligence Summaries are contained in F. S. Regs., Part II. and the Staff Manual respectively. Title pages will be prepared in manuscript.

Place	Date	Hour	Summary of Events and Information	Remarks and references to Appendices
CROIX du BAC	19/14 16 Dec	am	2nd Lieuts T.A. FRANCIS, F.C. PHEYSEY, 3 NCOs & men proceeded on 7 days leave to ENGLAND. Three untrained Drivers joined joining from Base R.D. Depot. Three trained Drivers transferred to Base R.D. Depot today. Received order from Dir. Transportation to debar on Train mules as for those men owing to breakdown. Forwarded report on "Empire" repairs by Train to D.D.S. & T. 1st Army of grain being rail authorised. Cables HALLOBEAU & JESUS FARM area— Transport 19 lorries breakdowns, 7 R.E. Weather fine — ERQUINGHEM Bridge repairs for dipper.	
	17 Dec	am	Vet. Officer inspected half the horses of Nos. 41, 192 & 193 Companies, nil reacted — Units 191, 192 & 193 Cos. Transport 17 lorries breakdowns, 8 from R.E. Weather — fine	
	18 Dec	am	Lieut Goyett of 15.6 Temp Recd H. MORTHEN to be Company Captain. Sgt. J.A FRANCIS to L. Corpl. Returned. Vet. Officer inspected remaining horses of No. 191, 192 & 193 Companies, nil reacted. Inspected billets. FORT ROMPU & DOR MOIRE area. Transport 14 breakdowns, 4 R.E. Weather fine.	

WAR DIARY
or
INTELLIGENCE SUMMARY

Army Form C. 2118

Place	Date	Hour	Summary of Events and Information	Remarks and references to Appendices
CROIX du BAC 134c	19/12	am	Sunday, no Church Parade. Vet. Officer inspected half the horses of 19 Co. MTC & marked ones to be cast. A.F. B213 & 2 folios B.C. rendered as a result of Inspection of Horses, and up by Corporal Tindles Parties. Transport 4 from RE, 2 from Slaughter. Some Officers & men of Train, slightly affected by gas in billets. Weather fine and dry.	
	20 Dec		Capt N. NORTHEN took over duties of S.O. 6th S. Bgade vice 2/Lt R.V. HOLMES L'expecting orders (probably) to have Transport Parks. 63rd & 69th G Bgade. Transport 10 from Slaughter, 4 R.E., 2 from Bagan. Weather fine.	
	21 Dec		Capt. T.W.C. AGATE proceeded by motor to THEROUANNE & took over Transport for 2nd F. Bay. Machine Gun Company vice 1 F.S. Wagon, 4 G.S. Limbered Wagon, 1 Cook cart, 1 water cart, 13 horses, 7 men. 2/Lieut. L.C. Osborne, 1 W.O., 3 N.C.Os proceeded on 7 days leave to ENGLAND. Transport 10 from Slaughter, 8 from R.E. Weather still good.	

Army Form C. 2118

WAR DIARY
or
INTELLIGENCE SUMMARY.
(Erase heading not required.)

Instructions regarding War Diaries and Intelligence Summaries are contained in F. S. Regs., Part II. and the Staff Manual respectively. Title pages will be prepared in manuscript.

Place	Date	Hour	Summary of Events and Information	Remarks and references to Appendices
C.Rock An 13AC	1915 22nd Dec	9 am	Conference at Divl. Headquarters, as to future system of —	
			Following officers reconnoitred for future line. Lt Capron, Lieut R.J. Lloyd-Davis, E.A. Smythe, H. Berryman	(3)
			Inspected billets. R.A. wagon lines	
			Transport 10 horse breakers, 8 horse C.R.E., 10 horse Wass, 15 horse shoeshs.	Div Quarterm No. 24
			Weather dull.	
	23rd Dec		Inspected billets. R.A. wagon lines	
			Transport 10 horse breakers, 6 R.E. 3 S.S.O.	
			Weather fine, wet.	
	24th Dec		Inspected billets. R.A. wagon lines	
			Transport 7 horse R.E.	
		5pm	Church Parade in Leese of 193 C. + 200 Officers NCOs from "Royal Scots" —	
			Weather fine	
	25th Dec		Transport 2 horse R.E.	
			FRAMINGHAM gun sheds	
			Cross Country 5km followed by Company Crunch.	
			Weather fine	

Army Form C. 2118

WAR DIARY
or
INTELLIGENCE SUMMARY.
(Erase heading not required.)

Instructions regarding War Diaries and Intelligence Summaries are contained in F. S. Regs., Part II. and the Staff Manual respectively. Title pages will be prepared in manuscript.

Place	Date	Hour	Summary of Events and Information	Remarks and references to Appendices
CROIX du BAC	1915 26 Dec	a.m.	Sunday - 2 Lieut R.W. HOLMES and 4 N.C.O.s Lincolns and 7 days leave to England. Three mechanics drivers joined from Base M.T. Depot. Transport 4 horse, R.E., 4 horse stores, 5 horse baggage. Weather fine day, wet at night.	
	27 -	a.m.	Inspected vehicles D.A.C. Three drivers Hampshires 6 - 7 D.V. Team. Transport 8 horse LA MOTTE, 6 horse R.E. Weather wet.	
	28 -		Visited by Dir. Transporation to find vehicles for 3 Machine Gun Companies. Visited 1st A.C. & No. 3 Co. Transport 8 horse Police etc., 7 R.E. Weather fine showers. Forwarded report to Dir. Transportation on purchases made by French authorities, and other than in the Divisional Area, owing to men in the party of regulate it.	

2353 Wt.W2544/1454 700,000 5/15 D. D. & L. A.D.S.S./Forms/C. 2118.

Army Form C. 2118

WAR DIARY
or
INTELLIGENCE SUMMARY.
(Erase heading not required.)

Instructions regarding War Diaries and Intelligence Summaries are contained in F. S. Regs., Part II. and the Staff Manual respectively. Title pages will be prepared in manuscript.

Place	Date	Hour	Summary of Events and Information	Remarks and references to Appendices
CROIX du BAC	1915 29th Dec	12.45am	Fire at billets occupied by 19th C. M.C. exhibited and on Cookers & showrooms destroyed.	(*)
		am	Inspected and reported on billets for two Machine Gun Companies	See Appendix No. 25
			Transport: 10 pairs La MOTTE, 7 pairs R.E. 5 pairs baggage. (*) Am. Transport Co. provided 16 pairs for the shift. Am. Transport Co. provided 16 pairs for the shift. Over No. 25.
			Remainder of horses of 19th C. exercised by Vet. Officers and noted -
	30th Dec	10 am	Court of enquiry on Fire at 19th C's billets. Fire, on evidence one to a rat having hung to kerosene tin from a hen plug (tench) parting.
			19th C. M.C. took over 8 wagons (sig) from D.A.C. to assist the transport.
		pm	Inspected billets - 65 F and 76 F Field Ambulances. 110th Heavy Battery.
			Transport: 10 pairs. LA MOTTE, 8 pairs R.E. 4 horses, 3 pairs Baggage.
			Weather fine.
	31st	am	Fired off Cos and 1 trumrs (Canadian Forces) on 7 day's leave to ENGLAND
			Visited billets 19th and 192 Coys ???
			Transport 8 pairs transport etc, 9 pairs C.R.E. 1 baggage
			Weather fine
	6-1-1916		

A. Mondsley
Lieut C. Grant
A.D.C
Army 23rd Div ???

Appendix (1)

SECRET. Copy No. 7

23rd DIVISION OPERATION ORDER NO 22.

December 1st 1915.

1. The 69th Bde will relieve the 24th Bde in the Right Section of the 23rd Division Line on the night of 6th/7th December. The frontage is from Trench I.31/4 to I.26.4. both inclusive.

2. After relief the 24th Brigade will withdraw into Divisional Reserve to billets as under :-

    H.Q.   ERQUINGHEM.
    1 Bn.   FORT ROMPU.
    1 Bn.   RUE DORMOIRE.
    1 Bn.   JESUS FARM.
    1 Bn.   HALLOBEAU.

The D.A.Q.M.G. will point out billeting areas.

3. All trench stores, bombs etc., will be handed over by daylight.

4. All details of the move will be arranged by the Brigadiers of 24th Bde & 69th Bde.

5. No movement of troops South of the railway, either to or from the trenches, is to commence before 4 p.m.

6. The 12th Trench Mortar Battery, 102nd Fd. Co. R.E. & one Company 9th S. Staffords Regt will come under the orders of G.O.C. 69th Bde.

7. No Trench is to be vacated by 24th Brigade until occupied by 69th Bde.

8. Brigadier General Oxley will remain in Command of the Right Section until the relief is completed.

9. ACKNOWLEDGE.

C.F. Watson.
Major.
General Staff 23rd Division.

H.Q. 23rd Division.
Issued at 5.30 p.m.
S.G. 172.

SECRET.   COPY NO. 7

23RD DIVISION OPERATION ORDER NO. 23.

December 10th, 1915.

1. The 24th Bde. will relieve the 68th Bde. in the LEFT SECTION of the 23rd Division Line on the night of 14th/15th December. The frontage is from Trench I.26/5 to I.16 inclusive.

2. After relief the 68th Brigade will withdraw into Divisional Reserve to billets as under :-

    H.Q.   ERQUINGHEM.
    1 Bn. FORT ROMPU.
    1 Bn. RUE DORMOIRE.
    1 Bn. JESUS FARM.
    1 Bn. HALLOBEAU.

    The D. A. Q. M. G. will point out billeting areas.

3. All trench stores, bombs, etc., will be handed over by daylight.

4. All details of the move will be arranged by the Brigadiers of 24th and 68th Brigades.

5. No movement of troops South of RUE MARLE, either to or from trenches, is to commence before 4 p.m.

6. The 21st Trench Mortar Battery, 128th Fd. Co. R.E. and one Company 9th South Staffords. Regt. will come under the orders of Brig. Genl. OXLEY.

7. No Trench is to be vacated by 68th Brigade until occupied by 24th Brigade.

8. Brigadier General SEROCOLD will remain in Command of the LEFT SECTION until the relief is completed.

9. ACKNOWLEDGE.

                                    A Blair   Lieutenant Colonel,
Issued at 6 p.m.   General Staff, 23rd Division.

S.G.3.

Appendix (3)

SECRET.   COPY NO. 10

23RD DIVISION OPERATION ORDER NO. 24.

December 18th, 1915.

1. The 68th Bde. will relieve the 69th Bde. in the RIGHT SECTION of the 23rd Division Line on the night of 22nd/23rd December. The frontage is from Trench I.31/1 to I.26/4 inclusive.

2. After relief the 69th Bde. will withdraw into Divisional Reserve to billets as under:-

        H.Q. ERQUINGHEM.
        1 Bn. FORT ROMPU.
        1 Bn. RUE DORMOIRE.
        1 Bn. JESUS FARM.
        1 Bn. HALLOBEAU.

The D.A.Q.M.G. will point out billeting areas.

3. All details of the move will be arranged by the Brigadiers of 68th and 69th Bdes.

4. No movement of troops South of LA ROLANDERIE, either to or from the Trenches, before 4 p.m.

5. The 12th Trench Mortar Battery, 102nd Fd. Co. R.E. and one Company 9th South Staffords Regt. will come under the orders of Brigadier General SEROCOLD.

6. No Trench is to be vacated by the 69th Bde. until occupied by the 68th Bde.

7. Brigadier General DERHAM will remain in Command of the RIGHT SECTION until the relief is completed.

                              A. Blair   Lieut-Colonel,

Issued at 6 p.m.   General Staff, 23rd Division.

SECRET   COPY NO. 10

Appendix (4)

23RD DIVISION OPERATION ORDER NO. 25.

1. The 69th Bde. will relieve the 24th Bde. in the LEFT SECTION of the 23rd Division Line on the night of 29th/30th December. The Frontage is from Trench I.26/5 to I/16, both inclusive.

2. After relief the 24th Bde. will withdraw into Divisional Reserve to billets as under :-

        H. Q. .... ERQUINGHEM.
        1 Bn. .... FORT ROMPU.
        1 Bn. .... RUE DORMOIRE.
        1 Bn. .... JESUS FARM.
        1 Bn. .... HALLOBEAU.

    The D. A. Q. M. G. will point out billeting areas.

3. All details of the move will be arranged by the Brigadiers of 24th and 69th Bdes.

4. No movement of troops South of RUE MARLE, either to or from the trenches, is to commence before 4 p.m.

5. The 128th Fd. Coy. R. E. and one company 9th South Staffords. Regt. will come under the orders of Brigadier General DERHAM.

6. No trench is to be vacated by the 24th Bde. until occupied by the 69th Bde.

7. Brigadier General OXLEY will remain in Command of the LEFT SECTION until the relief is completed.

8. Acknowledge.

                                                  A Blair
Issued at 8 p.m.   Lieut. Colonel,
25/12/1915.   General Staff, 23rd Division.

        Copies to :-
            No. 1.   24th Bde.   No. 5,6,7   R.A.
               2.   68th Bde.   8   R.E.
               3.   69th Bde.   9   9th S. Staffords.
               4.   "Q"   10   Train.
                                              11   Diary.

23rd Strike Pain
vol. 5
TAN.

On His Majesty's Service.

Confidential

War Diary
of
Lt. Colonel A. Northen.
Commanding
23rd Divisional Train A.S.C.

From 1st to 31st January 1916

WAR DIARY
or
INTELLIGENCE SUMMARY.

Army Form C. 2118.

Place	Date	Hour	Summary of Events and Information	Remarks and references to Appendices
CROIX du BAC	1916 1st Jan		Transport 11 faim R.E., 8 faim LA MOTTE 3 faim various - health fair.	
	2nd Jan		Sunday - No Church Parade. Transport 4 faim R.E., 2 faim blankets - health, drill and rain -	
	3rd Jan		Transport 13 faim R.E. 6 faim baggage, 6 faim stores - health fair.	
	4 "	5.15pm	Lecture by A.P.M. 23rd Division to Officers & NCOs of Tun, subject "Road Discipline".	
		10 am	Lt. Col. NORTHEN, President of F.G.C.M.	
		"	Board of Officers on Shorey Smith for 12hrs Transport in East of 1916 & ASS	
			Transport 13 faim R.E. 5 faim smith coal health fair	
	5 "	9 am	Captain Du Margarlin. Question of allowance of Col. SCC 14 th. owing to requirement of Div. Batt. having WO not act of weekly allowance of 86 km. 5 N.COs proceeded on 7 days leave to ENGLAND.	

WAR DIARY
or
INTELLIGENCE SUMMARY.
(Erase heading not required.)

Army Form C. 2118.

Place	Date	Hour	Summary of Events and Information	Remarks and references to Appendices
CROIX du BAC	1916 5 Jan (cont)		Transport 15 hours R.E. 3 hours sacks. Weather fine & mild.	
	6.		Compiled & despatched War Diary for Dec. 1915. Capt. Hyde inspects 1st Line Transport 24 6/17 Brigade. Capt. Montgomery inspects 1st Line Transport of A.S. Staff Hqrs. Transport - 15 hours R.E. 6 hours thaw, 3 hours harrow. Weather - dull.	(1) Sparrin orders No 26 of 4.1.16
	7.		Transport :- 2.18 hours R.E. 12 hours baggage & ammunition, 24 hours from him H.T.G. Blankets 24 hours from H.T.G. Weather wet & stormy.	(1) Spec. Order No.1 of 5/1/16 etc.
	8.		Capt. KESSALL inspects 1st Line Transport 6.9. Lz. Brigade. Lieut. J.F.BARRY rejoins from No.9 Stationary Hospital, HAVRE. 12. H.D. horses received from Remount Depot. Transport: 32 hours R.E. 1 truck. Weather - fine & cold.	

WAR DIARY
or
INTELLIGENCE SUMMARY.

Place	Date	Hour	Summary of Events and Information	Remarks and references to Appendices
CROIX du BAC	1916 9 Jan.		Sunday, No Church Parade. Lieut A.G. EDEN granted sick leave in ENGLAND b. 21st inst. W.O. letter 3836/4 (A.M.G. 6-) of 3-1-1916 Transport: 26 fam R.E. 4 fam Rns. Weather fine & dry.	
	10		Received from Divl. Headquarters orders to inspect billets of Heavy & Siege Artillery attacks to Division, re accommodation & accessory buildings, repairs & N.Cos. proceeded on 7 days leave to ENGLAND. Transport 19 fam R.E. 10 fam blankets. weather fine	
	11		Capt. AGATE to BOULOGNE to Officer R.A under arrest. Transport 27 fam R.E.; 8 fam blankets; 6 fam Rns 3 fam rations weather fine	
	12	9am	Sent in report on billets of Heavy & Siege Batteries. Conference Divl. Headquarters re engineers; in event of severe frost & ensuing thaw for traffic etc.	

Army Form C. 2118.

WAR DIARY
or
INTELLIGENCE SUMMARY.
(Erase heading not required.)

Place	Date	Hour	Summary of Events and Information	Remarks and references to Appendices
CROIX du BAC	1916 12 Jan (cont.)		Transport – 40 horses R.E. 3 horses various. Weather, stormy.	
	13 –		Forwarded to Div. Headquarters report on Transport & Supply arrangements in event of Fins 2 & 3 arr. Transport 32 horses R.E., also 2 horses. Weather stormy.	
	14 –		Capt. C. LANGFORD P.S.O. employed at Div. Headquarters "D" March for the day. Capt. AGATE returns from BOULOGNE. Received orders from Div. Headquarters to find billets for two Brigade Machine Gun Companies. Transport 28 horses R.E. 2 horses Supply Col. Weather, fair.	
	15 –		Forwarded report in detail for Machine Gun Companies. Transport 28 horses R.E. 12 horses Photo, 12 horses baggage, 24 horses from Arri R.T.C. Weather, wet. 8 N.C.Os who were warranted on 7 days leave to ENGLAND	(2). Upon Order No. 28 of 11-1-16

Army Form C. 2118.

WAR DIARY
or
INTELLIGENCE SUMMARY.
(Erase heading not required.)

Place	Date	Hour	Summary of Events and Information	Remarks and references to Appendices
CROIX de BAC	1916 16 Jan		R.A.M.C. Capt. A.C.W. KNOX admits 71st F. Ambulance, 2nd Lieut. No. 2 C.C.S. BAILLEUL. Lieut. PHEYSEY proceeds to BOULOGNE for medical treatment, returns same day. 3 Supply men reported from 432 M.T.C.(2) and 3rd C. A.S.C.(1). Transport 14 horse R.E., lorries trucks. Weather - fair.	
	17.	10 am	Capt. KNOX evacuated from No 2 C.C.S. BAILLEUL to BOULOGNE. Board of Officers on Shoeing Smith in lines of 19th C. M.T.C. S.S.O. visits advance posts for inspection of reserve supplies. Transport 23 horse R.E. Weather dull.	
	18.		Transport 24 horse R.E. Weather wet.	
	19.		Conference Div. Headquarters, subject of move to Rest Area discussed. Transport 20 horse R.E., 14 horse baggage + blankets, 4 horse chai. Weather fair.	

Army Form C. 2118.

WAR DIARY
or
INTELLIGENCE SUMMARY.
(Erase heading not required.)

Place	Date	Hour	Summary of Events and Information	Remarks and references to Appendices
CROIX du BAC	1916 20th Jan		8 N.Co. then proceeded on 7 days leave to ENGLAND. Lt. Col. NORTHEN proceeded with S.S.O. to Rest Area, to obtain information as S.&T. Services. 9 drivers and 3 Supply men reported from BASE M.T. Depot as reinforcements. Transport 32 train R.E. Weather - fine.	
	21st "		Received orders from Divn. Headquarters to find billets for incoming Units of 34th Divn. Transport 30 train R.E., 7 lorries. Weather - not noted.	
	22nd "		Took Off. Lyon 24th Sept. Bayart round reports leave to 34th Divn. 2 Lieut. F.C. PHEYSEY promoted Temp. Lieut. Lrn Gazette of 22-1-1916. Transport 20 train R.E., 5 lorries LA MOTTE. Weather - fine.	
	23rd "		3 Supply men who arrived on 20th inst, returned to H.T. Depot Base as surplus. 1 Lt. H.D. Turner and 3 Riders received from Remount Depot.	

Army Form C. 2118.

WAR DIARY
or
INTELLIGENCE SUMMARY.
(Erase heading not required.)

Instructions regarding War Diaries and Intelligence Summaries are contained in F. S. Regs., Part II. and the Staff Manual respectively. Title pages will be prepared in manuscript.

Place	Date	Hour	Summary of Events and Information	Remarks and references to Appendices
CROIX du BAC	1916 23rd Jan (cont)		Transport 11 horses R.E., 14 horses baggage, 4 horses officers, 5 horses police, 24 horses Amm. H.T.C. weather dull.	(3) Opn Orders No.29 of 18.1.16 blanks
	24.		Reinforcement of 4 horses from B.A.I.G. H.T. Depot. Capt. H.T. MONTGOMERY recommended for promotion to Temp. Major. Transport 20 horses R.E. 5 horses trucks. weather dull.	
	25.		9 N.C.Os horses forwarded on 7 day's leave to ENGLAND. Transport 21 horses R.E. weather dull.	
	26.	9 a.m.	Conference Div. Headquarters, question of supply of hay, only 6 lbs. per horse and a Pack Train. Strs. arrived in turn. H.D. Batts. L.D. rations 6 lbs., ½ wheat, ½ oat, Hqs. 101st Inf. Bde & 2 Bns; 207 F.G. R.E. and a detachment of 231 C. Coy., all of 34th Division attached for rations from this date.	
			Transport 26 horses R.E. weather dull.	

Army Form C. 2118.

WAR DIARY
or
INTELLIGENCE SUMMARY.
(Erase heading not required.)

Place	Date	Hour	Summary of Events and Information	Remarks and references to Appendices
CROIX du BAC	1916 27ᵗʰ Jan		S.S.M. McDonnell admitted to 71ˢᵗ Field Ambulance. Transport 2/ham R.E, 6/ham char, 2/ham baggage. Weather fine/rain, dull.	
	28.		Transport 12/ham R.E. Weather fine.	
	29.		Transport 14/ham R.E, 3 various. Weather dull.	
	30.		Lieut. Col. A. WORTHEN and 8 NCOs men proceeded on 7 days leave to ENGLAND. Transport 6/ham R.E. Weather fair, cold.	
	31.		Lieut. A.G. EDEN struck off strength of B.E.F. unfit for general service. Transport 14 R.E., 11/ham char, 14 returned baggage, 24/ham blankets Ammᵗⁿ H.T.C. Weather dull cold.	D.D.S+T. No. ST Nov/369 of 25.1.16 # (4) Div Spares Brca No 31 Date 26-1-16
	1-2-1916		During the month the baggage wagons of 4 Artillery Brigades were overhauled & repaired by 190 C. APP.	

Gw Worthen Lieut Colonel
Comdg. 23ʳᵈ Divᶦ Train

SECRET. COPY NO. 10.

Appendix (1)

23RD DIVISION OPERATION ORDER NO. 26.

1. The 24th Bde. will relieve the 68th Bde. in the RIGHT SECTION of the 23rd Division line on the night of 7th/8th January. The frontage is from Trench I.31/1 to I.26/4 inclusive.

2. After relief the 68th Bde. will withdraw into Divisional Reserve to billets as under

    H. Q..........ERQUINGHEM.
    1 Bn..........FORT ROMPU.
    1 Bn..........RUE DORMOIRE.
    1 Bn..........HALLOBEAU.
    1 Bn..........JESUS FARM.

    The D.A.Q.M.G. will point out billeting areas.

3. All details of the move will be arranged by the Brigadiers of 24th and 68th Bdes.

4. No movement of Troops South of LA ROLANDERIE, either to or from the Trenches before 4.15 p.m.

5. The 12th Trench Mortar Battery, 102nd Field Coy. R. E. and one Coy. 9th South Staffords. Regt. will come under the orders of Brigadier General OXLEY.

6. No Trench is to be vacated by the 68th Bde. until occupied by the 24th Bde.

7. Brigadier General SEROCOLD will remain in command of the RIGHT SECTION until the relief is completed.

8. Acknowledge.

Issued at 1 p.m.

A Blair. Lieut. Colonel,
General Staff, 23rd Division.

Headquarters 23rd Div.
4/1/1916.
S. G. 74.

Copies to:

    No. 1...... 24th Bde.
        2...... 68th Bde.
        3...... 69th Bde.
        4...... "Q".
        5)
        6).... R. A.
        7)
        8...... R. E.
        9...... 9th South Staffords.
        10..... Train.
        11)... "G".
        12)
        13)... Diary.
        14)
        15..... 3rd Corps.

SECRET.   Appendix (2)   COPY NO. 10

23RD DIVISION OPERATION ORDER NO. 28.

1. The 68th Bde. will relieve the 69th Bde. in the LEFT SECTION of the 23rd Division line on the evening of the 15th. The frontage is from Trench I.26.5 to I.16, inclusive.

2. After the relief the 69th Bde. will withdraw into Divisional Reserve to billets as under :

    H.Q...................ERQUINGHEM.
    1 Bn..................FORT ROMPU.
    1 Bn..................RUE DORMOIRE.
    1 Bn..................HALLOBEAU.
    1 Bn..................JESUS FARM.

    The D.A.Q.M.G. will point out billeting areas.

3. All details of the move will be arranged by the Brigadiers of 68th and 69th Bdes.

4. No movement of troops South of RUE MARLE, either to or from the trenches, is to commence before 4.30 p.m.

5. No. 21 Trench Mortar Battery, 128th Fd. Coy. R.E. and one Coy. 9th South Staffords Regt. will come under the orders of Brigadier General SEROCOLD.

6. No trench, or billet, is to be vacated by the 69th Bde. until occupied by the 68th Bde.

7. Colonel HOLMES will remain in command of the LEFT SECTION until the relief is completed.

8. Acknowledge.

Arthur Blair
Lieut. Colonel,
General Staff, 23rd Division.

Issued at 9 a.m.

Headquarters 23rd Div.
11/1/1916.
S.G.88.

    Copies to :

        No. 1 .... 24th Bde.
            2 .... 68th Bde.
            3 .... 69th Bde.
            4 .... "Q".
            5)
            6)..... R.A.
            7)
            8 .... R.E.
            9 .... 9th South Staffords.
           10 .... Train.
           11 .... "G".
           12 .... "G".
           13 .... Diary.
           14 .... Diary.
           15 .... 3rd Corps.

SECRET.   COPY NO. 11.

23RD DIVISION OPERATION ORDER NO. 29.

1. The 69th Bde. will relieve the 24th Bde. in the RIGHT SECTION of the 23rd Division line on the evening of the 23rd January. The frontage is from Trench I.31.1. to trench I.26.4. both inclusive.

2. After relief the 24th Bde. will withdraw to Div. Reserve.

    H.Q. ....ERQUINGHEM.
    1 Bn ....ERQUINGHEM.
    1 Bn ....RUE DORMOIRE.
    1 Bn ....HALLOBEAU.
    1 Bn ....JESUS FARM.
    Bde. Machine Gun Company FARM at B.26.a.7.6.

3. All details of the move will be arranged by the Brigadiers of the 24th and 69th Bdes.

4. No movement of troops South of LA ROLANDERIE, either to or from the trenches before 4.45 p.m.

5. The 12th Trench Mortar Battery, 102nd Fd. Coy. R.E. and one Coy. 9th South Staffords Regt. will come under the orders of Brigadier General DERHAM.

6. No trench or billet is to be vacated by the 24th Bde. until occupied by the 69th Bde.

7. Brigadier General OXLEY, will remain in command of the RIGHT SECTION until the relief is completed.

8. Acknowledge.

Arthur Blair Colonel,
General Staff, 23rd Division.

Issued at 8 p.m.

H.Q. 23rd Division,
18/1/16.
S.G.107.

Copies to :-

    No. 1 ....24th Bde.
        2 ....68th Bde.
        3 ....69th Bde.
        4 ...."Q".
        5)........R.A.
        6)........R.A.
        7)........R.A.
        8)........R.E.
        9)
        10 ....9th South Staffords.
        11 ....Train.
        12 ...."G".
        13 ...."G".
        14 ....Diary.
        15 ....Diary.
        16 ....12th T.M.Bty.
        17 ....3rd Corps.

Appendix 4

SECRET.   COPY NO. 10.

23RD DIVISION OPERATION ORDER NO.31.

Headquarters 23rd Division.
26/1/1916.

1. 24th Inf. Bde. will relieve 68th Inf. Bde. in left section of 23rd Division line on evening of 31st January, 1916. Frontage from Trench I.26.5. to Trench I.16, both inclusive.

2. After relief 68th Inf. Bde. withdraws to Divisional Reserve billets as under :-

    H. Q. .... ERQUINGHEM.
    1 Battn............ FORT ROMPU.
    1 Battn............ RUE DORMOIRE.
    1 Battn............ HALLOBEAU.
    1 Battn............ JESUS FARM.

3. All details of move will be arranged by Brigadiers of 24th and 68th Inf. Bdes.

4. No movement of troops South of RUE MARLE, either to or from trenches, to commence before 5 p.m.

5. No. 21 Trench Mortar Battery, 128th Fd. Co. R. E. and one Company 9th South Staffords. will come under orders of Brigadier General Oxley.

6. No trench or billet to be vacated by 68th Inf. Bde. until occupied by 24th Inf. Bde.

7. Brigadier General Serocold will remain in command of left section until relief completed.

8. Acknowledge.

                                            ARTHUR BLAIR,
                                              Colonel,
Issued at 6 p.m.   General Staff, 23rd Division.
    S.G. 128.

    Copies to :-

        No. 1   24th Bde.   No. 8   R.E.
            2   68th Bde.   9   9th S. Staffords.
            3   69th Bde.   10   Train.
            4   "Q".   11   "G".
            5)   12   "G".
            6 - R.A.   13   Diary.
            7)   14   Diary.
                   No.15   3rd Corps.

23/23 Div
grain
Vol. 6

Army Form C. 2118.

WAR DIARY
or
INTELLIGENCE SUMMARY.
(Erase heading not required.)

Instructions regarding War Diaries and Intelligence Summaries are contained in F. S. Regs., Part II. and the Staff Manual respectively. Title pages will be prepared in manuscript.

Place	Date	Hour	Summary of Events and Information	Remarks and references to Appendices
CROIX du BAC.	1916 1st Feb.		Transport 14 pairs R.E. Weather fair - cold	
"	2nd Feb.	9 a.m.	Conference Divl. Headquarters. Transport 12 pairs R.E. 2 baggage. Weather wet, snowy	
"	3rd		Transport 14 pairs R.E. 4 baggage 4 vanners. Weather wet, snowy	
"	4th		Lieut. H.P. BARUGH joined train from 17th Reserve Park, posted to 190 C. APA Capt. T.H. MONTGOMERY, 2 Lt. W.G. LACEY, 7 N.C.O's men proceeded on 7 days' leave to England. Transport 20 pairs R.E. 8 pairs baggage. Weather fair; rain at night.	
"	5th		Transport 12 pairs R.E. 2 pairs vanners. Weather - mild.	
"	6th		Sunday, no Church Parade. S.S.M. McDonnell discharged from Field Ambulance. Transport 6 pairs R.E. Weather - fine.	

2353 Wt. W2544/1454 700,000 5/15 D. D. & L. A.D.S.S./Forms/C. 2118.

Army Form C. 2118.

WAR DIARY
or
INTELLIGENCE SUMMARY.
(Erase heading not required.)

Instructions regarding War Diaries and Intelligence Summaries are contained in F. S. Regs., Part II and the Staff Manual respectively. Title pages will be prepared in manuscript.

Place	Date	Hour	Summary of Events and Information	Remarks and references to Appendices
CROIX du BAC	1916 7th Feb		Transport 12 fmn R.E. 2 fmn Div. Weather fine	
	8	6-	Major C.D.E. UPTON and Capt. CRAWFORD proceeded on 7 days leave to England. Capt. H. WORTHEN took over duties of S.S.O., 2 Lt. V. HOLMES acting Adjutant. Lt. Col. NORTHEN inspected 1st Line Transport 24th & 68th Inf. Brigade, broken 6F" WD on last order # Transport 20 fmn R.E. 8 fmn 6 S. Inf. 13 Bde, 4 fmn 6 S. Inf. Bde, 8 fmn Div. Weather wet.	(1) # Div. Off. Orders No. 32 copy to (?)
	9	9 am	Conference Div. Headquarters; question of Transport for men of Division to Rest Area. Lt. Col. NORTHEN inspected 1st Line Transport 6 S. Inf. Brigade, many broken in last order. Arrival in area of first King of 34 S. Division; army arm 2/232 G MT attacked 151y G. MT. Transport 22 fmn R.E. 3 fmn Div. Weather fine. 8 NCO men on leave to England	
	10		Lieut. LLOYD DAVIS to Rest Area. S.O.f.R.A. Arrangements for move to Rest Area at Div. Headquarters. Transport 20 fmn R.E. 3 fmn Div. Weather fine; very cold.	

Army Form C. 2118.

WAR DIARY
or
INTELLIGENCE SUMMARY.
(Erase heading not required.)

Instructions regarding War Diaries and Intelligence Summaries are contained in F.S. Regs., Part II. and the Staff Manual respectively. Title pages will be prepared in manuscript.

Place	Date	Hour	Summary of Events and Information	Remarks and references to Appendices
CROIX du BAC	1916 11 Feb.	am	Repelling Point BAC ST MAUR and ERQUINGHEM Shelled. Supply Station of Train under fire. Casualties nil. Further Supp. 34 G Div arrived. Same station RA to Rest Area. Transport 15 pairs R.E. 11 pairs shoes. Weather wet & cold.	
	12 "		Received order to inspect building shed by night Brigade in forward area. LAROIANDERIE, GRIS POT wing agreed to washhouses & latrines occupied all day. Transport 14 pairs R.E. 2 pairs shoes. Weather wet roads.	
	13 "	pm	BAC ST MAUR again shelled, and bombs dropped. Further move R.A. to Rest Area. Transport. Nil. Weather fair.	
	14 "		8 Mtr. Posn. 6 leave to England. 69, 9, 13 & 192 C. FAC left area, and marched to VIEUX BERQUIN 6 miles. Transport for above 28 pairs baggage, 16 wagons from 3rd Corps Amm H.T.C. for blankets. Weather wet roads. Repelling Point advanced to 7 a.m. on account of shelling.	(2) Div. Op. Order 34 Copy No. 8.

Army Form C. 2118.

WAR DIARY
or
INTELLIGENCE SUMMARY.

(Erase heading not required.)

Instructions regarding War Diaries and Intelligence Summaries are contained in F.S. Regs., Part II. and the Staff Manual respectively. Title pages will be prepared in manuscript.

Place	Date	Hour	Summary of Events and Information	Remarks and references to Appendices
CROIX du BAC	1916 15th Feb.		6 9th Inf. Bde. & 192 Co. ASC from VIEUX BERQUIN to STEENBECQUE Area - 8 miles. Mm Sectin R.A. 34th Div. arrived in Area. Weather - Snow, very cold.	
	16th	9 am	Conference Divl. Headquarters - Question of transport for further move to Rest Area, move of Indian lorries necessary for Indian baggage. Weather, very rough. 8 Section R.A. to Rest Area, 6 Section R.A. 34th Div. arrived. Transport 8 Section baggage 6 Section Phas. Weather very rough.	
	17th		Divl. Remounts Transfer to Rest Area. Transport 7 Section R.E. 6 Section R.A. baggage. Weather, wet enough.	
	18th		Indian baggage 20th Inf Brigade moved by Indian lorries of Horse Park to Rest Area. D.A.C. moved to 8th Div. Area with their train wagons. Lieut. H.P. BARUGH and 7 NCOs leave to England on 7 days leave.	(3) Div. Order No. S.G. 180 copy
	19th		Transport 11 Section R.E. Weather - fair.	

Army Form C. 2118.

WAR DIARY
or
INTELLIGENCE SUMMARY.
(Erase heading not required.)

Instructions regarding War Diaries and Intelligence Summaries are contained in F. S. Regs., Part II. and the Staff Manual respectively. Title pages will be prepared in manuscript.

Place	Date	Hour	Summary of Events and Information	Remarks and references to Appendices
CROIX du BAC	1916 20. Feb.		Reinforcement of 3 drivers from Base H.T. Depot.	(A) Div. Orders W.O. S.G. 128
			24th Inf. Bde. to VIEUX BERQUIN en route to Rest Area, 16 Elephant wagons from Army H.T.C.	
			193 C. de Rav Area MORBECQUE 18 miles – W	
			S.S.O. & Adjt proceed to Rest Area re S. & T. arrangements & billets ordered.	
			Self details to arrange billets for 9th Div. Hd. at STEENWERCK	
			Transport 6 hami R.E. found by 232 C. H.T.C.	
			Weather fair.	
	21st		Transport 6 hami R.E. formerly 232 C. H.T.C., 8 hami 60th Bde. baggage	(B) Div. Op. Order 35 Copy No. 9
			weather fair, cold. 230 C. H.T.C. 34th Div. Train arrived & took over billets of 193 C. H.T.C.	
	22nd		190 C. H.T.C. marched to VIEUX BERQUIN en route to Rest Area	
			Transport 6 hami R.E.	
			Weather fair, mild.	
	23rd		190 C. H.T.C. remained at VIEUX BERQUIN	(C) Div. Order S.G. 205 –
			192 C. H.T.C. marched with 69th Inf. Bde from STEENBECQUE area to ESTAIRES 11 miles	
			Railhead changed to LA GORGUE	
			Refilled from D.S. Col. on STEENWERCK – TROIS ARBRES road	
			Weather heavy snow.	

WAR DIARY
or
INTELLIGENCE SUMMARY.
(Erase heading not required.)

Army Form C. 2118.

Place	Date	Hour	Summary of Events and Information	Remarks and references to Appendices
CROIX du BAC	1916 24. Feb.		Railhead changed to RUE ST MAUR. 190 C. A.P.C. marched from VIEUX BERQUIN to ESTAIRES 6 miles. Train Hospital moved with Div. Headquarters to ESTAIRES. Field Stores A.V.C. posts & Train on Vet Office moved - cold & snow. Infield LESTREM a railhead with A.D.M.S.	
ESTAIRES	25th		Railhead changed to LESTREM Halte — R.R. ESTAIRES to NEUF BERQUIN road. 191 C. A.P.C. marched from STEENWERCK to DOULIEU 3 miles. Weather cold & snow.	
Do.	26th		Div. Headquarters & H.Q. Train to BLARINGHEM. 190 C. A.P.C. marched from ESTAIRES to LE PARC (Forest de NIEPPE) 12 miles. 191 C. A.P.C. marched from DOULIEU to PAPOTTE 10 miles. Supply & baggage wagons with 68. Inf. Bde. Lu SAILLY L. MORBECQUE, 20 miles. Weather cold, snow, and thaw.	
BLARINGHEM	27 F.		Railhead STEENBECQUE also R.P. — R.P. for R.A. WITTES. 192 C. A.P.C. marched with 69. J. Inf. Bde. from ESTAIRES to STEENBECQUE 11 miles. 190 C. A.P.C. marched from LE PARC to BLARINGHEM, 9 miles. 9 H.D. horses received from Remount Depot. Weather cold & raw.	

2353 Wt. W2544/1454 700,000 5/15 D. D. & L. A.D.S.S./Forms/C. 2118.

Army Form C. 2118.

WAR DIARY
or
INTELLIGENCE SUMMARY.

(Erase heading not required.)

Instructions regarding War Diaries and Intelligence Summaries are contained in F. S. Regs., Part II. and the Staff Manual respectively. Title pages will be prepared in manuscript.

Place	Date	Hour	Summary of Events and Information	Remarks and references to Appendices
BLARINGHEM	1916			
	28 Feb		Arrangements for move of Division to BRUAY area. Weather mild.	Div. Op. Order No.36 copy No.15
"	29 Feb		Division moved to BRUAY area & to be under IV Corps.	
		8.45 am	191, 192, 193 Cos. Train (Company headquarters only) leaves, marching from STEENBECQUE station all under Capt HADDEN.	
			LANGFORD	
		9.50 am	190 Co. and Supply Section 191,192,193 Cos. under Capt. transport farms to -	
		11.15 am	Supply Section H.Q. group under 2nd Lt HOLMES do-	
			190 C. A.S.C. marches to CAUCHY RICOUART 23 miles	
			191 C. A.S.C. marches to do- 20 miles	
			192 C. A.S.C. marches to CAMBLAIN CHATELAIN 20 miles	
			193 C. A.S.C. marches to PERNES (via BRUAY) 28 miles	
			Baggage Section accompanies Units -	
			Supply Section H.Q. group marches to PERNES -	
			Weather fine & mild.	
	18th March 1916			

A. Norlett
Lieut Col.
A.D.S.T.
Comp. 23rd Div. Train

SECRET   Appendix I

                                                     COPY NO. 10

23RD DIVISION OPERATION ORDER NO. 32.

                                                   H.Q. 23rd Div.
                                                   4/2/1916.   S.G.148.

1.   68th Bde. will relieve 69th Bde. in Right Section of the 23rd Division line on evening of 8th February, 1916.   Frontage from Trench I.31/1 to I.26/4 (both inclusive).

2.   After relief the 69th Bde. withdraws to Divisional Reserve billets as under :-

                   H.Q.................ERQUINGHEM.
                   1 Battn..............FORT ROMPU.
                   1 Battn..............RUE DORMOIRE.
                   1 Battn..............HALLOBEAU.
                   1 Battn..............JESUS FARM.

3.   All details of the move will be arranged by Brigadiers of 68th and 69th Bdes.

4.   No movement of troops SOUTH of LA ROLANDERIE, either to and from trenches, to commence before 5.30 p.m.

5.   No. 12 T.M.B., 102nd Fd. Co. and 1 Co. 9th South Staffords will come under orders of O.C. 68th Bde.

6.   No trench or billet to be vacated by 69th Inf. Bde. until occupied by 68th Bde.

7.   Brigadier General Derham will remain in command of Right Section until relief completed.

8.   Acknowledge.

                                              ARTHUR BLAIR,
Issued at 12, noon.   Colonel,
                            General Staff, 23rd Division.

       Copies to :-

           No. 1 24th Bde.   No. 8 R.E.
                2 68th Bde.   9 9th South Staffords.
                3 69th Bde.   10 Train.
                4 "Q"   11 "G".
                5)   12 "G".
                6 - R.A.   13 Diary.
                7)   14 Diary.

                   No. 15   3rd Corps.

SECRET.

COPY NO. 8

Appendix (2)

23RD DIVISION OPERATION ORDER NO. 34.

Headquarters, 23rd Division,
9/2/1916.   S.G. 162.

Ref: Map,
1/40,000,
Sheets 36
and 36A.

Inf.

1. The 69th Bde. will march to the RESERVE AREA, H.Q. at STEENBECQUE. March to commence on the 14th February, in accordance with attached Table "A". All details to be arranged by G.O.C. 69th Infantry Brigade.

2. The G.O.C. 69th Infantry Bde. will make all arrangements for billeting in the VIEUX-BERQUIN Area on the night of the 14th/15th February.

3. Advanced parties will be sent to the STEENBECQUE Area to take over billets, etc., from the 102nd Infantry Bde. on February 12th.

4. Acknowledge.

Issued at 1 p.m.

ARTHUR BLAIR,
Colonel,
General Staff, 23rd Division.

Copies to:-

No.		No.	
1	24th Bde.	7	R.E.
2	68th Bde.	8	Train.
3	69th Bde.	9	"G"
4	102nd Bde.	10	"G"
5	"Q".	11	Diary.
6	R.A.	12	Diary.
13	3rd Corps.		
14	34th Division.		

TABLE 'A'.

DATE	UNIT	MOVES TO	ROUTE	TIME	REMARKS.
14th Feb.	Two Bns. billeted at HALLOBEAU and JESUS FARM.	VIEUX-BERQUIN AREA	L'HALLOBEAU-LE MENEGATE-STEENWERCK-LE VERRIER-CROSS-ROADS F.13.A.		To march by coys., with half hour intervals between coys. Last Coy. to clear HALLOBEAU by 2p.m.
14th Feb.	Two Bns. billeted at DORMOIRE and ROMPU	VIEUX-BERQUIN AREA	FORT POMPU-CROIX-DU-BAC-STEENWERCK-LE VERRIER-CROSS ROADS F.13.A.	10 p.m.	
15th Feb.	69th Infantry Bde.	STEENBECQUE	VIEUX BERQUIN-LA MOTTE-ROAD JUNCTION, D.24.a.1.1-PAPOTE.		

Appendix (3)

SECRET.

To ~~D.M.T.~~
~~35th Mobile Vet. Section.~~
~~Train.~~
~~54th Division.~~
~~3rd Corps.~~

1. With reference to Divisional O.O. No. 53 of 9th Feb.
(Table B) :-

The D.M.T. and 35th Mobile Vet. Section will march direct to their billets in the Reserve Area on February 18th. These units will march independently.

2. Please acknowledge.

C.F. Watson

Lt. Colonel,
General Staff, 23rd Division.

Headquarters
23rd Division,
15/2/1916.
S.G.180.

Appendix (4)

To
~~34th Division.~~
~~24th Infantry Bde.~~
~~101st Infantry Bde.~~
~~C.R.A.~~
Train.
~~3rd Corps.~~

REFERENCE DIVL. OPERATION ORDER NO. 33
(TABLE B.)

1. The 101st Infantry Bde. will relieve the 24th Infantry Bde. in the Div. Reserve Area on the 20th.
The head of the Bde. will reach CROIX-DU-BAC (G.6.c.) at 12 noon. The leading Bns. are to be those whose billets are S. of R. LYS.

2. (a) The two Bns. 24th Infantry Bde., N. of the R. LYS, will march via HALLOBEAU - LA MENEGATE - STEENWERCK - LE VERRIER - Crossroads F.13.a to the VIEUX BERQUIN AREA. The last Coy. from these Bns. will leave HALLOBEAU Road Junction at 12.30 p.m.

(b) The two Bns. 24th Infantry Bde., S. of R. LYS, will march via ERQUINGHEM BRIDGE - Road Junction B.14.c - LE MENEGATE - STEENWERCK - LE VERRIER - Crossroads F.13.a. to the VIEUX BERquin Area. The last Coy. from these Bns. will leave RUE DORMOIRE at 1.0 p.m.

3. Bns. are to march by companies at intervals of 10 minutes.

4. Acknowledge.

Lt. Colonel,
General Staff, 23rd Division.

Headquarters
23rd Division.
16/2/1916.
G.128.

SECRET.   COPY NO. 9

23RD DIVISION OPERATION ORDER NO. 35.

Ref. Map
1/20,000
Sheet 36
N.W.

1. The 101st Infantry Brigade will relieve the 68th Infantry Brigade in the Right Section of the 23rd Division line on the evening of 21st February, 1916. Frontage from Trench I.31/1 to I.26/4 (both inclusive).

2. After relief the 68th Infantry Brigade will withdraw to the Divisional Reserve Billets as under :-

    H.Q.....................ERQUINGHEM.

    1 Battn..................FORT ROMPU.

    1 Battn..................RUE DORMOIRE.

    1 Battn..................HALLOBEAU.

    1 Battn..................JESUS FARM.

3. All details of the move will be arranged by Brigadiers of 68th and 101st Brigades. Trench stores, etc., will be taken over by day.

4. No movement of troops SOUTH of LA ROLANDERIE, either to or from trenches, to commence before 5.45 p.m.

5. No trench or billet to be vacated by the 68th Infantry Brigade, until occupied by the 101st Infantry Brigade.

6. No. 12 Trench Mortar Battery will be relieved on the evening of 22nd February.

7. One Company Pioneers will come under the command of G.O.C. 101st Infantry Brigade.

8. Brigadier General PAGE-CROFT will remain in command of the Right Section until relief is completed.

9. ACKNOWLEDGE.

                                                F. Watson.

H.Q. 23rd Division,   Lt.Colonel,
16th February,1916.
S.G.182.   General Staff, 23rd Division.

Issued at 1 p.m.

Copies to:-

No. 1.	R.A.	No. 8 "Q".
2.	R.E.	9 Train.
3.	34th Div.	10 Pioneer Bn. 34th Div.
4.	34th Div.	11 "G".
5.	68th Bde.	12 "G".
6.	101st Bde.	13 Diary.
7.	103rd Bde.	14 Diary.
	No. 15	3rd Corps.

SECRET.

To. R.A., 23rd Divn.
~~H.Q., 23rd Divn.~~
68th Inf. Bde.
~~" "~~
~~" "~~
~~" "~~
Train.

PRELIMINARY ORDER.

1. A redistribution takes place on 24th.

2. On 23rd, 69th Bde. and 128th Fd. Coy., R.E. march to ESTAIRES.

3. On 24th (a) Div. H.Q. move to ESTAIRES and at 12 noon takes over the new Divisional Area.

   (b) R.A., 24th Inf. Bde. and 102nd Fd. Coy. R.E. march to ESTAIRES.

   (c) 69th Inf. Bde. and 128th Fd. Coy. R.E. relieve 23rd Inf. Bde. (8th Div).

4. 69th Inf. Bde. remains temporarily under command of 34th Division.

5. Detailed orders will follow.

H.Q. 23rd Division,　　　　　　　　　　　　　Lt.Colonel,
23rd February, 1916.
S.G.205.　　　　　　　　　　　　General Staff, 23rd Division.

SECRET

COPY NO 15

Appendix 7

23RD DIVISION OPERATION ORDER NO. 36.

Reference Map:
HAZEBROUCK 5A
and LENS 11
1/100,000

1. The 23rd Division will join the 4th Corps to-morrow and will be billeted round BRUAY (See March Table).

2(a) Infantry will proceed according to the attached Railway Time Table.

(b) The remainder of the Division will march in accordance with attached March Table.

3. One blanket will be carried on the man by units proceeding by rail.

4. A goods train will leave STEENBECQUE STATION to-morrow at a time to be notified later, for the conveyance of the 2nd blanket and all surplus baggage.

5. Each unit will detail a fatigue party of 1 N.C.O. and 6 men to load blankets and surplus baggage into the goods train. One Officer will be detailed by each Bde. to be in charge of these parties.

6. Billeting parties in charge of Staff Captains of Bdes. and one officer of other units will leave for the new area at 7 a.m. to-morrow. Ambulances will be provided for them at the above hour as follows :-

    1 for each Bde. at Bde. H.Q.
    1 for R.A. at R.A. H.Q.
    1 for R.E., D.M.T., 9th South Staffords Regt.
      Fd. Ambs. at C.R.E.'s Office.
    1 Divl. H.Q. at D.H.Q.
Report to 4th Corps H.Q. near BRUAY.

7. All trench stores on list No. O.S. 27, dated 23rd December, 1915, Trench Mortars complete with parts, trench handcarts and bomb stores, will be handed in to the Ordnance Dump at MORBECQUE.

8. Transport for services mentioned in "5" and "8" will be placed at the disposal of units at 8 a.m. This transport is on no account to leave this area.

9. Div. H.Q. will be at BRUAY at 11 a.m.

10. Acknowledge.

                              C.F. WATSON,

Issued at 12 p.m.
S.G. 208.
                          Lt. Colonel,
              General Staff, 23rd Division.

Copies to :
No. 1	3rd Corps.	No. 8	A.D.M.S.
2	4th Corps.	9	A.D.V.S.
3	R.A.	10	D.A.D.O.S.
4	R.E.	11	"Q"
5	24th Bde.	12	9th S. Staffords.
6	68th Bde.	13	"G"
7	69th Bde.	14	Diary.
		No. 15	Train.
		16	D.M.T.
		17	Signals.

UNIT	HOUR OF STARTING	ROUTE	BILLETING AREA	REMARKS.
D.M.T. CYCLISTS	7.30 a.m.	BLARINGHEM - WITTES - AIRE - ST. HILAIRE - FERFAX - PERNES.	CAMBLAIN-CHATELAIN	Under orders of Lt. Col. TILNEY.
R.A. (Less 102nd Bde. C/105 and D/104.	8 a.m.	WITTES - AIRE - ST. HILAIRE - FERFAY - PERNES	PERNES	Under orders of C.R.A. 102nd Bde. R.F.A. C/105 and D/104. March to join Division on March 1st.
1st line Transport 24th Inf. Bde. 1st line Transport 9th S. Staffords.	8.30 a.m.	ditto.	BRUAY CAMBLAIN-CHATELAIN.	
Div. H.Q.	9.30 a.m.	ditto.	BRUAY.	

H.Q. + Supply Section of Train march under orders M.C. Train - T. Baker M.

UNIT	HOUR OF STARTING	ROUTE	BILLETING AREA	REMARKS.
24th Bde. M.G. Coy	8 a.m.	MORBECQUE - ST VENANT - LILLERS - BRUAY	BRUAY	Independently.
1st Line Transport 68th Bde.	8.15 a.m.	ditto.	MARLES-LES-MINES	ditto.
1st Line Transport 69th Bde.	8.30 a.m.	ditto.	HESDIGNEUL— HALICOURT-RUITZ	ditto.
Baggage Section of Train	8.45 a.m.	ditto.	CAMBLAIN-CHATELAIN	ditto.
69th Fd. Amb.	9 a.m.	ditto.	ditto	ditto.
70th Fd. Amb.	9.15 a.m.	ditto.	ditto.	ditto.
Sanitary Section	9.15 a.m.	ditto.	BRUAY	ditto.
Mobile Vet. Section	9.30 a.m.	ditto.	CAMBLAIN- CHATELAIN	Under orders of C.R.E.
R.E.	10. a.m.	ditto		
71st Fd. Amb.	8.30 a.m.	MERVILLE- ST VENANT - LILLERS- BRUAY	BRUAY	Independently.
D.A.C.	10 a.m.	ditto.	To be allotted by C.R.A. on arrival.	ditto.

ENTRAINING TABLES.

UNIT.	ENTRAINING STATION.	Time of arrival at Station.	ROUTE.	Time of departure of Train.	Detraining Station.	BILLETING AREA	REMARKS.
Headquarters 69th Bde. "A" Bn.	STEENBECQUE.	7.30 a.m.	DIRECT.	8 a.m.	CALONNE RICQUART.	HAILLICOURT – RUITZ and HESDIGNEUL.	and personnel T.M.B.
"B" Bn. 69th Bde.) Dismounted men "A" Coy) R.E.	" "	7.50 a.m. "	" "	8.20 a.m. "	" "	CAMBLAIN – CHATELAIN. "	(for R.E.)
"C" Bn. 69th Bde.) Dismounted men "B" Coy) R.E.	" "	8.10 a.m. "	" "	8.40 a.m. "	" "	As for "A" Bn. As for R.E.	
"D" Bn. 69th Bde.) Dismounted men "C" Coy) R.E.	" "	8.30 a.m. "	" "	9 a.m. "	" "	As for "A" Bn. As for R.E.	
Headquarters 24th Bde. "A" Bn. "A" Coy. 9th S.Staffs.	THIENNES. " "	10.30a.m. " "	ROMAN ROAD – THIENNES. " "	11a.m. " "	" " "	BRUAY. " CHAMBLAIN – CHATELAIN.	and personnel T.M.B.
"B" Bn. 24th Bde.	"	10.50a.m.	"	11.20 a.m.	"	As for "A" Bn.	

UNIT.	Entraining Station.	Time of arrival at Station.	ROUTE.	Time of departure of Train.	Detraining Station.	Billeting Area.	Remarks.
H.Q's 9th South Staffs.	THIENNES.	10.50a.m.	ROMAN ROAD - THIENNES.	11.20 a.m.	CALONNE RICQUART.	CHAMBLAIN-CHATELAIN.	
"B" Coy. 9th S.Staffs.	"	"	"	"	"	"	
"C" Bn. 24th Bde.	"	11.10a.m.	"	11.40 a.m.	"	As for "A" Bn.	
"C" Coy. 9th S.Staffs.	"	"	"	"	"	CHAMBLAIN-CHATELAIN.	
"D" Bn. 24th Bde.	"	11.30a.m.	"	12 noon.	"	As for "A" Bn.	
"D" Coy. 9th S.Staffs.	"	"	"	"	"	CHAMBLAIN-CHATELAIN.	
H.Q's 68th Bde.	STEENBECQUE.	1.30 p.m.	DIRECT.	2 p.m.	"	MARLES-LES-MINES.	and any dismounted units in the area (i.e. T.M.Batteries).
"A" Bn.68thBde.	"	"	"	"	"	CALONNE-RICQUART.	
"B" Bn.	"	1.50 p.m.	"	2.20 p.m.	"	"	

UNIT.	Entraining Station.	Time of arrival at Station.	ROUTE	Time of departure of train.	Detraining Station.	Billeting Area.	Remarks.
"C" Ba. 60th Bde.	STEENBEC-QUE.	2.10 LATER p.m.	DIRECT.	2.40 p.m.	CALONNE-RICOUART.	CALONNE-RICOUART.	
"D" Bn.	"	2.30 p.m.	"	3 p.m.	"	"	

Confidential

23rd Divl
Train
Vol T

War Diary

By Lt Colonel A. Norton

Commanding 23rd Divisional Train A.S.C

The D.A.G.
3rd Echelon

From 1st to 31 March 1916

Army Form C. 2118.

WAR DIARY
or
INTELLIGENCE SUMMARY.
(Erase heading not required.)

Instructions regarding War Diaries and Intelligence Summaries are contained in F. S. Regs., Part II. and the Staff Manual respectively. Title pages will be prepared in manuscript.

Place	Date	Hour	Summary of Events and Information	Remarks and references to Appendices
BRUAY - PAS DE CALAIS	1916 Feb 1st		H.Q. and Nos. 2 & 3 at CALONNE-RICOUART, No. 4 C PERNES - Baggage wagons and body No. 3 C. marched to PERNES, 4 miles. Third Train Officers in Div Headquarters. Following names taken for Despatches, Major C.D.E.UPTON (for D.S.O.), Capt. C.LANGFORD, Capt. R.I. HADDEN and S.S.M. McDonnell (for mention) - Weather dull. Railhead LILLERS.	
"	2nd		Inspected H.Q. C. & No. 2 at CALONNE RICOUART. Weather wet.	
"	3rd		Lt.Col. NORTHEN proceeded F.G.C.M. at R.Q. R.E. CAMBRIN CHATELAIN. Lieut. E.A. SOUTHEE promoted Captain ex 1.2.1916. Weather wet.	
"	4th	1am	9 drivers arrived from Base H.T. Depot as reinforcements. Inspected Div. Headquarters at move to forward area. Weather snowing.	

Army Form C. 2118.

WAR DIARY
or
INTELLIGENCE SUMMARY.
(Erase heading not required.)

Instructions regarding War Diaries and Intelligence Summaries are contained in F. S. Regs., Part II. and the Staff Manual respectively. Title pages will be prepared in manuscript.

Place	Date	Hour	Summary of Events and Information	Remarks and references to Appendices
BRUAY	1916 5.6." 7. March		Arrangements for move to forward area. Weather - snow & rain -	
"	8"		Team H.Q. moved with Div. H.Q. to MAISNIL-BOUCHE. Div. H.Qrs. to Chateau de la HAIE. No.1 & No.2 marched from CAUCHY RICOURT to LA COMTE - 6 miles - Nos. 3 & 4 marched from PERNES to LA COMTE - 10 miles - Baggage & supply wagons met their units - Snow.	Appendix (1) Divl. order Nos - 37 -
MAISNIL BOUCHE	9"		Transport - 6 wagons for R.E. Railhead HERSIN Weather. Snow.	
"	10"		H.Q. marched from LA COMTE to ROCOURT, 2 miles. Nos. 2, 3 & 4 Coys. marched from LACOMTE to MAISNICOURT - 2 miles. Weather. Snow.	
"	11"		Weather - thawing -	
"	12"		9 H.D. horses received from Remounts. Ira D.A.C. all for cookers and 6 wire carts an to M.V. Sec. Weather thawing.	

2353 Wt. W2344/1454 700,000 5/15 D. D. & L. A.D.S.S./Forms/C. 2118.

Army Form C. 2118.

WAR DIARY
or
INTELLIGENCE SUMMARY.
(Erase heading not required.)

Instructions regarding War Diaries and Intelligence Summaries are contained in F. S. Regs., Part II. and the Staff Manual respectively. Title pages will be prepared in manuscript.

Place	Date	Hour	Summary of Events and Information	Remarks and references to Appendices
MAISNIL BOUCHÉ	1916 July 13th	8.15 a.m.	German Biplane No C 447 B descended in difficulties 700 yds rear of Train Office, two occupants were arrested by S.S.M. McDonnell & handed over to Guards of 9 G.S. Supply Coy 2. manoeuvres —	Appendices 2 Div. G. Anno 70.39
			No.3 C. marched from MAISNICOURT to DIVION, & took over duties of No.3 C. 47th Div. Train Supply wagon upward — breakdown. Four —	
	14th 15th		breakdown. Four —	
		16.5.	Hd. Qrs. Train moved into Div. Headquarters to BRUAY	
			No. 2 C. marched from MAISNICOURT to BARLIN 6 miles, supply wagon upward —	
			No. 4 C. from MAISNICOURT to DIVION, 5 miles breakdown Four —	
BRUAY	17.6.		Hd.Qrs. Company marched from ROCOURT to DIVION 4 miles breakdown Four	
	18.6.		No. 2 C. marched to Brickfields (K28.a.6.c) 3/4 mile, baggage wagon collects No. 3 C. marched from DIVION to BARLIN 6 miles Do - Report to Div. Headquarters a certain of which breakdown Four —	

4353 Wt. W2544/1454 700,000 5/15 D.D.&L. A.D.S.S./Forms/C. 2118.

Army Form C. 2118.

WAR DIARY
or
INTELLIGENCE SUMMARY.
(Erase heading not required.)

Instructions regarding War Diaries and Intelligence Summaries are contained in F. S. Regs. Part II. and the Staff Manual respectively. Title pages will be prepared in manuscript.

Place	Date	Hour	Summary of Events and Information	Remarks and references to Appendices
BRUAY	1916 18th cont		Comdt of Supply on enquiry D. R. Williams 19°C. Transport 3 wagons R.E.	
"	19th		Lieut. Simon A.V.C. admitted to Hospital. Weather very fine	
"	20th		No. 4 C. motors from DIVION to BARLIN. Removing baggage upon call. Forwards following names of officers for promotion: 2 Lieuts. HOLMES, MITCHELL and LODGE. Weather very fine	
"	21st		6 M.Cars were forwarded on 7 days' leave to England - 5 trains' baggage, 5 trains' civil authorities HERSIN and BARLIN. Transport 4 trains baggage.	
"	22nd	6.30 p.m	Trans Headquarters' moved (with Div. Headquarters) to BARLIN - Div Hqrs to SAINS-en-GOHELLE. Appendix (3) Weather wet. Transport 10 from R.E. 3 from HERSIN. Conference Div. Headquarters garden 7 officers of Headquarters Company, machines for DIVION to BARLIN	Div. Order No. 40
BARLIN	23rd		Transport 13 from R.E., 4 train baggage, 2 lorries. Weather wet	

Army Form C. 2118.

WAR DIARY
or
INTELLIGENCE SUMMARY.
(Erase heading not required.)

Instructions regarding War Diaries and Intelligence Summaries are contained in F. S. Regs., Part II. and the Staff Manual respectively. Title pages will be prepared in manuscript.

Place	Date	Hour	Summary of Events and Information	Remarks and references to Appendices
BARLIN	1916 Feb 24th		Called in Supply wagon of Div. Troops (Railhead) BARLIN	
"	25th		Transport 18 from R.E. 3 vanners. Weather fair & frost.	
			Terp. Lieut. H.T. HEWARD DAVIS promoted T/Captain 11th March. Lieut. P.A. CARROLL AVC. appointed Vet Officer y/c Train.	
			Capt. T.H. MONTGOMERY wounded 7 F.G.C.M.	
"	26th		Transport 6 from R.E. 8 baggage, 2½ vanners. Weather wet and raw.	
			Capt. H. MATTHEW 2nd L. M.C.O. proceeded on 7 days leave to England.	
			Transport 14 from R.E. 1 hour stale. Weather snow & sleet.	
	27th	3.30pm	Church Parade in Perrenchin Room	
	21st		Transport 12 from R.E. Weather rain	
"	28th		Capt. M. MURPHY RAMC appointed M.O. y/c Train	
			Transport 14 from R.E. 3½ from vanners. Weather - wet.	

Army Form C. 2118.

WAR DIARY
or
INTELLIGENCE SUMMARY.
(Erase heading not required.)

Instructions regarding War Diaries and Intelligence Summaries are contained in F. S. Regs., Part II. and the Staff Manual respectively. Title pages will be prepared in manuscript.

Place	Date	Hour	Summary of Events and Information	Remarks and references to Appendices
BARLIN	1916			
	29. Fed.		Capt. T.L.R. PHILIP relieves Capt. H. MURPHY as M.O. of Train.	
			Transport 12 horses R.E., 6 horses Mechists, 3 vans	
		6.30p	Weather fine. × Confirms Div. Headquarters, quarters of Transport, changes to M. Hope Farm.	
	30. "		Capt. T.H. MONTGOMERY member of F.G.C.M.	
			Transport 12 horses R.E. 3 vans	
			Weather fine.	
	31. "		Capt. J.L.G. AGATE and H. MCGOWMAN proceeded on 10 and 7 days leave to England respectively.	
			Transport 12 horses R.E., 4 for Div. Bakery & Laundry, 8½ vans.	
			Weather fine. Sunny.	
			Forwarded to Div. Headquarters the name of Capt. CLIFFORD DSO. for command of a Reserve Park.	

April 3rd 1916

A. Winchester
Lieut Col.
Comy. 23rd Div. Train.

Appendix (1)

SECRET.   COPY NO. 7
                23RD DIVISION OPERATION ORDER NO. 37.

Reference   1.   In accordance with 4th Corps Order No. 102, of
Map: 1st March, the relief of the French from the
Sheet 36c   SOUCHEZ RIVER as far as approx. S.15.a.3.2.
1/40,000.   (BOYAU de l'ERSATZ) will be completed by 10 a.m.
                    8th March.

             2.   The 69th Inf. Bde. will hold this Sector with 3
                    Bns. in the front line; half Bn. in support and
                    half Bn. in CARENCY.   H.Q. 69th Inf. Bde. will
                    be in ABLAIN ST. NAZAIRE.

             3.   The 24th Inf. Bde. will be in support, the 68th
                    Bde. in Divisional Reserve.

             4.   The garrison of the hill NOTRE DAME de LORETTE
                    will consist of one Bn. from the Bde. in support.

             5 (a). The relief will commence on the night of 6th/7th
                    March.

                    One Bn. 69th Inf. Bde. will take over from the
                    Left French Bn. and one Bn. 24th Inf. Bde. will take
                    over the trenches of NOTRE DAME de LORETTE.

                    These two Bns. will move into billets at Gd. and
                    Pt. SERVINS (Q.34) on the 5th.   Billeting par-
                    ties will proceed on the 4th.

             (b)   All details will be arranged between the
                    O.C. French Left Sector and G.Os.C. 24th and 69th
                    Inf. Bdes.

             (c)   The remaining Bns. of 69th Inf. Bde. will billet
                    at Gd. and Pt. SERVINS on the 6th and take over
                    the remaining French line on the night of the
                    7th/8th. Billeting parties will proceed on the 5th

             (d)   No reliefs will take place in daylight.

             6.   The line taken over will be under command of
                    the G.O.C. 17th French Division until 10 a.m.
                    March 8th.

             7.   The Artillery reliefs will be arranged between the
                    Commanders of the Artillery of the French 17th
                    Division and British 23rd Division.

             8.   Further orders for the relief will be issued later.

             9.   Acknowledge.

                    Issued at 1.45 p.m.

                                                      for Lt. Colonel,
                                               General Staff, 23rd Division

H.Q. 23rd Div.
3/3/1916.
S.G.210.   Copies to :-

        No. 1 R.A.   No. 6 A.D.M.S.   No.11 17th Div. d'Inf-
            2 24th Bde.   7 Train.   anterie.
            3 69th Bde.   8 4th Corps.   12 Diary.
            4 Signals.   9 4th Corps.   13 Diary.
            5 "Q".   10 17th Div. d'Inf.   14 "G".

Operation order
31. Copy no 7
3.3.16

APPENDIX II. - MOVES ON 8TH AND 9TH.

UNIT.	DATE.	FROM.	8/9	9/10	REMARKS.
Div. H.Q.	8	BRUAY	CH. de la HALE. (10 a.m.)		
68th Bde.	8	Reserve Area (C.30.d.)	1 Bn. VERDREL. 1 Bn. FRESNICOURT. 1 Bn. HERMIN.	1 Bn. ESTREE CAUCHIE.	68 M.G.Co. to billet with 68th Bde. H.Q.
128th Fd. Co. R.E. (less 100 men) 9th S.Staffords.	8	CAMBLAIN-CHATELAIN.	CARENCY.		Transport to remain at GOUY SERVINS.
	8		2 Cos. MESNIL BOUCHE. H.Q. & 2 Cos.la COMTE.		
D.M.T. Train.	8	Rest Area. (PERNES).	BAJUS. la COMTE. (O.18) CAUCOURT.		
35th Mob.Vet.Sec. R.A.		Reliefs arranged by G.O.C. R.A.			(Wagon Lines. (1 Bde. CAUCOURT. (1 Bde. ESTREE CAUCHIE. (1 Bde. GAUCHIN LEGAL.
Reserve Group. (Col. Hobday). D/102 D/103 D/104	8		BARAFFLE. OLHAIN. (Until the 12th when FREVILLERS is empty.)		
D.A.C.	8		CAUCOURT.		
Fd. Amb.	8		1 Sec.Fd.Amb. QUATRE VENTS. 1 3.Fd.Amb. GD. SERVINS.	2 Sec.Fd.Amb. ESTREE CAUCHIE. 1 Fd. Amb. GAUCHIN-LEGAL.	

SECRET   COPY NO. 17

23RD DIVISION OPERATION ORDER NO. 39.

12TH MARCH, 1916.

1. The 23rd Division will be relieved by the 47th Division in the Right Sector (CARENCY) of the IVth Corps Front.

2. (i) R.E. and Infantry reliefs will be carried out in accordance with attached table and will be completed by 12 noon March 16th. Details to be arranged direct between G.O's.C. Brigades concerned.

   (ii) The Reserve Group R.A. will relieve the Artillery of 47th Division attached to the 2nd Division on nights 14/15 and 15/16.
   Other Artillery reliefs will be arranged direct between G.O's.C. R.A. 23rd and 47th Divisions; the relief will commence on night March 17/18.
   The guns in each case will be left in their positions.

   (iii) Relief of Medical Units will be arranged direct between the A.D.M.S. concerned and Div. H.Q. informed.

3. The moves of other units of the Division will be notified later.

4. Refilling tomorrow will be at 7 a.m. at the same place.

5. Div. H.Q. will move to BRUAY at 10 a.m. March 16th at which hour G.O.C. 47th Div. will assume command of the CARENCY SECTOR.

6. Acknowledge.

Issued at 2.20 p.m.

C. F. Watson.

Headquarters,
23rd Division.   Lt. Colonel,
S.G.241.   General Staff, 23rd Division.

Copies to :-

No. 1.- 6.	C.R.A.	16. Signals.
7.	C.R.E.	17. Train.
8.	24th Bde.	18. Train.
9.	68th Bde.	19. A.D.M.S.
10.	69th Bde.	20. A.D.V.S.
11.	9th S.Staffs.	21. D.A.D.O.S.
12.	D.M.T.	22. Diary.
13 - 15.	"Q".	23. Diary.
	24. "G".	
	25. 2nd Div.	
	26. 46th Div.	
	27. 47th Div.	
	28. 4?th Div.	
	29 - 30. IVth Corps.	

SECRET.   COPY NO. 18.

23RD DIVISION OPERATION ORDER NO. 40.

14th March, 1916.

1. The 23rd Division will relieve the 2nd Division in the Left Sector of 4th Corps front.

2. (a) Infantry reliefs will be carried out in accordance with attached Table and will be completed on the night of the 21st/22nd inst. Details of relief will be arranged between G.Os. C. Brigades concerned.

    (b) Artillery reliefs will be arranged direct between G.Os.C. R.A. 2nd and 23rd Divisions. The relief will commence on the night of the 22nd/23rd and will be completed on the night of the 23rd/24th. Guns will be left in their positions. On completion of relief the 24th Siege Battery will be attached to 23rd Division.

    (c) Relief of Medical Units will be arranged direct between A.D.M.S. concerned and Div. H.Q. informed.

    (d) The relief of R.E. and Pioneers will be arranged direct between the C.R.Es. concerned and Div. H.Q. informed.

3. Moves of other units of the Division will be notified later.

4. The 2nd Division will hand over all maps, photographs, log books, trench stores and mortars to the 23rd Division.

5. Div. H.Q. will open at SAINS-EN-GOHELLE at 10 a.m. March 22nd, at which hour G.O.C. 23rd Division will assume command of the Left Sector.

6. Acknowledge.

Issued at 4 p.m.   C.F. Watson.
                                         Lt. Colonel,
H.Q. 23rd Division.   General Staff, 23rd Division.
S.G. 246.

Copies to :-

Nos. 1 - 6	C.R.A.	No. 19	A.D.M.S.
No. 7	C.R.E.	20	A.D.V.S.
8	24th Inf. Bde.	21	D.A.D.O.S.
9	68th Inf. Bde.	22	A.P.M.
10	69th Inf. Bde.	23	Diary.
11	9th S. Staffords.	24	Diary.
12	D.M.T.	25	"G".
Nos. 13-15	"Q"	26	2nd Division.
No. 16	Signals.	27	47th Division.
Nos. 17-18	Train	28	4th Corps.

W 74—664 250,000 3/15 L.S. & Co.   Army Form W. 3091.

Cover for Documents.

Nature of Enclosures.

Confidential

War Diary

of

Lt Colonel A Northen Comdg. 23rd Div Train A.S.C

From 1st to 30th April 1916

The D.A.G.
3rd Echelon

Notes, or Letters written.

Army Form C. 2118.

WAR DIARY
or
INTELLIGENCE SUMMARY.
(Erase heading not required.)

Instructions regarding War Diaries and Intelligence Summaries are contained in F. S. Regs., Part II. and the Staff Manual respectively. Title pages will be prepared in manuscript.

Place	Date	Hour	Summary of Events and Information	Remarks and references to Appendices
BARLIN	1916 1st April		Reached BARLIN Railway Station; Refilling Point, BARLIN Railway Station. Divl Supply Column arrived. 1 day's supplies. Transport:- 12 four R.E., 4 pair Laundry, 4 pair Sanitary Duty, 1 for Stores. Weather fine.	
"	2"	8 am	Insp'cd inspection "Geographic" Company.	
		3-30 pm	Church Parade for Troops in Marralles Ronson Barns.	
			Transport: 12 four R.E., 8 four blankets etc., 4 four Laundry, 4 four Sanitary. Weather fine.	
"	3rd	10 am	Lt. Col. NORTHEY inspected F.O. C.M. HERSIN. 8 am. Medical inspection Nos 2,3 & 4 Cos. Transport:- 21 four R.E., 4 four Laundry, 2 four to MARQUEFFLES for 10 days washing.	
"	4 "		Lt. DAVIDSON R.A.M.C. 7th F.A. took over temporary M.O.C. charge of TRAIN. Transport: 21 four R.E., 4 Laundry, 4½ four Sanitary, 1 pair Blankets. Weather fine.	
"	5"		7. H.D. Truscs from Remount Depot. 2 Pte MITCHELL, Lt. BERRYMAN, 4 M. Cs'men proceeded on 7 days leave to England. Transport: 22 four R.E., 4 Laundry, 4½ four Sanitary, 2 four Blankets.	

Army Form C. 2118.

WAR DIARY
or
INTELLIGENCE SUMMARY.
(Erase heading not required.)

Instructions regarding War Diaries and Intelligence Summaries are contained in F. S. Regs., Part II. and the Staff Manual respectively. Title pages will be prepared in manuscript.

Place	Date	Hour	Summary of Events and Information	Remarks and references to Appendices
BARLIN	1916			
	6.4.April	9.30 am	Cond. of Injury or Injuries – No T.S. 9/20 Fan. Cpl. A. GUMBRILL 190 C. A.S.C.	
			Transfers 10 from R.E., 4 Laundry, 4½ from Sanitary, 6 from 51 S.I.f. Brigade.	
			Weather fine.	
	7. April	9.30 am	Cond. of Injury or Injuries – No. 2 029231 Dr. D. PUGH, 190. C. R.E.	
			Transfers – 20 from R.E., 4 Laundry, 1½ Sanitary, 3 baggage.	
			Weather – fair.	
	8. April	10 am	Lt. Col. MATTHEW, President F.G.C.M. SAINS.	
			Transfers 14 from R.E., 4 Laundry, 1½ Sanitary, 2 from baggage.	
			Weather fine – cold Tillifula P.HESTE (190.C.120) return from Town.	
	9.April	8 am	Medical inspection. Inspection Corps.	
		3.30 pm	Church Parade for Town, Bunston Room.	
			Transfers 14 from R.E., 6 from Laundry, 1½ Sanitary.	
			Weather fine.	
	10. April		Passed inspection Nos. 2.3 & 4 Companies.	
			Capt. HADDEN and 4 NCOs men proceed on 7 days leave to England.	
			Transfers – 12 from R.E., 4 Laundry, 4½ Sanitary.	
			Weather fine.	

Army Form C. 2118.

WAR DIARY
or
INTELLIGENCE SUMMARY.
(Erase heading not required.)

Instructions regarding War Diaries and Intelligence Summaries are contained in F. S. Regs., Part II. and the Staff Manual respectively. Title pages will be prepared in manuscript.

Place	Date	Hour	Summary of Events and Information	Remarks and references to Appendices
BARLIN	1916 11th April	11 a.m.	Horse Inspection by DDVS, 1st Army.	
			Transport 20 from R.E, 4 laundry, 1½ from Sanitary, 2 baggage. Weather - wet. Two Indian orderlies from Train, 4 each cycles were ill L.S	
	12		Transport 22 from R.E, 4 from Laundry, 1½ Sanitary. Weather wet.	
	13		All tins cancelled, officers were seen to open 18c. Transport 22 from R.E, 4 Laundry 1½ Sanitary. Weather wet.	
	14	4.15	A. a. 13 S —	
	16		Inspection for move C. Rest line. Report by DDVS 1st Army, horses 23rd Div Train were very good. Baggage wagons 69th Inf Bgde found slack. Transport 6 from R.E, 6 from Vernon. Weather wet	
	17	6	192. C. M.C. marched to LA COUCHETTE near DIVION — 6 miles, & took over billets from No. 2 C. 2nd Div. Train. Baggage section marches with 1st line of 69th Inf Bgde. Transport 4 from R.E. 2 from Vernon. Weather - wet.	Appendices ① 23rd Div Operation Order No. 2 and Route Table

Army Form C. 2118.

WAR DIARY
or
INTELLIGENCE SUMMARY.
(Erase heading not required.)

Place	Date	Hour	Summary of Events and Information	Remarks and references to Appendices
BARLIN	1916 18th April		Railhead BARLIN. Ripley Pont 69th Bde. DIVISION, remainder of Division BARLIN Railway Pt.	
			193 Co. marches to DIVION - 6 miles - with 24th Inf. Bde., & took over billets of No. 3 Co.	
			2nd Divl. Train	
			Transport Officers R.E. & train returns	
			Weather wet.	
"	19		Divl. Headquarters & Headquarters Train moved to BRUAY. Railhead BARLIN.	
			190 Co. marches to LA COUCHIETTE (DIVION) & took over billets of 2.A.C. 2nd Divl. Train	Appendix 2
			192 Co. marches with 69th Inf. Brigade to Monceur area, and took over billets of BEF. G.S. Sc. 91	
			7 H.D. horses cast from Remount Depot	Cert 2 15th April
			2nd Lieut. A.W. HOOLEY admitted to 23 C.C.S. LOZINGHEM from -	
			Weather wet. Lieut. PRESSEY attacks for duty to Salvage Corps	
BRUAY	20th & 21st		Inspected billets. 190 + 193 Cos. LA CAUCHIETTE and DIVION. Railhead BRUAY	
			Weather wet. RPs 6 1st Bn. HALLICOURT, 69 LAIRES, 24th BRUAY Ry. Pnr. R+ OURTON	
	22nd	10am	F.G.C.M. on 74/59/796 Pr. R. STUART 190 C.	
			1 Sergt & 3 Issuers detached for duty with extra Cashier Coys Paymaster's Office - for share -	
			Weather wet	
	23rd		Weather well. Company Church Parade.	

WAR DIARY
or
INTELLIGENCE SUMMARY.

Army Form C. 2118.

Place	Date	Hour	Summary of Events and Information	Remarks and references to Appendices
BRUAY	1916 April 24		Lieut R.A WARTERS R.A.M.C appointed M.O. of Train. Weather - fine.	
	25		Transport 4 pair CC.R.O (plrs) 3 pair Vermin weather fine	
	26	11a	2nd Lt A. NORTHEN assumes duty of 2nd C.M. 191 Co. marched with 68th Inf. Bgde from Bruay to BERLIN & DIVION 192 Co. from with 69 Inf. Bde from FIEFS to BARLIN 193 Co. with 24th Inf. Bde from DIVION to FIEFS 2Lt BERRY to THERUANNE to collect transport for 23rd Tunnelling Company. Transport 4 wagons CC.R.O (plrs) weather fine warm.	
	27		1 Sub: Car detached for duty with CC.R.O (plrs). Weather fine warm	
	28		6 drivers evacuated Base H.T. Depot HAVRE - Transport for 23rd Tunnelling Co. arrived Capt KELSALL and 3 Drivers on 7 days leave to England - Transport - 8 wagons CC.R.O Weather fine warm	

Army Form C. 2118.

WAR DIARY
or
INTELLIGENCE SUMMARY.
(Erase heading not required.)

Instructions regarding War Diaries and Intelligence Summaries are contained in F. S. Regs., Part II. and the Staff Manual respectively. Title pages will be prepared in manuscript.

Place	Date	Hour	Summary of Events and Information	Remarks and references to Appendices
BRUAY	1916 29 April		1 wagon (R.T.) arrived from XV Divl Train for use of Divl Band — Weather fine warm	
	30.		Company Church Parade. Transport 6 p.m. service. Weather fine warm	
			During the month majority of vehicles of the Train were repainted and wheels stoved.	

France
1st May 1916

A. Noakes
Lieut. Colonel
Comdg 23rd Divl Train

SECRET.   COPY NO. 17

23rd DIVISION OPERATION ORDER NO.42.

                                                    12th April, 1916.

1. The 23rd Division will be relieved by the 2nd Division in the NOULETTE SECTOR as under. The moves will take place as in the attached March Table.

2. (a) The 69th Inf.Bde. will be relieved by the 5th Inf.Bde. on night 16/17th.
   The 24th Inf.Bde. (less 1 Bn.)   "   99th   "   " 17/18th.
   The 68th Inf.Bde. will be relieved by the 6th   "   " 18/19th.

   (b) Details of relief will be arranged between Brigadiers concerned. On completion of reliefs the relieving Brigadier will assume command of the Section.

   (c) The Coys. of 9th South Staffords will come out of the Sections on the same day as the Inf. Bdes. in the Sections and march independently to near RUITZ where they will be billetted under orders of C.R.E.
   Hd. Qrs. will move on the 16th.

   (d) Artillery reliefs will be carried out on evening of 19/20th; details to be arranged direct between G.O's C.R.A. concerned. Guns will be left in the line. Reliefs will be completed by 10 a.m. on 20th.

   (e) All Medium Trench Mortar Batteries will be left in the line. The personnel of the French Mortars will be relieved by the infantry of 2nd Div. on the same day the infantry in the sections are relieved and will be disposed of by G.O.C., R.A. The personnel of the 2 inch mortars will be relieved by the R.A. 2nd Div., under arrangements between G.O's C.R.A.

   (f) One Field Company R.E. at a time will go into rest billets near RUITZ under orders of C.R.E. The C.R.E. will hand over command of the R.E. in the NOULETTE SECTOR at 10 a.m. on 19th to C.R.E. 2nd Div.

   (g) Relief of Medical Units will be arranged direct between the A.D.M.S. concerned and Div. H.Q. informed.

   (h) The remainder of the Division (less R.A. & D.M.T.) will move on the 19th.

3. All maps, photographs, log books, trench stores & mortars in the trenches will be handed over to the 2nd Division.

4. The 68th Bde. will be attached to 2nd Div. from 10 a.m. 19th April and will supply working parties required by that Division.

5. Div. H.Q. will open at BRUAY at 10 a.m. on 19th, at which hour the G.O.C. 2nd Div. will assume command of the NOULETTE SECTOR.

6. Acknowledge.

                              C.F. Watson
   Issued at 4 p.m.   Lt.Colonel,
                                          General Staff, 23rd Division.

Headquarters,
23rd Division.
S.G.44/9.   P.T.O.

Copies to :-

No. 1 - 6.	C.R.A.	16.	Signals.
7.	C.R.E.	17.	Train.
8.	24th Bde.	18.	Train.
9.	68th Bde.	19.	A.D.M.S.
10.	69th Bde.	20.	A.D.V.S.
11.	9th S.Staffs.	21.	D.A.D.O.S.
12.	D.M.T.	22.	Diary.
13 - 15.	"Q".	23.	Diary.
		24.	"G".
		25.	2nd Div.
		26.	1st Div.
		27.	47th Div.
		28.	IVth Corps.
		29.	IVth Corps.

March Table issued with 23rd Division Operation Order.

Date.	Unit.	From.	Starting Pt.	Time of Passing S.P.	Route.	Destination.	Remarks.
16/4/16	69th Inf. Bde.	ANGRES SECTION	—	On relief.	PETIT SAINS.	HERSIN AREA.	H.Q. COUPIGNY. 1 Bn. FOSSE 10. M.G. 1 Bn. COUPIGNY. Coy. 2 Bns. HERSIN. HERSIN.
16/4/16	H.C.9/S.S.	HERSIN.	—	2 p.m.	Direct.	RUITZ.	
16/4/16	1 Coy. 9/S.Staffs	BULLY.	—	3.30 p.m.	Rd.Junction L.33.b. - PETIT SAINS.	RUITZ.	Sections at 5 minutes interval.
17/4/16	69th Inf. Bde.	HERSIN AREA.	Road Junction K.34.d.7.1.	Leading Bn. 12 noon remaining units at ¼ Hr. intervals.	BARLIN - HALLICOURT.	DIVION AREA. (Bde. Area Commander G.O.C. 69th Inf. Bde.)	H.Q. DIVION. 2 Bns. DIVION. 1 Bn. OURTON. 1 Bn. LA COMTE. Bde. M.G. Coy. BEUGIN.
17/4/16.	24th Inf. Bde. (less 1 Bn.)	SOUCHEZ SECTION.	—	On relief.	PETIT SAINS.	HERSIN AREA.	
17/4/16	2 Coys. 9/L.Staffs	—do—	—	By arrangement with G.O.C. 24th Bde.	—do—	RUITZ AREA.	
18/4/16	24th Inf. Bde. (less 1 Bn)	HERSIN AREA.	Road Junction K.34.d.7.1.	Leading Bn. 12 noon remaining units at ¼ Hr. intervals.	BARLIN - HALLICOURT.	BRUAY AREA. (Bde. Area Commander G.O.C. 24th Inf. Bde.)	H.Q. BRUAY. 2 Bns. BRUAY. 1 Bn. CALONNE. Bde. M.G. Coy. BRUAY.

2.

Date.	Unit.	From.	Starting Pt.	Time of Passing S.P.	Route.	Destination.	Remarks.
18/4/16	68th Inf.Bde.	CALONNE SECTION.	-	On relief.	PETIT SAINS	HERSIN AREA.	
18/4/16.	1 Coy. 9/S.Staffs.	-do-	-	By arrangement with G.O.C. 68th Bde.	-	RUITZ AREA.	
19/4/16	69th Inf.Bde.	DIVION AREA.	-	-	-	MANOEUVRE AREA.	Transport by road. Dismounted personnel by rail.
19/4/16	H.Q.	SAINS-EN-GOHELLE.	-	-	Direct.	BRUAY.	
20/4/16.	F.A.	-	-	On relief.	Direct.	H.Q.BRUAY. 1 Bde.R.F.A. DIEVAL. 1 Bde.R.F.A. DIVION. 1 Bde.R.F.A. CAMBLAIN. 1 Bde.R.F.A. CALONNE. D.A.C.BRUAY.	In consultation with G.O.C. Inf. Bde. and Town Major in whose area these towns are situated.

GENERAL STAFF No. P991 21 APR. 1916 23rd DIVISION

SECRET

Appendix (2)

To. ~~R.A.~~   S.S.O.
   ~~24th Bde.~~   ~~Signals.~~
   ~~68th Bde.~~   ~~A.D.M.S.~~
   ~~69th Bde.~~   ~~IVth Corps.~~   )
   ~~"Q".~~   ~~2nd Division.~~) For information.
   ~~Train.~~   ~~Corps School.~~)

With reference to 23rd Division "TRAINING PROGRAMME" issued on 13th April the following moves will take place on the 26th :-

(1). 24th Inf. Bde. from BRUAY AREA will march to 1st Army Training Area under Brigade arrangements. 2/Northampton Regiment from PERNES will rejoin the Brigade.

   68th Inf. Bde. from HERSIN AREA will march to DIVION AREA, sending one Battalion to PERNES for duty at Corps School. The dismounted personnel of this Bn. will go by train.

   69th Inf. Bde. will march to PERNES and will send dismounted personnel by train from PERNES to HERSIN AREA for attachment to 2nd Division. Transport will march to HERSIN area.

(2). 1st train leaves PERNES 11.37., 2nd train leaves PERNES 12.37., arriving HERSIN at 14.06 and 15.06 respectively.
   Train time table from HERSIN to PERNES will be notified later.

(3). In accordance with Instructions No.2 "G.H.Q. Movement" para 14 (i), each Infantry Brigade will hand over 40 boxes S.A.A. to the relieving Brigade.
   This will simplify transport if a sudden move is ordered.

(4). (i) The loads on vehicles of 69th Inf. Bde. should be as light as possible. The Brigade supply wagons will be available to lighten the loads.
   The usual number of lorries will be provided.
   Supplies for consumption on 27th will be dumped on 26th at HERSIN - COUPIGNY - FOSSE 10 for units billetted in those areas. Particulars will be sent to Supply Officers of Brigades as early as possible.

   (ii) Supplies for 68th Inf. Bde. (less Bn. proceeding to PERNES) will accompany units, those for Bn. at PERNES will be dumped at the MAIRE on 26th.
   Supply wagons of the Bn. proceeding to PERNES may be used by that Battalion so as to lighten loads.
   The usual number of lorries will be provided.

   (iii) The 24th Inf. Bde. (including Bn. at PERNES) will take their supplies with them.
   The usual number of lorries will be provided.

C.F.Watson.
Lt.Colonel,
General Staff, 23rd Division.

Headquarters,
23rd Division.
21st April, 1916.

W 74—664 250,000 3/15 L.S. & Co.   **Secret**   Army Form W. 3091.

Cover for Documents.

Nature of Enclosures.

War Diary

By Lieut. Colonel. A. Northen D.S.O.

Commanding 23rd Divisional Train A.S.C.

6th June 1916   The D.A.G.
In the Field   3rd Echelon

Notes, or Letters written.

[margin: 23 Div Train Vol 9]

Army Form C. 2118.

WAR DIARY
—or—
INTELLIGENCE SUMMARY.
(Erase heading not required.)

Place	Date	Hour	Summary of Events and Information	Remarks and references to Appendices
Bruay	1916 May 1		Railhead Bruay. Transport 11 wagons for Corps Ordnance Requisitioning Officer. The other Evenerly attached to Divisional Salvage Corps. Weather fine.	
	" 2		Railhead Bruay. L'Col A.V. Olton R.C. Present H.Q. CMV at Spencer Hospital Bruay "Spy in Police Van no." Transport 1 wagon for Army Corps. Weather fine.	
	" 3		Railhead Bruay. Transport 1 wagon Salvage Corps. One Officer & 3 men Return on leave to England. Mons of Brigades arranging to emp for over the 5th Inst. Weather fine.	
	" 4		Railhead Bruay. Transport 4 wagons for Corps & Divisional Stables. 1 man sent to Corps School of Lootery. Weather fine.	

WAR DIARY or INTELLIGENCE SUMMARY

Army Form C. 2118.

Place	Date	Hour	Summary of Events and Information	Remarks and references to Appendices
Bruay	1916 May 5		18th Brigade went 1916 minus from Divion to Corps Training area. 69th Brigade and 192nd moved from BARLIN to DIVION. 24th Brigade and 193rd moved from training area to BARLIN. One horse reported from Boat H.T. 8957. Major Upton prisoner of T.G.C.M. at Special Hospital Busnes. Weather fair.	
"	6		Self Wheeler moved for Bruay. Weather fair. Allotment of land received to 2 acres every Salvage Transport 5 wagons. C.R.E. Ord Town Major Bruay.	
"	7		Transport 3 wagons. C.R.E. H. to Corps Requisitioning Oficer. Weather wind. Clear stone dried.	
"	8		Wheeler arrived from Boat H.T.8957.	
"	9		Transport 6 wagons. C.R.E. 3 wagons Corps Requisitioning Officer 1 wagon Salvage Corps 2 Busnes (Sergt W Richardson). Major Upton Present. T.G.C.M. ad Busnes. Weather fair.	

WAR DIARY
or
INTELLIGENCE SUMMARY.

(Erase heading not required.)

Army Form C. 2118.

Place	Date	Hour	Summary of Events and Information	Remarks and references to Appendices
Bruay	1916 May 10		Transport 9 wagons. C.R.E. 1 Divisional Luncheon. 2 Heavy Draught horses received from Remount Depot for 190 Co. Weather fine.	
	" 11		Transport 4 wagons. Divisional horse. 192 Co. with by 4th Brigade work from Divion to BARLIN. Count of Engineer Officers in the 91 Co. Bruay at FES ordered by letter G. S. O., D.R.O. 1297. Weather fine.	
	12		Transport 3 wagons. Divisional Laundry. Major Upton breaks A.G. C.M. Brenen Whyte recommended. Weather fine.	
	13		Transport 4 wagons. Divisional work. Hd. Qrs. Tennis with the Brigadier, and Division R.A. in the fortress area. 190 Co. Moved from Divion to BARLIN. 4 Men from Base Reporting. Weather fine.	

Army Form C. 2118.

WAR DIARY
or
INTELLIGENCE SUMMARY.
(Erase heading not required.)

Instructions regarding War Diaries and Intelligence Summaries are contained in F. S. Regs., Part II. and the Staff Manual respectively. Title pages will be prepared in manuscript.

Place	Date	Hour	Summary of Events and Information	Remarks and references to Appendices
BERLIN	14th May		Transport, 3 from R.E., 4 Laundry, 12 Sanitary. Weather warm.	
	15.		Capt SOUTHEE taken duties of S.O. 2nd Inf Bde, vice Lieut BERRYMAN to 59 Fd Amb. Major UPTON proceeded on 10 days leave to England. Capt. HUNTER TODD on his return to STO	
			Transport 9 from R.E. 4 Laundry, 2 from reserve. Weather dull.	
	16.	11am	Lieut Col NORTHEY, Assistant P.O.M. BOULOGNE	
			Capt LANGFORD proceeded on 10 days leave to England. 2Lt HOLMES taken over duties of Adjutant	
			Transport 9 from R.E., 4 Laundry, 6 other. Weather fine warm.	
	17th		Shell fire near Dunkirk-Dieppe [?] road & fire brigade turned out	
			Transport H Waggons Divisional Ammunition, 6 Waggons for ORE, 8 Waggons for Asylum R.S.C. 6 Waggons for Sheur Corps Dumps, 2 Waggons H Wates [?]	
			2 Waggons 8.11/12 0	
			Weather Showery	
			Gas alarm.	
			Lieut BURNS [?] nov [?] the men protected to England on Army leave	
	18"		Newport 13 Waggons Divisional [?]	

Army Form C. 2118.

WAR DIARY
or
INTELLIGENCE SUMMARY.
(Erase heading not required.)

Instructions regarding War Diaries and Intelligence Summaries are contained in F. S. Regs., Part II. and the Staff Manual respectively. Title pages will be prepared in manuscript.

Place	Date	Hour	Summary of Events and Information	Remarks and references to Appendices
Bulscamp	18th May		Weather fair.	
	19		Nieuport 22 wagons for Divisional works. 68th Brigade sent 191 O.R.s for a forward area to form an area. Lt Col A Nother proceeded to GHQ at HESDIN. Owing to moonlight up to Wed and Artillery train between Nieuport and Furnes to proceed at G.3 hr/ms.	
	20 "		Revd allotment increased to 4 pr/men. Nieuport 19 wagons for Divisional works. 10 Heavy Arty. U know hours from Beer. Weather fine.	
	21		S.O.S. for alarm received at 7.30 pm. Cancelled 8 pm. Lt Col A Nother proceed to G.P.M. Nieuport 18 wagons for Divisional works. Weather fair.	
	22		All out (except Special Coys) Churches. Nieuport 18 wagons for Divisional works.	

WAR DIARY
or
INTELLIGENCE SUMMARY.

Army Form C. 2118.

Place	Date	Hour	Summary of Events and Information	Remarks and references to Appendices
Berlin	22 May		2 Coys S/d [?] move to VIVIERS au Bois. 1 Supply wagon attached him. Wither fine.	
	23		Lt Francis proceeds England on leave. A.S.C Reserve [?] Vehicle [?] relieved by 1 G.S. & 2 [?] for ambulance. 3 Sgts + 1 driver transferred to Base. 2 drivers returned to complete establishment.	
			Transport 20 wagons f.o.d. Divisional work. Weather fine.	
	24		Transport 22 [?] Divisional work. Weather fine.	
	25		Captain Darragh proceeds Eng[?] leave. M. O'Hary & Lead. Bowes &[?] head accident [?] K.[?] — Sgt Shillitt[?] escort [?]. Nine of Polwagmy[?] Divisional work. Weather fine.	

Army Form C. 2118.

WAR DIARY
or
INTELLIGENCE SUMMARY.
(Erase heading not required.)

Instructions regarding War Diaries and Intelligence Summaries are contained in F. S. Regs., Part II. and the Staff Manual respectively. Title pages will be prepared in manuscript.

Place	Date	Hour	Summary of Events and Information	Remarks and references to Appendices
Boleen	26.5.16		Transport & Transport Division War D. Some men proceeded to Bughmen on Lorry. Weather fine	
	27.		Transport 31 wagons on Divisional work. Reinforcement incoming to 8 may 5 days. Weather fine	
	28.		Transport H.Q. wagons on Divisional work. Weather fine	
	29.		Transport – 29 wagons Divisional work. & Brucek Divisional Headquarters moves to Barlin from forward area owing to King Shelled. They take own wheeled transport by Farrier Hanguarters. Weather fair	
	30.		The 69 Brigade relieved 24th Brigade in line	
	30		Transport 25 wagons for Divisional work. Weather fine	

T2134. Wt. W708-776. 500000. 4/15. Sir J. C. & S.

Army Form C. 2118.

WAR DIARY
or
INTELLIGENCE SUMMARY.
(Erase heading not required.)

Instructions regarding War Diaries and Intelligence Summaries are contained in F. S. Regs., Part II. and the Staff Manual respectively. Title pages will be prepared in manuscript.

Place	Date	Hour	Summary of Events and Information	Remarks and references to Appendices
Berlin	31/5		Transport & transport & general work Lt Lodge and 9 N.C.O's men posted in to work. Inspected Water Guns	

18 June 1916

A. Norther
Lt Col
Comg 23rd Dn Train

Army Form W. 3091.

Cover for Documents.

Nature of Enclosures.

War Diary
By Lt Colonel A. Northen D.S.O.
Commanding 23rd Divisional Train A.S.C.
B.E.F. France.

From 1st to 30th June 1916
In the Field

The D.A.G.
3rd Echelon
Base

June 23 Div Train Vol. 10

Notes, or Letters written.

Army Form C. 2118.

WAR DIARY
or
INTELLIGENCE SUMMARY.
(Erase heading not required.)

Instructions regarding War Diaries and Intelligence Summaries are contained in F. S. Regs., Part II. and the Staff Manual respectively. Title pages will be prepared in manuscript.

Place	Date	Hour	Summary of Events and Information	Remarks and references to Appendices
Berlin	1916 1.6		Railhead Berlin. Transport- 34 wagons Divisional work. 3 lorries returned from Base. Weather fine.	
"	2.6		Railhead Berlin. Transport- 29 wagons for Divisional work. Weather fine.	
"	3.6		Railhead Berlin. Transport- 46 wagons for Divisional work. Two Mechanical Transport 180 men Naval Brigade working party of 45 Wenches. Weather fine.	
"	4.6		Railhead Berlin. Transport- 58 wagons for Divisional work. Including 25 wagons for taking working party of Naval Brigade to trenches. Weather fair. Orders 10am.	

Army Form C. 2118.

WAR DIARY
or
INTELLIGENCE SUMMARY.
(Erase heading not required.)

Place	Date	Hour	Summary of Events and Information	Remarks and references to Appendices
Berlin	1916			
	5.6		Raikeen Berlin. Transport 65 wagons including 25 G.S. working parties of Batt. brigade to Trenches. Lieut Holmes and 9 men proceeded overland to Dyphera. Weather fair. Some showers.	
"	6.6		Rachan Berlin. Transport of wagons including 23 G.S. working parties of Brigade trenches. Major McGrenery proceeded overland to Dyphera. Wse the Rain	
"	7.6		Raikeen Berlin. Transport 57 wagons in ordnance 25 G.S. working parties of Naval Brigade to Trenches. L.G.C. trailed on down 85 lie 170 C. Weather dull.	

T2134. Wt. W708-776. 500000. 4/15. Sh J. C. & S.

Army Form C. 2118.

WAR DIARY
or
INTELLIGENCE SUMMARY.
(Erase heading not required.)

Place	Date	Hour	Summary of Events and Information	Remarks and references to Appendices
Berlin	1916			
	8.6		Railhead Berlin	
			Newport 29 Wagons to SWB/oval work	
			Matter Fine	
	9.6		Railhead Berlin	
			Newport 61 Wagons to Divisional works	
			Weather fine	
			Railhead Berlin	
	10.6		Newport 22 Wagons to Divisional work	
			2nd L. Horse & 5 N.Z. Coy men proceeded on leave	
			Water MT	
	11.6		Railhead Berlin	
			Newport 15 Wagons to Divisional works	
			191 Coy made with 68th Brigade to FIÉFFES, this commences a	
			m.m. of 23rd Division from Lines of Cg. H.d. Reserve	
			Weather fine	

WAR DIARY
or
INTELLIGENCE SUMMARY.
(Erase heading not required.)

Army Form C. 2118.

Place	Date	Hour	Summary of Events and Information	Remarks and references to Appendices
	1916			
Barlin	12.6		Ruthern Barlin. Transport 10 wagons for divisional work. 3 Report near reporting from Bras. Weather wet.	Appendix I
	13.6		Ruthern - Barlin. Transport - 7 wagons divisional work. 9 Nieuport - 7 wagons divisional work. *193bn with 24th Bgde moved to PERNES in route for 9 H.Q. Reserve area. All leave cancelled. Weather hot.	Operation Order No 4 & 8
Bruay	14.6		Railhead moved to Bruay. *9mm Headquarters moved to Bruay. *190.Co. moved to La Comette 19.2 horses both by Bruay to PERNES in route to G.H.Q. Reserve area. Weather dull.	

WAR DIARY
or
INTELLIGENCE SUMMARY.

(Erase heading not required.)

Army Form C. 2118.

Place	Date	Hour	Summary of Events and Information	Remarks and references to Appendices
Bruay	19.6		Railhead Bruay	
	15.6		2.190 mules met to Westrees	Appendix I
			Winter wet	
Bomy	16.6		Railhead Bruay	Operation order No 46
			19.1, 19.2, 19.3 all went in lorries with Brigade	
			The Divn Headquarters moved to Bomy.	
			Winter fine	
"	17.6		Railhead Bruay	
			Transport 3 wagons per Bn.s, one MTR	
			Railhead AIRE	
"	18.6		Winter fine	
"	19.6		Railhead AIRE	
			Winter fine	

Army Form C. 2118.

WAR DIARY
or
INTELLIGENCE SUMMARY.
(Erase heading not required.)

Instructions regarding War Diaries and Intelligence Summaries are contained in F.S. Regs., Part II. and the Staff Manual respectively. Title pages will be prepared in manuscript.

Place	Date	Hour	Summary of Events and Information	Remarks and references to Appendices
Barry	1916			
	20.6		Railhead AIRE	
			Weather fine	
"	21.6		Railhead AIRE	
			One number to attend a course of instruction in boots artie	
			2nd Lt Berry H. No 0 proceeded to area around AMIENS for billeting	
			Weather fine	
"	22.6		Railhead AIRE	
			Lt. Col A. Norton proceeded to G.H.Q.	
			2nd Lt O Thomas + 2nd Lt Hosley's names submitted for promotion to Lieut	II
			Weather Showery	
"	23.6		Railhead AIRE	
			Weather fine	
"	24.6		Railhead AIRE	
			Lt. Col. Norton + Adjutant with S.S.O + 3 Buyers Supply Officers	23 personal
			proceeded to AIRE by hand VAUX near AMIENS	instructions
			Weather Showery Shaving	Appx No 2
				20.4.16

Army Form C. 2118.

WAR DIARY
or
INTELLIGENCE SUMMARY.
(Erase heading not required.)

Instructions regarding War Diaries and Intelligence Summaries are contained in F.S. Regs., Part II. and the Staff Manual respectively. Title pages will be prepared in manuscript.

Place	Date	Hour	Summary of Events and Information	Remarks and references to Appendices
VAUX EN AMIENOIS	25.6		Railhead VAGNICOURT. A Company of train entrained at LILLERS Station under Command of Major Montgomery, and one entire party in first train Mourlu partie in 2nd train. Weather fine	Appendix II. 23rd Divisional Instructor Aug 25.6 to 30.4.16
"	26.6		Railhead VAGNICOURT. Company arrived about 7am. and proceeded to Pujincee. Area. Detrainment took place at LONGUEAU. Weather fine	
"	27.6		Railhead. VAGNICOURT. Rifles twice, 8am & 9pm. Weather showery	
"	28.6		Railhead VAGNICOURT. Rifles 9pm. Men previously orders cancelled. Weather showery	

Army Form C. 2118.

WAR DIARY
or
INTELLIGENCE SUMMARY.
(Erase heading not required.)

Instructions regarding War Diaries and Intelligence Summaries are contained in F. S. Regs., Part II. and the Staff Manual respectively. Title pages will be prepared in manuscript.

Place	Date	Hour	Summary of Events and Information	Remarks and references to Appendices
VAUX EN AMIENOIS	29.6		Railhead VAGNICOURT. Fresh orders to be prepared to march tomorrow. Refilling 5pm. Water Supply.	Appendices III
"	30.6		Railhead kept VAGNICOURT. Refilling at 9pm. All Companies move forward. Weather fine.	23 S/118.10 D/L A2. Order 30.6.16

A. Walker Lt Colonel
COM G. 23rd DIVISIONAL TRAIN A.S.C.

Appendix I

SECRET

Copy No. 16

23RD DIVISION ORDER NO. 48.

13th June, 1916.

1. The Division will continue its march to the 1st Army Training Area in accordance with the attached revised March Table.

2. Companies of the Train will march with the Brigades to which they are affiliated.

3. Reports to BRUAY up to 9 a.m. on 16th, after which hour to BOMY.

4. Acknowledge.

Issued at 9 a.m.

C. F. Watson.
Lt. Colonel,
General Staff, 23rd Division.

Headquarters
23rd Division.

Copies to :-

Nos. 1 - 6	R.A.	No. 23	A.P.M.
7	R.E.	24	A.D.V.S.
8	Signals.	25	D.A.D.O.S.
9 - 10	24th Inf. Bde.	26	Camp Commandant.
11 - 12	68th Inf. Bde.	27	Diary.
13 - 14	69th Inf. Bde.	28	Diary.
15	9th S. Staffords. R.	29	File.
16	Train	30	"G".
17 - 20	"Q".	31	Town Major, PERNES.
21	A.D.M.S.	32	Town Major, BRUAY.
22	S.S.O.	33	IVth Corps.

No 34   9th Division.

MARCH TABLE TO ACCOMPANY 23RD DIVISION ORDER NO.48.

DATE.	UNIT.	TIME.	ROUTE.	BILLETING AREA.	REMARKS.
14th June.	H.Q.Division. H.Q.&.H.Q.Coy A.S.C. 35th Mob.Vet.Sect.	9 a.m.	HERSIN - BARLIN - BRUAY.	BRUAY.	
	9/S.Staffs.	As arranged by O.C.	PERNES - SAINS-LEZ-PERNES FIEFS.	BEAUMETZ LEZ AIRE.	To be clear of PERNES by 8 a.m.
	24th Inf.Bde. 71st Fd.Amb. 193 Co. A.S.C	As arranged by G.O.C. 24th Inf.Bde	SAINS LEZ PERNES FIEFS.	H.Q. FONTAINE LEZ BOULANS, 1 Bn. LAIRES, 1 Bn. LIVOSSART, 1 Bn. PREDEFIN, 1 Bn. FIEFS, M.G.Coy. FIEFS, Fd.Amb. LAIRES, Coy.A.S.C. PALFART.	Not to be West of PERNES before 8.15 a.m.
	69th Inf.Bde.	As arranged by G.O.C.	Direct.	H.Q. DIVION, 1 Bn. SAINS LEZ PERNES & TANGRY. 1 Bn. CAMBLAIN CHATELAIN. 1 Bn. CALONNE RICOUART. 1 Bn. PERNES.	M.G.Coy. in this area.
15.	68th Inf.Bde. 191 Co.A.S.C. 70 Fd. Amb.	As arranged by G.O.C. 68th Inf.Bde	LUGY -MATRING-HEM - RECLING-HEM.	H.Q. & 1 Bn. DELETTE, 1 Bn. COVECQUE, 1 Bn. DENNEBOROUCQ, LILLETTE, CAPELLE SUR LA LYS, 1 Bn. RECLINGHEM. Bde.M.G.Coy. VINCLY, Coy.A.S.C. on main road near COVECQUE Field Amb. NOUVEAUVILLE.	FIEFS
16.	24th Inf.Bde. 71st Fd. Amb. 193 Coy.A.S.C.	As arranged by G.O.C. 24th Inf.Bde.	CUHEM - ERNY ST JULIEN.	H.Q. & 1 Bn. ERNY ST. JULIEN. 1 Bn. FLECHIN, 1 Bn. BONCOURT LE PIOUY, PIPPEMONT, 1 Bn. ENGUINEG- attc. Bde.M.G.Coy. GREUPPE, Fd. Amb. ERNY ST. JULIEN, Coy.A.S.C CUHEM.	

DATE.	UNIT.	TIME.	ROUTE.	BILLETING AREA.	REMARKS.
15th June. 16	69th Inf.Bde) 69th Fd.Amb.) 192 Coy.A.S.C.)	As arranged) by G.O.C.) 69th Inf.Bde	FERFAY - ESTREE BLANCHE.	H.Q. & 1 Bn. ESTREE BLANCHE. 1 Bn. 2 Bns. ENQUIN LES MINES. SERNY. Bde.M.G.Coy. LIETTRES. Fd. Amb. LIETTRES. Coy.A.S.C. FLECHINELLE.	
15-6	R.E.	As arranged by C.R.E.	VALHOUN - BERQUENEUSE.	VERCHIN.	
16th June.	Div. H.Q.) H.Q. & H.Q.) Coy.Train.) 31th Mob.) Vet. Sect.)	9 a.m.	DIVION - PERNES - BOMY.	BOMY. Cheerves -	
	R.E.	As arranged by C.R.E.	LUGY - MATRING-HEM.	MATRINGHEM.	

SECRET. 13/6/1916.
G.I.

Reference 23rd Division Order No. 48, of to-day's date, following alterations are made in March Table :-

68th Inf. Bde. Group stands fast 14th; moves 15th.
24th and 69th Inf. Bde. Groups stand fast 15th;
   move 16th.
All other moves will take place on dates ordered.

Acknowledge.

                         for Lt. Colonel,
                     General Staff, 23rd Division.

H.Q. 23rd Div.

Copies to :-

R.A.	A.P.M.
R.E.	A.D.V.S.
Signals.	D.A.D.O.S.
24th Inf. Bde.	Camp Comdt.
68th Inf. Bde.	Diary.
69th Inf. Bde.	Diary.
9th S. Staffords.	File.
Train.	"G".
"Q".	Town Major, PERNES.
A.D.M.S.	Town Major, BRUAY.
S.S.O.	IVth Corps.
9th Division.	

Appendix II

Officers for duty at entraining Stations will be detailed as follows:—

    1 Officer R.A.
    1   "   2" Inf Bde } Lillers

    1 Officer R.A.
    1   "   69 Inf Bde } Berguette

    1 Officer R.A.
    1   "   68" Inf Bde } Aire

These Officers will act in Co-operation with R.T.O. They will proceed by the last Train leaving their respective Stations. The R.A. Officers will also assist in entraining the D.A.C.

Two N.C.O's & 25 other ranks will be detailed by R.A. to assist in entraining the D.A.C. at each station

SECRET.
S.G.254

FOLLOWING AMENDMENTS WILL BE MADE TO 23RD DIVISION INSTRUCTIONS
NO.2. DATED 20TH APRIL,1916.

Para 1. for 10 a.m. 21st April read 6 p.m. 16th June.

Para 3.(a) revised table "A"   (to follow).

Para 3.(b) (ii), Entraining Stations are (A) LILLERS (B) BERGUETTE
(C) AIRE.

Para 7. Officers for duty at entraining stations will be detailed as
follows :-

        1 Officer R.A.   ) LILLERS.
        1   "   24th Inf. Bde.)

        1 Officer R.A.   ) BERGUETTE.
        1   "   69th Inf. Bde.)

        1 Officer R.A.   ) AIRE.
        1   "   68th Inf. Bde.)

These Officers will act in co-operation with the R.T.O. They will proceed by the last train leaving their respective stations. The R.A. Officers will also assist in entraining the D.A.C. Two N.C.Os and 25 other ranks will be detailed by R.A. to assist in entraining the D.A.C. at each station.

Para 9. Alter names of stations to read LILLERS, BERGUETTE and AIRE.

Para 12. Delete whole of para 12 - and substitute :- One lorry per Bn. will be provided to carry steel helmets.

Para 14 (iv) delete.

Para 16. Delete and substitute new para.

    16. In all cases Advanced parties will take with them an "Entraining
        State" giving total personnel, animals, vehicles and approx:
        weight of baggage.

Delete Table "B" (i) & (ii) and substitute revised table "B" (Entraining programme).

Delete Entraining March Table and substitute "Entraining Routes".

                                F. Watson
                                Lt. Colonel,
16th June, 1916.   General Staff 23rd Division.

ENTRAINING ROUTES

1. **LILLERS STATION**

    All troops entraining at LILLERS Station will use roads SOUTH of the line:—

    BOMY – CUHEM – RÉLY – ST. HILAIRE – LILLERS (all inclusive).

    Troops coming from ENGUINE GATTE and ERNY ST. JULIEN will march via CUHEM and thence as ordered.

2. **BERGUETTE STATION.**

    All troops entraining at BERGUETTE Station will use roads NORTH of the line given in para 1 (exclusive) to SOUTH of the line BLESSY – ISBERGUES (exclusive).

    102nd Field Company will march via BOMY – ENQUIN-LES-MINES, thence direct to BERGUETTE.

3. **AIRE STATION.**

    All troops entraining at AIRE will use the road DELETTE – THÉROUANNE – MAMETZ – AIRE.

    R.A. will select their own routes.

F. Watson
Lt. Colonel,
General Staff 23rd Division.

16th June, 1916.

SECRET.

23rd DIVISION INSTRUCTIONS NO.2.

Reference Map, 1/40,000   20th April, 1916.
Sheet 36.B.

SCHEME G.H.Q.

1.   23rd Division will be in G.H.Q. Reserve from 10 a.m. 21st [6 pm 16 June] April until further notice.

2.   During the period of being in G.H.Q. Reserve the Division will be prepared to move by road or rail at nine hours notice. Period of notice (9 hours) is calculated from the hour at which the notice reaches First Army H.Q. (Units may only have about 6 hours notice).

3.   The movement of the Division will be carried out in one of the following alternative manners according to the circumstances which exist at the time.

     (a). <u>By route march.</u>

         23rd Division will be prepared to march at 9 hours (See para 2) notice under orders which will be issued at the time.
         The grouping of formations and units for the purposes of this move is shown in Table "A" attached hereto.

[S.G 104/2 29/4/16]

     (b). <s>By rail (strategical trains).</s> *Complete Strategical Move by Rail (Strategical Trains)*

         (i). 23rd Division will be prepared to entrain as a whole.

         (ii). Entraining Stations are (A) <s>BERLIN</s> (B) <s>BRUAY</s> (C) <s>PERNES</s>. *Lillers (B) Bruette (C) Aire*

         (iii). The first train at each entraining station will be ready at 9 hours notice from the time of receipt of such notice at 1st Army H.Q. Subsequent trains leave at <u>one hour intervals.</u>

         (iv). In this case, the Division will entrain as in Table "B" attached hereto.

         (v). The table is calculated from an hour 0.00 (zero). Zero will be the hour at which the first train will leave. The hour of zero will be notified by Div. H.Q. to all concerned.

     (c). By Route March and Rail.
         (The grouping being similar to Tables "A" & "B").

         (i). By tactical trains.

[104/2 25/4/16] *(d) In the event of any Brigade having moved by tactical trains before the rest of the Division is ordered to move by strategical or Modified Strategical Move, such portions of units detailed to entrain in the first 5 trains from the station allotted to that Brigade, as have not gone in the tactical trains will entrain in the first two trains from that station and the next 3 trains from that station will not be required.*

<u>NOTE.</u> A set of Tactical Trains consists of 3 trains; two trains for dismounted personnel only, which can be entrained or detrained anywhere on the line, and one train of 48 vehicles for transport. The first two trains will each take the personnel of two Battalions, without any transport or animals. The third train will take the personnel, animals and vehicles detailed in the attached Table "C" -

Accommodation........

........accommodation   2.
accommodation on this train is strictly limited to the detail given
in Table "C": no additional personnel, animals or vehicles can be
carried.

    Entraining Tables for the move by tactical trains and orders
for the movement of the remaining troops by road, will be issued when
the necessity arises.

    (ii). Modified Strategical Move.
        The Infantry Brigades and certain Divisional Troops,
including all men who would otherwise have to march on foot,
will move by rail. The remainder of the Division move by road.
The troops to move by rail are those detailed for the first
19 trains in the Standard Entraining Programme for a Complete
Strategical Move. All the units concerned entrain complete
with whole of their transport, except in the case of Field
Companies, R.E., and Field Ambulances, which units move partly
by rail and partly by road, as follows:-

	By Rail.	By Road.
Field Companies, R.E.	Whole unit except pontoons.	Pontoons.
Field Ambulances.	Dismounted personnel (not exceeding 170).	Remainder of unit.

    The Division will be prepared to march at 9 hours notice.
(See para.2.)
    The entraining Tables for this move are given in Table "B"
see footnote thereto.
    Orders for the move of troops by road will be issued when
required.

4.   All units will reconnoitre the routes allotted to them for movement to the entraining stations.

5.   All troops except the personnel of Infantry Battalions entraining in accordance with para. 3(b) and (c)(ii) will be at the entraining station 3 hours before the time at which their train is due to depart. Transport of Infantry Battalions with a strong loading party will be at the entraining station 3 hours before the time at which their train is due to depart, and the remainder of the Battalion 1 hour before that time.
    Arrangements for entraining in tactical trains - see para. 3(c)(i) - will be notified when required.

6.   The composition of strategical trains is as follows :-

    TYPE COMBATTANT - 33 Covered Trucks.
                         14 Open Flats.
                         1 Officers' Coach
    TYPE PARC.   - 24 Covered Trucks.
                         23 Open Flats.
                         1 Officers' Coach.

    All trains in Table "B" are "Type Combattant" unless specifically marked as "Parc".
    Covered Trucks take 40 men or 8 horses; 2 or 3 men can travel in each truck with the horses.
    Open flats vary in size, but 4 pairs of wheels can be taken with limbered vehicles (5 for guns and ammunition wagons); 3 pairs when 1 - 4wheeled vehicle is not limbered, and only one vehicle in the case of pontoons and ambulances.
    Officers' Coach cannot be taken as having more than 4 compartments

3.

Officers for duty at entraining stations will be detailed as follows :-

Royal Artillery.....................................PERNES.
Infantry Brigade Head Qrs in Rest Area...........BRUAY.
    "   "   "   "   in HERSIN AREA......BARLIN.

These officers will act in co-operation with the R.T.O. and railway entraining staff as may be required. They will proceed by the last train leaving their respective stations.

8. G.O.C., R.A. will detail one subaltern officer, 2 N.C.O's and 25 men at each of the following stations :-

PERNES.
BRUAY.
and BARLIN.

to assist in entraining B.A.C's and D.A.C., commencing with trains No.23, 24 and 25 respectively. These parties will proceed in the last train leaving their respective stations.
G.O.C.,R.A. will make all arrangements for rationing these parties.

9. O.C., Divisional Signal Co. will furnish one motor cyclist for permanent duty at each of the entraining stations PERNES, BRUAY and BARLIN. The cyclist will be at the disposal of the officer detailed by R.A. and Infantry Brigades mentioned in para. 7 above, for communication with billeting areas. He will proceed by the last train from the entraining station concerned.

10. Every unit will entrain its supply and baggage wagons (from 23rd Divl. Train) with its 1st Line Transport.

11. (i). Troops will in all cases move with one day's iron ration on the man and the unexpended portion of the current day's ration on the man or in the 1st Line Transport. Troops entraining after noon should have the following day's rations with them in addition to the day's rations in the supply vehicles of the Train.

(ii). Supply Vehicles of the train will move full.

(iii). To ensure this, O.C. Divl. Supply Column will arrange to have one day's supplies for each train load of troops entraining after midday, at the station 2 hours before the time of departure of the train. He will bring sufficient loaders to load up the supplies on the train.
Lorries used thus will be loaded up again at Supply Railhead before proceeding to the new area.
S.S.O. will submit a statement of the feeding strength of each train load to the O.C. Divnl. Supply Column as soon as possible and will keep him informed of any fluctuations.

12. One blanket per man will accompany units. Transport will be provided for these between billets and entraining stations under arrangements which will be made by Divisional Headquarters
Units will arrange to either carry or stack blankets at the journey's end. If blankets are stacked, a small party must be left in charge of them.
Units will submit to Divisional Headquarters demands for the amount of transport required for carrying blankets to the entraining station, and the place where the transport is to report.

One lorry per Bn. will be provided to carry steel helmets.

14............

13. Orders regarding the movement of units provided with motor transport will be issued when orders for the Division to move are actually received.

14. (i). All Lewis guns and half the S.A.A. will be carried on their G.S. limbered wagons. The remainder of the S.A.A. will be collected at once and kept near Bde. H.Q. with the Light T.M. Battery.
   In the event of a move one man per Battalion will be left in charge. This S.A.A. will be loaded on the lorries which take away the Light Trench Mortar Battery.

   (ii). The Light T.M. Battery will be collected and kept together near Brigade H.Q. In the event of a move one Officer per Brigade and 2 men per Battery will take charge of the guns. This Officer will also take charge of the S.A.A. mentioned in (i).

   (iii). Lorries for the Light Trench Mortars and half S.A.A. (para 14 (ii)) will be sent to Bde. H.Q. under Divisional arrangements. (Units having hand carts will take them with them).

   (iv). ~~The Medium Trench Mortar Batteries will be kept together. In the event of a move four men per Battery will be left in charge of the guns; and one Officer will be left in charge of all the Batteries. Lorries will be sent to pick up the guns and the party i/c S.A.A. and convoy them to their destination.~~

   (v). No Trench Mortar Ammunition will be taken.

15. The Division will be accompanied by "P" Cable Section as a proportion of Corps Signals.

    In all cases advance parties will take with them an entraining state

16. The D.H.T. ~~(if still away)~~ will move by special train from ~~S.M.E.~~ *giving total numerical animals, vehicles and approx. weight of baggage.*

                                    C. F. Watson.
                                    ──────────────── Lt. Colonel,
                                    General Staff, 23rd Division.

Issued to :-

    24th Inf. Bde.
    68th Inf. Bde.
    69th Inf. Bde.
    R.A., 23rd Divn.
    R.E., 23rd Divn.
    23/Div. Signal Co.
    D.L.O.Y.
    23/Div. Cyclist Co.
    A.D.M.S., 23rd Divn.
    A.P.M., 23rd Divn.
    A.D.V.S.,   "
    D.A.D.O.S.   "
    "Q"   "
    Camp Commandant.
    O.C. Train.
    S.S.O., 23rd Divn.
    23/Div. Supply Column.
    IVth Corps (For information).
    Corps Signals.(ditto   ).
    Southern Railheads.(,,   ).
    1st Cavy. Divn. (,,   ).

Appendix III

COPY NO 16

SECRET.
S.G.44/84

23RD DIVISION ORDER NO.50.

Reference Map AMIENS Sheet 17 1/100,000

1. The Division will march to the RAINNEVILLE Area on the night of 30th June/1st July, 1916 in accordance with the attached March Table.

2. Coys of the Train will move with the Brigades to which they are affiliated.

3. Divisional Headquarters remains at VAUX.

4. ACKNOWLEDGE.

C.F. Watson
Lt.Colonel,
General Staff 23rd Division.

Headquarters 23rd Division.
30th June, 1916.

Issued at 12 noon.

Copies to :-

Nos. 1 - 6	R.A.	No. 23	A.P.M.
7	R.E.	24	A.D.V.S.
8	Signals.	25	D.A.D.O.S.
9 - 10	24th Inf. Bde.	26	Camp Commandant.
11 - 12	68th Inf. Bde.	27	Diary.
13 - 14	69th Inf. Bde.	28	Diary.
15	9th S.Staffords.	29	File.
16	Train.	30	"G".
17 - 20	"Q".	31	IInd Corps.
21	A.D.M.S.	32	Supply Column.
22	S.S.O.	33	D.A.C.

MARCH TABLE TO ACCOMPANY 23RD DIVISION ORDER NO.50.

UNIT.	STARTING POINT.	TIME.	ROUTE.	BILLETING AREA.	REMARKS
24th Bde. Group. 9th S.Staffords 24th Inf. Bde. 71st Fd. Amb. 193rd Coy. A.S.C. 190th Coy. A.S.C.	Cross Rds. just South of G. in LONGPRE.	6 p.m.	POULAINVILLE - COISY - RAINNE-VILLE.	RAINNEVILLE & MOLLIENS au BOIS.	
	St.SAUVEUR.	6 p.m.	Ditto.	RAINNEVILLE.	To follow 24th Bde.Group.
68th Bde. Group. 68th Inf. Bde. 70th Fd. Amb. 191 Coy. A.S.C.	BRELLY.	3.30 p.m.	AILLY - St.SAUVEUR.- LONGPRE - POULAINVILLE.	POULAINVILLE - ALLONVILLE.	
69th Bde. Group. 69th Inf. Bde. 69th Fd. Amb. 192 Coy. A.S.C.	To be arranged by 69th Inf. Bde.		Direct.	BERTANGLES - COISY.	
R.E. Group. 101 Fd. Co. R.E. 102nd Fd. Co. R.E. 128th Fd. Co. R.E.	To be arranged by C.R.E.		ST. SAUVEUR - LONGPRE - AMIENS - ALLONVILLE.	ALLONVILLE.	To be clear of LONGPRE by 4 p.m.
R.A. Group.	PICQUIGNY Station.	3.30 p.m.	PICQUIGNY - DREUIL - AMIENS - CARDONNETTE.	CARDONNETTE.	
A.C.	DREUIL.	4 p.m.	AMIENS - ALLONVILLE.	ALLONVILLE.	

W. 15517—M. 141. 250,000. 1/16. L.S.&Co. Forms/W 3091/2.   Army Form W. 3091.

Cover for Documents.

Nature of Enclosures.

Confidential   War Diary

By Lt. Colonel. A. Northen. D.S.O.
Commanding 23rd Divisional Train A.S.C

From 1st to 31 July 1916

Notes, or Letters written.

Army Form C. 2118.

WAR DIARY
or
INTELLIGENCE SUMMARY.
(Erase heading not required.)

Instructions regarding War Diaries and Intelligence Summaries are contained in F. S. Regs., Part II. and the Staff Manual respectively. Title pages will be prepared in manuscript.

Place	Date	Hour	Summary of Events and Information	Remarks and references to Appendices
	1916			
VAUX	July 1		Railhead VIGNACOURT	
			Train Headquarters moved to BAIZIEUX	23 Divisional
			190 Co at MOLLIENS AU BOIS	Duty No 50
			191 " at POULAINVILLE	3 b 16
			192 " COISY	Sgt with
			193 " MOLLIENS AU BOIS	last works
			Instruction	Scary
BAIZIEUX	" 2		3 Brigade Companies moved to BRESLE	
			Weather fine	
"	" 3		Yesterday and today, when here reconnoitred	
			Water fine	
"	" 4		Main Headquarters moved to DERNANCOURT	
			3 water units begun with Kerrs ofst horse attached to 191 Co	Appendix No I
			1 water tank wagon and lorry ofst horse attached to 192 Co	Appendix No II
			Very heavy rain	

WAR DIARY or INTELLIGENCE SUMMARY

Army Form C. 2118.

Place	Date	Hour	Summary of Events and Information	Remarks and references to Appendices
DERNANCOURT	July 5		Railway work to DERNANCOURT. 2 vets had 6 wagons with teams 9th horse attached to 193 Coys. Own whilst using this Railway host hautspoot was used to draw in there at 7 min intervals. The tractor & wire lathes to Courcelles drawn by ano issued to units during the evening morning	
"	6		Hayworth 2 units to BVIRE. 9th Brigade Companies out to meet DERNANCOURT. Transport Transport for work at Bourcelles and by RE work. (men around 28 reinforcements from Base 1 Pioneer and 12 HD horses received from Base. No temporary attached during action of operation. 1 water tank began work. Team 9th horse attached to 193 Coy. Weather fine.	
"	7		Transport 6 hay or cloth & pairs up ready for RE work 2 wagons for Bourrolles. Weather wet.	

WAR DIARY or INTELLIGENCE SUMMARY.

Army Form C. 2118.

Place	Date	Hour	Summary of Events and Information	Remarks and references to Appendices
DERNANCOURT	July 8		Transport 6 wagons with relief parts for R.E. works. 2 wagons for Bond School.	
			2 Supply Clerks transferred to A.G's Office Base	
			17 men as reinforcements arrived	
			2 Lt. W.F. Lacy temporarily attached to assist in working light tramways and to train NCOs in forward area.	
			Weather wet	
"	" 9		RAILHEAD moved to ALBERT. Horse transport there.	
			Transport. 6 wagons & helps for R.E. work. 2 wagons for 12nd.	
			Store. 2 wagons for Salvage work.	
			Weather fine	
"	" 10		Transport 4 wagons for X division work	
			Lt Col. A. Northen. President. + G.C.M	
			2 Supply Clerks transferred to Base	
			2 hoods of wheeled transport attached to Trans. Killed in Becourt Wood by shell fire	
			Weather fine	

T2134. Wt. W708—776. 500000. 4/16. Sir J.C. & S.

Army Form C. 2118.

WAR DIARY
or
INTELLIGENCE SUMMARY.
(Erase heading not required.)

Instructions regarding War Diaries and Intelligence Summaries are contained in F. S. Regs., Part II. and the Staff Manual respectively. Title pages will be prepared in manuscript.

Place	Date	Hour	Summary of Events and Information	Remarks and references to Appendices
DERNANCOURT	July 11		Main Headquarters moved to ST GRATIEN. 193 Company march to BRESLE. Railway moved to FRECHENCOURT. Weather fine.	Appendix No II Divisional Order No 3
ST GRATIEN	" 12		Supply Column 4 hours late dumping owing to ham trying late. 190 & 192 Companies march to BRESLE. 193 moved to MOLLIENS au Bois. Lt. A.C.Phepey wounded whilst supplying with Salvage Company. 2nd Lt. St. Barry reported at Battalion for ten as to qualifications for R.F.C. Weather fine.	
"	" 13		4 Supply men arrived from Base. 192 Co. moved to MOLLIENS au Bois. Weather fine.	
"	" 14		Weather fair some rain.	

WAR DIARY
or
INTELLIGENCE SUMMARY.
(Erase heading not required.)

Army Form C. 2118.

Place	Date	Hour	Summary of Events and Information	Remarks and references to Appendices
S^T GRATIEN	July 15		24th Infantry Brigade transferred to 8th Division and 70th Infantry Brigade to	
"	" 16		Physical training 2.3rd Division. The only A.S.C. personnel to remain were the 5 men with Brigade Hd. Qrs. Inactive front.	
"	" 17		70th Infantry Brigade reported 2.3 Division Board of Officers examined 190 to 5 gunner stokey sights. Weather fair & some rain. Transport - 8 wagons R.E. work. Weather very wet.	
"	" 18		Transport - 6 wagons A.E. work. 19 O.R. men to hosp. ALBERT 2 Lieut from L. from Gazette - Lt. A.E. Bergman to be Captain 2 Lt. K. Berry to be Lieutenant. Weather wet.	

WAR DIARY or INTELLIGENCE SUMMARY

Army Form C. 2118.

Place	Date	Hour	Summary of Events and Information	Remarks and references to Appendices
ST GRATIEN	1916 July 19		Received warning orders to be prepared to move on 21st inst. Then notified that establishment of A Horse would be reduced by 30 Hoses HR to be replaced by 35 Leyds Lays. Weather fine.	
"	20		19th Company moved to FRANVILLERS. Captain R.A. Spurke takes over duties of Supply Officer by Brigade. Captain A.D. Burgmann takes over duties of supply officer 19th Brigade. Weather fine.	Appendix No II Divisional Orders No. 1
"	21		Train Headquarters moved to HENENCOURT. 191, 192, 193 Comp moved North to BRESLE. 6 R.D. horses and 1 rider received from Remounts. 1 Bugger Wagon attached A/102 Rt.a. auth'sn by ACE [illegible] Weather fine.	
HENENCOURT	22		4 mares received from Base. Weather fine.	

Army Form C. 2118.

WAR DIARY
or
INTELLIGENCE SUMMARY.
(Erase heading not required.)

Instructions regarding War Diaries and Intelligence Summaries are contained in F.S. Regs., Part II. and the Staff Manual respectively. Title pages will be prepared in manuscript.

Place	Date	Hour	Summary of Events and Information	Remarks and references to Appendices
	1916			
HENENCOURT	23 July		Those losing the Lient Lt Phipsley had been evacuated to England. Machine gun	
"	24"		section arrived with Lewis Churges for Reclaimers One. Waiting fire	
"	25.		1 & 3 Company moved from Bresle to Camps near Albert. Machine fire	
"	26		Rather moved to ALBERT. Lapphin trains instructing Openwur horse transport event 2 AM. Moved in Company Each will Not Known to trucks during the morning. Krums	
"			Main Headquarters moved from HENENCOURT to Camps near ALBERT. Nailing	
"			1, 2 + 1 Companies moved from BRESLE with same Camps of Main Headquarters.	
"			2nd Lt Lacey detached for special duties with Motor truck wagons in forward area	

T2134. Wt. W708-776. 500000. 4/15. Sir J.C. & S.

Army Form C. 2118.

WAR DIARY
or
INTELLIGENCE SUMMARY.
(Erase heading not required.)

Instructions regarding War Diaries and Intelligence Summaries are contained in F. S. Regs., Part II. and the Staff Manual respectively. Title pages will be prepared in manuscript.

Place	Date	Hour	Summary of Events and Information	Remarks and references to Appendices
ALBERT	1916 July 26		Lt. Barry transferred to R.F.C. on probation as an observer. Machine gun instruction.	
"	" 27		Transport wagons to Suzanne R.E. works. Instruction.	
"	" 28		Two men Sub Barrett attached to 19th C according to orders in Bacon room through explosion of bomb ammunition. injuries received by L.A. 13 wagons transport division works. Machine gun.	
"	" 29		Transport wagons to divisional works. 4 G.S. in the district to carry bombs to forward area. Instruction.	
"	" 30		4 wagons of R.E. works. Instruction.	
"	" 31		Transport 5 wagons to Divisional works.	

WAR DIARY
or
INTELLIGENCE SUMMARY.

Army Form C. 2118.

Place	Date	Hour	Summary of Events and Information	Remarks and references to Appendices
ALBERT	31st July		Lieut L. P. Gilbert joined for duty from 47 Reserve Park and proceeded to 195 Co. as Reconnoitring Offr. Lieut S. C. Anderson joined for duty from 32 Reserve Park and posted to 19 Co. as temporary Officer. Water fine.	

3-9-19 GG

A. Walker

COM G. 23rd DIVISIONAL TRAIN A.S.C.

COPY NO. 16

Appendix No I

SECRET
S.G.44/85.

23RD DIVISION ORDER NO. 51.

1. The 23rd Division will relieve the 34th Division in the Line.

2. The 69th Inf. Bde. is placed under the orders of 34th Division and will take over the Advanced Line to-night.

3. The 24th Inf. Bde. will move to bivouacs in the vicinity of DERNANCOURT to-morrow. The Bde. will move at intervals, but will be in bivouacs by 10.30 a.m.

4. The 23rd Divisional Artillery will gradually relieve that of the 34th Division under arrangements to be made between the Cs. R. A. concerned. 23rd Divisional Artillery Brigades may billet in DERNANCOURT for the purpose of relief, moving up via BUIRE.

5. 102nd Fd. Coy. R.E. will march under the orders of the C.R.E.

6. The Fd. Ambs. will move under the orders of the A.D.M.S.

7. All R. E. stores, tools, ammunition, rations, water, bombs and Stokes Mortar ammunition in the area will be taken over by the 69th Inf. Bde.

8. The Mobile Vet. Section will remain at ST. GRATIEN.

9. The baggage and supply sections of H.Q. Coy. will remain at ST. GRATIEN.
The baggage and supply sections of the remaining companies will remain at BRESLE.

10. The G.O.C. will assume command of the front held by the 34th Division at 3 p.m. to-morrow.

    Divisional H.Q. will be at VIVIER MILL.

11. Acknowledge.

Headquarters 23rd Division.
3/7/1916.

F. Watson
Lt. Colonel,
General Staff, 23rd Division.

Issued at 9 p.m.

Copies to :-

Nos. 1 - 6	R.A.	No. 23	A.P.M.
7	R.E.	24	A.D.V.S.
8	Signals.	25	D.A.D.O.S.
9 -10	24th Inf. Bde.	26	Camp Commandant.
11-12	68th Inf. Bde.	27	Supply Column.
13-14	69th Inf. Bde.	28	D.A.C.
15	9th S. Staffords.	29	Salvage Coy.
16	Train.	30	"G".
17-20	"Q".	31	Diary.
21	A.D.M.S.	32	Diary.
22	S.S.O.	33	File.
		No. 34	IIIrd Corps.
		35	19th Division.
		36	21st Division.
		37	34th Division.

SECRET.   Appendix No ~~III~~ 4 Cb   COPY NO. 16

23RD DIVISION ORDER NO.54.   24th July, 1916.

Reference 1/20,000 Map.

1. The 23rd Division will relieve the 1st Division in the Left Sector of the 3rd Corps front as under :-

2. (a) On the 25th the 70th Inf. Bde. will relieve the 1st Inf. Bde. (H.Q. SHELTER WOOD) and will come under orders of 1st Division.
The G.O.C. will assume command of the Sector on completion of relief.
Details of reliefs to be arranged between Brigadiers.

(b) On the 26th the 69th Bde., relieving the 2nd Inf. Bde., will be in Divl. Reserve with H.Q. at ALBERT. It will march off at 8 a.m., 5 minutes intervals to be kept between Bns. and 1 min. between Coys.

(c) Orders for the move of the 68th Bde. on the 26th will be issued later.

3. The 1st Division will hand over all R.E.Stores, Ammn. rations, water in the area, together with all maps, photographs, etc.

4. The R.E. and Pioneers will move on the 26th. Orders for this move will be issued later.

5. The A.D.M.S. will arrange the reliefs of the Fd. Ambulances.

6. Train Coys. will take over the lines of the Train Coys. they relieve under orders from O.C. Train.

7. Two troops, 3rd Corps Cav. Regt. and the Sections 3rd Corps M.M.G. Bty. at present with 1st Division will be attached to 23rd Division.

8. G.O.C. 23rd Division will take over command of the Left Sector 3rd Corps Front at 12, noon, 26th. Div. H.Q. will be in ALBERT.

9. Acknowledge.

[signature]
for Lt. Colonel,
General Staff, 23rd Division.

Issued at 6 p.m.

Copies to :-

Nos. 1-6	R.A.	No. 27	Supply Column.
7	R.E.	28	D.A.C.
8	Signals.	29	Salvage Coy.
9-10	68th Inf. Bde.	30	"G".
11-12	69th Inf. Bde.	31	Diary.
13-14	70th Inf. Bde.	32	Diary.
15	9th S. Staffs. R.	33	File.
16	Train.	34	3rd Corps.
17-20	"Q".	35	1st Division.
21	A.D.M.S.	36	34th Division.
22	S.S.O.	37	19th Division.
23	A.P.M.	38	1st Australian Div.
24	A.D.V.S.	39	3rd Corps Cav. Regt.
25	D.A.D.O.S.	40	3rd Corps M.M.G.Bty.
26	Camp Comdt.	41	Town Major, Albert.
		No. 42	Town Major, Baizieux.

Army Form W. 3091.

Cover for Documents.

Nature of Enclosures.

Confidential

War Diary

By Lt Colonel A. Northen D.S.O.

Commanding 23rd Divisional Train a.s.c

1st to 31st August 1916

A.H.Q.
3rd Echelon

Notes, or Letters written.

Army Form C. 2118.

WAR DIARY
or
INTELLIGENCE SUMMARY.
(Erase heading not required.)

Place	Date	Hour	Summary of Events and Information	Remarks and references to Appendices
Albert	1916 Aug 1		Railhead Albert. Supplies drawn in trucks by horse transport and issued from railway points near Company lines. Court of Inquiry assembled to investigate injuries received by T.2/29858 Driver Barrett in forward area. Newport 4 G.S. wagons R.E. tools into town area. No T/127947 Driver W. Hutchinson tried by F.G.C.M. Weather Hot.	
"	" 2		Newport 5 G.S. wagons & Divisional work. M. Col. A Northern S.O. trainers F.G.M. at Divisional Bomb store. Weather Hot.	
"	" 3		Newport 4 G.S. wagons R.E. work forward area. Weather very hot.	
"	" 4		Newport 8 G.S. wagons R.E. work forward area. Weather fine very hot.	

WAR DIARY or INTELLIGENCE SUMMARY

Army Form C. 2118.

Place	Date	Hour	Summary of Events and Information	Remarks and references to Appendices
Whit Hips	Aug		Newport - 8 G.S. Wagons R.E. works in forward area. Weather fine, very hot.	
"	6		Newport - 6 G.S. Wagons R.E. work in forward area. Weather fine, hot. Lieut D Hutchen took charge of 50 G.S. Bns.	
"	7		Major C.D.S. Upton left to take over Command 55th Divisional Train. Capt H Norton took over duties S.S.O. Re- Field Note I 1375 & 7 8 moves to Hutchinson by L.C.M. to see two Companies. Captain Burgh th. J.A. Francis who Present to march of a Comt of Infantry escort the at Divisional Headquarters. Weather fine, very hot.	Appendix No. I Divisional Order No 59 5.8.16
"	8		Train Headquarters move in to Bergues. 191 & 193 Companies march to Brede Woods. 193 Company moved to Brede. 190 Company no move. Weather fine.	

Army Form C. 2118.

WAR DIARY
or
INTELLIGENCE SUMMARY.
(Erase heading not required.)

Instructions regarding War Diaries and Intelligence Summaries are contained in F.S. Regs., Part II. and the Staff Manual respectively. Title pages will be prepared in manuscript.

Place	Date	Hour	Summary of Events and Information	Remarks and references to Appendices
	1916			
Baizieux	Aug 9		Railway arrangements for aug. Reclincourt Supply Column again taken into use.	
			190 Company remains at ALBERT	Appendix II
			3 Officers and 3 men proceeding with Divisional Billeting Party to reconne. Intraine at Mericourt at 4 pm.	Division Order A/2793/4 8.8.16
			Weather hot	
	" 10		Main headquarters move to St Sauveur by train	
			191 and 193 Companies move to St Sauveur	Appendix III
			192 Co. move to Allonville	
			Weather fine	
St Sauveur	" 11		Main headquarters move to Ailly le Haut Clocher	
			191 Co. move to Gorenflos, 192 Co. move to Vauchelles	
			193 Co. move to Pont-Remy.	
			All Supply Wagons moved on full, and rations were delivered to Units on arrival. Wagons refueling again at 7 pm.	Appendix III
			Weather hot	

WAR DIARY or INTELLIGENCE SUMMARY

Army Form C. 2118.

Place	Date	Hour	Summary of Events and Information	Remarks and references to Appendices
Ailly le haut Clocher	Aug 12		Railhead Hangest-Sur-Somme for Brigade groups for All 4 190 Co Heilly. Winter very hot	
"	" 13		3rd Coy headquarters marched to Longpré and entrained there for Bailleul. En route for Flêtre. Train left 9.20 am. 19 & Co also moved from Longpré to Flêtre. Train left 12.20 pm. 19 3 C.S. entrained at Pont-Remy detained at Bailleul en route for Meteren. 190 Co moved to Beaucourt. Railhead for 19 o C and R.A. Mechincourt. Weather fine.	
FLÊTRE	" 14		Railhead for Brigades Caestre 192 Co moved by rail from Longpré to Bailleul en route for Meteren. 193 Co moved to La Creche. 2ndLt Lacey reported to intervening Officer R.E. was not accepted by Leasy. Weather fine	Appendix II R.A. Order II 12 Aug 16

Army Form C. 2118.

WAR DIARY
or
INTELLIGENCE SUMMARY.
(Erase heading not required.)

Instructions regarding War Diaries and Intelligence Summaries are contained in F. S. Regs., Part II. and the Staff Manual respectively. Title pages will be prepared in manuscript.

Place	Date	Hour	Summary of Events and Information	Remarks and references to Appendices
FLETRE	Aug 15		191 Company moved to La Creche. 190 Company refilled twice. Weather fine	
"	16		190 Company moved to Overview. Weather fine	
"	17		Railhead Steenwerck. Supplies drawn in lorries by Companies from Railhead. Headquarters of transport to Steenwerck. 192 Company to La Creche. 190 Co. entrained at Salenet and detrained at Bailleul. On route for EECKE. The 23rd Supply Column did last mail with 8 wagons and after arrival opened at Bailleul the H.1st Supply Column. Was here to replenish. Weather fine	Appendix IX Room 59/15/8/16

WAR DIARY or INTELLIGENCE SUMMARY

Army Form C. 2118.

Place	Date	Hour	Summary of Events and Information	Remarks and references to Appendices
STEENWERCK	1916 Aug 18		Railhead for R.B. H9 & Cavalry. Nieuport 4 wagons for R.E. works. Weather fine a little rain	
"	" 19		Nieuport 26 wagons R.E. works. 2 wagons g.H.Q. for Lancs Supply Section of 19th Cmmds to La Creche. Weather hot	
"	" 20		Railhead for 19 Div & R.A. moved to Steenwerck. Baggage Section 19 G.mrds to La Creche. Nieuport 15 wagons for R.E. works 5 G.S. wagons for other divisional works. Weather fine	
"	" 21		Nieuport 21 G.S. wagons R.E. works 3 G.S. wagons for other divisional works. Weather fine and dull	

WAR DIARY
or
INTELLIGENCE SUMMARY.

Army Form C. 2118.

Place	Date	Hour	Summary of Events and Information	Remarks and references to Appendices
Slenystrete	1916 Aug 22		Nieuport 24 G.S. Wagons for R.E. and Divisional work. Lt. Col Nathan present. 19 O.R. admitted to Divisional Wagonners. Lt. A.C. Anderson admitted to hospital. Weather fine. 5mm rain.	
"	" 23		Nieuport 28 G.S. wagons for R.E. & Divisional work. Weather fine.	
"	" 24		Nieuport 27 G.S. Wagons for R.E. & Divisional work. Lt. Col Nathan proceed to G.H.Q. Court of Enquiry at 19.20 to investigate minor accident accidentally by Driver E. Nader. Weather fine.	
"	" 25		Nieuport 28 G.S. Wagons for R.E. & Divisional work. Weather fine.	
"	" 26		Nieuport 26 G.S. Wagons for R.E. & Divisional work. 3 H.D. horses received from Remounts. Weather fine. Drew Rum.	

Army Form C. 2118.

WAR DIARY
or
INTELLIGENCE SUMMARY.
(Erase heading not required.)

Instructions regarding War Diaries and Intelligence Summaries are contained in F.S. Regs., Part II. and the Staff Manual respectively. Title pages will be prepared in manuscript.

Place	Date	Hour	Summary of Events and Information	Remarks and references to Appendices
	1916			
Steenwerck	Aug 27		Nieuport 30 G.O. wagons for R.E. & Divisional work	
			Weather fine	
"	28		Nieuport 26 G.O. wagons for R.E. & Divisional work	
			Lt Col Norton attended G.O.C.'s at Divisional Headquarters	
			Weather fine	
"	29		Main Headquarters moved by lorry to Bailleul	
			All companies moved to new camps in main van Militair	
			Drills and musketry	
			Nieuport 26 G.O. wagons to Nieuport R.E. work	
			Weather dull. Some rain	
Bailleul	" 30		Nieuport 18 G.O. wagons for R.E. & Divisional work	
			Weather very hot	
"	31		Nieuport 25 G.O. wagons for R.E. & Divisional work	
			9 G.O. wagons went to Divisional work	
			2 G.O. wagons took 15 men by 33 Room pick to escort in Kinsworth area	
			Weather fine	

A. Norton Lt. Col.
COM. G. 23rd DIVISIONAL TRAIN A.S.C.

SECRET   *Appendix No I*   COPY NO. 16

23RD DIVISION ORDER NO. 59.

1. (a) The 23rd Division (less R.A.) will be relieved by the 15th Division (less R.A.) in the left sector of the Corps front on the 7th and 8th inst.

   (b) The 23rd Division will be prepared to move from 3rd Corps area as under :
   - Transport on 10th inst.
   - Infantry by tactical trains on 11th inst.

2. Reliefs will take place as follows :-

   (a) On the 7th inst.:
   - 70th Bde. will be relieved by 46th Bde. in Right Section.

   On the 8th inst.:
   - 69th Bde. will be relieved by 45th Bde. in Left Section.
   - 68th Bde. will be relieved by 44th Bde. in Reserve.

   All details of reliefs to be arranged by G.Os.C. Brigades concerned.

   (b) Relief of R.E. and Medical Units will be arranged direct between Cs.R.E. and A.Ds.M.S. concerned and Div. H.Q. informed.

   (c) 9th S. Staffords will be relieved on the 8th by 9th Gordons --- All details to be arranged between C.Os.

3. Orders for relief of R.A. will be issued later.

4. On completion of relief Brigades will move to billets as follows, marching by the MILLENCOURT - LAVIEVILLE - BRESLE Road :-
   - 70th Inf. Bde. to FRANVILLERS.
   - 68th Inf. Bde. to BEHENCOURT and LA HOUSSOYE.
   - 69th Inf. Bde. to BRESLE.
   - 9th S. Staffords. to BEHENCOURT to be billeted by 68th Bde.

5. Train companies will move with the Brigades to which they are affiliated. The H.Q. Coy. of the Train and the Mobile Veterinary Section will remain with D.A.C.

6. G.O.C. 15th Div. will take over command of the Sector from G.O.C. 23rd Division at 6 p.m. on 8th inst. at which hour Div. H.Q. will open at BAZIEUX CHATEAU.

7. Acknowledge.

Issued at 4.30 p.m.
5/8/1916.

F. Watson,
Lt. Colonel,
General Staff, 23rd Division.

Copies to :-

Nos. 1 - 6	R.A.	23.	D.A.D.O.S.
7	R.E.	24.	Camp Cmdt.
8	Signals.	25.	Supply Column.
9-10	68th Inf. Bde.	26.	D.A.C.
11-12	69th Inf. Bde.	27.	Salvage Coy.
13-14	70th Inf. Bde.	28.	"G"
15	9th South Staffs.	29.	Diary.
16	Train.	30.	Diary.
17-18	"Q"	31.	File.
19	A.D.M.S.	32.	III Corps.
20	S.S.C.	33.	15th Division.
21.	A.P.M.	34.	2nd Australian Div.
22	A.D.V.S.	35.	34th Division.

"A" Form.   Army Form C. 2121.
MESSAGES AND SIGNALS.   No. of Message..........

Prefix...... Code......m.	Words	Charge	This message is on a/c of:	Recd. at..........m.
Office of Origin and Service Instructions.		Sent		Date..........
From	At..........m.		..........Service.	6. III. 16
	To			From
	By		(Signature of "Franking Officer.")	By

TO: KT / KE / KT — Train

| Sender's Number | Day of Month | In reply to Number | |
| Q 671 | 6 | | AAA |

Reference 23rd Div. Order No 59 dated 3rd inst Para 5 aaa Train companies should read Baggage sections of Train Companies

From 23rd Div.
Place
Time

The above may be forwarded as now corrected.   (Z)

Censor.   Signature of Addressor or person authorised to telegraph in his name.

* This line should be erased if not required.
(A1) O. Ltd., London— W.14042/M.44. 150,000 Pads. 12/15. Form C.2121.

SECRET.   23rd Division
                                                 No. A/27907/4
VERY URGENT.   Appendix II

O.C. Train

MOVE TO XTH CORPS AREA.

With reference to 23rd Divn. Order No.60 dated 8.8.16, an acting Staff Officer from each Infantry Brigade will leave MERICOURT Station for LONGPRE Station on the 10th instant by the train leaving at 7.30 a.m. and proceed on arrival as follows :-

    68th Infantry Bde to GORENFLOS,
    69th Infantry Bde to VAUCHELLES,
    70th Infantry Bde to PONT REMY.

Chargers to be sent on by road on 9th instant.

Advance Parties from each Brigade Group strength as below will leave MERICOURT Station on the 10th instant as follows :-
                                      LONGPRE arr.
68th Bde Group and ½ 69th Bde Group at 7.30 am. 1.15 pm. on 10th inst.
½ 69th Bde Group and 70th Inf.Bde Group at 5.15pm. 1.15 am." 11th inst.

The acting Staff Officer of each Brigade will arrange to meet the advance parties on arrival at LONGPRE.

Rations for consumption on 11th and 12th insts will be carried :-

Off.	O.R.	
1	4	Per Battn.
1	2	" M.G. Co.
-	2	" T.M. Bty.
1	2	" Field Co. R.E.
1	2	" Fd. Ambulance.
1	2	" A.S.C. Co.

1 Interpreter,
and in the case of 70th Inf.Bde Group
1 Off.   4 O.R. Per Pioneer Battn.

Acknowledge by wire.

                                     A.H.Randolph
8th August, 1916.   Lieut-Colonel,
                              D.A.A. & Q.M.G. 23rd Division.

Copy to :-

    68th Inf.Bde.
    69th Inf.Bde.
    70th Inf.Bde.
    R.E.
    A.D.M.S.
    O.C. Train.

SECRET.

Appendix III COPY NO. 16

23RD DIVISION ORDER NO. 60.

Ref. Map: 1/100,000.

1. The moves for the 10th and 11th are as follows:-

    (a) All mounted personnel, transport and detachments of T.M.Bs. and Lewis guns, with handcarts, will move in accordance with March Table "A".

    (b) All other dismounted personnel will move in accordance with Table "B".

2. Administrative Instructions for move on 10th and 11th Aug.

    (a) Two lorries will be sent to each Bde. H.Q. on 10th for carriage of Lewis guns which cannot be carried on the Lewis Gun S.A.A. limbered wagons and for Trench Mortars. These will convey the above mentioned guns and mortars to Bde. H.Q. in the new area.

    (b) Each Lewis gun handcart will carry one box of ammunition.

    (c) G.S.L. wagons with Lewis gun detachments will carry as many guns as possible and no ammunition.

    (d) Ammunition for Lewis guns surplus to above will be returned to ammunition railhead CONTAY or to the Div. Bomb Store on the 8th at Gunpits, B.5.a.7.0 (Sheet 62.D).

    (e) Trench Mortar carts will carry no ammunition.

    (f) The teams of all the Lewis gun and T. M. handcarts will pull their carts and move with the transport to POULAINVILLE, where they will be billeted by the Officer detailed by the Bde. Area Comdr.

3. 2 G.S. water wagons, 2 water lorries, will be provided for each Bde. area for the use of all the troops (23rd Div.) in their area on 10th in lieu of watercarts which have proceeded with transport and will be allotted by Bde. Area Comdr. They will be returned to 3rd Corps Camp Comdt.

4. ~~Bully beef in lieu of fresh meat will be issued on 10th for consumption on 11th.~~ Care will be taken to ensure that personnel marching and the dismounted personnel moving by train have their rations with them.

5. ~~Rations for consumption on 12th will be dumped in the new area at a place to be notified later.~~

6. Bde. Area Comdr. BEHENCOURT – LA HOUSSOYE will arrange for the accommodation of the personnel and transport of units moving to POULAINVILLE on the night of the 10th/11th Aug.

    Bde. Area Comdrs. at FRANVILLERS and BRESLE will similarly arrange for billets of personnel and transport of units moving to ALLONVILLE and CARDONNETTE respectively on the night of the 10th/11th August.

7. Bde. Area Comdrs. will detail an Officer not below rank of Captain to command the whole of the personnel and transport of their group.

    O.C. units will detail an officer to command their own echelon of personnel and transport and hand cart detachments.

P.T.O.

2.

8. Div. H.Q. will move to AILLY-LE-HAUT CLOCHER on the 11th.

9. ACKNOWLEDGE.

Issued at 8.30 p.m.
8/8/1916.

C.F. Watson
Lt. Colonel,
General Staff, 23rd Division.

Copies to :-

Nos.	
1 - 6	R.A.
7	R.E.
8	Signals.
9 -10	68th Inf. Bde.
11-12	69th Inf. Bde.
13-14	70th Inf. Bde.
15	9th South Staffords. R.
16	Train.
1, 17-18	"Q".
19	A.D.M.S.
20	S.S.O.
21	A.P.M.
22	A.D.V.S.
23	D.A.D.O.S.
24	Camp Comdt.
25	Supply Column.
26	D.A.C.
27	Salvage Coy.
28	"G".
29	File.
30	File
31	Diary.
32	Diary.
33	III Corps.
34	X Corps.
35	R.T.O. MERICOURT.
36	R.T.O. FRESCHINCOURT.
37	R.T.O. AMIENS.
38	Reinforcement Camp, 23rd Division.
39	A.P.M. III Corps.
40	A.P.M. X Corps.

TABLE "A".

UNITS AT	HOUR OF START ON 10TH	ROUTE	BILLETS	HOUR OF START ON 11TH	ROUTE	NEW AREA (See Table "B" for details)	REMARKS.
BRESLE	3 p.m.	QUERRIEU	ALLONVILLE	5.30 a.m.	ARGOEUVRES FLIXECOURT	VAUCHELLES-les-QUESNOY, &c.	Columns to move under orders of senior officer. ※ See remarks re T.M.B. and Lewis gun teams.
FRANVILLERS	3 p.m.	QUERRIEU	CARDONETTE	5 a.m.	do.	PONT REMY &c.	
LA HOUSSOYE	3 p.m.	QUERRIEU	POULAINVILLE	5 a.m.	do.	GOREMFLOS &c.	
BEHENCOURT	2.30 p.m.	MONTIGNY	POULAINVILLE	5 a.m.	do.	do.	
All detachments of ※ T.M. Btys. & Lewis guns.	----	----	POULAINVILLE	5 a.m.	do.	BOUCHON.	

TABLE "B".

MOVE BY RAIL ON 11TH --- DISMOUNTED PERSONNEL ONLY, NO VEHICLES, BAGGAGE OR HORSES.

UNIT	ENTRAINING STATION	DETRAINING STATION	NEW AREA	REMARKS.
69th Bde. ※ 69th Fd. Amb. 123th Fd. Coy. Coy. Train	MERICOURT	PONT REMY	VAUCHELLES-les-QUESNOY - YAUCOURT - BUSSUS - BELLANCOURT - BINGNY - l'ABBE.	Time of Train will be notified later.
68th Bde. ※ 102nd Fd. Coy. 71st Fd. Amb. Coy. Train	FRECHINCOURT	LONGPRE	GORENFLOS - AILLY -le- HAUT CLOCHER - ERGNIES - VILLERS-sous-AILLY - FAMECHON.	do
70th Bde. ※ 101st Fd. Coy. 70th Fd. Amb. Coy. Train	do	do	PONT REMY - FRANCIERES - COQUEREL.	do
Div. H.Q.	do	LONGPRE	AILLY-le-HAUT CLOCHER.	do
9th S. Staffords	do	LONGPRE	BUSSUS.	do

※ (Less detachments of T.M.B. and Lewis guns with handcarts.)

SECRET.
5/3/48.

Appendix IV

COPY NO: 28

R.A. 23RD DIVISION ORDER NO: 58.

12th August, 1916.

RELIEF.	1.	R.A. 23rd Division will be relieved by Sections on 13th & 14th August by 3 Brigades of 47th Divisional Artillery and one Brigade 34th Divisional Artillery. Relief each day to be completed by 6 p.m. Table of Reliefs attached.
MARCH.	2.	On the morning following relief, each Section will march back to Rest Billets under Brigade arrangements. Route will be via ALBERT main road to LA HOUSSOYE and thence to billets. Order of march 102nd, 103rd, 104th and 105th Brigades. First named to start each day at 9 a.m. remainder at half an hour's interval. Billeting parties will proceed ahead on 14th instant reporting to the Town Major at the following places:-

All Brigades and)
Mob: Vet: Section)   BEHENCOURT.

D. A. C.   )
H.Q. Coy: Train)   BEAUCOURT.

For allotment of billets see Table.

GUNS.	3.	All guns in action (except as below) will be handed over stripped of sights, stores, etc, to relieving Batteries, and an equal number will be taken over at wagon lines. The following unserviceable guns will not be handed over

        No: 4969 of B/103
             1802 of C/102
             3352 of C/102
             2256 of B/104
             3451 of A/105.

MAPS.	4.	All 1/10,000 and 1/20,000 maps, sketches, photos registrations, etc, will be handed over.
WIRE.	5.	All wire laid down will be handed over as it stands and none taken in exchange.
AMMUNITION.	6.	All units will move out filled to establishment. Surplus dumped at guns will be handed over, and receipts obtained. Where batteries are not relieved, ammunition will be taken to nearest occupied pits of the Brigade. 23rd D.A.C. will hand over ammunition dumped at Refilling Point and obtain receipts. Units will report to H.Q. R.A. total ammunition in possession at noon 14th and at noon 15th.

SUPPLIES.	7.	Refilling point B 17 A (Sheet 62 D) on 14th and subsequent days. Supplies to be delivered to present wagon lines on 13th and to new wagon lines on 14th and subsequent days. "X", "Y" and "Z" T.M. Batteries will be attached to 23rd D.A.C. for rations from 13th instant inclusive. Detachment of 23rd Signal Coy: R.E. will be attached H.Q. R.A. for rations from 14th inst:
TRANSPORT.	8.	Baggage wagon horses will join units on evening of 13th.
TRENCH MORTARS.	9.	Two medium T.M. Batteries 47th Division will relieve "X" and "Y"/23 on 13th instant. "X" and "Y"/23 will hand over their mortars to relieving Batteries. Details of exchange of other parts will be arranged between Staff Captain R.A. 23rd Division and D.T.M.O. 47th Divn: Personnel of "X" and "Y"/23 will return to 23rd D.A.C. All 3 T.M. Batteries of 23rd Division with equipment will proceed by lorry to FRECHINCOURT on 14th.
ATTACHED UNITS.	10.	H.Q. Coy: 23rd Divisional Train will march to BEAUCOURT on evening of 13th. 35th Mobile Veterinary Section will march to FRECHINCOURT on morning of 14th.
REPORTS.	11.	H.Q. R.A. close at W.26.c.3.3. at 6 p.m. and re-open at BEHENCOURT CHATEAU at the same hour.
	12.	ACKNOWLEDGE.

A. K. Hay.
Major,
Bde: Major R.A. 23rd Division.

Issued at 7.0 p.m.

Copy: No: 1 to R.A. 3rd Corps.
        2   15th Division.
        3   1st Divisional Arty:
        4   34th Divisional Arty:
        5   47th Divisional Arty:
        6   LAHORE ARTILLERY.
   7 to 11 102nd Brigade R.F.A.
 12 to 16 103rd Brigade R.F.A.
 17 to 21 104th Brigade R.F.A.
 22 to 26 105th Brigade R.F.A.
     27 23rd D. A. C.
     28 190th Coy: A.S.C.
     29 35' Mobile Vety: Section.
     30 X/23 T.M. Battery.
     31 Y/23 T.M. Battery.
     32 Z/23 T.M. Battery.
     33 Staff Captain R.A.

S E C R E T.
S/3/49.

Appendix V

COPY NO: 6

R.A. 23rd Division Order No: 59.

Reference:- AMIENS 1/100000.   15th August, 1916.

ENTRAINMENT. 1. The 23rd Divisional Artillery, H.Q. Coy: 23rd Train and No: 35 Mobile Veterinary Section will entrain as per Entrainment Table alreay issued, commencing on 16th instant.

ROUTE. 2. Routes to both entraining stations will be via ALLONVILLE - AMIENS - to either LONGEAU or SALEUX.

START. 3. The hour of start for each party will be minus 6 hours, reckoning the scheduled time of departure of train as "zero". Each party must reach the entraining station at minus two hours before "zero".

PORTIONS OF D.A.C. TO ACCOMPANY BATTERIES. 4. O.C. 23rd D.A.C. will ensure that the portions of the D.A.C. detailed to accompany each Battery, move off from camp with the Battery with which they entrain. Hours of start must therefore be strictly adhered to by all units.

D.A.C. WAGONS. 5. Each Battery will provide the necessary men to entrain and detrain the D.A.C. Vehicles which accompany it. O.C. D.A.C. will retain sufficient men to entrain the half of No: 4 Section travelling by the last train.

TRENCH MORTARS 6. Trench Mortar Batteries will proceed to entraining stations by motor lorries. One lorry per Battery will report at road junction just N. of the last U in QUERRIEU at 5 a.m. on 17th instant.

ENTRAINING & DETRAINING OFFICERS. 7. Reference para 2 of 23rd Division Letter No: A.Q. 2790/7 of 10th August (issued with Entrainment Table):-
Brigades and D.A.C. will detail officers as under -

ENTRAINMENT DUTIES.

SALEUX. 1 Officer 104th Bde:) To report to R.T.O.
LONGUEAU 1 Officer 105th Bde:) 4 hours before
) departure of 1st
) Train. They will
) travel by last train
DETrainment Duties.) from their station.

102nd Bde: 1 Officer to accompany A/102.) To report
103rd Bde: 1 Officer to accompany A/103.) to R.T.O.
D.A.C.   1 Officer to accompany A/104.) at
) detraining
) station.
They will remain on duty there till all trains have arrived.

SURPLUS BAGGAGE.	8.	A lorry will report at road junction just N. of the last U in QUERRIEU at 7 a.m. on 16th. 104th Brigade will send a guide and conduct the lorry to baggage dump at LA CHAUSSEE. The baggage will be collected and taken to SALEUX station in charge of the present baggage party. This bagge will be placed on the train conveying H.Q's of Brigades.
BAGGAGE SUPPLY.	9.	All units will entrain with baggage and supply wagons full.
	10.	UNITS will receive further instructions from a Staff Officer 23rd Division, and their own Advanced Parties on arrival at Detrainment Stations.
COMMAND.	11.	Lieut; Colonel P.W.B.Henning will be in command of 23rd Divisional Artillery and attached units from 9 a.m. on 16th instant.
H.Q. R.A.	12.	H.Q. R.A. will close at BEHENCOURT CHATEAU at 11 a.m. 16th inst; and re-open at the camp N of QUERRIEU at 12 noon 16th instant.
	13.	ACKNOWLEDGE.

A.K.Hall
Major,

Issued at 2.15 p.m.   Brigade Major R.A. 23rd Division.

Copy: No: 1   102nd Brigade R.F.A.
       2   103rd   "   "
       3   104th   "   "
       4   105th   "   "
       5   23rd Divisional Ammunition Column.
       6   190th Company A.S.C.
       7   35th Mobile Vetinary Section.
       8   Staff Captain R.A.
       9   A.D.C. R.A.
   10 & 11   Diary.

ENTRAINMENT TABLE.
23rd DIVL. R.A.

Unit.	Stn. of Entrainment.	Date.	Time of Departure.
A Battery 102 Bde. ¼ No.1 Sect. D.A.C.	LONGUEAU.	Aug.16th	20.13.
A Battery 103 Bde. ¼ No.2 Sect. D.A.C.	"	"	21.13.
A Battery 104 Bde. ¼ No.3 Sect. D.A.C.	SALEUX.	"	22.16.
B Battery 102 Bde. ¼ No.1 Sect. D.A.C.	LONGUEAU.	"	22.53.
B Battery 103 Bde. ¼ No.2 Sect. D.A.C.	"	Aug.17th.	0.03.
B Battery 104 Bde. ¼ No.3 Sect. D.A.C.	SALEUX.	"	1.16.
C Battery 102 Bde. ¼ No.1 Sect. D.A.C.	LONGUEAU.	"	2.13.
C Battery 103 Bde. ¼ No.2 Sect. D.A.C.	"	"	3.03.
C Battery 104 Bde. ¼ No.3 Sect. D.A.C.	SALEUX.	"	4.16.
D Battery 102 Bde. ¼ No.1 Sect. D.A.C.	LONGUEAU.	"	5.03.
D Battery 103rd Bde. ¼ No.2 Sect. D.A.C.	"	"	6.03.
D Battery 104 Bde. ¼ No.2 Sect. D.A.C.	SALEUX.	"	7.16.
A Battery 105 Bde. 12 wagons & teams No.4 Section.	LONGUEAU.	"	8.03.
B Battery 105 Bde. 12 wagons & teams No.4 Section.	"	"	8.43.
H.Q. R.A. 102,103,104/105 Bdes. Part of No.1 Sect Divl. Signal Co.	SALEUX.	"	9.56.
C Battery 105 Bde. 12 wagons and teams No.4 Section.	LONGUEAU.	"	10.23.
D Battery 105 Bde. 4 G.S. wagons, teams and drivers additional.	"	"	12.13.

Unit.	Stn. of Entrainment.	Date.	Time of Departure.
H.Q. Co. Train, Mob. Voty. Sect. X/23, Y/23 T.M. Batteries.	SALEUX.	Aug. 17th.	13.16.
Z/23 T.M. Battery. ½ H.Q. D.A.C.	LONGUEAU.	"	14.13.
½ H.Q. D.A.C. ½ No. 4 Sect. D.A.C.	"	"	15.13.

JOURNEY TAKES ABOUT 8 HOURS.

(signed)
Major.
D.A.Q.M.G. 23rd Division.

10th August, 1916.

W. 15517—M. 141. 250,000. 1/16. L.S.&Co. Forms/W 3091/2.   Army Form W. 3091.

Vol 13

Confidential

Cover for Documents.

Nature of Enclosures.

War Diary

By Lt Colonel. A. Northen D.S.O.

Commanding 23rd Divisional Train A.S.C

From 1st to 30th Sept 16

The D.A.G
3rd Echelon Base

Notes, or Letters written.

WAR DIARY
or
INTELLIGENCE SUMMARY.
(Erase heading not required.)

Army Form C. 2118.

Place	Date	Hour	Summary of Events and Information	Remarks and references to Appendices
Ballieul	1916 1.9		Routine Staff workers	
"	2 "		Transport 25 G.S. wagons for Divisional works Weather fine	
"			Transport 27 wagons for Divisional works Reserve one G.S. wagon (Complete transport) to 3rd Div three wagons had been attached to applied work Weather fine	
"	3 "		Transport 10 wagons for Div Road works Sam Commences to work into 34th Army Gunning area 19.30 Marched to war hollow Alopel Weather fine	Appendix Z
"	4 "		Transport 11 G.S. wagons for Div road works 19.30 Officers at hollow Copse them move on by noon to Clairmarais Notification received that Mr A.C. Anderson has been invalided to England to return men	

Army Form C. 2118.

WAR DIARY
or
INTELLIGENCE SUMMARY.
(Erase heading not required.)

Place	Date	Hour	Summary of Events and Information	Remarks and references to Appendices
Bailleul	5.9		Transport H.Q. & wagons & H.T. Wis. Med. units	
			19.1 Co & 19.2 Co proceeded by road to Slatsoro. One Supply wagon per Battalion went in train with Troops.	
			1st line transport went with Companies & also 19 & 6 officers men Limbers and horses on to Leulene	
			Divisional personnel of 19.1 & 19.2 Companies proceeded by rail from Bailleul	
			12 wagons lent by 32nd Reserve Park handed on to 36th Div. Ctn.	
			19.0 Co. Water WSC	
			Train Headquarters moved by Road to T. Eynes	
"	6		19.1 Co moved to Nordausques	
			19.2 Co moved to Yperlegues	
			Rations delivered to units in horses by Lorry	
			Weather fine	
T.Eynes	7		Railhead watton	
			Weather fine	

Army Form C. 2118.

WAR DIARY
or
INTELLIGENCE SUMMARY.
(Erase heading not required.)

Instructions regarding War Diaries and Intelligence Summaries are contained in F. S. Regs., Part II. and the Staff Manual respectively. Title pages will be prepared in manuscript.

Place	Date	Hour	Summary of Events and Information	Remarks and references to Appendices
Giques	8-9		Went to H.Q. Army A.S.C. Rouen. Sgt Elliot & 3 N.C.O.s went on 15 minutes by him for interesting. Rejoined horse to-day. Weather fine.	
"	9		Headquarters to return from Camp near Buire to Camp near Méteren. 191 Company moved from Marcelcave to Flipon. The resignation of Divisional R.A. Mess Establishment reduced by 9 Compt. est. Turns Out (G.S. wagons). These sent to-day to ABBEVILLE. Under command of Lt. Antoine. Capt. Birdwant & Mr Coulte left here by J.C.M. Weather fine. Lt. Giliard's gaulin 10 days Special leave to England. From Headquarters return 2/Lt St Mais returned at Longueau transported to Abbeville. Three Brigade Companies entrained at Argues & detrained at Longueau. 191 marched to Méteren au Bois. 19 Marched to	
"	10			Appendix I.

Army Form C. 2118.

WAR DIARY
or
INTELLIGENCE SUMMARY.

(Erase heading not required.)

Instructions regarding War Diaries and Intelligence Summaries are contained in F. S. Regs., Part II. and the Staff Manual respectively. Title pages will be prepared in manuscript.

Place	Date	Hour	Summary of Events and Information	Remarks and references to Appendices
Rhyno	10.9		(Continued) Marched to Cosy and 19 & Company marched to Corronette. Weather fine	
Alloweele	11.9		Railhead Tricourcourt Weather fine	
"	12.9		Main Headquarters moved to Burignet Three Brigade Coys moved to Bude	
			19 Co to entrainer at Bulwell to Longueau arrived early morning 13th. 190 Co arrived at Longueau marched to Moreuil en Pons Two sping carts. One p.m R.A. the other to Brigade HQ Co with 8 water wagons connected to spare have been attached to Train from III Corps water wagon section. Weather fine	
Bingum	13."			
Biagueux	14.		a second issue was made to-day to infantry firms 24 most violent only 5 mts arrived from Base weather fine	

WAR DIARY
or
INTELLIGENCE SUMMARY.
(Erase heading not required.)

Army Form C. 2118.

Place	Date	Hour	Summary of Events and Information	Remarks and references to Appendices
Busnes	15.9		Owing to a more My Anticipated all baggage wagons loaded were withdrawn from units	
"	16.9		Horses returned from Altrice Tractor fire. Captain C. Gayford appointed a member of a General Court Martial	
"	17.9		Tractor fire. 4 H.D. horses + 2 Mules received from Remounts Tractor fire	
"	18.9		191 Composing work Stamp on Albert Millencourt road. N. Osborne went to Decourt town in charge of water wagons Water W.F.	
"	19.9		Main Headquarters, 190, 192 & 193 Companies work on Albert-Millencourt road in relief of 15th Divisional Train. Tractor W.F. Dr Girrand team returned to 2Ld. work by W.O.	appendix III

Army Form C. 2118.

WAR DIARY
or
INTELLIGENCE SUMMARY.
(Erase heading not required.)

Instructions regarding War Diaries and Intelligence Summaries are contained in F. S. Regs., Part II. and the Staff Manual respectively. Title pages will be prepared in manuscript.

Place	Date	Hour	Summary of Events and Information	Remarks and references to Appendices
Nr Albert	20.9		Received Albert. Transport 6 G.S. wagons R.E. work. Sgt Cainer, Corpl Hutchings Smith Pleisher Finch by S.G.C.M. All rations drawn in bulk at Méthries by horse transport even dumps for issue at Outable Depots near Camp. Weather hot.	
"	21.9		Transport 10 G.S. wagons R.E. work. Lt Cuthbert admitted to X division Ror Station. Weather fine	
"	22.9		Transport 16 G.S. wagons R.E. work. Weather fine	
"	23.9		Transport 8 wagons R.E. work. Weather fine	
"	24.9		Transport 8 wagons R.E. work. Church parade 5 pm. Weather fine	

Army Form C. 2118.

WAR DIARY
or
INTELLIGENCE SUMMARY.
(Erase heading not required.)

Instructions regarding War Diaries and Intelligence Summaries are contained in F.S. Regs., Part II. and the Staff Manual respectively. Title pages will be prepared in manuscript.

Place	Date	Hour	Summary of Events and Information	Remarks and references to Appendices
Mr Albert	25.9		Transport 10 G.S. wagons for X Divisional work. Weather fine.	
"	26		Transport 20 G.S. wagons to X Divisional work. W.S.P. Gillman returned from Specialhurst. Weather hot.	
"	27		Transport 24 G.S. wagons Divisional work front of Brigades. Weather hot.	
"	28		Transport 24 G.S. wagons for Divisional work front of Brigades. Weather fine.	
"	29		Transport 11 G.S. wagons for Divisional work. Lt. Col. Lodge discharged to Divisional Rest Station. Captain A.C. Burgess admitted to Divisional Rest Station. Weather fine.	
"	30		Transport 14 G.S. wagons to Divisional work. Weather fine.	

A. Voiller
Lt. Col. MO
Comg. 23rd Div. Train

4-10-1916

Appendix I

SECRET.   COPY NO. 12

23RD DIVISION ORDER NO.66.

1. (a) The 23rd Division will be relieved in the Right Sector of IXth Corps front by the 51st and 19th Divisions. Moves will take place as in attached March Table.

   (b) 154th Inf. Bde. is placed under the orders of 23rd Division from 9 a.m. today.

2. (a) 70th Inf. Bde. will be relieved by 154th Inf. Bde.(51st Div) on 2nd instant.
   68th Inf. Bde. will be relieved by 154th Inf. Bde.(51st Div) on night of 3rd/4th instant.
   69th Inf. Bde. will be relieved by "A" Bde. 19th Division on night of 4th/5th instant.

   (b) Details of relief will be arranged direct by Brigadiers concerned. On completion of relief relieving Brigadiers will assume command of the Section.

   (c) Further orders will be issued as to relief of R.A., R.E. and Medical Units.

3. All photographs, log books and trench stores in the trenches will be handed over to relieving Brigades.

4. Div. H.Q. will close at BAILLEUL ux at 10 A.M. 6th September and open at same hour at FLETRE.

5. ACKNOWLEDGE.

                                        C.F. Watson
                                                   Lt.Colonel,
2nd September, 1916.   General Staff, 23rd Division.

   Issued at 11:45 AM.

      Copies to :-

         Nos. 1 - 6   R.A.   18. "G".
              7   R.E.   19 19th Div.
              8   68th Bde.   20 36th Div.
              9   69th Bde.   21 51st Div.
             10   154th Bde.   22 A.P.M.
             11   9th South Staffords. 23 Signals.
             12   Train.   24 Camp Comdt.
             13   "Q".   25 IXth Corps.
             14   A.D.M.S.   26 A.D.V.S.
             15   S.S.O.   27 70th Inf. Bde.
             16   Diary.
             17   Diary.

MARCH TABLE TO ACCOMPANY DIVISIONAL ORDER NO.66.

DATE.	UNIT.	FROM.	TO.	TIME.	REMARKS.
2nd Septr:	70th Inf.Bde.	Reserve Area RUE du SAC, PAPOT, SOYER, PONT de NIEPPE.	METEREN AREA.	1 p.m.	H.Q. X.20.a.7.2., 1 Bn. X.22.c.2.5., 1 Bn. COURTE CROIX, 1 Bn. FLETRE, 1 Bn. X.8.Central, M.G.Coy.& T.M.B. METEREN.
	154th Inf. Bde.		RESERVE AREA.	1 p.m.	H.Q. BRUNE GAYE, 1 Bn. RUE du SAC, 1 Bn. PAPOT, 1 Bn. SOYER, 1 Bn. PONT de NIEPPE
3rd Septr:	70th Inf. Bde. 154th Inf. Bde.	METEREN AREA. RESERVE AREA.	STAPLE AREA. Trenches (Right Sector)	To be arranged by G.O.C's concerned.	Relieves 68th Inf. Bde.
	68th Inf. Bde.	TRENCHES.	2nd ANZAC TRAIN-ING AREA.	After relief.	
4th Septr:	68th Inf. Bde. 69th Inf. Bde.	2nd ANZAC TRAIN-ING AREA. 2nd ANZAC T. AREA. TRENCHES.	METEREN AREA. 2nd ANZAC T. AREA.		Move to be completed by 12 noon. Relieved by "A" Bde. 19th Division.
	70th Inf. Bde.	STAPLE AREA.	ARQUES.	After relief.	
5th Septr:	70th Inf. Bde.	ARQUES.	TILQUES AREA.		

NOTE. The PONT D'ARCHELLES - LA RUE DU SAC road will be used from WEST to EAST only and the BRUNE GAYE - LES TROIS ARBRES (B.15.b.4.8.) road from EAST to WEST only.

All moves E. of BAILLEUL will be by Coys. at 100 yards interval.
1 Fd. Amb. will move to METEREN today and will accompany the 70th Inf. Bde.

"A" Form.
Army Form C. 2121.
MESSAGES AND SIGNALS.

No. of Message 180

Prefix .... Code .... m. | Words 104 | Charge | This message is on a/c of: | Recd. at .... m.
Office of Origin and Service Instructions. | | | | Date 2 IX
| | Sent | | From
| | At .... m. | |
| | To | |
| | By | (Signature of "Franking Officer.") | By

TO — 101st Bde.
       102 Bde.   103rd Div. ~~~~~~
       Div. Hq. Train

Sender's Number   Day of Month   In reply to Number   AAA
G295

In continuation of Div. Order 66 of todays date
following moves will take place tomorrow 3rd
inst. AAA 101 Field Coy. to LA BOURSE (O.B)
on relief by 81 Field Coy AAA 102 Field Coy.
to W.11.a.2.2. on relief by 81 Field Coy. AAA
103 Field Coy to K.2.d.7.9. on relief by 94 Field
Coy AAA 9th South Staffords to R.33.b on relief
by 5th S.W.B. AAA All above reliefs will take
place about noon AAA. Movements EAST of
D.11.3.UL will be by companies at 100 yards
interval AAA Addressed to all recipients of
23rd Div. Order No. 66.

AAA Acknowledge

From 23rd Division
Place
Time

The above may be forwarded as now corrected.   (Z)

Censor.   Signature of Addressor or person authorised to telegraph in his name.
* This line should be erased if not required.

"A" Form.
MESSAGES AND SIGNALS.
Army Form C. 2121.

Prefix......Code......m.	Words	Charge	This message is on a/c of:	Recd. at............m.
Office of Origin and Service Instructions.				Date............
Priority	Sent		............Service.	From............
	At............m.			
	To............		(Signature of "Franking Officer.")	By............
	By............			

TO { 70th Inf Bde   51st Div   Sig's
     154 "   "   Q   ADMS
                     Train

Sender's Number.	Day of Month.	In reply to Number.	
G283	2		AAA

70th Inf Bde will move today
to METEREN area being relieved
by 154th Inf Bde aaa
Both Bdes will march at 1 pm with
100 yards interval between Coys aaa
Addressed to 70th & 154th Inf Bdes
repeated 51st Div Q Train Sigs
ADMS

From 23rd Div.
Place
Time 9.30 am

"A" Form.
Army Form C. 2121.

MESSAGES AND SIGNALS.

No. of Message _____

Prefix ___ Code ___ m.	Words	Charge	This message is on a/c of:	Recd. at ___ m.
Office of Origin and Service Instructions.		.		Date ___
SECRET.	Sent At ___ m.		___ Service.	From ___
D.R.L.S.	To ___			
	By ___		(Signature of "Franking Officer.")	By ___

TO { ~~...~~ ~~...~~ ~~...~~ R.A.
~~...~~ ~~...~~ Train.

Sender's Number	Day of Month	In reply to Number	**AAA**
G.342.	7th.		

Warning Order AAA 23rd Division less R.A. will be prepared to entrain for the South on the 10th inst. AAA Destination and entraining stations will be notified later AAA R.A. will move about the 12th AAA Addressed all concerned.

From 23rd Division "G".
Place
Time 11.0 A.M.

Major G.S.

SECRET.   COPY NO. 11

appendix II

23RD DIVISION ORDER NO. 67.

Ref. Map: 1/40,000.

1. The Division (less 70th Bde) is in Army Reserve; the 70th Bde. is in Corps Reserve.

2. On the 12th the Division (less Arty. & 2 Bns. 70th Bde.) will move to the BAIZIEUX AREA in accordance with attached March Table.

3. At 8.30 a.m. on the 12th, 2 Bns. 70th Bde. will proceed in busses to BECOURT, (route via QUERRIEU) and will come under the orders of 15th Division. Column not to enter ALBERT before 10 a.m. Four lorries per Bn. for carriage of Lewis Gun handcarts will be at CARDONETTE CHURCH at 7.30 a.m.

4. (a) Baggage wagons of train will accompany units as far as their billets, - when horses will be sent to rejoin the Train at BRESLE.

   (b) Orders for the transport of the 2 Bns. 70th Bde. proceeding to BECOURT will be issued later.

5. Group Commanders will be responsible for the billeting of their Groups; Town Majors are to be consulted.

6. Halts will take place at 10 minutes before the clock hour and the march will be resumed at the clock hour.

7. The Corps Area WEST of ALBERT and EAST of the line - WARLOY - through centre of BAIZIEUX - HENLEY is at the disposal of the Division for training purposes.

8. Div.H.Q. will close at 9.30 a.m. & open at BAIZIEUX at 10 a.m.

9. ACKNOWLEDGE.

C. F. Watson,
Lt. Colonel,
General Staff, 23rd Division.

Issued at 10 a.m.

11/9/1916.

Copies to :-

Nos.
1. R.A.
2. R.E.
3. Signals.
4 - 5 68th Inf. Bde.
6 - 7 69th Inf. Bde.
8 - 9 70th Inf. Bde.
10. 9th South Staffords.
11. Train.
12. A.D.M.S.
13 - 14 "Q".
15. S.S.O.
16. A.P.M.
17. A.D.V.S.
18. D.A.D.O.S.
19. Camp Comdt.
20. Supply Column.
21. D.A.C.
22. Salvage Coy.
23. "G".
24. File.
25. Diary.
26. Diary.
27. IIIrd Corps.
28. 15th Division.

23rd Division
No. A/2790/13.

The dismounted portion of the Division less the 70th Inf Brigade and 70th Fd Ambl. will proceed to the Back Area by tactical trains as under :-

No. of Train.	Unit.	Station of entrainment.	Date.	Time.	Station of detrainment.	Date.	Time.	Remarks.
1	2 Bns 68th Bde. 68th Bde HQ. Dismounted personnel of 71st F.A. & 191 & 192 Co A.S.C.	BAILLEUL.	Sept 5th.	13.28	ST.OMER.	Sept 5th.	14.48	
2	2 Bns 68th Bde. Dismounted personnel of R.E. Coys.	"	"	14.28	"	"	15.48	
3	Transport of above.	"	"	16.18	WIZERNES.	"	17.14.	
4	69th Bde HQ. 2 Bns 69th Bde. HQ 9/S.Staffs. 2 Coys 9th S.Staffs. Divl.H.Q.	"	Sept 6th	9.28	ST.OMER	Sept 6th.	10.48.	
5	2 Bns 69th Bde. 2 Coys 9th S.Staffs. Dismounted personnel of 69th F.A.	"	"	10.28	"	"	11.48.	
6	Transport of above.	"	"	11.28	"	"	12.48.	

All trains for personnel leave BAILLEUL Main Station.
All Trains for transport leave BAILLEUL West Station.

2. The cookers, water carts, mess carts, Trench Mortar carts, and one G.S. Wagon or limber (for rations) for units entraining on the 5th only will be taken on the Transport Trains, Nos. 3 & 6. Lewis Gun handcarts will be taken with the infantry on trains Nos. 1, 2, 4 & 5.

3. Units will be at the Station one hour before time of departure in the case of trains Nos. 1, 2, 4 & 5.

P. T. O.

(2)

All transport and parties for loading same on to trains Nos. 3 & 6 will be at station 3 hours before time of departure.

4. The capacity of Trains Nos. 1, 2, 4 & 5 is each 64 Officers and 2,200 O.R, reckoning 10 men to a compartment.
The Capacity of trains Nos. 3 & 6 is each 300 men, 144 LD horses and 92 axles.

5. Billeting Parties will proceed from Bde H.Q. at 6 am on the 5th instant. Two lorries will be at each Bde H.Q. and one lorry at H.Q. 101st Fd Co. R.E. to convey parties to Backward Area. The R.E. lorry will also convey billeting party of 9th South Staffords, arrangements to be made direct by C.R.E. with 9th South Staffords.
Staff Captains will arrange the billeting of the Field Ambulances.
The A.D.M.S. will arrange to send on billeting parties on the morning of the 5th inst.

6. Vehicles and transport not being sent by rail will proceed by road as follows :-

Unit.	Starting Point.	Time.	Commander.
68th 1st Line Transport. 191 Co. A.S.C. 71st Fd Ambl. 9th S. Staffs. 1st Line Transport	W18 b 3.2 X.19.c.2.8. Sheet 27. COURTE CROIX	1 p.m. Sept 5th.	O.C. 191 Co. A.S.C.
69th 1st Line Transport. 192 Co. A.S.C. 69th Fd Ambl. Divl. H.Q.	S.20.d.6.6. Sheet 28.	1 p.m. Sept 5th.	O.C. 192 Co. A.S.C.
R.E. Companies.	ROUGE CROIX W.10.c.1.0. Sheet 27.	12 noon Sept. 5th.	To be detailed by C.R.E.

The route will be via STRAZEELE, HAZEBROUCK, WALLON CAPPEL, EBBLINGHEM, ARQUES, ST. OMER.
All transport will halt for night of 5/6th inst at WALLON CAPPEL and will march on the 6th inst. as under :-

       68th Bde. etc.   7.30 am) Starting Point
       69th "   "   9. 0 am)
       R.E. Companies.   10.30 am) EBBLINGHEM

Destinations will be according to billeting list.

C.R.E. and O.C. Train will arrange for billeting parties to proceed to WALLON CAPPEL on the morning of the 5th inst. They will apply at the Mairie for instructions. The C.R.E. will detail an officer not below the rank of Captain who will supervise the billeting of all units.

7. The 68th Brigade will detail an officer to supervise the entrainment of trains Nos. 1 & 2 and the 69th Brigade will detail an officer to supervise the entrainment of trains Nos. 4 & 5 at BAILLEUL Main Station. They will report to the R.T.O. BAILLEUL Main Station one hour before departure of first train on each day and leave on the second train.

   The 68th Brigade will detail an officer to supervise the entrainment of train No. 3 and the 69th Brigade will detail an officer to supervise the entrainment of No. 6 at BAILLEUL West Station. They will report to the R.T.O. BAILLEUL West 3 hours before departure of trains No. 3 & 6.

   The necessary loading parties will be detailed by Brigades for trains Nos. 3 & 6. These parties will hand over to the R.T.O. detailed states of transport to be entrained.

   The Officers and parties detailed above for entraining will be responsible for detraining at detraining Stations.

8. Refilling on the 5th will be as usual for all units in the present area.

   Units entraining on the 5th will arrange to distribute their supplies at the Refilling Point partly on vehicles to go by train and partly on vehicles to march with transport.

   Units entraining on the 6th will also arrange for their transport proceeding by road to carry rations for the 6th.

   Rations for consumption on the 7th will be distributed by lorries direct to billets in the Backward area.

   Separate orders have been issued to 70th Inf Brigade.

4th September, 1916.

Major,
D.A.Q.M.G. 23rd Division.

Copy to:

68th	C.R.A.	Train.
69th Inf Brigade.	C.R.E.	41st D.S.C.
70th	A.D.M.S.	Camp Commdt.
9th S.Staffs.	A.D.V.S.	

Doullens 3-15

ARRIVAL OF 23rd DIVISION.

S E C R E T.   III Corps
                               No. A.Q.3/14/16.

ADMINISTRATIVE INSTRUCTIONS
No.21 dated 9/9/1916.
-:-:-:-:-:-:-:-:-

Railhead.   FRECHENCOURT from 11th September, 1916.

2.   M.T. Supply Column will be located temporarily near B.21 central, on AMIENS – CONTAY Road. Workshop may use HOLLIENS-au-BOIS – ST. GRATIEN Road, if desired.

A. S. P. HOLLIENS-au-BOIS. O.C. to report to O.C. III Corps Ammunition Park, FRANVILLERS.

3.   Supply Refilling Points and Divisional Train will be located under Divisional arrangements, location being reported to Corps Headquarters.

4.   23rd Division to acknowledge.

                                     [signature]

Issued at 5-45 p.m.   BRIGADIER GENERAL,
9/9/1916.   D.A.& Q.M.G., III Corps.

DISTRIBUTION:-
         Normal plus one copy to Staff Officer,
                 23rd Division, c/o.
                   A.D.R.T., AMIENS.

MARCH TABLE TO ACCOMPANY DIVISIONAL ORDER NO.67.

UNIT.	FROM.	ROUTE.	TO.	STARTING POINT.	TIME.	REMARKS.
68th Bde. Group. 68th Bde. 71st Fd. Amb.	MOLLIENS-au-BOIS.	MONTIGNY BAIZIEUX.	MILLENCOURT.	EAST exit of MOLLIENS.	8.25 a.m.	Not to enter BAIZIEUX before 10.30 a.m.
69th Bde. Group. 69th Bde. 69th Fd. Amb.	COISY.	RAINNEVILLE MOLLIENS MONTIGNY BAIZIEUX.	HENENCOURT WOOD.	On road by Y of COISY.	8.5 a.m.	
H.Q.Group.(under G.R.E) Div.H.Q. 101, 102, 128th Field Coys. Mob. Vet. Sect:	ALLONVILLE	MONTIGNY BAIZIEUX	BAIZIEUX	Rd.Junction SOUTH of last E in CARDONETTE.	9.30 a.m.	
70th Bde. Group. 70th Bde.(less 2 Bns.) 9th S.Staffs. 70th Fd. Amb.	CARDONETTE	MONTIGNY BAIZIEUX	BRESLE	Rd.Junction SOUTH of last E in CARDONETTE.	10 a.m.	

Train (less baggage wagons). will follow immediately in rear of 70th Bde. Group - marching under orders of O.C.Train.

SECRET. COPY NO. 11

Appendix III

23RD DIVISION ORDER NO. 68.

1. (a) The 23rd Division will relieve the 15th Division in the Left Sector of the IIIrd Corps front (taking over PRUE TRENCH to M.33.b.4.7. from 50th Division) in accordance with attached March Table.

   (b) Details of relief will be arranged direct between Brigadiers concerned. On completion of the relief the G.O.C. 69th Bde. will assume command of the front line.

2. All maps, plans, photographs, trench stores &c will be handed over by 15th Division.

3. R.E. reliefs will be arranged between C.R.E's concerned and will take place after the Infantry reliefs are completed.

4. The 9th South Staffords (Pioneers) will be relieved tomorrow and bivouac at BECOURT WOOD. They will be at the disposal of the C.R.E.

5. Reliefs of R.A.M.C. units to be arranged between the A.D.M.S. concerned.

6. (a) All tents and "bivouac shelters" of 68th & 70th Bdes. will be handed over to 1st Division, and those of 69th Bde. to 15th Division. Clearing up parties will take charge and hand the above over. Orders as to tents and shelters of 1st Line Transport will be issued later.

   (b) Move of the Train will be notified later.

   (c) Divisional Bomb Store is at E.5.a.7.1. Dump A at X.25.c.7.6. and Dump B at X.16.d.7.4., Dump C at CONTALMAISON VILLA.

7. The G.O.C. 23rd Division will take over command of the line at 10 a.m. on 19th. H.Q. will close at BAIZIEUX at 10 a.m. and open at W.26.c.0.4. at same hour.

8. ACKNOWLEDGE.

for. Lt.Colonel,
General Staff, 23rd Division.

17/9/1916.

Issued at 7.30 p.m.

Copies to :-

Nos.	1	R.A.	Nos.	16	A.P.M.
	2	R.E.		17	A.D.V.S.
	3	Signals.		18	D.A.D.O.S.
	4 - 5	68th Inf. Bde.		19	Supply Column.
	6 - 7	69th Inf. Bde.		20	"G".
	8 - 9	70th Inf. Bde.		21	File.
	10	9th South Staffords.		22	Diary.
	11	Train.		23	Diary.
	12 - 13	"Q".		24	Camp Commandant.
	14	A.D.M.S.		25	34th Sqdn. R.F.C.
	15	S.S.O.		26	15th Division.

Nos. 27 50th Division.
     28 2nd Canadian Division.
     29 III Corps.

MARCH TABLE TO ACCOMPANY DIVISIONAL ORDER NO.68.

UNIT.	WILL RELIEVE.	NEW AREA.	ROUTE.	TIME.	REMARKS.
70th Inf. Bde.	46th Inf. Bde.	H.Q. SHELTER WOOD. 'C' Bn. SHELTER WOOD. 'D' Bn. SCOTS REDOUBT. 'A' Bn. E. of)CONTAL- 'B' Bn. W. of)MAISON.	Via BECOURT WOOD.	Reliefs to be completed by 10 a.m.	"RESERVE BDE".
68th Inf. Bde.	45th Inf. Bde.	H.Q. CONTALMAISON. 'A' Bn. WELCH ALLEY AREA 'B' Bn. GLOSTER ALLEY AREA. 'C' Bn. PEARL ALLEY AREA 'D' Bn. BLACK WATCH ALLEY AREA.	-do-	Commence noon. Complete by 6.0 p.m.	"SUPPORT BDE". (1 Bn. rejoins on 19th).
69th Inf. Bde.	44th Inf. Bde.	H.Q. VILLA WOOD.	-do-	Commence 6.0 p.m.	

Army Form C. 2118.

Vol 14

Train.

WAR DIARY
or
INTELLIGENCE SUMMARY.
(Erase heading not required.)

Instructions regarding War Diaries and Intelligence Summaries are contained in F. S. Regs., Part II. and the Staff Manual respectively. Title pages will be prepared in manuscript.

Place	Date	Hour	Summary of Events and Information	Remarks and references to Appendices
ALBERT	1916 Oct 1		Reached ALBERT. Natives drawn in met by horse transport and taken to refilling points. Church parade 5.15pm. Watches time from army clock put back one hour. Weather fine	
"	" 2		Transport 89 Dragons for R.E. work. Lieut J. H. Mitchell admitted to C.C.S. CORBIE. Weather wet	
"	" 3		Train office moved into hut vacated by Q Branch. Transport 99 Dragons for R.E. work. Weather wet	
"	" 4		Transport 15 Dragons for Divisional work. Weather wet	
"	" 5		Transport 11 Dragons for Divisional work. Weather fine	

Army Form C. 2118.

WAR DIARY
or
INTELLIGENCE SUMMARY.
(Erase heading not required.)

Instructions regarding War Diaries and Intelligence Summaries are contained in F.S. Regs., Part II. and the Staff Manual respectively. Title pages will be prepared in manuscript.

Place	Date	Hour	Summary of Events and Information	Remarks and references to Appendices
ALBERT	Oct 6		Newport 8 hayrops for R.E. work. Weather fair some rain	
"	7		Newport 8 hayrops for R.E. work. Lieut Ent Mitchell discharged from hospital. Lieut S.K. Walton joined from 3rd K.S.Wo' Mont train. Lieut J.L. Morrison proceeded to A.C. B Wore Depot Havre. Weather fine.	
"	8		Warning Order received that Division would being withdrawn from the line. Two Brigades of Artillery to remain in line. Sent are baggage wagons to inside. Weather fine.	Appendix No. 1 Appendix No. 73
"	9		Headquarter Company moved to Molliens au Bois leaving an detachment in present Camp under command of Lieut Holmes. 15 Battn's the Artillery remaining in action. Weather fair some rain	

Army Form C. 2118.

WAR DIARY
or
INTELLIGENCE SUMMARY.
(Erase heading not required.)

Place	Date	Hour	Summary of Events and Information	Remarks and references to Appendices
ALBERT	Oct 10		Two trains of natives who made to escape to all went to Depot R.A. The natives for R.A. out of the line are being sent to R.A. rear area by lorry and replied by horse transport. The R.A. in forward area are fed by detachment near Lieut. Holmes. Supplies driven by horse transport from ALBERT station. 193 Company moved to BRESLE. Weather fine. 191 Co. then headquarters Man then to ARGOEUVES en route for X Corps area. Appendix (1) 192 + 193 Companies moved by road to St SAUVEUR in the left X Corps area. Up from 70 to 74. Weather fine. Main headquarters AILLY LE HAUT CLOCHER. 191 Co arrived at GORENFLOS.	
AILLY LE HAUT CLOCHER	Oct 12	1920	VAUCHELLES. 1936. Reached PONT REMY. Railhead VIGNACOURT. Repairing been FLIXECOURT. During these marches the 1st line transport of Companies marches under command of the O.C's. These A.S.C. Brigade Companies. Weather fine.	

Place	Date	Hour	Summary of Events and Information	Remarks and references to Appendices
ST. RICQUIER	Oct 13		Main headquarters moved to St. Ricquier. 191 Co moved to Neuville. 192 Co moved to Vurenchuex. 193 Co Nuisance at Pont Remy. Lieuts Lodge, Osborne, & West proceeded by Motor Car to Bailleul. Report to DAA & QMG 2nd Division to arrange billets for new H.Q.'s today, one for 88 Reg Bus is to be for 90th Brigade. Two refilling points to-day, one 91 Brigade. There were 2 cases of scabies to-day. Weather fine	
"	" 14		193 Company moved to Millencourt. 191 Co Nuisance at St. Ricquier and Nuisance at Proven. 192 Co Nuisance at Conteville and Nuisance at Houpoutre. The supply wagon of H.Q.s Company entrained Supply ready to join the infantry on arrival. Whether fine marches to Camps near Busseboom	Appendix (3) of War No 71
" Busseboom	" 15		Main headquarters entrained at Conteville and Nuisance at Houpoutre. 193 Co Nuisance at St. Ricquier & Nuisance at Proven. Supply wagon entrained Infantry. Weather fair. Main headquarters 1193 Co marched to Busseboom	

Army Form C. 2118.

WAR DIARY
or
INTELLIGENCE SUMMARY.
(Erase heading not required.)

Instructions regarding War Diaries and Intelligence Summaries are contained in F. S. Regs., Part II. and the Staff Manual respectively. Title pages will be prepared in manuscript.

Place	Date	Hour	Summary of Events and Information	Remarks and references to Appendices
POPERINGHE Reninghelst	1916 Oct 16		Railhead RENINGHELST. Supplies drawn in trolls by horse transport and taken to ruling points for issue. 1 W.O. 3 Wheelers & 7 arm'rs arrived from Base. Weather fine.	Appx (1) 6 of our Men
"	" 17		Transport 10GS wagons for Divisional work. Weather wet.	
"	" 18		Transport 14 G.S. wagons for Divisional work. Lieut. Cuff Lodge proceeded on 10 days leave to England. Weather wet.	
"	" 19		Transport 19. G.S. wagons for Divisional work. Weather wet.	
"	" 20		Transport 15 G.S. wagons for Divisional work. Capt. H. Norton proceeded on 10 days leave. Capt. ER Lowestoft to took over duties of S.S.O. temporarily. Lieut Ockroid took over duties of S.O.O. by Bn temporarily. Weather fine.	

Army Form C. 2118

WAR DIARY
or
INTELLIGENCE SUMMARY

(Erase heading not required.)

Place	Date	Hour	Summary of Events and Information	Remarks and references to Appendices
BUSSEBOOM	1916 Oct 21		Train Head quarters moved from POPERINGHE to BUSSEBOOM.	
"	22		Transport 21 F.S. wagons for Divisional work. Weather fine.	
"	23		Transport 23 F.S. wagons for Divisional work. Weather fine. Transport 12 F.S. wagons for Divisional work. O.C. Train motored to MOLLIENS-au-BOIS to inspect 190 b.o. Lt. Hooley & 1.C.S.S.M. McDonnell proceeded on leave to United Kingdom. 4 H.D. horses arrived from Remounts. Weather fine.	
	24		Transport 24 F.S. wagons for Divisional work. Weather wet.	
	25		Transport 27 F.S. wagons for Divisional work. Lt. Col. A. Forshaw D.S.O. inspected at F.g.C.M. at Div. H.Qrs. Weather fair.	

WAR DIARY
or
INTELLIGENCE SUMMARY

Army Form C. 2118

Place	Date	Hour	Summary of Events and Information	Remarks and references to Appendices
BUSSEBOOM.	1916 Oct 26		Transport 50 G.S. Wagons for Divisional work. Lt. Col. A. Tooher, President of F.G.C.M. at H.Q. Ors. Train. Weather wet.	
	27		Transport 26 G.S. Wagons for Divisional work. Capt. L. Langford D.S.O. & 1 Man from 192 Co. Proceeded on leave. Lt. W.G. Yoxley took over duties of Adjutant. Weather fair.	
	28		Transport 25 G.S. Wagons for Divisional work. Weather rain.	
	29		Transport 34 G.S. Wagons for Divisional work. Weather wet.	
	30		Transport 42 G.S. Wagons for Divisional work. Weather wet.	
	31		Transport 24 F.B. Wagons for Divisional work. 4/Lt. R.A.S. Elliot & 1 Man from 191 Co. Proceeded on leave. Brooch of Meritorious Service Medal awarded to Jun. & Sgt. of 191 & 193 Cos.	A. Tooher Lt Col Comdg 23rd Div Train 1-11-1916

SECRET.   Copy No. 20

23rd DIVISION OPERATION ORDER No 73.

1.   23rd Division (less R.A.) will be relieved in the Left Sector of III Corps front by the 15th Division on the 8th and 9th instant.

2.   Reliefs will be carried out as under :-

   On the 8th instant.

   (a)   The 68th Infantry Brigade will be relieved by 44th Infantry Brigade (at BECOURT WOOD). 68th Infantry Brigade on relief will move to BECOURT WOOD.

   (b)   69th Infantry Brigade will be relieved by 45th Infantry Brigade (at about X.27. central). 69th Infantry Brigade on relief will move to Reserve Bde. area about X.27. central.

   (c)   The 70th Infantry Brigade will not be relieved by a Brigade, but will vacate their trenches in time to arrive at the station at X.29. Central as follows :-

          2 Bns. (dismounted personnel only) at 4 p.m.
          2 Bns. (do   do   do) at 6 p.m.

   These battalions will detrain at VIVIER MILL and march to BRESLE.
   All mounted personnel will proceed by road.

   On the 9th instant.

          69th Infantry Brigade will be relieved in Reserve Area by 46th Infantry Brigade. 69th Infantry Brigade on relief will move to ALBERT. To be clear of bivouacs by 10 a.m.

3.   Details of above reliefs will be arranged direct between Brigadiers concerned. On completion of reliefs, relieving Brigadiers will assume command of the Sections.

4.   Reliefs of Pioneers, R.E. and Medical units will be arranged direct between C.R.Es. and A.Ds. M.S. concerned, and Divisional Head-Quarters informed.

5. (a).   All tents and bivouacs in area east of ALBERT will be handed over, on present sites, to 15th Division by units concerned of 23rd Division on relief.

    (b).   Pack animals and pack saddlery will be handed over to 15th Division by Brigades and Field Ambulances concerned on relief.

    (c).   All equipment taken over by units from 50th Division will be handed over to relieving units of 15th Division.

    (d).   In all above cases receipt will be obtained by units concerned.

6. G.O.C. 15th Division will take over command of the Sector at 9 a.m. on the 9th instant, at which hour Divisional Head-Quarters will close at SHELTER WOOD and re-open at MONTIGNY.

7. A C K N O W L E D G E.

F. Watson
Lieutenant-Colonel,
General Staff, 23rd Divn.

7/10/16.
Issued at 7.30 p.m.

Copies to :-

```
        Nos.  1 - 10   R.A.
                 11   R.E.
                 12   Signals
             13 - 14   68th Inf. Bde.
             15 - 16   69th   "     "
             17 - 18   70th   "     "
                 19   9th S.Staffs.
                 20   Train
             21 - 22   "Q"
                 23   A.D.M.S.
                 24   S.Supply Offr.
                 25   A.P.M.
                 26   A.D.V.S.
                 27   D.A.D.O.S.
                 28   41st Supply Col.
                 29   File
             30 - 31   Diary
                 32   Camp Commdt.
                 33   15th Division
                 34   47th Division
                 35   1st Can. Division.
             36 &  37   III Corps.
```

S E C R E T.   Copy No. 11

Appendix (2)

23rd DIVISION OPERATION ORDER No. 74.

1. 23rd Division (less Royal Artillery) will be transferred to X Corps at midnight 11th/12th October, and will move to AILLY-le-HAUT-CLOCHER area. On the 14th the Division will entrain for another area.

2. Moves will take place as follows :-

   (a) 68th Infantry Bde. Group.
       68th Infantry Bde.
       71st Field Ambulance
       102nd Fd. Company, R.E.
       190th Company, A.S.C.
       } Will move by tactical trains from ALBERT on the 11th instant.

   (b) 69th Infantry Bde. Group.
       69th Infantry Bde.
       69th Field Ambulance
       101st Fd. Company, R.E.
       191st Coy. A.S.C.
       } Will move by tactical trains from ALBERT on the 12th instant.

       70th Infantry Bde. Group.
       70th Infantry Bde.
       70th Field Ambulance
       128th Field Coy. R.E.
       9/S.Staffs. Regt.
       Divn. Head-Quarters
       192nd Company, A.S.C.

3. (a) All transport will move by road.

   (b) Detailed arrangements for all moves will be issued by "Q".

4. Orders for the move of the Artillery will be issued later.

5. Divisional Head-Quarters will close at MONTIGNY at 9 a.m. on the 12th instant and re-open at AILLY-le-HAUT-CLOCHER on arrival.

6. A C K N O W L E D G E.

                                    F.H. Moncheif
10th October, 1916.   Lieutenant-Colonel,
                                    General Staff.

Issued at 12 700 Z
Copies to:-
No. 1 -   R.A.   20   File
    2 -   R.E.   21 - 22   Diary
    3 -   Signals   23   Camp Commandant
    4 - 5 68th Inf. Bde.   24   Town Major, ALBERT
    6 - 7 69th Inf. Bde.   25   R.T.O. ALBERT
    8 - 9 70th Inf. Bde.   26 - 27   III Corps.
     10   9/S.Staffs R.   28   X Corps.
     11   Train
   12-13 "Q"
     14   A.D.M.S.
     15   Senior Supply Offr.
     16   A.P.M.
     17   A.D.V.S.
     18   D.A.D.O.S.
     19   41st Supply Col.

Appendix (3)

SECRET.   COPY No. 18

23rd DIVISION OPERATION ORDER No. 75.

Reference 1/100,000 Map.

1. Preparatory to entrainment on the 14th instant, the Division (less R.A.) will move to the area HIERMONT - CONTEVILLE - COULONVILLERS - St. RIQUIER - NEUF MOULIN - ARGENVILLERS - GAPENNES - MAISON PONTHIEU on the 13th instant.

2. Moves will take place in accordance with the attached March Table.

3. Divisional Head-Quarters will close at AILLY-le-HAUT-CLOCHER at 9.30 a.m. on 13th instant and re-open at same hour at St. RIQUIER.

4. ACKNOWLEDGE.

                                        C. F. Watson
                                        Lieutenant-Colonel,
11th October, 1916.   General Staff.

Issued at 4.30 p.m.

Copies to :-

    No. 1   R.A.
       2   R.E.
       3 & 4   68th Inf. Bde.   5 Signals.
       6 & 7   69th Inf. Bde.
       8 & 9   70th Inf. Bde.
       10   9/S.Staffs R.
       11   X Corps.
       12   Third Army.
       13   File
       14 & 15 Diary
       16 & 17 "Q"
       18   Train
       19   S.S.O.
       20   41st Sup. Col.
       21   A.D.M.S.
       22   Camp Commandt:
       23   A.D.V.S.
       24   D.A.D.O.S.

SECRET   Copy No. *Assheton* (4)

23rd Divisional Operation Order No. 76.

Reference :-
     Trench Map, Sheet 28 N.W., Scale 1:20,000.

1. (a)   23rd Division, less Artillery, is to relieve the 2nd Australian Division in the left sector, 1st ANZAC Corps from Trench I.29.8. to Trench I.17.4, both inclusive, commencing on the 16th instant.

   (b)   One Brigade 47th Division is to take over the remainder of the 2nd Australian Division front from Trench I.29.8., exclusive, to VERBRANDENMOLEN Road, Trench I.35.1, inclusive, on the night of the 19th/20th.

2. (a)   Reliefs will take place in accordance with attached March Table.

   (b)   The 68th Infantry Brigade will relieve the 6th and 7th Australian Brigades in Trenches I.24.4. to I.17.4., both inclusive. The 70th Infantry Brigade will relieve the 7th Australian Brigade in Trenches I.29.8. to I.24.3., both inclusive.

   (c)   The dividing line between brigades will be the junction of Trenches I.24.3. and I.24.4. thence along VIGO STREET, FORT STREET, to the trench tram-line through I.24 and I.23; VINCE STREET to be common to both Brigades.

   (d)   All details of relief will be arranged direct between Brigadiers concerned. G.Os. C. relieving Brigades will assume command of their sector on completion of relief.

   (e)   Relief of Pioneers, R.E. and Medical units will be arranged direct between C.R.Es. and A.Ds. M.S. concerned. Reliefs to be complete by 6 a.m. on the 19th instant.

   (f)   Infantry will proceed to and from YPRES by train. Transport by road. Train time-table will be issued by A.A.& Q.M.G.

3.   The 2nd Australian Division will hand over all air photos, defence schemes and 1/10,000 maps to relieving brigades.

4.   The 69th Infantry Brigade will remain at POPERINGHE and be in Corps Reserve.

5.   The 2nd Australian Division Artillery will remain covering the Divisional Front until the night of 22nd/23rd, when it will be relieved by the 47th Divisional Artillery.

6.   After relief, the Divisional boundaries will be as shown on map issued to all concerned.

7.   G.O.C. 23rd Division will assume command of the Divisional Sector at 8 a.m. on the 20th instant, at which hour Divisional Head-Quarters will open at RENINGHELST.

     ACKNOWLEDGE.

                                             Lieut.-Colonel,
15.10.16.   General Staff.
Issued at 5 p.m.
Copies to :-

1	R.E.	11 2nd Aust. Divn.	20 Supply Col.
2 - 3	68th Inf. Bde	12 55th Division.	21 A.D.M.S.
4 - 5	69th Inf. Bde.	13 File	22 Camp Commdt.
6 - 7	70th Inf. Bde.	14 - 15 Diary.	23 A.D.V.S.
8.	9/S.Staffs.	16 - 17 Q.	24 D.A.D.O.S.
9.	1st Anzac Corps.	18 Train	25 2nd Aust. Divl.
10.	47th Division.	19 S.S.O.	Artillery.

W. 15517—M. 141. 250,000. 1/16. L.S.&Co. Forms/W 3091/2.   Army Form W. 3091.

Vol 15

Cover for Documents.

Secret

Nature of Enclosures.

War Diary
By Lt Colonel A. Northen
Commanding 23rd Divisional Train
A.S.C

From 1st to 30th Nov 1916

The D.A.Q.
3rd Echelon
Base

Notes, or Letters written.

WAR DIARY or INTELLIGENCE SUMMARY

Army Form C. 2118

Place	Date	Hour	Summary of Events and Information	Remarks and references to Appendices
Busseboom	1916. Jan 1		Railhead RENINGHELST. Transport 42 G.S. Wagons for Divisional work. Weather wet.	
	2		Transport 30 G.S. Wagons for Divisional work. Four Issuers joined from Base to relieve four clerks for transfer to fighting units. Weather wet.	
	3		Transport 30 G.S. Wagons for Divisional work. Capt. Burryman returned from Hospital & resumed duties of S.O. 70th Bde vice Lt. L.P. Gilliard to T.O. 192 Co.	
	4		Weather fair. Transport 28 G.S. Wagons for Divisional work. S.S.M. Watson & 1 man from 193 Co. proceeded on leave. Weather wet.	
	5		Transport 26 G.S. Wagons for Divisional work.	

WAR DIARY
or
INTELLIGENCE SUMMARY
(Erase heading not required.)

Army Form C. 2118

Place	Date	Hour	Summary of Events and Information	Remarks and references to Appendices
BUSSEBOOM	1916. Mar 5.		1 Man & 19 OR proceeded on Special leave. 3 Clerks sent to Base for transfer to fighting units. Weather fair.	
	6.		Transport 28 G.S. wagons for Divisional work. Lt. J.P. Gilliard reported to D.D. of S.&T. II Army & commenced duties as temp. to R.O. 4 Reinforcements arrive from Base. Leave suspended. Weather wet.	
	7		Transport 25 G.S. wagons for Divisional work. Leave re-opens. Weather wet.	
	8		Transport 23 G.S. wagons for Divisional works. L'Col A Mutter, Capt Apgate & one more proceeded by train on leave. Weather fine	

Place	Date	Hour	Summary of Events and Information	Remarks and references to Appendices
BUSSEBOOM	1916 No 19		Transport 19 G.S Wagons for Divisional work. Capt Roughsen returned from leave and took on duties as O.C Trains. Weather fine	Appendix I
	10		Brigade Moving 2 G.S. Wagons for this purpose 4 G.O. Wagons from the Divisional works Weather fine	
	11		Transport 26 G.O. Wagons for Divisional work. Weather fine	
	12		Transport 16 G.O. Wagons for Divisional work. Lt Lacey and 9 men proceeded on leave to England. Two men of Train transferred to Base for posting to a lighter unit. Weather fine	
	13		Transport 33 G.O. Wagons for Divisional work Weather fine	

WAR DIARY
or
INTELLIGENCE SUMMARY

Army Form C. 2118

Place	Date	Hour	Summary of Events and Information	Remarks and references to Appendices
Bisse Boom Nully	15		Transport 30 G.S. Wagons for Divisional work. Started issuing supplies in field from Packtrain to units. 3 H.D. horse went up for 90 Co. from Nunney. Captain Barugh proceeded on 10 days leave to England. Weather fine.	
	16		Transport 30 G.S. Wagons for Divisional units. Lent accoutrement, increased to 3. Weather fine.	Appendix IV
			Relief of Brigades. 16 G.S. wagons detailed for this duty. 8 G.S. wagons for Divisional Transport units. Lieut. Mitchell and 2 men proceeded on leave to England. Weather fair.	
	17		Transport 32 G.S. wagons for Divisional work. Weather fine.	

WAR DIARY or INTELLIGENCE SUMMARY

Army Form C. 2118

Place	Date	Hour	Summary of Events and Information	Remarks and references to Appendices
Busseboom	No 1/18			
	19		Transport 86 G.S. Wagons for Divisional work. Lt Col A Norton granted extension of leave on medical certificate from 19 Nov to 25 Nov. Captain Argall granted extension of leave absent private affairs from 19 Nov to 25 Nov. Wrote Coln Pnr. Weather fine.	
	20		Transport 26 G.S. Wagons for Divisional work. Weather fine.	
	21		Transport 30 G.S. Wagons for Divisional work. Captain Souttar proceeded on 10 days leave to England. Driver Jennings 193 Coy killed by L.G. Car. Weather wet.	
	22		Transport 34 G.S. Wagons for Divisional work. Weather fine.	

Army Form C. 2118

WAR DIARY
or
INTELLIGENCE SUMMARY
(Erase heading not required.)

Place	Date	Hour	Summary of Events and Information	Remarks and references to Appendices
Busseboom	Nov 1916 22		Newport 14 G.S wagons & 4 G.S wagons for Divisional work. 3 H.D horses and 1 mule received from Remounts. Leave allotment increased to seven four days. Weather fine	appendix III
	23		Newport - 3 G.S wagons for Divisional work. Captain R.J. Harris & 6 other ranks proceeded to Boulogne on leave. Captain J. McAgate returned from leave struck off strength of Force from to-day, date authority Aug. A.S.C. 13/92 4/23.11.16. Weather fine	
	24		Newport - 36 G.D. wagons for Divisional work. Board of Officers assembled at 9.30 Change for purpose of testing Colic Shoes. Capt. R. Hughes Sub as Member of General Court Martial. Divine Service in S.S.S Office. Weather fine	

1875 Wt. W593/826 1,000,000 4/15 J.B.C. & A. A.D.S.S./Forms/C. 2118.

WAR DIARY or INTELLIGENCE SUMMARY

Army Form C. 2118

Place	Date	Hour	Summary of Events and Information	Remarks and references to Appendices
BUSSEBOOM No 135	1916			
	25		Transport. 33 G.S. wagons for Divisional work. 8 Mixer G. Hughes 1920. Tried by F.G.C.M. Weather hot.	
	26		Transport 30 G.S. wagons for Divisional work. Weather also fine.	
	27		Transport 3 S.G.O. wagons for Divisional work. Weather fine.	
	28		Transport 58 G.S. wagons for Divisional work. Captain Bergman + 70 other ranks proceeded to England on leave. Driver Jennings 1936. Committed to prison by Pres.Comp.H.L.	
	29		Transport- Nil 17 Bignaro 28 G.S.wagons. 9 S.S.wagons for Divisional work. Weather fine.	Appendix IV

WAR DIARY
or
INTELLIGENCE SUMMARY

(Erase heading not required.)

Army Form C. 2118

Place	Date	Hour	Summary of Events and Information	Remarks and references to Appendices
BUSSEBOOM	Nov 30		Runaford- 31 G.S. wagons to Divisional HQ. Captain Ingram received Court of Inquiry on a fire at No 4 Siege Co RE. Lt. Eliot detailed to determine tracing of rations on train at BRANDHOEK Siding Westoutre	

Signed A. Wickes
T.V. Clonel
COM G. 23rd DIVISIONAL TRAIN A.S.C.

SECRET.   COPY NO. 17

23RD DIVISION ORDER NO. 80.

Reference 1/10,000 Trench Map and 1/20,000 Map, Sheet 28 N.W.

1. (a).   The 69th Infantry Brigade will relieve the 68th Infantry Brigade in the Right Section 23rd Division front on the night of the 10th/11th November. The frontage is from BOSSEWAY to Trench I.24/4 (both exclusive).

   (b).   All details of relief will be arranged direct between Brigadiers concerned.

   (c).   Infantry will proceed to and from YPRES by train. Transport by road. Train time-table will be issued by A.A.&.Q.M.G.

   (d).   No trench will be vacated by 68th Infantry Brigade until occupied by 69th Infantry Brigade.

   (e).   G.O.C. 69th Infantry Brigade will assume command of the Right Section on completion of relief.

   (f).   All trench stores, photographs and trench maps will be handed over by 68th Infantry Brigade to 69th Infantry Brigade.

2.   After relief, the 68th Infantry Brigade will be in Corps Reserve and be billetted as follows.

   Brigade Headquarters   POPERINGHE.
   One battalion   WINNIPEG CAMP.
   One battalion   MONTREAL CAMP.
   One battalion   ST. LAURENCE CAMP.
   One battalion   ERIE and TORONTO CAMPS.

3.   One battalion of 69th Infantry Brigade quartered in YPRES will be in Divisional Reserve. The name of unit and C.O. will be forwarded to this office.

4.   ACKNOWLEDGE.

                                    F. Watson.
                                    Lieut-Colonel,
7th November, 1916.   General Staff.

Issued at 1.30 p.m.

Copies to :-
   No. 1   Lowe's Group R.A.   No. 15   A.P.M.
       2   R.E.   16   Camp Commandant.
       3   Signals.   17   Train.
       4 - 5 68th Inf. Bde.   18   S.S.O.
       6 - 7 69th Inf. Bde.   19   Area Commandant.
       8 - 9 70th Inf. Bde.   20 - 21   X Corps.
       10.   9th S.Staffs. R.   22   47th Division.
       11.   "Q".   23   File.
       12.   A.D.M.S.   24 - 25   Diary.
       13.   D.A.D.O.S.   26   Town Major, YPRES.
       14.   A.D.V.S.

appendix 11

SECRET.   COPY NO. 17.

23RD DIVISION ORDER NO. 81.

Reference 1/10,000 Trench Map and 1/20,000, Sheet 28 N.W.

1. (a).   The 68th Infantry Brigade will relieve the 70th Infantry Brigade in the Left Section 23rd Division front on the night of the 16th/17th November. The frontage is from Trench I.24.4. to BELLEWAARDE BEEK (I.12.c.½.1.) (both inclusive).

   (b).   All details of relief will be arranged direct between Brigadiers concerned.

   (c).   Infantry will proceed to and from YPRES by train. Transport by road. Train time-table will be issued by A.A.& Q.M.G.

   (d).   No trench will be vacated by 70th Infantry Brigade until occupied by 68th Infantry Brigade.

   (e).   G.O.C. 68th Infantry Brigade will assume command of the Left Section on completion of relief.

   (f).   All trench stores, photographs and trench maps will be handed over by 70th Infantry Brigade to 68th Infantry Brigade.

2.   After relief, the 70th Infantry Brigade will be in Corps Reserve and be billetted as follows :-

   Brigade Headquarters   POPERINGHE.
   One battalion.   WINNIPEG CAMP.
   One battalion.   MONTREAL CAMP.
   One battalion.   ST. LAURENCE CAMP.
   One battalion.   ERIE and TORONTO CAMPS.

3.   One battalion of 68th Infantry Brigade quartered in YPRES will be in Divisional Reserve. The name of unit and C.O. will be forwarded to this office.

4.   ACKNOWLEDGE.

                                          F. Watson.
                                          Lieut-Colonel,
13th November, 1916.   General Staff.

Issued at 1.30 p.m.

Copies to :-
No.		No.	
1.	Lowe's Group R.A.	15	A.P.M.
2.	R.E.	16	Camp Commandant.
3.	Signals.	17	Train.
4 - 5	68th Inf. Bde.	18	S.S.O.
6 - 7	69th Inf. Bde.	19	Area Commandant.
8 - 9	70th Inf. Bde.	20 - 21	X Corps.
10.	9th S.Staffs. R.	22	55th Division.
11.	"Q"	23	File.
12.	A.D.M.S.	24 - 25	Diary.
13.	D.A.D.O.S.	26	Town Major, YPRES.
14.	A.D.V.S.		

Appendix III

SECRET.   COPY NO. 17

23RD DIVISION ORDER NO. 82.

Reference 1/10,000 Trench Map and 1/20,000, Sheet 28 N.W.

1. (a).   The 70th Infantry Brigade will relieve the 69th Infantry Brigade in the Right Section 23rd Division front on the night of the 22nd/23rd November.

   (b).   All details of relief will be arranged direct between Brigadiers concerned.

   (c).   Infantry will proceed to and from YPRES by train. Transport by road. Train time table will be issued by A.A.&.Q.M.G.

   (d).   No trench will be vacated by 69th Infantry Brigade until occupied by 70th Infantry Brigade.

   (e).   G.O.C. 70th Infantry Brigade will assume command of the Right Section on completion of relief.

   (f).   All trench stores, air photos and Secret trench maps will be handed over by 69th Infantry Brigade to 70th Infantry Brigade.

2.   After relief, 69th Infantry Brigade will be in Corps Reserve and will be billetted as follows :-

   Brigade Headquarters.   POPERINGHE.
   One battalion.   WINNIPEG CAMP.
   One battalion.   MONTREAL CAMP.
   One battalion.   ST. LAURENCE CAMP.
   One battalion.   ERIE and TORONTO CAMPS.

3.   One battalion of 70th Infantry Brigade quartered in YPRES will be in Divisional Reserve. Name of unit and O.C. will be forwarded to Divisional Headquarters.

4.   ACKNOWLEDGE.

                                     F. Watson
                                                    Lieut-Colonel,
19th November, 1916.   General Staff.

Issued at 8.30 p.m.

Copies to :-
  No. 1.   Lowe's Group R.A.   No. 15   A.P.M.
      2.   R.E.   16   Camp Commandant.
      3.   Signals.   17   Train.
      4 - 5   68th Inf. Bde.   18   S.S.O.
      6 - 7   69th Inf. Bde.   19   Area Commandant.
      8 - 9   70th Inf. Bde.   20 - 21   X Corps.
      10.   9th S.Staffords.   22   47th Division.
      11.   "Q".   23   File.
      12.   A.D.M.S.   24 - 25   Diary.
      13.   D.A.D.O.S.   26   Town Major, YPRES.
      14.   A.D.V.S.

SECRET.

appendix IV

Copy No. 17

23rd DIVISION ORDER No. 83.

Reference: 1/10,000 Trench Map and 1/20,000 Sheet 28 N.W.

1. (a). The 69th Infantry Brigade will relieve the 68th Infantry Brigade in the Left Section, 23rd Division Front, on the night of the 29th/30th November.

   (b). All details of relief will be arranged direct between Brigadiers concerned.

   (c). Infantry will proceed to and from YPRES by train. Transport by road. Train time-table will be issued by A.A.&.Q.M.G.

   (d). No trench will be vacated by 68th Infantry Brigade until occupied by 69th Infantry Brigade.

   (e). G.O.C.69th Infantry Brigade will assume command of the Section on completion of relief.

   (f). All trench stores, air photos and secret trench maps will be handed over by 68th Infantry Brigade to 69th Infantry Brigade.

2. After relief the 68th Infantry Brigade will be in Corps Reserve and will be billetted as follows :-

Brigade Head-Quarters	POPERINGHE
One battalion	WINNIPEG CAMP.
One battalion	MONTREAL CAMP.
One battalion	St. LAWRENCE CAMP.
One battalion	ERIE & TORONTO CAMPS.

3. One battalion, 69th Infantry Brigade, quartered in YPRES, will be in Divisional Reserve. Name of unit and O.C. will be forwarded to Divisional Head-Quarters.

4. ACKNOWLEDGE.

F.Watson,
Lieutenant-Colonel,
General Staff.

26th November, 1916.

Issued at 4.30 p.m.

Copies to :-

No. 1	Lowe's Group R.A.	No. 15	A.P.M.
2	R.E.	16	Camp Commandant.
3	Signals.	17	Train
4 - 5	68th Inf. Bde.	18	S.S.O.
6 - 7	69th Inf. Bde.	19	Area Commandant.
8 - 9	70th Inf. Bde.	20 - 21	X Corps.
10	9th S.Staffs.	22	15th Division.
11	A & Q	23	File
12	A.D.M.S.	24 - 25	Diary.
13	D.A.D.O.S.	26	Town Major, YPRES.
14	A.D.V.S.		

Army Form C. 2118

WAR DIARY
or
INTELLIGENCE SUMMARY
(Erase heading not required.)

Instructions regarding War Diaries and Intelligence Summaries are contained in F.S. Regs., Part II. and the Staff Manual respectively. Title Pages will be prepared in manuscript.

Place	Date	Hour	Summary of Events and Information	Remarks and references to Appendices
BUSSEBOOM	1916 Sep 1		Railhead RENINGHELST. Still loading into G.S. wagons after detail issue from train. Transport 30 G.S. wagons for Divisional work. Started running of charcoal for Division for this purpose 6 men attached to 192 Co from Infantry. Weather fine	
"	2		Newport 29 G.S. wagons for Divisional work. 7 Men proceeded on leave. Colonel Northern returned from leave. Captain 2nd Sontree granted 4 days extension of leave by him Office. Weather fine	
"	3		Transport 31 wagons for Divisional work. Weather fine	
"	4		Transport 38 G.S. wagons for Divisional work. Weather rainy.	

Army Form C. 2118

WAR DIARY
or
INTELLIGENCE SUMMARY
(Erase heading not required.)

Instructions regarding War Diaries and Intelligence Summaries are contained in F. S. Regs., Part II. and the Staff Manual respectively. Title Pages will be prepared in manuscript.

Place	Date	Hour	Summary of Events and Information	Remarks and references to Appendices
BUSSEBOOM	1916 Dec 5		Transport - 24 G.S. wagons for Divisional work. Weather dull.	
"	" 6		Nieuport 28 G.S. wagons for Divisional work. 7 Men proceeded on leave. Weather fair.	
"	" 7		Nieuport 13 G.S. wagons for Divisional work. All wagons & horses of 65th & 90th Brigades sent to Mints for refit. A Board of Officers assembled to hand over 19,360 to Lt. France owing to Capt Agate being detained for duty in England. Weather fine.	Appendix I
"	" 8		Nieuport 26 wagons for Divisional work. 1 Rein. 1 H.S. horse received from Remounts. Weather fine.	

1875 Wt. W593/826 1,000,000 4/15 J.B.C. & A. A.D.S.S./Forms/C. 2118.

WAR DIARY
or
INTELLIGENCE SUMMARY

(Erase heading not required.)

Army Form C. 2118

Place	Date	Hour	Summary of Events and Information	Remarks and references to Appendices
BUSSEBOOM	1916 Dec 9		Transport & O.C. wagons for Divisional work. Capt Bergman granted extension of leave by War Office on written present of Court of Inquiry & Any Sheads by War Office on a fire in Toronto Camp. Commenced march to this area	Appendix II
"	" 10		23 Divisional R.A. Commenced march to this area. Railhead for R.A. Group BOVAUR MAISON. 190 Co marching with Divl to BARLY. Weather wet. Transport & G.O. wagons for Divisional work. advance party 1 N.C.O & R. of 190 Co arrived to take on Camp. Lt Gilliam relieved by 2nd Lt Elcoat as R.O. 2nd Army Purchase Board. 1 Senior Cpl, 1 Wheeler Cpl, & 1 driver arrived from Base. Lewis accoutrement for today Concience Port of Boulogne closed. Weather wet	
"	" 11		Transport & E.O. wagons in Divisional work. Railhead R.A. Group FREVENT. 190 Co Y Munched to MONCHEL SUR CHANCHE Weather fair	

Army Form C. 2118

WAR DIARY
or
INTELLIGENCE SUMMARY
(Erase heading not required.)

Instructions regarding War Diaries and Intelligence Summaries are contained in F.S. Regs., Part II. and the Staff Manual respectively. Title Pages will be prepared in manuscript.

23rd DIVISIONAL TRAIN A.S.C.
JAN 1916
ORDERLY ROOM

Place	Date	Hour	Summary of Events and Information	Remarks and references to Appendices
BUSSEBOOM	1916 Feb 12		Nieuport 3 G.S. wagons for Divisional work. 190 Co. marched to GUERNOVAL. Weather dull	
"	" 13		Nieuport 25 G.S. wagons for Divisional work. Lt. Osborne and 12 O.R. proceeded on Leave. Railhead for R.A. BRUAY. 190 Co. did not move. Weather fine	
"	" 14		Nieuport 40 G.S. wagons for divisional work. Railhead R.A. LILLERS. 190 Co. marched to RELY. Lt. Col. Nothen presided Court of Inquiry on fire in St Laurence Camp. Weather fine	
"	" 15		Nieuport 31 G.S. wagons for divisional work. 190 Co. marched to THIENNES. Weather fine	Appendix III

WAR DIARY
INTELLIGENCE SUMMARY

Army Form C. 2118

Place	Date	Hour	Summary of Events and Information	Remarks and references to Appendices
BUSSEBOOM	1916 Dec 16		Nieuport 22 G.S. wagons for Divisional work and 8 G.S. wagons for 68th (Brigade Supply Coy) Last allotment fixed at 14 men every 5 days. Weather fine.	
"	17		Nieuport 19 G.S. wagons for Divisional work. Purchase from R.A. RENINGHELST. 19 Co move to RWELD. 1st hr relaxation + 13 O.R. proceeded on leave. Weather fine.	
"	18		Nieuport 52 G.S. wagons for Divisional work. Weather fine.	
"	19		Nieuport 26 G.S. wagons for Divisional work. Weather fine.	
"	20		Nieuport 16 G.S. wagons for Divisional work + 8 G.S. wagons for 68 Inf. Brigade. Weather fine.	

WAR DIARY
or
INTELLIGENCE SUMMARY.

Army Form C. 2118.

Place	Date	Hour	Summary of Events and Information	Remarks and references to Appendices
BusseBoom	1916 Dec 21	—	Transport 26 G.S. Wagons for Divisional work. Capt Llewellyn R.A.M.C. to 11th West Yorks temporarily. Weather wet.	
	22		Transport 26 G.S. Wagons for Divisional work. Major Montgomery granted leave. Weather wet.	
	23		Transport 3 G.S. Wagons for Divisional work. All baggage wagons of 68th & 69th Bde. sent to units for Relief. 114 N.C.O's & men proceeded on leave. Mostly fair.	Appendices
	24		Transport 24 G.S. Wagons for Divisional work. Weather fair. Christmas Church Parade at 192 Coy.	
	25		Transport 7 T.S. Wagons for Divisional work. Weather fair.	
	26		Transport 27 G.S. Wagons for Divisional work. Hd Qrs Coy. moved from R.WELD J.27 m.b.27 to BussEBoom.	

WAR DIARY
or
INTELLIGENCE SUMMARY

Army Form C. 2118

Place	Date	Hour	Summary of Events and Information	Remarks and references to Appendices
BUSSEBOOM	Dec 26 1916	-	Lt. R.T. Holmes & 2/Lt. D.T's It Riders, 30 H.D. Horses proceeded with 104 Bde. R.F.A. to Calais. Halt on night 26/27 WULVERDINGHE. Weather fair. Lt.Col. Horner inspected the 69th Bde. first line transport.	
	27		Transport 31 G.S. Wagons for Divisional work. Detachment of 7 H.Q. Group halted at NORDAUSQUE for night 27.28. Lt.Col. Horner inspected the 70th Bde. first line transport. Weather fair.	
	28		Transport 32 F.S. Wagons for Divisional work. Detachment of 7 H.Q. Group arrived at CALAIS. Weather fair. Lt.Col. Horner inspected 69th Bde. first line transport.	
	29		Transport 31 G.S. Wagons for Divisional work. Lt.Col. A. Horner Capt. L. Langford, members of a General Court Martial at H7C70. Weather fair.	

WAR DIARY or INTELLIGENCE SUMMARY

Army Form C. 2118

Place	Date	Hour	Summary of Events and Information	Remarks and references to Appendices
Bus=es Boom	1916 Dec 30	—	Transport 30 G.S. wagons for Divisional work. Weather fair.	
	31		Transport- 7 G.S. wagons for Divisional work. All baggage wagons of 68th + 70th Bde. sent to units for relief. Lt. Col. A. Norton D.S.O. President of F.G.C.M. at 68th Bde. HQrs. Church of England parade at 193 Coy. Weather fine.	Appendix V

4-1-1917

A. Norton
CDM G. 23RD DIVISIONAL TRAIN A.S.C.

Appendix I

<u>SECRET.</u> COPY NO. 17

<u>23rd DIVISION ORDER NO.84.</u>

Reference: 1/10,000 Trench Map.
1/20,000 Sheet 28 N.W.

1. (a) The 68th Infantry Brigade will relieve the 70th Infantry Brigade in the Right Section 23rd Division Front on the night of 7th/8th December.

   (b) All details of relief will be arranged direct between Brigadiers concerned.

   (c) Infantry will proceed to and from YPRES by train. Transport by road. Train time table will be issued by A.A.&.Q.M.G.

   (d) No trench will be vacated by 70th Infantry Brigade until occupied by 68th Infantry Brigade.

   (e) G.O.C. 68th Infantry Brigade will assume command of the Section on completion of relief.

   (f) All trench stores, air photos and Secret trench maps will be handed over by 70th Infantry Brigade to 68th Infantry Brigade.

2. After relief the 70th Infantry Brigade will be in Corps Reserve and will be billetted as follows :-

Brigade Headquarters	POPERINGHE.
One battalion.	WINNIPEG CAMP.
One battalion.	MONTREAL CAMP.
One battalion.	ST. LAWRENCE CAMP.
One battalion.	ERIE & TORONTO CAMPS.

3. One battalion 68th Infantry Brigade quartered in YPRES will be in Divisional Reserve. Name of unit and O.C. will be forwarded to Divisional Head Quarters.

4. ACKNOWLEDGE.

C.F. Watson
Lieut-Colonel,
5th December, 1916.   General Staff.

Issued at 1.30 p.m.

Copies to :-

No.	1.	Lowe's Group R.A.	No. 15.	A.P.M.
	2.	R.E.	16.	Camp Commandant.
	3.	Signals.	17.	Train.
	4-5	68th Inf. Bde.	18.	S.S.O.
	6-7	69th Inf. Bde.	19.	Area Commandant.
	8-9	70th Inf. Bde.	20-21	X Corps.
	10.	9th S.Staffs.	22.	47th Division.
	11.	A & Q.	23.	File.
	12.	A.D.M.S.	24-25	Diary.
	13.	D.A.D.O.S.	26.	Town Major, YPRES.
	14.	A.D.V.S.		

Appendix II

SECRET. G.H.Q. O.A.212.   23rd Division,
         Second Army G.900.   No. A/4147.
         X.Corps G.1/40/2.

Second Army.

1. The 23rd Divisional Artillery will be transferred by march route as shewn below from Fourth Army to Second Army (X.Corps).

Date.	March.	Administered by.
9th Dec.	From Fourth Army (VILLERS BOCAGE area) to Third Army (MEZEROLLES area). Detailed arrangements for this move will be made between Third and Fourth Armies direct in consultation with Fifth Army.	Third Army.
10th Dec.	Halt.	Third Army.
11th Dec.	Under orders of Third Army to BOUBERS-sur-CANCHE area.	Third Army.
12th Dec.	Under orders of First Army to area VALHUON-CONTEVILLE-TROISVAUX.	First Army.
13th Dec.	Halt.	First Army.
14th Dec.	Under orders of First Army to area AUCHY-au-BOIS - WESTREHEM.	First Army.
15th Dec.	Under orders of First Army to area BOESEGHEM - THIENNES - STEENBECQUE.	First Army.
16th Dec.	Halt.	First Army.
17th Dec.	Under orders of Second Army to Second Army area.	Second Army.

2. All grenades and ammunition will be left behind in Fourth Army.
 Fourth Army will arrange suitable storage.

3. Acknowledge by wire.

G. H. Q.   Sd. R. BUTLER, M.G. for
26th November, 1916.   Lieut. General. C.G.S.

X.Corps.
        Forwarded for information. Further details will be communicated by Second Army Q,

27th November, 1916.   Sd. C.H. HARINGTON, M.G.G.S.
                                            Second Army.

Appendix III

SECRET.   COPY NO. 17

23rd DIVISION ORDER NO.85.

Reference: 1/10,000 Trench Map.
           1/20,000 Sheet 28 N.W.

1. (a) The 70th Infantry Brigade will relieve the 69th Infantry Brigade in the Left Section 23rd Division Front on the night of 15th/16th December.

   (b) All details of relief will be arranged direct between Brigadiers concerned.

   (c) Infantry will proceed to and from YPRES by train. Transport by road. Train time table will be issued by A.A.&.Q.M.G.

   (d) No trench will be vacated by 69th Infantry Brigade until occupied by 70th Infantry Brigade.

   (e) G.O.C. 70th Infantry Brigade will assume command of the Section on completion of relief.

   (f) All trench stores, air photos and Secret trench maps will be handed over by 69th Infantry Brigade to 70th Infantry Brigade.

2. After relief the 69th Infantry Brigade will be in Corps Reserve and will be billetted as follows :-

Brigade Headquarters.	POPERINGHE.
One battalion.	WINNIPEG CAMP.
One battalion.	MONTREAL CAMP.
One battalion.	ST. LAWRENCE CAMP.
One battalion.	ERIE & TORONTO CAMPS.

3. One battalion 70th Infantry Brigade quartered in YPRES will be in Divisional Reserve. Name of unit and O.C. will be forwarded to Divisional Head Quarters.

4. ACKNOWLEDGE.

                                        F.H. Moore
                                        for. Lieut-Colonel,
14th December, 1916.   General Staff.

        Issued at 9.15 a.m.

Copies to :-

No.			No.		
1.	Lowe's Group R.A.		15.	A.P.M.	
2.	R.E.		16.	Camp Commandant.	
3.	Signals.		17.	Train.	
4-5	68th Inf. Bde.		18.	S.S.O.	
6-7	69th Inf. Bde.		19.	Area Commandant.	
8-9	70th Inf. Bde.		20-21	X Corps.	
10.	9th S.Staffs.		22.	55th Division.	
11.	A & Q.		23.	File.	
12.	A.D.M.S.		24-25	Diary.	
13.	D.A.D.O.S.		26.	Town Major, YPRES.	
14.	A.D.V.S.				

Appendix IV.

S E C R E T.   COPY No. 17

23rd DIVISION ORDER No. 86.

Reference :-   1/10,000 Trench Map and 1/20,000, Sheet 28.N.W.

1. (a).   The 69th Infantry Brigade will relieve the 68th Infantry Brigade in the Right Section 23rd Division front on the night of 23rd/24th December.

   (b).   All details of relief will be arranged direct between Brigadiers concerned.

   (c).   Infantry will proceed to and from YPRES by train. Transport by road. Train time-table will be issued by A.A.&Q.M.G.

   (d).   No trench will be vacated by 68th Infantry Brigade until occupied by 69th Infantry Brigade.

   (e).   G.O.C.69th Infantry Brigade will assume command of the Section on completion of relief.

   (f).   All trench stores, air photos and secret trench maps will be handed over by 68th Infantry Brigade to 69th Infantry Brigade.

2.   After relief the 68th Infantry Brigade will be in Corps Reserve and will be billetted as follows :-

   Brigade Head-Quarters ... ... POPERINGHE
   One Battalion ... ... WINNIPEG CAMP.
   One Battalion ... ... MONTREAL CAMP
   One Battalion ... ... St. LAWRENCE CAMP
   One Battalion ... ... ERIE & TORONTO CAMPS.

3.   One battalion 69th Infantry Brigade quartered in YPRES will be in Divisional Reserve. Name of Unit and O.C. will be forwarded to Divisional Head-Quarters.

4.   A C K N O W L E D G E.

20th December, 1916.
   Issued at 4.30 p.m.

J.H. Moore
Major,
General Staff.

Copies to :-

No.			
1	Lowe's Group R.A.	15	A.P.M.
2	R.E.	16	Camp Commandant
3	Signals	17	Train
4 - 5	68th Infantry Brigade	18	S.S.O.
6 - 7	69th Infantry Brigade	19	Area Commandant.
8 - 9	70th Infantry Brigade	20 - 21	X Corps
10	9/S.Staffordshire Regt.	22	47th Division
11	A. & Q.	23	File
12	A.D.M.S.	24 - 25	Diary
13	D.A.D.O.S.	26	Town Major, YPRES.
14	A.D.V.S.		

Appendix V

SECRET.   COPY NO. 17.

23rd DIVISION ORDER NO.88.

Reference :- 1/10,000 Trench Map and 1/20,000, Sheet 28.N.W.

1. (a)   The 68th Infantry Brigade will relieve the 70th Infantry Brigade in the Left Section 23rd Division front on the night of 31st Dec./1st Jan.1917.

   (b)   All details of relief will be arranged direct between Brigadiers concerned.

   (c)   Infantry will proceed to and from YPRES by train. Transport by road. Train time-table will be issued by A.A.&.Q.M.G.

   (d). No trench will be vacated by 70th Infantry Brigade until occupied by 68th Infantry Brigade.

   (e)   G.O.C. 68th Infantry Brigade will assume command of the Section on completion of relief.

   (f)   All trench stores, air photos and secret trench maps will be handed over by 70th Infantry Brigade to 68th Infantry Brigade.

2. After relief, the 70th Infantry Brigade will be in Corps Reserve and will be billetted as follows :-

Brigade Headquarters … …	POPERINGHE.
One Battalion. … … …	WINNIPEG CAMP.
One Battalion. … … …	MONTREAL CAMP.
One Battalion. … … …	ST. LAWRENCE CAMP.
One Battalion. … … …	ERIE & TORONTO CAMPS.

3. One battalion 68th Infantry Brigade quartered in YPRES will be in Divisional Reserve. Name of Unit and O.C. will be forwarded to Divisional Headquarters.

4. ACKNOWLEDGE.

                                                    Major,
                                       General Staff, 23rd Division.

28.12.16.
   Issued at 1.30 p.m.

Copies to :-

No.			
1	R.A. 23rd Div.	15	A.P.M.
2	R.E.	16	Camp Commandant.
3	Signals.	17	Train.
4-5	68th Inf. Bde.	18	S.S.O.
6-7	69th Inf. Bde.	19	Area Commandant.
8-9	70th Inf. Bde.	20-21	X Corps.
10	9th S.Staffs.	22	55th Division.
11	A & Q.	23	File.
12	A.D.M.S.	24-25	Diary.
13	D.A.D.O.S.	26	Town Major, YPRES.
14	A.D.V.S.		

W. 15517—M. 141. 250,000. 1/16. L.S.&Co. Forms/W 3091/2.   Army Form W. 3091.

Cover for Documents.

Confidential

Nature of Enclosures.

War Diary

By Lt Col. A. Northen D.S.O.

Commanding 23rd Divisional Train A.S.C

From 1st to 31 Jan 1917.

The D.A.G.
3rd Echelon
Base

Notes, or Letters written.

WAR DIARY or INTELLIGENCE SUMMARY

Army Form C. 2118.

Place	Date	Hour	Summary of Events and Information	Remarks and references to Appendices
BUSSEBOOM	1917 July 1	—	Railhead RENINGHELST Siding. Transport 15 G.S. Wagons for Divisional work. Major Montgomery granted extension of leave until 11th inst. Fair allotment of leave. 3 per day. New Years Honours & Rewards. Lt. W.G. Lacy, Military Cross, — Lt. Nothen, Major Montgomery, Capt. Langford & Capt. Nadden, Mentioned. Weather fair.	
	2		Transport 7 G.S. Wagons for Divisional work. Weather fair.	
	3		Transport 11 G.S. Wagons for Divisional work. Capt. R. Langford left to take command of 205 Reserve Park. Lt. Col. A. Nothen, President of F.G.C.M. held at Train H.Qrs. ↖BUSSEBOOM. 2/Lt. P.W. Leycester A.S.C. joined from 1st Cavalry Divisional A.S.C. Lt. W.G. Lacy took over duties of Adjudant.	

Army Form C. 2118.

WAR DIARY
or
INTELLIGENCE SUMMARY.
(Erase heading not required.)

Place	Date	Hour	Summary of Events and Information	Remarks and references to Appendices
BUSSEBOOM	1916 Jan 4th		Transport 17 G.S. Wagons for Divisional work. Weather fair.	
	5		Transport 21 G.S. Wagons for Divisional work. Lt. Osborne, Lt. Hooley, Lt. Watson & Lt. Gay attended lecture on "Horse Mastership" at 55th Divisional Cinema. Weather wet.	
	6		Transport 25 G.S. Wagons for Divisional work. Weather fair, some rain.	
	7		Transport 26 G.S. Wagons for Divisional work. Capt. Kelsall proceeded on leave. C. of E. Service at 10.2 Coy. Camp. Weather wet.	
	8		Transport. P. & G.S. wagons to 70th Bde. & 9 G.S. wagons to 69th Bde. for Relief. 21 G.S. wagons for Divisional work. A.D.M.S. 23rd Division inspected company camps. Weather fair.	Appendix I

Army Form C. 2118.

WAR DIARY
or
INTELLIGENCE SUMMARY.
(Erase heading not required.)

Instructions regarding War Diaries and Intelligence Summaries are contained in F.S. Regs., Part II. and the Staff Manual respectively. Title pages will be prepared in manuscript.

Place	Date	Hour	Summary of Events and Information	Remarks and references to Appendices
Busseboom	1917 Jany 9.	—	Transport 26 F.S. wagons for Divisional work. Weather fine.	
		10	Transport 9 F.S. wagons for Divisional work. Weather fair.	
		11	Transport 29 F.S. wagons for Divisional work. Weather fine.	
		12	Transport 20 F.S. wagons for Divisional work. Twelve W. carts taken over from 2nd Canadian Reserve Park. Fd. (A Graces, granted leave. Weather fair.	
		13	Transport 10 G.S. wagons for Divisional work. 8 tip carts for conveying road Material to HELL FIRE CORNER. 1 Driver, 1 Bn. H.D. horses & 1 G.S. wagon attached to 194th M.G.C. taken on the strength of the Train & posted to 190 Coy. 2t. Col Northen proceeded on 2 days leave to PARIS. Weather wet	

Army Form C. 2118.

WAR DIARY
or
INTELLIGENCE SUMMARY.
(Erase heading not required.)

Place	Date	Hour	Summary of Events and Information	Remarks and references to Appendices
BUSSEBOOM	1917 Jan. 14	—	Transport 6 G.S. Wagons for Divisional work. Detachment of Roadmakers Coy. with 104 Bde. R.F.A. returned to STEENVOORDE. Weather fair.	
	15		6 T.E. Service at 192 Coy. Camp. Transport 16 GS wagons & 8 lt.f. carts for Divisional work. Weather wet.	
	16		Transport all baggage wagons to 68th & 69th Bdes. for relief. 11 G.S. Wagons & 8 lt.f. carts for Divisional work. 3 Men joined from Base. Weather fine.	APPENDIX I
	17		Transport 6 G.S. Wagons & 8 lt.f. carts for Divisional work. Weather fine.	
	18		Transport 33 G.S. Wagons & 4 lt.f. carts for Divisional work. Weather fine.	

Army Form C. 2118.

WAR DIARY
or
INTELLIGENCE SUMMARY.

(Erase heading not required.)

Instructions regarding War Diaries and Intelligence Summaries are contained in F. S. Regs., Part II. and the Staff Manual respectively. Title pages will be prepared in manuscript.

Place	Date	Hour	Summary of Events and Information	Remarks and references to Appendices
Busse Boom	1916 Jan. 19	—	Transport. 8 G.S. Wagons & 8 l/b carts for Divisional work. Weather fine.	
	" 20	—	Transport 24 G.S. Wagons & 9 l/b carts for Divisional work. 13 Drivers joined from Base. Lt. J.P. Pillard wounded on leave. Dr. N. McLaren 191 Coy. tried by F.G.C.M. case dismissed. Weather fine.	
	21	—	Transport 17 G.S. Wagons for Divisional work. Gas precautions taken. 2 days issue of Coal, 2 days issue of hay & 1 day's issue of Oats, dumped at Transport Lines of all units. No. 6 F. Service at 192 Coy. Camp. 14 Combats. Linnets transferred to 104 Bde. R.F.A. from 2nd Army Troops Bde R.F.A. Weather fine.	Authority Q.M.G. No. O.3472 (Q.A.1) 4-20-12-15

Army Form C. 2118.

WAR DIARY
or
INTELLIGENCE SUMMARY.
(Erase heading not required.)

Instructions regarding War Diaries and Intelligence Summaries are contained in F. S. Regs., Part II. and the Staff Manual respectively. Title pages will be prepared in manuscript.

Place	Date	Hour	Summary of Events and Information	Remarks and references to Appendices
BUSSEBOOM	1917. Jan 22	—	Transport 10 G.S. wagons & 8 lt. carts for Divisional work. Weather fine.	
	23	—	Transport 12 G.S. wagons & 8 lt. carts for Divisional work. Lt. Col. A. Nother, President F.G.C.M. assembled at Train Headquarters. Court reassembled on 25th inst.	APPENDIX III
	24	—	Transport 10 baggage wagons to 68th & 70th Bdes. for riding. 7 G.S. Wagons & 8 lt. carts for Divisional work. Lt. Nothen proceeded on leave. Weather fine.	
	25	—	Transport 21 G.S. Wagons & 8 lt. carts for Divisional work. Capt. Barugh took over command of 192 Coy. from Capt. L.J. Kidall. Weather fine.	
	26	—	Transport 12 G.S. Wagons & 8 lt. carts for Divisional work. Weather fine.	

WAR DIARY
or
INTELLIGENCE SUMMARY.

Army Form C. 2118.

Place	Date	Hour	Summary of Events and Information	Remarks and references to Appendices
BUSSEBOOM	1917 Jan (cont) 28	-	Transport: 12 G.S. Wagons & 8 lt. carts for Divisional work. Weather fine.	
	28	-	Transport 27 G.S. Wagons & 8 lt. carts for Divisional work. Lt. E.P. Caddell joined from Base & posted to 190 Coy. Capt. J. Kilwall proceeded to England on transfer to R.F.A. 6 O.R. to service at 192 Coy. camp. Weather fine.	
	29	-	Transport 21 G.S. Wagons for Divisional work. Weather fine.	
	30	-	Transport 24 G.S. Wagons & 8 lt. carts for Divisional work. Weather fair.	
	31	-	Transport 21 G.S. Wagons & 8 lt. carts for Divisional work. Weather fine.	

1-2-1917

B. Moseley Lt. Col.
COM G. 23rd DIVISIONAL TRAIN A.S.C.

APPENDIX I

SECRET.   Copy No. 17

23rd DIVISION ORDER No. 89.

Reference :-   1/10,000 Trench Map and 1/20,000, Sheet 28. N.W.

1. (a)   The 70th Infantry Brigade will relieve the 69th Infantry Brigade in the Right Section, 23rd Division front on the night of the 8th/9th January, 1917.

   (b)   All details of relief will be arranged direct between Brigadiers concerned.

   (c)   Infantry will proceed to and from YPRES by train. Transport by road. Train time-table will be issued by A.A.&.Q.M.G.

   (d)   No trench will be vacated by 69th Infantry Brigade until occupied by 70th Infantry Brigade.

   (e)   The G.O.C.70th Infantry Brigade will assume command of the Section on completion of relief.

   (f)   All trench stores, air photos and secret trench maps will be handed over to the 70th Infantry Brigade by 69th Infantry Brigade.

2.   After relief the 69th Infantry Brigade will be in Corps Reserve and will be billetted as follows :-

Brigade Head-Quarters	POPERINGHE.
One battalion	WINNIPEG CAMP
One battalion	MONTREAL CAMP
One battalion	ST. LAWRENCE CAMP
One battalion	ERIE & TORONTO CAMPS.

3.   One battalion 70th Infantry Brigade quartered in YPRES will be in Divisional Reserve. Name of unit and O.C. will be forwarded to Divisional Head-Quarters.

4.   A C K N O W L E D G E

                                                 J. H. Morse,
5th January, 1917.   Major,
Issued at 4 p.m.   General Staff.

    Copies to :-
    No. 1   R.A.   15   A.P.M.
         2   R.E.   16   Camp Commdt.
         3   Signals   17   Train
         4 - 5   68th Inf. Bde.   18   S.S.O.
         6 - 7   69th Inf. Bde.   19   Area Commdt.
         8 - 9   70th Inf. Bde.   20 - 21   X Corps
         10   9th S.Staffs. R. 22   47th Divn.
         11   A.&.Q.   23   File
         12   A.D.M.S.   24 - 25   Diary.
         13   D.A.D.O.S.   26   Town Major, YPRES.
         14   A.D.V.S.

APPENDIX II

S E C R E T.   23rd DIVISION ORDER No. 91.   Copy No. 17

Reference :- 1/10,000 Trench Map and 1/20,000 Map, Sheet 28, N.W.

1. (a). The 69th Infantry Brigade will relieve the 68th Infantry Brigade in the Left Section 23rd Division front on the night of the 16th/17th January, 1917.

    (b). All details of relief will be arranged direct between Brigadiers concerned.

    (c). Infantry will proceed to and from YPRES by train. Transport by road. Train time-table will be issued by A.A.& Q.M.G.

    (d). No trench will be vacated by the 68th Infantry Brigade until occupied by 69th Infantry Brigade.

    (e). The G.O.C.69th Infantry Brigade will assume command of the Section on completion of relief.

    (f). All trench stores, air photos and secret trench maps will be handed over to the 69th Infantry Brigade by the 68th Infantry Brigade.

2. After relief, the 68th Infantry Brigade will be in Corps Reserve and will be billetted as follows :-

    Brigade Head-Quarters ... POPERINGHE
    One Battalion ... ... WINNIPEG CAMP.
    One Battalion ... ... MONTREAL CAMP.
    One battalion ... ... ST. LAWRENCE CAMP.
    One Battalion ... ... ERIE & TORONTO CAMPS.

3. One battalion 69th Infantry Brigade quartered in YPRES will be in Divisional Reserve. Name of unit and O.C. will be forwarded to Divisional Head-Quarters.

4. ACKNOWLEDGE.

12. 1. 17.
    Issued at 8.15 p.m.   F. Watson
                                                        Lieut.-Colonel,
                                                        General Staff.

Copies to :-

    No. 1.   R.A.23rd Divn.   15. A.P.M.
        2.   R.E.   16. Camp Commandant.
        3.   Signals.   17. Train
     4 - 5.   68th Inf. Bde.   18. S.S.O.
     6 - 7.   69th Inf. Bde.   19. Area Commandant.
     8 - 9.   70th Inf. Bde.   20 - 21. X Corps.
       10.   9th S. Stafford. R.   22. 39th Division.
       11.   A.& Q.   23. File.
       12.   A.D.M.S.   24 - 25. Diary.
                                       26. Town Major, YPRES.
       13.   D.A.D.O.S.
       14.   A.D.V.S.

APPENDIX III

SECRET.   COPY NO. 17

23rd DIVISION ORDER NO.92.

Reference :- 1/10,000 Trench Map and 1/20,000 Map, Sheet 28, N.W.

1. (a).   The 68th Infantry Brigade will relieve the 70th Infantry Brigade in the Right Section 23rd Division front on the night of the 24th/25th January, 1917.

    (b).   All details of relief will be arranged direct between Brigadiers concerned.

    (c).   Infantry will proceed to and from YPRES by train. Transport by road. Train time-table will be issued by A.A.& Q.M.G.

    (d).   No trench will be vacated by the 70th Infantry Brigade until occupied by 68th Infantry Brigade.

    (e).   The G.O.C. 68th Infantry Brigade will assume command of the Section on completion of relief.

    (f).   All trench stores, air photos and secret trench maps will be handed over to the 68th Infantry Brigade by the 70th Infantry Brigade.

2.   After relief, the 70th Infantry Brigade will be in Corps Reserve and will be billetted as follows :-

    Brigade Headquarters   ...   POPERINGHE.
    One Battalion.   ...   WINNIPEG CAMP.
    One Battalion.   ...   MONTREAL CAMP.
    One Battalion.   ...   ST. LAWRENCE CAMP.
    One Battalion.   ...   ERIE & TORONTO CAMPS.

3.   One battalion 68th Infantry Brigade quartered in YPRES will be in Divisional Reserve. Name of unit and O.C. will be forwarded to Divisional Headquarters.

4.   ACKNOWLEDGE.

                                    C.F. Watson.
20.1.1917.
    Issued at 9.15 a.m.   Lieut-Colonel,
                                            General Staff.

Copies to :-

No. 1.	R.A. 23rd Divn.	15.	A.P.M.
2.	R.E.	16.	Camp Commandant.
3.	Signals.	17.	Train.
4 - 5.	68th Inf. Bde.	18.	S.S.O.
6 - 7.	69th Inf. Bde.	19.	Area Commandant.
8 - 9.	70th Inf. Bde.	20 - 21.	X Corps.
10.	9th S.Staffs.	22.	47th Division.
11.	A.& Q.	23.	File.
12.	A.D.M.S.	24 - 25.	Diary.
13.	D.A.D.O.S.	26.	Town Major, YPRES.
14.	A.D.V.S.		

Army Form W. 3091.

W. 15517—M. 141. 250,000. 1/16. L.S.&Co. Forms/W 3091/2.

Vol 18

Cover for Documents.

Nature of Enclosures.

War Diary

By Lt Col. A Northen D.S.O.
Commanding 23rd Div Train A.S.C

1st to 28 Feby 1917

Notes, or Letters written.

Army Form C. 2118.

WAR DIARY
or
INTELLIGENCE SUMMARY.
(Erase heading not required.)

Instructions regarding War Diaries and Intelligence Summaries are contained in F. S. Regs., Part II. and the Staff Manual respectively. Title pages will be prepared in manuscript.

Place	Date	Hour	Summary of Events and Information	Remarks and references to Appendices
BUSSEBOOM	July 1	-	Railhead RENINGHELST. Transport 13 F.S. wagons & 8 t.s. carts for Divisional work. All baggage wagons to units of 69th & 70th Brigades, for relief. Spare COULTER E, 190 boys filed by F.G. & M. Leave allotment, 2 men per day.	Appendix I Authority DDS.T Second Army B.3960 d/30/6
	" 2	-	Lt. L.P. GILLIARD, returned in England for Home Service. Weather fine. Transport 21 G.S. wagons & 8 t.s. carts for Divisional work. Weather fine.	
	" 3	-	Transport 15 G.S. wagons & 8 t.s. carts on Divisional work. Weather fine.	
	" 4	-	Transport 42 F.S. wagons & 8 t.s. carts for Divisional work. Church of England Service held at 192 Coy Camp.	
	" 5	-	Transport 20 G.S. wagons for Divisional work. 1 T.C.O. & 2 men sent to No 5 F.N.Q. Ammunition Park, BAINCOURT for duty under Second Army Purchase Board.	

Army Form C. 2118.

WAR DIARY
or
INTELLIGENCE SUMMARY.
(Erase heading not required.)

Instructions regarding War Diaries and Intelligence Summaries are contained in F.S. Regs., Part II. and the Staff Manual respectively. Title pages will be prepared in manuscript.

Place	Date	Hour	Summary of Events and Information	Remarks and references to Appendices
BUSSEBOOM	Feby 6	-	Transport 7 G.S. Wagons for Divisional work. Weather fine.	
"	7	-	Transport 15 G.S. wagons for Divisional work. 2/Lt. W.G. LACEY, appointed Adjutant with effect from 3rd January 1917. Weather fine.	Authy A.Q.M.G L76 d/6/2/17
"	8	-	Transport 9 G.S. Wagons for Divisional work. Double issue of rations to all units, was issue from Supply Column reserve, consequent on daily late arrival of Pack trains & one from Supply. Weather fine.	
"	9	-	Transport 11 G.S. wagons & 8 L.L. carts for Divisional work. All baggage wagons to units of 128 & 69th Brigades for relief leave cancelled. Fire at 192 Coy. Officers Quarters, some R.E. & Officers Kits & other Government & private property destroyed.	Appendix II
"	10	-	Transport 21 G.S. Wagons for Divisional work. 2/Lt. D.M. WATSON left to report to M.T. School of Instruction, ROUEN.	Authy A.M.G M/91225 ASC/4/2/17

Army Form C. 2118.

WAR DIARY
or
INTELLIGENCE SUMMARY.
(Erase heading not required.)

Place	Date	Hour	Summary of Events and Information	Remarks and references to Appendices
BUSSEBOOM	July 10	—	Weather fine.	
"	" 11	—	Transport 6 G.S. wagons & 8 lt. carts for Divisional work. Two bomb-lote turnouts transferred to Army R.F.A. Brigade "6" Battery, 104 Brigade. Weather fine.	Q.M.G. M25972 (Q.A.I.)
"	" 12	—	Transport 21 G.S. wagons & 8 lt. carts for Divisional work. Weather fine.	
"	" 13	—	Transport 18 G.S. wagons & 8 lt. carts for Divisional work. Lt. F. Ball. A. St. G. ADAMS. joined from 55th Divisional Train. 1 man & 1 Q.C. wounded & 1 horse killed by shell fire at YPRES. Weather fine.	Ref to Q.D.D.975T AP2229 d/9.2.17
"	" 14	—	Transport 11 G.S. wagons & 8 lt. carts for Divisional work. Court of Enquiry assembled at Divisional Rest Station, Tournigut circumstanced of fire at Officers Quarters, 192 Coy. Weather fine.	
"	" 15	—	Transport 24 G.S. wagons & 8 lt. carts for Divisional work.	

Army Form C. 2118.

WAR DIARY
or
INTELLIGENCE SUMMARY.
(Erase heading not required.)

Instructions regarding War Diaries and Intelligence Summaries are contained in F.S. Regs., Part II. and the Staff Manual respectively. Title pages will be prepared in manuscript.

Place	Date	Hour	Summary of Events and Information	Remarks and references to Appendices
BUSSEBOOM	July 15	—	Lt. Col. A. NORTHEN, President of 3. G.C.M. assembled at D.H.Q. Weather fine	
"	16	—	Transport 18 G.S. wagons & 8 lt. carts for Divisional work. Lt. Col. A. NORTHEN. Proceeded on leave to England. Orders re "Imposed Straw Restrictions" received.	
"	17	11.30 a.m.	Transport 10 G.S. wagons for Divisional work. All baggage wagons to units of 68th & 90th Brigades for relief. Weather fair.	Appendix III
"	18	—	Transport 7 G.S. wagons for Divisional work. Church of England Service at 192 Company. Weather fair.	
"	19	—	Transport 36 G.S. wagons & 4 lt. carts for Divisional work. D.H.Q. wired for Lt. Col. NORTHEN to return. Weather fine.	
"	20	—	Transport 9 G.S. wagons & 4 lt. carts for Divisional work. Lt. Col. NORTHEN, rejoins from leave.	

Army Form C. 2118.

WAR DIARY
or
INTELLIGENCE SUMMARY.
(Erase heading not required.)

Place	Date	Hour	Summary of Events and Information	Remarks and references to Appendices
Bossboom	Feby 20.	—	Lt. H.T. GILCHRIST joined from Base Horse Trans. sort Depot ref. GILLIARD. Weather wet.	A/Lt/Lt, DDS&T 2nd Army P.2229 d/4.2.17
	" 21	—	Transport - 23 G.S. wagons for Divisional work. All 6 J.L.E. Rifles for charge of Train, exchanged for S.E. rifles. Weather fair.	
	" 22	—	Transport 69 G.S. wagons for Divisional work	
		6 am.	Thaw restrictions removed. Weather wet.	
	" 23	—	Transport 16 G.S. wagons for Divisional work. Twelve (12) Carts returned to 2nd Canadian Reserve Park (Div.).	
		part	Thaw restrictions imposed.	
		—	Weather fair.	
	" 24	—	Transport - 32 G.S. wagons for Divisional work. 193 Company, Move to LEDERZEELE, Infantry moved by rail. Weather fine. Railhead for 193 Coy., PROVEN.	Appendix IV

Army Form C. 2118.

WAR DIARY
or
INTELLIGENCE SUMMARY.
(Erase heading not required.)

Place	Date	Hour	Summary of Events and Information	Remarks and references to Appendices
BUSSEBOOM	Feb 25	—	Transport 14 G.S. wagons for Divisional Train. All baggage wagons to units of 69th Brigade for relief 103 Coy. move to WATTEN. Railhead for 193/Coy...PROVEN. Weather fine.	Appendix V.
	"26	—	Transport 2 G.S. wagons for Divisional cyclists. 193 Company move to TOURNEHEM. Railhead for 193 Coy. ST OMER. Weather fine. Lieut. A.W.R. Müller joined from 1st Divisional Cavalry A.S.C.	
	"27	—	Train Headquarters move by motor lorry to ST OMER. 192 Company move to HERZEELE. 191 Company move to PROVEN. Railheads:- 103 Coy. ST OMER, 191 & 192 Companies PROVEN, 190 Coy. RENINGHELST. Thaw restrictions removed. Weather fine.	
ST OMER	"28	—	191 Coy. move to HERZEELE. 192 Coy. move to LEDERZEELE.	

Army Form C. 2118.

WAR DIARY
or
INTELLIGENCE SUMMARY.
(Erase heading not required.)

Instructions regarding War Diaries and Intelligence Summaries are contained in F. S. Regs., Part II. and the Staff Manual respectively. Title pages will be prepared in manuscript.

Place	Date	Hour	Summary of Events and Information	Remarks and references to Appendices
ST OMER	Feb 28	—	Railheads:- 191 & 192 Companies, PROVEN, 193 Coy. ST OMER, 190 Coy. RENINGHELST. Weather fair.	
			March 1st 1917.	

A. Noches
Lt. Col.
COM G. 23rd DIVISIONAL TRAIN A.S.C.

APPENDIX I

SECRET.

23rd DIVISION ORDER No. 93.

Copy No. 17

Reference :- 1/10,000 Trench Map and 1/20,000 Map, Sheet 28, N.W.

---

1. (a). The 70th Infantry Brigade will relieve the 69th Infantry Brigade in the Left Section 23rd Division Front on the night of the 1st/2nd February, 1917.

   (b). All details of relief will be arranged direct between Brigadiers concerned.

   (c). Infantry will proceed to and from YPRES by train: transport by road. Train time-table will be issued by A.A.&Q.M.G.

   (d). No trench will be vacated by the 69th Infantry Brigade until occupied by 70th Infantry Brigade.

   (e). The G.O.C. 70th Infantry Brigade will assume command of the Section on completion of relief, and will report to this office the hour at which he assumes command.

   (f). All trench stores, air photographs and secret trench maps will be handed over to the 70th Infantry Brigade by the 69th Infantry Brigade.

2. After relief, the 69th Infantry Brigade will be in Corps Reserve and will be billotted as follows :-

Brigade Head-Quarters ...	POPERINGHE.
One battalion	WINNIPEG CAMP.
One battalion	MONTREAL CAMP.
One battalion	ST. LAWRENCE CAMP.
One battalion	ERIE & TORONTO CAMPS.

3. One battalion 70th Infantry Brigade quartered in YPRES will be in Divisional Reserve. Name of unit and O.C. will be forwarded to Divisional Head-Quarters.

4. ACKNOWLEDGE

Evans.

28th January, 1917.
Issued at 8 p.m.

Lieut.-Colonel,
General Staff.

Copies to :-

No 1	R.A. 23rd Divn	15	A.P.M.
2	R.E.	16	Camp Commandant.
3	Signals	17	Train.
4 - 5	68th Inf. Bde.	18	S.S.O.
6 - 7	69th Inf. Bde.	19	Area Commandant.
8 - 9	70th Inf. Bde.	20 - 21	X Corps.
10	9/S.Staffs. R.	22	39th Division.
11	A.&Q.	23	File
12	A.D.M.S.	24 - 25	Diary.
13	D.A.D.O.S.	26	Town Major, YPRES.
14	A.D.V.S.		

APPENDIX II

SECRET.   COPY NO. 17

23rd DIVISION ORDER   No.95.

Reference :- 1/10,000 Trench Map and 1/20,000 Map, Sheet 28, N.W.

1. (a).   The 69th Infantry Brigade will relieve the 68th Infantry Brigade in the Right Section 23rd Division Front on the night of the 9th/10th February, 1917.

   (b).   All details of relief will be arranged direct between Brigadiers concerned.

   (c).   Infantry will proceed to and from YPRES by train: Transport by road. Train time-table will be issued by A.A.&Q.M.G.

   (d).   No trench will be vacated by the 68th Infantry Brigade until occupied by 69th Infantry Brigade.

   (e).   The G.O.C. 69th Infantry Brigade will assume command of the Section on completion of relief, and will report to this office the hour at which he assumes command.

   (f).   All trench stores, air photographs and secret trench maps will be handed over to the 69th Infantry Brigade by the 68th Infantry Brigade.

2.   After relief the 68th Infantry Brigade will be in Corps Reserve and will be billetted as follows :-

   Brigade Headquarters   ...   ...   POPERINGHE.
   One Battalion   ...   ...   WINNIPEG CAMP.
   One Battalion.   ...   ...   MONTREAL CAMP.
   One Battalion.   ...   ...   ST. LAWRENCE CAMP.
   One Battalion.   ...   ...   ERIE & TORONTO CAMPS.

3.   One battalion 69th Infantry Brigade will be in Divisional Reserve. Name of Unit and O.C. will be forwarded to Divisional Headquarters.

4.   The Headquarters of Battalion in Divisional Reserve, Right Brigade, will be in KRUISSTRAAT.

5.   The Headquarters of "A" Battalion, Left Brigade, will move to ZILLEBEKE BUND during the night of the 9th/10th instant and occupy Headquarters at the N. end of the BUND.

6.   ACKNOWLEDGE.

                                               Evans
                                                      Lieut-Colonel,
                                          General Staff.

7th February, 1917.
   Issued at 8 p.m.

Copies to :-

No. 1.	R.A. 23rd Divn.	15.	A.P.M.
2.	R.E.	16.	Camp Commandant.
3.	Signals.	17.	Train.
4 - 5.	68th Inf. Bde.	18.	D.S.O.
6 - 7.	69th Inf. Bde.	19.	Area Commandant.
8 - 9.	70th Inf. Bde.	20-21.	X Corps.
10.	G/S. Staffs.	22.	47th Division.
11.	A.G.Q.	23.	File.
12.	A.D.M.S.	24-25.	Diary.
13.	D.A.D.O.S.	26.	Town Major, YPRES.
14.	A.D.V.S.		

APPENDIX III

S E C R E T.   COPY NO. 17

23rd DIVISION ORDER   No. 96.

Reference :- 1/10,000 Trench Map and 1/20,000 Map, Sheet 28, N.W.

1. (a).   The 68th Infantry Brigade will relieve the 70th Infantry Brigade in the Left Section 23rd Division Front on the night 17th/18th February, 1917.

   (b).   All details of relief will be arranged direct between Brigadiers concerned.

   (c).   Infantry will proceed to and from YPRES by train: Transport by road. Train time-table will be issued by A.A.&.Q.M.G.

   (d).   No trench will be vacated by the 70th Infantry Brigade until occupied by 68th Infantry Brigade.

   (e).   The G.O.C. 68th Infantry Brigade will assume command of the Section on completion of relief, and will report to this office the hour at which he assumes command.

   (f).   All trench stores, air photographs and secret trench maps will be handed over to the 68th Infantry Brigade by the 70th Infantry Brigade.

2.   After relief the 70th Infantry Brigade will be in Corps Reserve and will be billetted as follows :-

Brigade Headquarters	POPERINGHE.
One Battalion.	WINNIPEG CAMP.
One Battalion.	MONTREAL CAMP.
One Battalion.	ST. LAWRENCE CAMP.
One Battalion.	ERIE & TORONTO CAMPS.

3.   One battalion 68th Infantry Brigade will be in Divisional Reserve. Name of Unit and O.C. will be forwarded to Divisional Headquarters.

4.   ACKNOWLEDGE.

                                                Evans.
                                                Lieut-Colonel,
14th February, 1917.   General Staff.
   Issued at 4 p.m.

Copies to :-

No.				
1.	R.A. 23rd Divn.		15.	A.P.M.
2.	R.E.		16.	Camp Commandant.
3.	Signals.		17.	Train.
4 - 5.	68th Inf. Bde.		18.	S.S.O.
6 - 7.	69th Inf. Bde.		19.	Area Commandant.
8 - 9.	70th Inf. Bde.		20-21.	X Corps.
10.	9/S.Staffs.		22.	39th Division.
11.	A.&.Q.		23.	File.
12.	A.D.M.S.		24-25.	Diary.
13.	D.A.D.O.S.		26.	Town Major, YPRES.
14.	A.D.V.S.			

Appendix IV

SECRET.

COPY NO. 11

23rd DIVISION ORDER NO. 97.

1. The 23rd Division is to be relieved by 39th Division. The relief will commence on February 24th in accordance with the attached Table.

2. The Division will occupy billets or huts in BOLLEZEELE and TILQUES Training Areas.

3. Brigade Groups in these areas will be composed as follows:-

   (a) 68th Infantry Brigade. 101st Field Company R.E., 70th Field Ambulance, 191st Company A.S.C.

   (b) 69th Infantry Brigade. 128th Field Company R.E., 69th Field Ambulance, 192nd Company A.S.C.

   (c) 70th Infantry Brigade. 102nd Field Company R.E., 71st Field Ambulance, 193rd Company A.S.C.

4. The 9th South Staffords will be attached to 69th Brigade Group.

5. Artillery Reliefs will take place on nights 27th/28th and 28th/1st March.

6. Further orders will be issued as soon as the necessary instructions have been received.

7. ACKNOWLEDGE.

19th February, 1917.
Issued at 1.30 p.m.

General Staff.   Lieut-Colonel,

Copies to :-

No.	
1.	"Q"
2.	C.R.A.
3.	C.R.E.
4 - 5.	68th Inf. Bde.
6 - 7.	69th Inf. Bde.
8 - 9.	70th Inf. Bde.
10.	A.D.M.S.
11.	Divisional Train.
12.	Signals.
13.	A.D.V.S.
14.	A.P.M.
15.	D.A.D.O.S.
16.	File.
17 - 18.	Diary.
19.	Camp Commdt.
20.	Area "

MARCH TABLE.

DATE.	UNIT.	FROM.	TO.	
Feb. 24th	70th Brigade Group.	OUDERDOM Area.	BOLLEZEELE Area.	Train or Bus.
25/26.	(9th Brigade Group) (9th S.Staffs.)	Trenches.	OUDERDOM Area.	" " "
26/27.	68th Brigade Group.	Trenches.	Huts A.30.	" " "
27.	69th Brigade Group.	OUDERDOM Area.	Huts L.Y.Z.	" " "

Should it be more convenient to Brigades of 23rd Division will be moved by VIII Corps direct from OUDERDOM Area to TILQUES.

Appendix V.

SECRET.   COPY NO. 17

23rd DIVISION ORDER   NO. 99.

Reference :- 1/10,000 Trench Map and 1/20,000 Map, Sheet 28, N.W.

1. (a).   The 116th Infantry Brigade will relieve the 69th Infantry Brigade in the Right Section 23rd Division Front on the night 25th/26th February, 1917.

   (b).   All details of relief will be arranged direct between Brigadiers concerned.

   (c).   Infantry will proceed to and from YPRES by train: Transport by road. Train time-table will be issued by A.A.&Q.M.G.

   (d).   No trench will be vacated by the 69th Infantry Brigade until occupied by 116th Infantry Brigade.

   (e).   The G.O.C. 116th Infantry Brigade will assume command of the Section on completion of relief, and will report to this office the hour at which he assumes command.

   (f).   All trench stores, air photographs and secret trench maps will be handed over to the 116th Infantry Brigade by the 69th Infantry Brigade.

2.   After relief the 69th Infantry Brigade will be billetted as follows :-

   Brigade Headquarters   ...   POPERINGHE.
   One Battalion.   ...   ...   WINNIPEG CAMP.
   One Battalion.   ...   ...   MONTREAL CAMP.
   One Battalion.   ...   ...   ST. LAWRENCE CAMP.
   One Battalion.   ...   ...   ERIE & TORONTO CAMPS.

3.   One battalion 116th Infantry Brigade will be in Divisional Reserve. Name of unit and O.C. will be forwarded to Divisional Headquarters.

4.   ACKNOWLEDGE.

                                        Evans.
                                        Lieut-Colonel,
22nd February, 1917.   General Staff.
     Issued at 1.30 p.m.

Copies to :-

No.1.	R.A. 23rd Divn.	15.	A.P.M.
2.	R.E.	16.	Camp Commandant.
3.	Signals.	17.	Train.
4 - 5.	68th Infantry Brigade.	18.	S.S.O.
6 - 7.	69th Infantry Brigade.	19.	Area Commandant.
8 - 9.	116th Infantry Brigade.	20-21.	X Corps.
10.	9th S. Staffords.	22.	39th Division.
11.	A.D.M.S.	23.	47th Division.
12.	A.D.M.S.	24.	File.
13.	D.A.D.O.S.	25-26.	Diary.
14.	A.D.V.S.	27.	Town Major, YPRES.

Vol 19

War Diary

By Lt Col A. Nortton D.S.O.

Commanding 23rd Divisional Train A.S.C

From 1st to 31 March 1917

The D.A.G.
3rd Echelon
B.E.F

Army Form C. 2118.

WAR DIARY
or
INTELLIGENCE SUMMARY.
(Erase heading not required.)

Instructions regarding War Diaries and Intelligence Summaries are contained in F. S. Regs., Part II. and the Staff Manual respectively. Title pages will be prepared in manuscript.

[Stamp: 23rd DIVISIONAL TRAIN A.S.C. 5 APR 1917 ORDERLY ROOM]

Place	Date	Hour	Summary of Events and Information	Remarks and references to Appendices
ST OMER	March 1st	-	191 Coy. move to VOLKERINCKHOVE. 190 Coy. move to HERZEELE. 192 Coy. move to SALPERWICK. Railhead WATTEN. Weather fair.	
	2	-	190 Coy. move to ZEGGERS-CAPPEL. Weather fair.	
	3	-	190 Coy. move to RECQUES. Dispositions of Companies :- 190 Coy. VOLKERINCKHOVE, 192 Coy. SALPERWICK, 193 Coy TOURNEHEM. Capt. H. NORTHEN, proceeded on leave.	
	4	-	Weather fair.	
	5	-	Weather fine. Recommendations for Mentions, forwarded to D.H.Q. Weather fair.	
	6	-	Weather fair.	

Army Form C. 2118.

WAR DIARY
or
INTELLIGENCE SUMMARY.
(Erase heading not required.)

Place	Date	Hour	Summary of Events and Information	Remarks and references to Appendices
ST OMER	March 7th	—	Lt. COVENTRY, K.O.Y.L.I. attached to Train Headquarters for instructional purposes.	
"	8	—	Lieutenant PERRONEAU. returned to Train Headquarters for duty from Lieutenant DESHAYES, to 2nd Army Purchase Board. Preserved Meat & Biscuit ration, issued to Units of the 68th Infantry Brigade & 101 Field Coy. R.E. Weather fair.	
"	9	—	Lt. Col. A. NORTHEN. member of General Court Martial. Weather wet.	
"	10	—	Weather fair.	
"	11	—	Weather fair.	
"	12	—	Weather fair.	
"	13	—	Lt. Col. A. NORTHEN proceeded on leave. Major T.H. MONTGOMERY. took over command of Train. Weather wet.	

Army Form C. 2118.

WAR DIARY
or
INTELLIGENCE SUMMARY.
(Erase heading not required.)

Instructions regarding War Diaries and Intelligence Summaries are contained in F.S. Regs., Part II. and the Staff Manual respectively. Title pages will be prepared in manuscript.

Place	Date	Hour	Summary of Events and Information	Remarks and references to Appendices
ST OMER	Nov 14th	—	Weather wet.	
	"15	—	Weather fair.	
	"16	—	Batt. LESTER, 10th West Ridings, attached to train Headquarters for instructional purposes.	
			Weather fair	
	"17	—	Weather fine	
	"18	—	Weather fine	
	"19	—	191 Coy. moved from VOLKERINCKHOVE to HERZEELE, refilled at BOLLEZEELE en route & refilled again later in HERZEELE Square & remained Appendix I loaded overnight.	
			192 Company moved to BOLLEZEELE, refilled at WATTEN prior to march.	
			193 Company moved to TOURNEHEM, via MOULLE & TILQUES, refilled at NORDAUSQUES - St OMER Rd. en route	
			Weather fine	
	"20	—	Train Headquarters moved from ST OMER to ESQUELBECQ	"

T2134. Wt. W708-776. 500000. 4/15. Sir J.C. & S.

Army Form C. 2118.

WAR DIARY
or
INTELLIGENCE SUMMARY.
(Erase heading not required.)

Instructions regarding War Diaries and Intelligence Summaries are contained in F.S. Regs., Part II. and the Staff Manual respectively. Title pages will be prepared in manuscript.

Place	Date	Hour	Summary of Events and Information	Remarks and references to Appendices
ST. OMER	March 20th	—	Railhead WATTEN.	
			190 Coy. moved from RECQUES via FORET D'ÉPERLECQUES, WATTEN to WULVERDINGHE. Supply wagons billed at BOLLEZEELE & delivered rations to Units same day.	Appendix I
			191 Coy. Moved to PROVEN via HOUTKERQUE - WATOU to E22 b 6.3 (Sheet 27)	"
			192 Coy. moved to HERZEELE D9 d 10.7 Sheet 27	"
			193 Coy. Moved to VOLKERINCKHOVE. Refilled at BOLLEZEELE. Weather wet.	"
ESQUELBECQ	„ 21	—	Railhead PROVEN.	
			190 Coy moved via LEDERZEELE - LE MENEGAT - ARNEKE - LEDRINGHEM - WORMHOUDT - HERZEELE - HOUTKERQUE to PROVEN. Refilled at HERZEELE.	
			191 Coy. moved from PROVEN to F14 C 8.6 Sheet 27. & took over billets from 331 Coy., 38th Div'l Train.	
			192 Coy. Moved to PROVEN E12 b 5.2 Sheet 27.	
			193 Coy. moved via ZEGGERS - CAPPEL - ESQUELBECQ - WORMHOUDT -	

Army Form C. 2118.

WAR DIARY
or
INTELLIGENCE SUMMARY.
(Erase heading not required.)

Instructions regarding War Diaries and Intelligence Summaries are contained in F. S. Regs., Part II. and the Staff Manual respectively. Title pages will be prepared in manuscript.

Place	Date	Hour	Summary of Events and Information	Remarks and references to Appendices
ESQUELBECQ	Sept 21st	—	HERZEELE to PROVEN. Refilled en route at HERZEELE. Weather wet.	
	"22	—	Dispositions of Companies. - 190 Coy. PROVEN - E12d3.9, 191 Coy. on Main PROVEN - POPERINGHE Rd. F14 c 8.6., 192 Coy. PROVEN E12 c 5.2. 193 Coy. PROVEN E12 d 3.9. System & points of Refilling. - Rations for R.A. less D.A.C. drawn by horse transport from Railhead. - D.A.C. rations dumped by lorries at HERZEELE. - 68th Bde. rations drawn by lorries from Railhead & dumped at G2a S6 Sht 28. - 69th Bde. drawn by horse transport from Railhead. - 70th Bde. & Div Headquarters drawn by lorry from Railhead & dumped at HERZEELE. Weather wet.	
	"23	—	68th Infantry Brigade & 191 Coy. A.S.C. attached to 38th Division for rations. Railhead PESELHOEK. 113th Infantry Brigade & 331 Coy. A.S.C. attached to 23rd Division for rations. Rations drawn by lorries at BOLLEZEELE.	

T2134. Wt. W708—776. 500000. 4/15. Sir J. C. & S.

Army Form C. 2118.

WAR DIARY
or
INTELLIGENCE SUMMARY.
(Erase heading not required.)

Place	Date	Hour	Summary of Events and Information	Remarks and references to Appendices
ESQUELBECQ	March 23rd	—	Cont: Weather fair.	
"	24	—	Lt Col. A. Northen rejoined from leave. Summer time. At 11 p.m. all clocks to be advanced one hour.	
	25	—	Weather fair.	
	26	—	Weather fine. Weather wet. Rations drawn by light railway for groups refilling at HERZEELE & BOLLEZEELE.	
	27	—	Weather fair.	
	28	—	Weather fair.	
	29	—	Weather fair.	
	30	—	Transport 3 G.S. wagons for Divisional work. Weather wet.	
	31	—	Transport 3 G.S. wagons for Divisional work. Weather wet.	

3-4-1917

A. Northen Lt Col.
OC No 2. 23rd DIVISIONAL TRAIN A.S.C.

Appendix I

S E C R E T.   Copy No. 17

23rd DIVISION OPERATION ORDER No. 101.

Reference: Maps Sheets 27 and 28, Scale 1/40,000.

1. The 23rd Division will move on 19th March and subsequent days in accordance with the attached March Table.
    The 69th Brigade Group will be clear of its present area by mid-day.

2. The Divisional Machine Gun Company and 9th South Stafford. Regt. will be attached to 70th Brigade Group from 20th instant.

3. Divisional Head-Quarters will close at St. OMER at 11 a.m. and open at ESQUELBECQ at the same hour on the 20th instant.

4. Separate instructions as to billeting, supply and other administrative arrangements will be issued by A.A.&.Q.M.G.

5.   ACKNOWLEDGE.

                                    Evans
                                    Lieutenant-Colonel,
16th March, 1917.   General Staff.
    Issued at 11.30 p.m.

Copies to :-

No.	
1	R.A.
2.	R.E.
3	Signals
4 - 5	68th Inf. Bde.
6 - 7	69th Inf. Bde.
8 - 9	70th Inf. Bde.
10	9/S.Staffs. R.
11	A. &. Q.
12	A.D.M.S.
13	D.A.D.O.S.
14	A.D.V.S.
15	A.P.M.
16	Camp Commdt.
17	Train ✓
18	S.S.O.
19	VIII Corps.
20	X Corps.
21	File.
22 - 23	Diary.
24	17th Supply Column.
25.	D.S. of Posts.
26	194 M.G.Coy.

M A R C H   T A B L E (continued).

U N I T.	19th March.	20th March.	21st March.	22nd March.	23rd March.
Divisional Artillery & portion of Train.			) WULVERDINGHE) LEDERZEELE) BROXEELE and) RUBROUCK.	H.Q. Chateau, WORMHOUDT. HERZEELE – HOUTQUERQUE – VaTOU.	HERZEELE Area.
Divnl. Amm.) Column) Mob. Vet.) Section.)				LEDERZEELE Area	

MARCH 1918.

UNIT	19th March.	20th March.	21st March.	22nd March.	23rd March.
Divisional Hd-Qrs.	H(OUTQUERQUE ~~BOLLEZEELE~~ Area. HERZEELE	ESQUELBECQ.			
68th Brigade Group.		H.Q. POPERINGHE. 1 Bn. Camp P.(A.15.d). 1 Bn. Camp L.(L.3.c.) 2 Bns.) Camps Y & Z M.G.Coy.)(F.25.b.&.c.) T.M.Bty.) 101st Fd.Coy. E. side HOUTQUERQUE Area. 191 Coy.Train PROVEN (E.12.central) 70th Fd. Amb. WATOU.	192 Coy. Train PROVEN.		
69th Brigade Group.	JOLLEZEELE Area.	H.Q. HERZEELE. HERZEELE area. 69th Fd. Amb. WORMHOUDT.			
70th Brigade Group.	EPERLECQUES Area.	H.Q. BOLLEZEELE. BOLLEZEELE Area. 71st Fd. Amb.(less 1 Sec.) RUBROUCK & HOGEN HILL (possibly WORMHOUDT) 1 Sec. 71st F.A. BOLLEZEELE.			
9th S.Staffs.	ZEGGERS CAPPEL Area.				
Div. M.G.Coy.	MILLAIN.				

Over.

23rd Divnl Train

Army Form C. 2118.

WAR DIARY
or
INTELLIGENCE SUMMARY.
(Erase heading not required.)

April 1917

Place	Date	Hour	Summary of Events and Information	Remarks and references to Appendices
ESQUELBECQ	1st April		Railhead PROVEN. System & Points of Refilling:- PROVEN:- 70th Brigade (including D.A.C. & D.H.Q. Group) Supplies conveyed by Light Railway to HERZEELE, where they are drawn by Horse Transport. Divisional Troops (2 Bdes R.A.) drawn by Horse Transport from PROVEN. 114th Inf. Brigade, 39th Division (attached to 23rd Division for rations) Supplies conveyed by Light Railway to BOLLEZEELE, where Rations are drawn by Horse Transport. 68th Brigade, attached to 39th Division, for Supplies. Weather wet.	
	2nd "		Weather wet.	
	3 "		Capt Tyldes, 11th Sherwood Foresters, attached to the Train for instruction & is posted to 190 Coy A.S.C. Weather fine.	
	4 "		193 Coy. moved from PROVEN to BUSSEBOOM, G.15.b.10.3. Sketch 28 Appendix I & took over camp from 104 Coy. 39th Divisional Train.	

T2134. Wt. W708—776. 500000. 4/15. Sir J. C. & S.

WAR DIARY
or
INTELLIGENCE SUMMARY.
(Erase heading not required.)

Army Form C. 2118.

Place	Date	Hour	Summary of Events and Information	Remarks and references to Appendices
ESQUELBECQ	July 5th	—	Weather wet.	
		—	191 Coy. moved from PROVEN (F14C.8.6) to BOLLEZEELE (H25C.7.8) 70th Brigade supplies drawn by Horse Transport 77th 70th Brigade - 114th Inf Brigade rationed by 38th Division. - 68th Brigade	
			PROVEN. - 114th Inf Brigade supplies conveyed by Light Railway to BOLLEZEELE, where they are drawn by Horse Transport.	
	"6	—	Weather fine. 192 Coy., moved from PROVEN to BUSSEBOOM, G15 b 1-7 Sheet 27 Appendix I	
	"7	—	Weather fine. 6a.t. H.T. Lloyd-Davis. Proceeded on leave. Railhead RENINGHELST. 69th & 70th Brigades draw supplies by Horse Transport from RENINGHELST. - Divisional Troops & 68th Inf Brigade attached to 39th Division for rations. - 39th Divisional Troops & 116th Inf Bde. (attached to 23rd Division for supplies) draw by Horse Transport from RENINGHELST.	

Army Form C. 2118.

WAR DIARY
or
INTELLIGENCE SUMMARY.

(Erase heading not required.)

Instructions regarding War Diaries and Intelligence Summaries are contained in F. S. Regs., Part II. and the Staff Manual respectively. Title pages will be prepared in manuscript.

Place	Date	Hour	Summary of Events and Information	Remarks and references to Appendices
ESQUELBECQ	Oct 7th	-	Weather fair	
PROVEN	" 8	-	Train Headquarters move from ESQUELBECQ to No 66 RUE DE LA GARE, PROVEN. Weather fine.	
	- 9	-	2/Lt. P.H. LEYCESTER reported to D.D. of S. & T. II Army. reversion to temporary rank. Transport 4 G.S. wagons for Divisional work. Weather wet.	
	-10	-	Headquarters & No 1 Coy Train moved to BUSSEBOOM G.16.c.5.5. Transport 13 G.S. wagons for Divisional work. Weather wet.	Appendix II
	-11	-	Headquarters Train moved to G.16.C.6.2. Two hors. of H.D. horses attached to 3rd R.W. Surrey Labour Coy., two hors. to 28th R.W. Surrey Labour Coy. & two hors. to 1st Hants Labour Coy. Transport 18 G.S. wagons for Divisional work	

T2134. Wt. W708—776. 500000. 4/15. Sir J. C. & S.

Army Form C. 2118.

WAR DIARY
or
INTELLIGENCE SUMMARY.
(Erase heading not required.)

Place	Date	Hour	Summary of Events and Information	Remarks and references to Appendices
BUSSEBOOM April 1st	-	-	Divisional troops draw supplies from RENINGHELST by Horse Transport. Weather wet.	
"	12th	-	Transport 18 G.S. wagons for Divisional work. Weather fine.	
"	13th	-	Lt. SAVAGE, 10th North'd Fusiliers, attached to Train for Instruction. Capt Fyldes to Headquarters 103rd Bde. R.F.A. Transport 19 G.S. wagons for Divisional work. 191 Coy. moved from BOLLEZEELE to PROVEN. Weather fine.	Appendix II
"	14th	-	All baggage wagons sent to Units of 69th & 70th Brigades for relief. Weather wet.	Appendix II
"	15th	-	191 Coy. moved from PROVEN to BUSSEBOOM G.9.c.6.6. Transport 20 G.S. wagons for Divisional work. Weather wet.	Appendix III
"	16th	-	68th Brigade draw supplies by Horse Transport from RENINGHELST.	

Army Form C. 2118.

WAR DIARY
or
INTELLIGENCE SUMMARY.
(Erase heading not required.)

Place	Date	Hour	Summary of Events and Information	Remarks and references to Appendices
Busseboom	April 16th	—	116th Bde Brigade rationed by 39th Division. Transport 18 G.S. wagons for Divisional work. Divisional Gas Officer inspected 190 & 193 Companies. Weather wet.	
"	17	—	Transport 24 G.S. wagons for Divisional work. Weather wet.	
"	18	—	Transport 23 G.S. wagons for Divisional work. Capt. H.T. LLOYD-DAVIS returned from leave. Weather wet.	
"	19	—	Transport 31 G.S. wagons for Divisional work. Weather fine.	
"	20	—	Transport 31 G.S. wagons for Divisional work. Weather fine.	
"	21	—	Transport 29 G.S. wagons for Divisional work. Weather fair.	
"	22	—	2/Lt SAVAGE, 10th North'd Fusiliers, reported to HQrs R.F.A. to be attached for instruction.	

WAR DIARY
or
INTELLIGENCE SUMMARY.
(Erase heading not required.)

Army Form C. 2118.

Place	Date	Hour	Summary of Events and Information	Remarks and references to Appendices
BusseBoom	22 April	-	Cont.^d Church of England Service at 192 Coy. A.S.C. For Corporal Service at 193 Coy A.S.C. Transport 13 G.S. wagons for Divisional work. All baggage wagons sent to units of 69th & 70th Bdes. for relief. Weather fine	Appendices
	23 April		Transport 30 G.S. wagons for Divisional work. Lt. C.P. CADDELL reported to S.M.T.O. Xth Corps ABEELE ref^{ce}. transfer to M.T. Weather fair.	Authority 23rd Div. M.A. 4/335/7/24/4/16 transferring as Adjutant 1st Cavalry Div. A.S.C.
	24	-	Transport 25 G.S. wagons for Divisional work. T/Lieut. BROWN W.H. reported for duty from Base Horse Transport Depot & is posted to 193 Coy. for duty. Weather fine.	Authority 23rd Div. M9/339/372/4/4/16
	25	-	Transport 28 G.S. wagons for Divisional work. Weather fine.	
	26	-	Transport 18 G.S. wagons for Divisional work.	

Army Form C. 2118.

WAR DIARY
or
INTELLIGENCE SUMMARY.
(Erase heading not required.)

Place	Date	Hour	Summary of Events and Information	Remarks and references to Appendices
BUSSEBOOM	26 April	-	Weather fine.	
	27	-	Lt. E.H. MITCHELL proceeded on leave. Transport 31 G.S. wagons for Divisional work. Weather fine.	
	28	-	Transport 22 G.S. wagons for Divisional work. Weather fine.	
	29	-	C. of E. Service at 192 Coy A.S.C. Transport 15 G.S. wagons for Divisional work. All baggage wagons sent to units of 69th Brigade Appendix Y1. 192 Coy. moved to STEENVOORDE AREA, K.32.a. Weather fine.	
	30	-	191 Coy ASC move to STEENVOORDE AREA. K.34.c.6.8. All baggage wagons sent to Units of 68th Brigade for move Appendix Y1. Weather fine.	
	1-5-17			

A. Nodden Lt Col
O.C. 23rd DIVISIONAL TRAIN A.S.C

SECRET.   APPENDIX I   COPY NO: 17

23rd DIVISION OPERATION ORDER NO: 102.

Reference: Sheet 28, Scale 1/40,000.

1. The Division returns to the command of the X Corps forthwith but will be prepared to be withdrawn into Army Reserve at 48 hours notice.

2. The Division will take over the front from 47th and 39th Divisions from trench I.34.8. (HENRY STREET inclusive) to trench I.30.9. (ST. PETERS STREET inclusive).

3. The Southern Boundary will be HENRY STREET - GRAND FLEET STREET I.28.central - Junction of Squares I.27. and I.22. - thence along VERBRANDEN ROAD and YPRES - MENIN Railway to I.20.central - I.19. central - I.18.d.0.0.
   The Northern Boundary will be ST. PETERS STREET - ZILLEBEKE STREET - The PROMENADE - SHRAPNEL CORNER - I.13.c.0.6.

4. The dug-outs in ZILLEBEKE BUND and necessary accommodation in YPRES are placed at the disposal of the division.
   The 39th Division will have the right to use The PROMENADE and ZILLEBEKE STREET.

5. The 70th Infantry Brigade will take over that portion of the new front, now held by 39th Division, on night 6/7 and the remainder of the divisional front, at present held by 47th Division, on the night of 8/9th April.
   Details of relief will be settled with G.Os.C. Brigades concerned.

6. The division will move into its new area in accordance with the attached March Table.
   Columns will consist of units not larger than a Battalion. A distance of half a mile will be kept between battalions.
   The 70th Infantry Brigade will come under the orders of 39th Division from 6 p.m. 5th April.
   The 68th Infantry Brigade will move to BOLLEZEELE Area on 4th and 5th under separate orders.

7. Separate orders will be issued for the Artillery Reliefs.

8. The Brigade accommodated in the OUDERDOM Area will be in Corps Reserve.

9. Separate instructions regarding supply and other administrative details will be issued.

10. Divisional Headquarters will be established at BUSSEBOOM (G.16.c) by 6 a.m. on 9th April at which hour the G.O.C. will assume command of the divisional front.

11. ACKNOWLEDGE.

4th April, 1917.
Issued at 8-45 a.m.

C. Evans.
Lieut-Colonel,
General Staff.

Copies to :-

No.		No.	
1	R.A.	14	A.D.V.S.
2	R.E.	15	A.P.M.
3	Signals.	16	Camp Commandant.
4-5	68th Inf.Bde.	17	Train.
6-7	69th Inf.Bde.	18	S.S.O.
8-9	70th Inf.Bde.	19	VIII Corps.
10	9th S.Staffs.	20	X Corps.
11	A.&Q.	21	39th Division.
12	A.D.M.S.	22	47th Division.
13	D.A.D.O.S.	23	File.
27	104 M.G.Coy.	24-25	Diary.

MARCH TABLE.

DATE.	UNIT.	FROM.	TO.	REMARKS.
4th.	102nd Field Coy., R.E.	LEDRINGHEM.	S. of WATOU.	March independently.
	194 M.G. Company.	ZEGGERS CAPPEL.	(K.17.b.3.6. (K.17.b.2.1.	ditto.
5th.	70th Infantry Brigade. 194 Machine Gun Coy. 69th Field Ambulance.	HOUTKERQUE Area. Bde.H.Q. HOUTKERQUE.	OUDERDOM Area. Bde.H.Q. POPERINGHE.	Under orders of G.O.C. 70th Bde. Route via SOUTHERN SWITCH and OUDERDOM ROAD. To reach ABEELE - POPERINGHE Railway by 12 noon.
	102nd Field Coy., R.E.	S. of WATOU.	KENORA CAMP. M.3.central.	Under orders of C.R.E. by above route. To clear ABEELE - POPERINGHE Railway by 12 noon.
6th.	126th Field Coy., R.E. 101st Field Coy., R.E.	HOUTKERQUE Area	KENORA CAMP.) M.3.central.) R.E. Dump.)	Under orders of C.R.E.
~~7th.~~ 6th	69th Infantry Brigade. (less Bn. in L Camp). 9th South Staffords.	JANSTER BIEZEN Area. H.Q. POPERINGHE. ZEGGERS CAPPEL.	OUDERDOM Area. H.Q. POPERINGHE. Y Camp.	Under orders of G.O.C. 69th Bde. Under orders of O.C. Battalion.
8th.	9th South Staffords.	Y Camp.	Inf.Bks., Y PRES.	ditto.
9th.	Bn. in L Camp.	L Camp.	WINNIPEG CAMP.	ditto.

Appendix II

SECRET.   23rd Divn.No.S.G.330/6.

Continuation of 23rd Division Order No.102 dated 4th April, 1917.

(1). The 23rd Divisional Artillery will relieve three 18-pdr. batteries less 1 section and one battery 4.5" Howitzers of the Right Group of the 39th Division on the nights 8th/9th and 9th/10th April, and the Left Group of the 47th Division on the nights 10th/11th and 11th/12th April.

Headquarters of the Right Group will be temporarily at ~~LILLE GATE~~. I 14 a 9.8.

Headquarters of the Left Group will be temporarily at ~~I.14.a.9.8.~~ LILLE GATE.

(2). The 23rd Division will be supplied by "B" Echelon of the D.A.C. which will relieve "B" Echelon 39th D.A.C. in its present billets on 9th April.

"B" Echelon 39th D.A.C. will be withdrawn to the back area and temporarily attached to "A" Echelon 23rd D.A.C.

(3). All details of relief will be arranged direct between C.R.A's concerned, including reliefs of heavy and medium Trench Mortar Batteries.

(4). The G.O.C. 23rd Division will assume command of the artillery covering the Divisional front at 6 a.m. on 9th inst. but Group Commanders will not hand over to their successors until Artillery reliefs are complete.

(5). R.E. reliefs will take place under arrangements to be made by C.R.E's concerned.

On completion of reliefs, the 23rd Division R.E. will be distributed as follows :-

128th Field Company R.E. at KRUISSTRAAT.
(less 2 sections at TILQUES).

102nd Field Company R.E. at BELGIAN CHATEAU.

101st Field Company R.E. at R.E. DUMP. (H.13.d.3.5.)

The Infantry Brigade (69th) in OUDERDOM AREA will be in Divisional Reserve.

(6). The Infantry Brigade (68th) at BOLLEZEELE will be in X Corps reserve and not as stated in para. 9 of 23rd Division Order No.102.

(7). ACKNOWLEDGE.

23rd Division.
6/4/1917.

Lieut-Colonel,
General Staff.

Issued to all recipients of 23rd Division Order No.102.

S E C R E T.   *Appendix III*   COPY NO. 17

23rd DIVISION OPERATION ORDER NO: 103.

Reference: Sheet 28 N.W., Scale 1/20,000.

1. The 68th Infantry Brigade will relieve the 116th Infantry Brigade, 39th Division in the HOOGE SECTOR on the night of the 15th/16th except the Machine Gun Company whose relief will take place on the night 14th/15th.

2. The 68th Infantry Brigade (less transport) will move by train on 13th and 14th to POPERINGHE in accordance with telegraphic orders already issued and will relieve the 117th Infantry Brigade, 39th Division in Divisional Reserve.
   Accommodation will be allotted in the BRANDHOEK Area by A.A.&.Q.M.G., 23rd Division.

3. Details of reliefs of 116th Infantry Brigade will be arranged direct between G.Os.C. Brigades concerned.
   Arrangements must be made for Advance Parties of 68th Infantry Brigade to go round their battalion fronts 24 hours before they are taken over.

4. The following will be taken over :-
   (a). All trench, camp and village stores which are normally handed over on relief.
   (b). R.E. material in excess of units establishment.
   (c). Maps, plans, photos and summary of information regarding the front.
   (d). Statement of work under construction or proposed.

5. A working party of 2 officers and 75 other ranks will relieve a similar party 39th Division now with 2nd Canadian Tunnelling Company.

6. C.R.E. will arrange direct with C.R.E. 39th Division in regard to taking over work in hand and proposed.

7. Orders regarding the relief of the Artillery 39th Division will be issued later.

8. A.A.&.Q.M.G. will issue orders regarding administrative arrangements.

9. Completion of relief will be wired in code to D.H.Q.

10. ACKNOWLEDGE.

12th April, 1917.
   Issued at 8-30 p.m.

(signed)
Lieutenant-Colonel,
General Staff.

Copies to :-
Nos.		Nos.	
1	R.A.	15	A.P.M.
2	R.E.	16	Camp Commandant.
3	Signals.	17	Train.
4-5	68th Inf.Bde.	18	S.S.O.
6-7	69th Inf.Bde.	19	VIII Corps.
8-9	70th Inf.Bde.	20-21	X Corps.
10	9/S.Staffs.	22	39th Division.
11	A & Q.	23	47th Division.
12	A.D.M.S.	24	File.
13	D.A.D.O.S.	25-26	Diary.
14	A.D.V.S.	27	17th Supply Column.
		No. 28	194 M.G.Company.
		29	VIII Corps

Appendix IV

SECRET.   COPY NO: 17

23rd DIVISION OPERATION ORDER NO: 104.

Reference: Sheet 28 N.W., Scale 1/20,000.

1. The 69th Infantry Brigade will relieve the 70th Infantry Brigade in the trenches on night 14th/15th April.
   After relief the 70th Infantry Brigade will withdraw into the camps vacated by the 69th Infantry Brigade and will be in Divisional Reserve.

2. The 69th Machine Gun Company and Trench Mortar Battery will relieve the 70th Machine Gun Company and Trench Mortar Battery respectively on night 15th/16th instant.

3. All details of relief will be arranged direct between Brigadiers concerned.

4. Personnel of three battalions of the 70th Infantry Brigade and one battalion of the 69th Infantry Brigade will travel by train.
   Remaining personnel and transport will march via road I.13.b.0.7 - KRUISSTRAAT - H.16.d.1.1.

5. No trench will be vacated by the 70th Infantry Brigade until relieved by a similar garrison of the 69th Infantry Brigade.

6. All trench stores, photographs, etc. will be handed over and receipts taken.

7. The detachment of the 69th Infantry Brigade finding R.E. working parties which is accommodated in ZILLEBEKE BUND will rejoin its Brigade on 15th instant under orders from 69th Infantry Brigade.

8. Completion of relief and the passing of command of the Sector to G.O.C. 69th Infantry Brigade will be wired in code to Divisional Headquarters.

9. ACKNOWLEDGE.

                                                Charles
12th April, 1917.   Lieut-Colonel,
   Issued at 8.30 p.m.   General Staff.

Copies to :-

Nos.			Nos.		
1	R.A.		15	A.P.M.	
2	R.E.		16	Camp Commandant.	
3	Signals.		17	Train.	
4-5	68th Inf.Bde.		18	S.S.O.	
6-7	69th Inf.Bde.		19-20	X Corps.	
8-9	70th Inf.Bde.		21	39th Division.	
10	9/S.Staffs.		22	47th Division.	
11	A & Q.		23	File.	
12	A.D.M.S.		24-25	Diary.	
13	D.A.D.O.S.		26	17th Supply Column.	
14	A.D.V.S.		27	194 M.G.Company.	

SECRET.   COPY NO: 17

23rd DIVISION OPERATION ORDER NO: 105.

Reference: Sheet 28 N.W., Scale 1/20,000.

1. The 70th Infantry Brigade will relieve the 69th Infantry Brigade in the HILL 60 Sector on night ~~23rd/24th instant.~~ 22/23rd inst
   The 69th Infantry Brigade after relief will withdraw into Divisional Reserve and will take over the camp vacated by the 70th Infantry Brigade.

2. All details of relief will be arranged direct between Brigadiers concerned.

3. On relief, all working parties found by the Brigade in the Right Sector will be taken over by the Brigade in Reserve.
   Similarly all parties found by the Brigade in Reserve (including the party of 300 in RAILWAY DUG-OUTS) will be taken over by the Brigade in the Right Sector.
   Reliefs will be so arranged that there will be no cessation of work.

4. All train arrangements will be arranged between Brigades concerned and 23rd Division "Q".
   All troops not proceeding by train, and all transport will march via Road I.13.b.0.7. - KRUISSTRAAT - H.16.d.1.1.

5. The usual march precautions will be observed.

6. Completion of relief and the passing of command of the Sector will be wired in code to Divisional Headquarters.

7. Machine-gun Companies and Trench Mortar Batteries will carry out their reliefs on the night ~~24th/25th~~ 23rd/24th April.

8. ACKNOWLEDGE.
   21 April, 1917.
   Issued at 9.30 a.m.
                                                    Evans
                                                    Lieut-Colonel,
                                                    General Staff.

Copies to :-

    Nos. 1   R.A.
         2   R.E.
         3   Signals.   Nos. 15   A.P.M.
         4-5 68th Inf.Bde.   16   Camp Commandant.
         6-7 69th Inf.Bde.   17   Train.
         8-9 70th Inf.Bde.   18   S.S.O.
         10   9/S.Staffs.   19-20   X Corps.
         11   A & Q.   21   47th Division.
         12   A.D.M.S.   22   File.
         13   D.A.D.O.S.   23-24   Diary.
         14   A.D.V.S.   25   17th Supply Column.
                                          26   194 M.G.Company.

"A" Form.
MESSAGES AND SIGNALS.

Army Form C.2121 (in pads of 100).

Sender's Number.	Day of Month.	In reply to Number.	
G.B.398	21		A A A

O.O. No.105 of today AAA

Amend second line of para. 1 to read "22nd/23rd instant" AAA Amend second line of para 7. to read "23rd/24th instant" AAA Addressed all recipients. AAA Acknowledge

From: 23rd Div.
Time: 3.30 p.m.

Lieut-Colonel,
General Staff

Appendix VI

SECRET.   23rd DIVISION OPERATION ORDER NO.107.   COPY NO. 14

Reference. Sheet 27 and 28 1/40,000.

1. The 23rd Division will be relieved by the 19th Division and will go into Army Reserve in the STEENVOORDE Area.

2. The 69th Infantry Brigade will be relieved by the 58th Infantry Brigade in the OUDERDOM Area to-day.

3. The 68th Infantry Brigade will be relieved by the 58th Infantry Brigade in the Left Sector on the night 30th April/1st May. On relief, 68th Infantry Brigade will move to STEENVOORDE Area by train.

4. The 70th Infantry Brigade will be relieved by 57th Infantry Brigade, which will arrive in the OUDERDOM Area on 30th, on the night 1st/2nd May. On relief, 70th Infantry Brigade will move into OUDERDOM Area where it will be in Divisional Reserve.

5. The 70th Infantry Brigade will be replaced in the OUDERDOM Area by 56th Infantry Brigade on 2nd May and will march to the STEENVOORDE Area.

6. The 194th Machine Gun Company will be relieved by a M.G. company of 19th Division on 2nd/3rd May and will march on 3rd May to STEENVOORDE Area.

7. Details of above reliefs will be arranged by G.Os.C. concerned. All trench maps, photos, stores, etc. will be handed over and receipts taken.
Completion of reliefs will be reported to Divisional Headquarters by telegram in code.
Battalion Intelligence Officers and Observers of Battalions in the line will remain with incoming units for 24 hours after the relief has taken place.

8. The relief of the Divisional Artillery will be carried out so as to be complete by 3rd May under arrangements to be made by C.R.AS. concerned.

9. Each Brigade of 19th Division will be accompanied by a Field Company R.E. The details of reliefs will be arranged by C.R.Es. concerned.
The Field Company R.E. relieved on night of 30th April/1st May will move by train with 68th Infantry Brigade. Other companies will move by road.
Attached infantry will remain with their Field Companies.

10. The 9th Bn. South Staffords Regt. will be relieved by the Pioneer Battalion 19th Division on night 1st/2nd May and will move by train to STEENVOORDE Area.

(2).

11.   All working parties and detachments, except the detachments 68th Infantry Brigade at Corps Headquarters and 8 guns 69th Machine Gun Company at ABEELE, will be relieved by incoming brigades.

12.   Reliefs of Field Ambulances will be arranged by A.D.M.S concerned.

13.   Command of the Divisional Front will pass to G.O.C. 19th Division at 10 a.m. on 2nd May.

14.   ACKNOWLEDGE.

29th April, 1917.
 Issued at 4.30 p.m.

Lieut-Colonel,
General Staff.

Copies to :-

Nos.		Nos.	
1	R.A.	13	Camp Commandant.
2	R.E.	14	Train.
3	Signals.	15	S.S.O.
4	68th Inf.Bde.	16 - 17	X Corps.
5	69th Inf.Bde.	18	19th Division.
6	70th Inf.Bde.	19	47th Division.
7	9/S.Staffs.	20	55th Division.
8	A & Q.	21	File.
9	A.D.M.S.	22 - 23	Diary.
10	D.A.D.O.S.	24	17th Supply Column.
11	A.D.V.S.	25	194 M.G. Company.
12	A.P.M.		

Confidential.

D.A.G.
 G.H.Q.

Herewith copy of April War Diary, as requested in your letter d/23-6-17, please.

July 10th 1917.   [signature] Acting Lt. Adjt.
for O.C. 23rd Divisional Train A.S.C.

23

23 Div. Train
Vol 20

WAR DIARY
or
INTELLIGENCE SUMMARY.
Army Form C. 2118.

(Erase heading not required.)

Instructions regarding War Diaries and Intelligence Summaries are contained in F.S. Regs., Part II. and the Staff Manual respectively. Title pages will be prepared in manuscript.

Place	Date	Hour	Summary of Events and Information	Remarks and references to Appendices
Esquelbecq.	1st April	—	Marched PROVEN. Artillery and Infantry Billeting – 68th Brigade by motor transport from PROVEN. – 70th Brigade (including D.A.C. and D.I.S. Troops) entrained to Hopoutre. HERZEELE here two cars came by road without baggage wagons. (2 Coys H.Q. drew full day's rations from PROVEN. Supply Column) attached to 23rd Divisional train billets occupied by 68th Bde for 2 Coys to 39th Divisional train on return by motor trans. at 68th Brigade motors to 38th Divisional Artillery. Weather Wet.	
	2nd	—	Weather Wet.	
	3rd	—	Capt Zylstra, 11th Sherwood Foresters, attached to the train for instruction and inspected to 100 horses 26. Weather fine.	
	4th	—	103 Coy moved from PROVEN to Busseboom G15.c.10.a.3 sheet 28 and took over supply for No 4 Coy 39th Divisional train.	
	5th	—	104 Coy moved from PROVEN (F14.c.v.6) to BOLLEZEELE (H2s.c.7.2) 70th Brigade supplies drawn by horse transport from PROVEN. – 114th N Brigade	

WAR DIARY
or
INTELLIGENCE SUMMARY.
(Erase heading not required.)

Army Form C. 2118.

Place	Date	Hour	Summary of Events and Information	Remarks and references to Appendices
ESQUELBECQ	April 5th	—	rationed by 30th Division — 68th Brigade supplies conveyed by light Railway to BOLLEZEELE where they are drawn by Horse transport. Weather fine.	
	6	—	102 boys reported from PROVEN to BUSSE=BOOM, G.15.d.1.7 Sheet 27. Weather fine.	Appendix I
	7		Capt. A.J. Lloyd-Davies proceeded on leave. Railhead RENINGHELST. 60th and 70th Brigades drew supplies by Horse transport from RENINGHELST. Divisional troops and 68th Inf. Brigade attached to 30th Division for rations. 30th Divisional stores and 115th Inf. Brigade (attached to 23rd Division for supplies) draw by Horse transport from RENINGHELST. Weather fair.	
PROVEN	"8th"		Division Headquarters move from ESQUELBECQ to No. 66 RUE DE LA GARE PROVEN. Weather fine.	
	9	2 P.M	P.W. LEYCESTER reported to D.D. of S.& T. II Army reference excursion to temporary ranks.	

Army Form C. 2118.

WAR DIARY
or
INTELLIGENCE SUMMARY.
(Erase heading not required.)

Instructions regarding War Diaries and Intelligence Summaries are contained in F. S. Regs., Part II. and the Staff Manual respectively. Title pages will be prepared in manuscript.

Place	Date	Hour	Summary of Events and Information	Remarks and references to Appendices
PROVEN April	9th	—	Transport 4 L.L wagons for Divisional Work. Weather wet	
"	10th	—	Headquarters & No 1 horse train moved to BUSSEBOOM G 16 c 5.5. Transport 13 L.L wagons for Divisional work. Weather wet	Appendix II
"	11	—	Headquarters train moved to G 16 c 6.2. Two teams of R.H.D horses attached to 3rd R.W Surrey Labour Bn; two teams to 28 R.W Surrey & army two and two teams to 1st Hants Labourers. Transport 12 L.L wagons for Divisional Work. Divisional output supplies drawn by Horse transport from RENINGHELST. Weather wet	
"	12	—	Transport 118 L.L wagons for Divisional Work. Weather fine	
"	13	—	2nd Lt Colvin, 10th South Lancashire, attached to train for instruction. Left in order to Headquarters 103 Bde R.F.A. Transport 10 L.L wagons for Divisional work	

T2134. Wt. W708—776. 500000. 4/16. Sir J. C. & S.

Army Form C. 2118.

WAR DIARY
or
INTELLIGENCE SUMMARY.
(Erase heading not required.)

Instructions regarding War Diaries and Intelligence Summaries are contained in F. S. Regs., Part II. and the Staff Manual respectively. Title pages will be prepared in manuscript.

Place	Date	Hour	Summary of Events and Information	Remarks and references to Appendices
BUSSEBOOM	April 13	—	Coy moved from BOLLEZEELE to PROVEN. Weather fine	Appendix VII
	14	—	All baggage wagons sent to units of 69th and 70th Brigade for relief. Weather wet	Appendix VI
	15	—	Coy moved from PROVEN to BUSSEBOOM G.9.c.6.6. 1 wagon 20 L.S wagons for Divisional work. Weather wet	Appendix VII
	16	—	62nd Brigade drew supplies by their transport from RENINGHELST. 116th Brigade rationed by 39th Division. 18 N.S wagons, 1 wagons for Divisional work. Divisional Gas Officer inspected 190 and 193 companies. Weather wet	
	17	—	Transport 24 L.S wagons for Divisional work. Weather wet	
	18	—	Transport 23 L.S wagons for Divisional work. Capt. H T LLOYD-DAVIES returned from leave	

WAR DIARY
or
INTELLIGENCE SUMMARY.
(Erase heading not required.)

Army Form C. 2118.

Place	Date	Hour	Summary of Events and Information	Remarks and references to Appendices
BUSSEBOOM April 18th			Weather wet	
	19	-	Transport 31 C. Dragoons for Divisional work	
			Weather fine	
	20	-	Transport 31 C.S. wagons for Divisional work	
			Weather fine	
	21	-	Transport 29 C. Dragoons for Divisional work	
			Weather fair	
	22	-	2nd Lt SAVAGE 10th hussars received orders to Hd Qrs R.F.A. to be attached for instructions	
			Church of England Service at 1.92 on F.A.P.	
			Rgn. Conformist Service at 193 on F.A.P	
			Transport 13 C. Dragoons for Divisional work. All Baggage wagons sent to units of 69th and 70th Bdes for relief	Appendix V
			Weather fine	
	23rd	-	Transport 30 C. Dragoons for Divisional work	
			2nd Lt Cantrell P. attached to S.M.T.O. 1st bsps. ABEELE reference transfer to M.T.	

Army Form C. 2118.

WAR DIARY
or
INTELLIGENCE SUMMARY.

(Erase heading not required.)

Instructions regarding War Diaries and Intelligence Summaries are contained in F. S. Regs., Part II. and the Staff Manual respectively. Title pages will be prepared in manuscript.

Place	Date	Hour	Summary of Events and Information	Remarks and references to Appendices
BUSSEBOOM April	23	—	Weather fair	
		—	2nd Lt. M. LLEYCESTER transferred to 1st Cavalry Divn. A.S.C. for duty as adjutant. Authority 23-0-21 in No.A/32/372 of 12/4/12	
	24	—	Transport 25 G.S. wagons for Divisional Work	Authority 23-0 in No. A/32/37 of 24/4/17
		—	Lieut BROWN W.H. reported for duty from Base Horse Transport Depot, and reported to 192 Coy for duty	
	25	"	Weather fine	
		"	Transport 28 G.S. wagons for Divisional work	
	26	"	Weather fine	
		"	Transport 18 G.S. wagons for Divisional work	
	27	"	Weather fine	
		"	Lt. E.H. MITCHELL proceeded on leave	
		"	Transport 31 G.S. wagons for Divisional work	
	28	"	Weather fine	
		"	Transport 32 G.S. wagons for Divisional work	
	29	"	Weather fine	
		"	192 Coy E. arrived at 192 Coy A.S.C.	
		"	Transport 15 G.S. wagons for Divisional work	

WAR DIARY
or
INTELLIGENCE SUMMARY.

(Erase heading not required.)

Army Form C. 2118.

Place	Date	Hour	Summary of Events and Information	Remarks and references to Appendices
BUSSEBOOM	April 29	—	All baggage wagons to Units of 69th Brigade for move. 1.92 tow moved to STEENVOORDE Area K.32.a. Weather fine.	Appendix II
		30	19th boy H.Q. to move to STEENVOORDE area K.34.c.6.8. All baggage wagons sent to Units of 68th Brigade for move. Weather fine.	Appendix VI

M Montgomery Major

OOM G. 23rd DIVISIONAL TRAIN A.S.C.

Army Form C. 2118.

WAR DIARY
or
INTELLIGENCE SUMMARY.
(Erase heading not required.)

23 Div Train
Vol 21

Place	Date	Hour	Summary of Events and Information	Remarks and references to Appendices
	1917			
BUSSEBOOM	May 1st	-	Transport 4 F.S. wagons for Divisional pack.	
STEENVOORDE	2	-	Headquarters train moved to No 2 Rue des Cerdres, Steenvoorde.	
			193 Coy. A.S.C. moved to Boeschepe area. L19a.2d Sheet 2 Kuun (ABEELE).	
			T. Lieut. W. H. Brown admitted to 23rd Divl. Rest Station	
			Transport 2 F.S. wagons for Divisional pack	
	3	-	Railhead / WIPPEN HOEK.	
			Divisional troops draw supplies by lorry from Railhead & dump at Reddy Road J27/5.S.Sheet 27 (near RMELE). 68th, 69th, 70th Brigades draw supplies by horse transport from Railhead.	
			190 Coy. A.S.C. moved from Bussebooom, G16.c.55.Sheet 27 to P26.63 Sheet 27 (near Cassel).	
			T 3/Lt C. Bridges joined from B.H.T.D. for duty	Authority 23rd Divn. A331/36? 27/36-4-17
			T/C. P. Caddell is to be posted to 190 Coy A.S.C	Authority 23rd Divn. A331/36? 27/36-4-17
	4	-	T/C. P. Caddell proceeded to report to Second Army M.T.	

WAR DIARY or INTELLIGENCE SUMMARY

Army Form C. 2118.

Place	Date	Hour	Summary of Events and Information	Remarks and references to Appendices
STEENVOORDE	1917 May 4 (Cont'd)		School of Instruction & no struck off the strength on train.	Authority 23rd Division 9338/363 30-4-17
	" 5	-	Lt. R.A.S. ELLIOT (attached to Second Army Purchase Board) proceeded on leave. G.O.C. 23rd Division inspected 190, 191 & 193 Companies. 192 Coy. moved from STEENVOORDE K32.Z.59 Sheet 27 to CONNAUGHT LINES, Sheet 27, L.34.C.1.5 (near WIPPENHOEK.)	
	" 8	-	Lt. E.H. MITCHELL returned from leave.	
	" 9	-	191 Coy. Moved from STEENVOORDE K34.C.6.8 Sheet 27 Appendix I to BUSSEBOOM G.16.a.0.4 Sheet 28. Lt. L.C. OSBORNE admitted to 2nd Canadian C.C.S. Pte 302745 3 Dr. H. WALKER 193 Coy. A.S.C. tried by F.G.C.M. "when on active service using violence to his superior officer", Sentenced to 12 Months Imprisonment with Hard Labour.	
	" 10	-	Lt. L.C. OSBORNE evacuated from No 2 Canadian C.C.S. to Base	

WAR DIARY
or
INTELLIGENCE SUMMARY.
(Erase heading not required.)

Army Form C. 2118.

Place	Date	Hour	Summary of Events and Information	Remarks and references to Appendices
STEENVOORDE	1917 May 11	—	193 Coy A.S.C moved from L.19.a.2.4 (near ABEELE) Sheet 27 (near ABEELE) to G.9.c.6.6 Sheet 28 (near POPERINGHE). 190 Coy A.S.C. moved from P.2.c.6.3 Sheet 27 (near Abeele) CASSEL to BUSSEBOOM G.16.c.5.5. Sheet 28. Railhead RENINGHELST.	Sheet 1. Sheet 1.
BUSSEBOOM	" 12	—	Headquarters Train moved from N°2 RUE DES CENDRES, Sheet 1 STEENVOORDE to G.16.C.6.2 Sheet 28 BUSSEBOOM. 192 Coy. A.S.C. moved from CONNAUGHT LINES, L.34-15 Sheet 27 (near WIPPENHOEK) to BOESCHEPE, R.11.a.5.6 Sheet 27. 190 Coy A.S.C. moved from BUSSEBOOM G.16.c.5.5 Sheet 28 to G.26.d.0.2 Sheet 28 (near HOOGRAAF). 191 Coy A.S.C. moved from BUSSEBOOM G.16.a.0.4 Sheet 28 to G.27.c.0.3 Sheet 28 (POPERINGHE – RENINGHELST Rd.). All Companies of Train draw supplies by M.T. transport from RENINGHELST.	

WAR DIARY or INTELLIGENCE SUMMARY.

Army Form C. 2118.

Place	Date	Hour	Summary of Events and Information	Remarks and references to Appendices
BUSSEBOOM	1917 May 13	—	Five G.S. wagons, Com Plete turnouts from 1st Canadian Reserve Park, attached to train & posted to 191 Coy R.E.	
	14	—	Transport 10 G.S. Wagons for Divisional work. 192 Coy A.S.C. moved from R.11 a 56 Sheet 27 (BUSSCHER/Appendix II G.H.Q. Sheet 28 (POPERINGHE-RENINGHELST ROAD).	Appendix II
	15	—	Transport 29 G.S. Wagons for Divisional work. 193 Coy A.S.C. moved from G.9.C.6 Sheet 28 (near Appendix II POPERINGHE) to L.19.L.2.7 Sheet 27 (near ABEELE)	Appendix II
	16	—	Transport 30 G.S. wagons for Divisional work. Lt R.A.S. Elliot (attached to Second Army Purchase Board) returned from leave.	
	17	—	Transport 28 G.S. Wagons for Divisional work.	
	18	—	Transport 33 G.S. wagons for Divisional work.	
	19	—	Transport 22 G.S. wagons for Divisional work.	
	20	—	Transport 29 G.S. wagons for Divisional work. Capt A.C. BERRYMAN proceeded on leave	

Army Form C. 2118.

WAR DIARY
or
INTELLIGENCE SUMMARY.
(Erase heading not required.)

Instructions regarding War Diaries and Intelligence Summaries are contained in F. S. Regs., Part II. and the Staff Manual respectively. Title pages will be prepared in manuscript.

Place	Date	Hour	Summary of Events and Information	Remarks and references to Appendices
BUSSEBOOM	1917 May 20	-	Four men proceeded on leave. Transport 46 G.S. wagons for Divisional work.	
	" 21	-	Two O.R. proceeded on leave. Transport 39 G.S. wagons for Divisional work.	
	" 22	-	Transport 34 G.S. wagons for Divisional work.	
	" 23	-	16426 E.A. SOUTHEE proceeded on leave. Have allotment to the chain two men daily. Transport 21 G.S. wagons for Divisional work. 193 Coy. A.S.C. moved from L.19.c.2.7 Sheet 27 (Near Abeele II Road) to G.15.C.7.1 Sheet 28 (POPERINGHE-RENINGHELST Road)	
	" 24	-	Transport 30 G.S. wagons for Divisional work. Seventy five B.1 Men joined from 23rd Div. Employment Coy. in duty as loaders for Supply wagons. Headquarters train moved from BUSSEBOOM G.16.C.6.2 Sheet 28 to G.15.D.7.4 Sheet 28 (Near BUSSEBOOM)	
	" 25	-		

WAR DIARY
or
INTELLIGENCE SUMMARY.
(Erase heading not required.)

Army Form C. 2118.

Place	Date	Hour	Summary of Events and Information	Remarks and references to Appendices
Bussèboom	1917. May 25th	—	Companies commenced having all L.D Horses & Mules for Pack work	
			Transport 33 G.S. wagons for Divisional work	
	"26	—	All loaders of Infantry Brigades. Iron loader lorries for R.J.A. having been relieved by B1. Amn. from 23rd Divs. Employment Coy are returned to their units	
			Capt. R.J. HADBEN admitted to 23rd Divl. Rest Station	
			192 Coy relieved the 2nd Bucket to Railhead. Companies commenced fitting water carriers on all first line limbers, also twelve (12) extra G.S. wagon of the above for water on each G.S. wagon for Divisional work	
			Transport 33 G.S. wagons for Divisional work	
			191 Coy A.S.C. returned by Second Bucket to Railhead	
	"27	—	Transport 26 G.S. wagons for Divisional work	
	"28	—	190 & 193 Coys A.S.C. returned by Second Bucket to Railhead	

WAR DIARY
or
INTELLIGENCE SUMMARY.

Army Form C. 2118.

Place	Date	Hour	Summary of Events and Information	Remarks and references to Appendices
BUSSEBOOM	1917 May 28	—	Transport 30 G.S. wagons for Divisional work	
	29	—	Transport 28 G.S. wagons for Divisional work	
	30	—	Transport 20 G.S. wagons for Divisional work	
	31	—	Capt. A.E. Berryman returned from leave. Transport 12 G.S. wagons for Divisional work	

1st June 1917

A. Noller
O.C. G. 23rd DIVISIONAL TRAIN A.S.C.

Appendix I (a)

SECRET.　　　　　　　　　　　　　　　　　　　　　　　　　COPY NO. 14

23RD DIVISION OPERATION ORDER NO.108.

Reference: Sheet 28 N.W. 1/20,000.

1. The 23rd Division will relieve the 19th Division in the Left Divisional Area of the X Corps in accordance with the attached March Table.

2. The 69th Infantry Brigade will continue to work as at present and will rejoin the Division under orders which will be issued later.

3. The C.R.E. will arrange direct with C.R.E. 19th Division with regard to the relief of the Field Companies and Pioneers. Relief to take place by the morning of 11th instant.

4. Artillery reliefs will be carried out on nights 10th/11th and 11th/12th instant.
   All arrangements will be made between C.R.As. concerned.

5. R.A.M.C. reliefs will be carried out under arrangements to be made between A.D.M.S's concerned.

6. Defence Schemes, Trench Stores, aeroplane photos, maps and observers telescopes and compasses will be taken over from outgoing units, carefully checked and a receipt given.

7. Command of the Divisional Sector will pass to G.O.C. 23rd Division at 10 a.m. on 12th instant at which time Divisional Headquarters will open at BUSSEBOOM.

8. ACKNOWLEDGE.

　　　　　　　　　　　　　　　　　　　　　　　　　　　　Lieut-Colonel,
8th May, 1917.　　　　　　　　　　　　　　　　　　　　　General Staff.
Issued at 4-30 p.m.

Copies to :-

Nos.			Nos.		
1	R.A.		13	Camp Commandant.	
2	R.E.		14	Train.	
3	Signals.		15	S.S.O.	
4	68th Inf. Bde.		16-17	X Corps.	
5	69th Inf. Bde.		18	19th Division.	
6	70th Inf. Bde.		19	47th Division.	
7	9th S. Staffs.		20	55th Division.	
8	A & Q.		21	File.	
9	A.D.M.S.		22-23	Diary.	
10	D.A.D.O.S.		24	17th Supply Col.	
11	A.D.V.S.		25	194 M.G. Company.	
12	A.P.M.				

TABLE OF RELIEF
OF 19th DIVISION BY 23rd DIVISION.

Date.	Unit.	From.	To.	Relieving.	Route.	Remarks.
9th.	68th Brigade Group.	STEENVOORDE Area.	OUDERDOM Area.	56th Bde. Group.	ABEELE and HOPOUTRE Siding.	
9th.	194th M.G.Coy.	--do--	Right Sector.	57th M.G.Coy.	--do--	To march under orders of G.O.C.68th Bde.
10th.	9th S.Staffs.R. (less 2 Coys).	--do--	YPRES.	Pioneer Bn. 19th Div.		By train or lorry.
10/11th.	68th Inf. Bde. (less M.G.Coy & T.M.Batty).	OUDERDOM.	Right Sector.	57th Inf. Bde.		
11th.	70th Bde.Group. 69th M.G.Coy 69th T.M.Batty.	(STEENVOORDE (Area.	(OUDERDOM (Area.		ABEELE and HOPOUTRE Siding.	To march under orders of G.O.C.70th Bde.
11/12th.	68th M.G.Coy. & T.M.Batty.	OUDERDOM.	Right Sector.			
12/13th.	70th Inf. Bde.	OUDERDOM Area.	Left Sector.	58th Inf. Bde.		

SECRET.   Appendix II (a)   COPY NO. 14

23RD DIVISION OPERATION ORDER NO. 109.

Reference: Sheet 28 N.W. 1/20,000

1. The 70th Infantry Brigade (less M.G. Company and Observers) will be relieved by a Brigade of 24th Division in the OBSERVATORY RIDGE and HOOGE Sectors on the night of 14th/15th. The M.G. Company and Observers will be relieved on the night of 15th/16th. The dividing line between divisions in the front line will be the junction between trenches I.30.9. and I.24.1., ZILLEBEKE STREET and ST. PETERS STREET belonging to 23rd Division.
ZILLEBEKE BUND will be in the 23rd Divisional Area.

2. The two battalions 69th Infantry Brigade now working at HEKSKEN DUMP will be at the disposal of the Division from 6 p.m. to-day.

3. Moves will take place in accordance with the attached Table. Details of relief will be arranged by Brigades concerned.

4. Artillery reliefs will take place on completion of the Infantry Reliefs under arrangements between C.R.As. concerned. Plans for the preparation of battery positions for the HOOGE CORPS will be handed over.

5. The relief of R.E. and Pioneers will be arranged by C.R.Es. concerned. C.R.E. 23rd Division will hand over the plans for offensive preparations in the HOOGE SECTOR.

6. A.D.M.S. of Divisions will arrange for the relief of Medical Units.

7. The Tunnelled Dug-outs in the YPRES RAMPARTS are placed at the disposal of 23rd Division, except that accommodation in them for 1 Company Pioneers of the 24th Division is to be provided. The remaining accommodation in YPRES will be handed over to 24th Division.

8. The detachment 68th Infantry Brigade at X Corps Headquarters will be relieved by a similar party of 24th Division. Date will be notified later.

9. All maps, aeroplane photos, defence schemes, trench stores, etc. will be handed over by 70th Infantry Brigade and receipts taken.

10. ACKNOWLEDGE.

A.C. Richardson, Capt.
for Lieut-Colonel,
General Staff.

11th May, 1917.
Issued at 8.0 p.m.

Copies to :-

Nos.		Nos.	
1	R.A.	13	Camp Commandant.
2	R.E.	14	Train.
3	Signals.	15	S.S.O.
4	68th Inf. Bde.	16-17	X Corps.
5	69th Inf. Bde.	18	24th Division.
6	70th Inf. Bde.	19	47th Division.
7	9th S. Staffs.	20	55th Division.
8	A & Q.	21	File.
9	A.D.M.S.	22-23	Diary.
10	D.A.D.O.S.	24	17th Supply Column.
11	A.D.V.S.	25	104 M.G. Company.
12	A.P.M.		

Appendix II (b)

TABLE OF MOVEMENTS.

Date.	Unit.	From.	To.	Route.
May.				
13th.	1 Bn. 69th Bde.	HEKSKEN.	Divisional Area.	
13/14th.	1 Bn. 69th Bde.	HEKSKEN.	ZILLEBEKE BUND.	
14th.	1 Coy. Pioneers, 24th Division. 69th Bde. less 2½ Battns. 9th S.Staffords.	BRANDHOEK. Present Camps. Cavalry Bks., YPRES. YPRES.	Tunnelled Dug-outs, YPRES. 23rd Division Area. Tunnelled Dug-outs, YPRES. KRUISSTRAAT.	
	1 Field Coy. R.E.			
14/15th.	Bde. 24th Division. 70th Brigade.	BRANDHOEK. HOOGE Sector.	HOOGE Sector. BRANDHOEK.	
15th.	70th Brigade.	BRANDHOEK.	BOESCHEPE Area.	Via RENINGHELST.
15/16th.	70th M.G.Coy.	HOOGE Sector.	BRANDHOEK.	To BOESCHEPE Area on 16th May

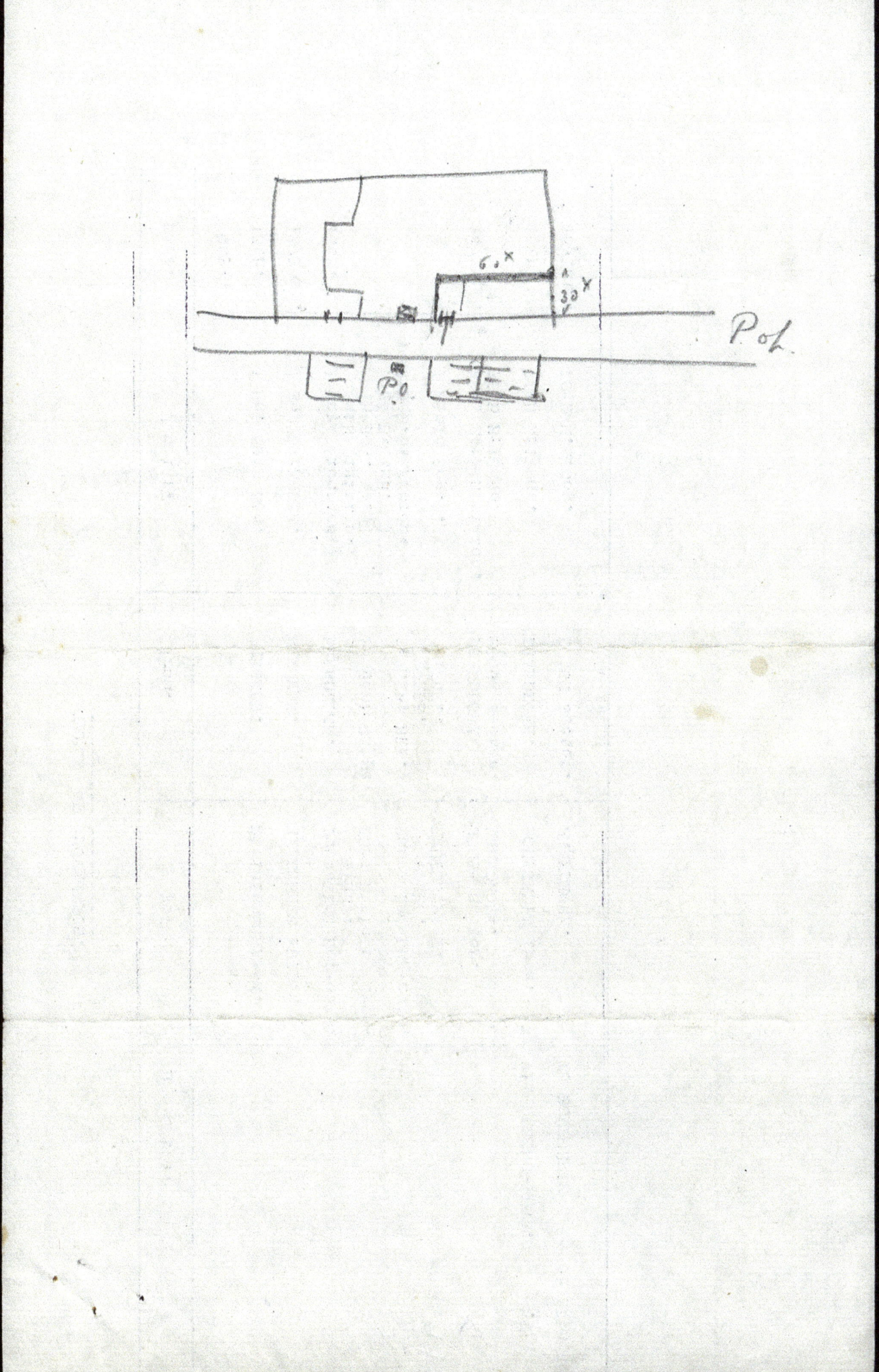

Appendix II (c)

SECRET
&
URGENT.

23rd Division
No. Q.S. 96.

69th Inf Brigade.
O.C. Train.   )
"G".   )   For information.
Area Commandant.   )
47th Division Q.   )

Reference 23rd Div. Operation Order No. 109 dated 12th inst.

<u>13th inst.</u>   The 9th Yorks will move from HEKSKEN to MONTREAL CAMP.   Transport will remain at HEKSKEN.

The 8th Yorks will move from HEKSKEN to ZILLEBEKE BUND.   Transport will move to H.20.a.8.5.

<u>14th inst.</u>   The 69th Bde H.Q. will move to Bde H.Q. Camp at G.22.b.3.4.   Transport will move to G.24.c.6.6. taking over after 4 p.m.

The 10th West Ridings will remain at SCOTTISH LINES with transport as at present.

The 11th West Yorks (less 2 Companies working under C.E. Xth Corps) will move from DEVONSHIRE CAMP to VANCOUVER CAMP.   Transport will move to H.13.d.8.3., taking over after 4 p.m.

Transport of 9th Yorks will move to H.13.d.7.1. taking over after 4 p.m.

69th M.G. Company will take over Transport Lines at G.24.d.2.9. after 4 p.m.

<u>15th inst.</u>   Transport of 10th West Ridings will take over Transport Lines of 68th M.G. Company at G.23.a.7.7.

George Hawes.
Major,
D.A.Q.M.G. 23rd Division.

12th May, 1917.

Appendix II (d)

SECRET   23rd Division
   &   No. Q.S. 97.
URGENT.

```
70th Inf Brigade.  )
"G"                )
O.C. Train.        )   For information.
69th Inf Brigade.  )
Area Commandant.   )
```

Reference 23rd Div. Operation Order No. 109 dated 12th inst.

1. Advanced Parties will proceed to the BOESCHEPE Training Area on the 14th inst.
2 lorries will be at Infantry Barracks at 8 am for this purpose.

2. Transport will proceed by road on the 14th and 15th inst. All Transport Lines will be vacated by 4 p.m. on those dates.
Those Transport Lines which are not taken over by units of the 69th Brigade (arrangements to be made direct between Brigades) will be handed over to the Area Commandant.

3. No area stores are under any circumstances to be taken out of the area.

4. The Brigade will proceed by train from YPRES as follows :-

     YPRES   1 a.m.   1000   detraining ABEELE.
     YPRES   3 a.m.   2000   "   POPERINGHE & ABEELE.

5. Lorries for advance parties and surplus kit will be arranged as follows :

14th.	2	Infantry Barracks YPRES.	8 a.m.
	6	MONTREAL CAMP.	8 a.m.
	3	Bde H.Q. Ramparts, YPRES.	9 p.m.
15th.	1	WINNIPEG Camp.	8 a.m.

                                 George Hawes
                                         Major,
13th May, 1917.   D.A.Q.M.G. 23rd Division.

Appendix III

SECRET.

COPY NO. 14

23RD DIVISION ORDER NO.112.
Reference: Sheet 28 N.W. 1/20,000.

1. The 70th Infantry Brigade will relieve the 69th Infantry Brigade in the line on night 24th/25th.
After relief, the 69th Infantry Brigade will withdraw into Corps Reserve and will take over the billets now occupied by the 70th Infantry Brigade in the BOESCHEPE Area.

2. All details of relief will be arranged direct between Brigadiers concerned.

3. The 70th Infantry Brigade will entrain at ABEELE and POPERINGHE for YPRES and the 69th Infantry Brigade, after relief, will be taken back to ABEELE by train.
Details will be arranged by "Q".

4. Defence Schemes, Trench stores, Aeroplane photos and Secret maps will be handed over and receipts taken.

5. Completion of relief and the passing of command of the Sector to G.O.C. 70th Infantry Brigade will be wired in code to Divisional Headquarters.

6. ACKNOWLEDGE.

22nd May, 1917.
Issued at 1.30 p.m.

A.C. Richardson Capt
for Lieut-Colonel,
General Staff.

Copies to :-

Nos.
1 R.A.
2 R.E.
3 Signals.
4 68th Infantry Brigade.
5 69th Infantry Brigade.
6 70th Infantry Brigade.
7 9th South Staffords R.
8 A & Q.
9 A.D.M.S.
10 D.A.D.O.S.
11 A.D.V.S.
12 A.P.M.
13 Camp Commandant.
14 Train.
15 S.S.O.
16-17 X Corps.
18 24th Division.
19 47th Division.
20 File.
21-22 Diary.
23 17th Supply Column.
24 194 Machine Gun Company.

Army Form C. 2118.

WAR DIARY
or
INTELLIGENCE SUMMARY.
(Erase heading not required.)

Vol 22

Place	Date	Hour	Summary of Events and Information	Remarks and references to Appendices
Busseboom	June 1st	—	Leave allotment two per day.	
	2nd	—	Transport 7 G.S. wagons for Divisional work.	
	3rd	—	Transport 18 G.S. wagons for Divisional work. Capt. E. A. Soulter returned from leave.	
			Transport 23 G.S. wagons for Divisional work.	
	4th	—	Extract from London Gazette dated 4-6-17:— T. Lt. J. A. Francis to be T. Captain. T. Lt. E. H. Mitchell to be T. Captain. Extract from Supplement to London Gazette giving Kings Birthday Honours:— Major T. Lt. Col. A. Northen to be Brevet Lt. Colonel. Mentions:— T. Capt. J. L. Kelsall, T. Lt. R. V. Holmes, & 1st C. S.S.M. N. McDonnell. Transport 6 G.S. wagons for Divisional work.	
	5th	—	Fire complete G.S. wagon burn-outs attached to the train from 1st Canadian Reserve Park are returned to their unit.	

Army Form C. 2118.

WAR DIARY
or
INTELLIGENCE SUMMARY.
(Erase heading not required.)

Instructions regarding War Diaries and Intelligence Summaries are contained in F. S. Regs., Part II. and the Staff Manual respectively. Title pages will be prepared in manuscript.

Place	Date	Hour	Summary of Events and Information	Remarks and references to Appendices
Busseboom	June 5 (cont.)		One driver & two pack mules of 193 Coy. A.S.C. killed by shell fire at H.16.d Sheet 28 (near DE GROENEN JAGER CABARET.) Transport 14 G.S. wagons for Divisional work.	
Busseboom	June 6	–	T. Lt. A.W. Hooley, proceeded to Divisional Bomb Store H.16.d.1.1 Sheet 28. for temporary duty, with 37 pack animals of the train for carrying Grenades, water etc. to forward area	
		–	Lt. Col. A. Northen, President of a Field General Court Martial. Transport 6 G.S. wagons for Divisional work	
	7th	–	Transport 3 G.S. wagons for Divisional work	
	11th	–	T. Lt. A.W. Hooley, returned from Divisional Bomb Store with 37 pack animals	
	12th	–	193 Coy. A.S.C. move from G.15.c.7.1. Sheet 28 (RENINGHELST. POPERINGHE ROAD), to X.4.a.8.6. (near FONTAINE HOUCK) Sheet 27.	
	13th	–	Train Headquarters move from G.15.d.7.4. Sheet 28 (near	

Army Form C. 2118.

WAR DIARY
or
INTELLIGENCE SUMMARY.
(Erase heading not required.)

Instructions regarding War Diaries and Intelligence Summaries are contained in F. S. Regs., Part II. and the Staff Manual respectively. Title pages will be prepared in manuscript.

Place	Date	Hour	Summary of Events and Information	Remarks and references to Appendices
METEREN	July 13th		Bussebroom to METEREN. 191 Coy A.S.C. move from G.21 a 4.3 Sheet 28 (RENINGHELST-POPERINGHE Road) to THIEUSHOUK. Q.34 d 8.4 Sheet 27 (Near CAESTRE). 192 Coy A.S.C. move from G.21 a 3.7 Sheet 27 (RENINGHELST-POPERINGHE Road) to R.32 d 9.5 Sheet 27.	
	14		T. Lt. C.W.G. LODGE, proceeded on leave. T. Capt. R. I. HADDEN, returned to duty from Hospital. 190 Coy A.S.C. moved from HOOGRAAF, G.26 d.0.2 Sheet 28 (near RENINGHELST) to M.4 Central Sheet 28 Railhead CAESTRE.	
	15		190 Coy A.S.C. draw supplies in bulk by lorry & refill by Horse Transport at N.1 d 5.7 Sheet 28 (OUDERDOM-MILLEKRUISSE Road). 191 & 193 Companies draw supplies in bulk by Horse Transport & refill all their respective Coy Camps.	

T2134. Wt. W708—776. 500000. 4/15. Sir J. C. & S.

WAR DIARY
or
INTELLIGENCE SUMMARY.

(Erase heading not required.)

Army Form C. 2118.

Place	Date	Hour	Summary of Events and Information	Remarks and references to Appendices
METEREN June 15 (Cont)	17	-	192 Coy. A.S.C. draw supplies & refill by Horse Transport & refill at Refilling Point. T. Capt. R.I. HADDEN, proceeded on leave. Lt. Col. A. NORTHEN took over duties of Divisional Claims Officer.	
	19	-	T. Lt. A.W. HOOLEY proceeded on leave.	
	23	-	190 Coy A.S.C. Move from M4 Central Sheet 28 (near RENINGHELST) to SCHAEXKEN R35a.5.0 Sheet 27. 190 Coy A.S.C. refill in detail by Horse Transport at CAESTRE.	
	24	-	Supplies for Divisional Troops, conveyed by lorry to Refilling Point R.27d (SCHAEXKEN - BERTHEN Road).	
	25	-	T. 2nd Lt. C.C.G. de WILTON, joined the Train from B.H.T.D. via T. Lt. L.C. OSBORNE. T. Lt. L.C. OSBORNE, having been invalided to England is struck off the strength of the Train.	Authority 2nd Svt Second Army No.2229 d/21.6.17. Authority O.M.G. A.S.C. H.Q. No 1698 d/22.6.17

WAR DIARY
or
INTELLIGENCE SUMMARY.
(Erase heading not required.)

Army Form C. 2118.

Place	Date	Hour	Summary of Events and Information	Remarks and references to Appendices
METEREN	June 25 (Cont⁴)		T/Lieut. C.W.G. LODGE, A.S.C., returned from leave. 23rd Divisional Horse Show held near BERTHEN. 23rd Divisional Train successful in gaining five (5) first prizes, two (2) second prizes and one third prize	
	26		193rd Coy. A.S.C. moved from FONTAINE-HOUCK - X.4.a.8.6. (sheet 27) to M5.c.2.9. (Sheet I) Sheet 28 (near RENINGHELST) Supplies for 70th Bde conveyed by lorry to refilling point at N.1.d Central (Sheet 28)	Appendix I
	27		193 Coy. A.S.C. moved from M5.c.2.9, Sheet 28 (near RENINGHELST) to N2.c.2.2. Sheet 28 (MILLEKRUISSE), taking over camp from 24 Divisional Train. Two A.F.A. Bdes attached to 70 Bde Group for rations	Appendix I
	28			Appendix I
	28		192 Coy. A.S.C. moved from R32.d.9.5. Sheet 27, to N2.c.2.2, Sheet 28. Supplies for 69th Bde conveyed by lorry to refilling point at N.7.b. Sheet 28 (near LA CLYTTE)	Appendix I
	29		T/Capt. R.I. HADDEN returned from leave	
	30		T/Major T.H. MONTGOMERY proceeded on leave. 191 Coy A.S.C. moved from THIEUSHOEK, Q.34.d.8.4. (Sheet 27) — near CAESTRE — to MILLEKRUISSE, N.2.c.2.2. (Sheet 28)	Appendix I

Army Form C. 2118.

WAR DIARY
or
INTELLIGENCE SUMMARY.
(Erase heading not required.)

Instructions regarding War Diaries and Intelligence Summaries are contained in F. S. Regs., Part II. and the Staff Manual respectively. Title pages will be prepared in manuscript.

Place	Date	Hour	Summary of Events and Information	Remarks and references to Appendices
METEREN	June. 30	(cont'd)	H.Q. TRAIN moved from Billet No 90, METEREN, to MILLEKRUISSE – N 2 c 2.2 (Sheet 28). Supplies for 68 Bde & Div H.Q. units (less H.Q. R.A.) conveyed by lorries to refilling point at N 7 b.	
MILLEKRUISSE				

A.W. ...
...

O.O.M.G. 23rd DIVISIONAL TRAIN A. S. C.

SECRET.   Copy No. 18.

23rd DIVISION OPERATION ORDER No. 123.

Reference Sheets 27 and 28, Scale 1/40,000.

1. The 23rd Division will relieve the 24th Division. Infantry Brigades will move in accordance with the attached table. Completion of reliefs will be notified in code to Head-Quarters 24th Division.

2. During the marches detailed in the table, intervals of ½ mile between battalions and of 200 yards between half battalions will be maintained.

3. Details of reliefs will be arranged by G.Os. C.Brigades concerned. All maps, photographs and trench stores will be taken over by relieving brigades and a receipt given.

4. A scheme of the preparations required for a future operation will be handed over by 72nd Brigade to 69th Brigade and by 73rd Brigade to 70th Brigade.

5. The Machine Gun Company and Observers of 17th Infantry Brigade will remain with 70th Infantry Brigade until the evening of 28th/29th June. G.O.C.70th Infantry Brigade will arrange for personnel to be attached to them from 27th/28th June.

6. G.O.C.69th Infantry Brigade will arrange for personnel to be attached to the Machine Gun Company and Observers of 72nd Infantry Brigade from night 28th/29th June.

7. Instructions regarding Artillery reliefs will be issued separately.

8. Relief of R.E. and Pioneers will be arranged by C.R.Es. concerned. This relief is to be completed on night 29th/30th June.

9. Relief of Field Ambulances will be arranged by A.D.M.S. concerned.

10. The G.O.C. will assume command of the Divisional front at 9 a.m. 30th June.

11. Acknowledge.

Evans
Lieutenant-Colonel,
General Staff.

24th June, 1917.

Issued at 9 a.m.

Distribution overleaf.

Copies to :-

1	R.A.
2	R.E.
3	68th Infantry Bde.
4	69th Infantry Bde.
5	70th Infantry Bde.
6	23rd Divnl. Signal Coy.
7	194th Machine Gun Coy.
8	A. & Q.
9	A.D.M.S.
10	X Corps.
11	X Corps.
12	24th Division.
13	30th Division.
14	47th Division.
15	File
16	Diary.
17	Diary.
18	Train.

DATE.	UNIT.	FROM.	TO.	REMARKS.
26th.	70th Infantry Brigade.	METEREN AREA.	CHIPPEWA, etc.	Route BERTHEN - R.16.c.3.6. - RENINGHELST.
27th/28th.	70th Infantry Brigade.	CHIPPEWA, etc.	LEFT SECTOR.	Relieves 17th Infantry Brigade (less M.G.Coy. & Observers). M.G.Coy. & Observers take over on 28th/29th.
28th.	69th Infantry Brigade.	ROUKLOSHILLE AREA.	CHIPPEWA, etc.	Route - GODEWAERSVELDE and RENINGHELST. Not to reach RENINGHELST till 11 a.m. Personnel of M.G.Coy. & Observers attached to 72nd Infantry Brigade from 28/29th.
29th/30th.	69th Infantry Brigade.	CHIPPEWA, etc.	RIGHT SECTOR.	Relieves 72nd Infantry Brigade.
July 1st.	68th Infantry Brigade.	THIEUSHOOK AREA.	MIC MAC.	Route GODEWAERSVELDE and RENINGHELST. To be clear of RENINGHELST by 3 p.m.

Headquarters
23rd Division

Herewith war diary for the
month of July 1917

By Lt Colonel A. Northen. D.S.O.
Commanding 23rd Divisional Train A.S.C

[signature]
Lieut Adjutant
for COM. G. 23rd DIVISIONAL TRAIN A.S.C.

4th August 1917.

Army Form C. 2118.

23D Train
Vol 23

WAR DIARY
or
INTELLIGENCE SUMMARY.
(Erase heading not required.)

Instructions regarding War Diaries and Intelligence Summaries are contained in F.S. Regs., Part II. and the Staff Manual respectively. Title pages will be prepared in manuscript.

Place	Date	Hour	Summary of Events and Information	Remarks and references to Appendices
	1917			
MILLEKRUISSE	July 1st	—	T.H.C. BRIDGES proceeded by motor lorry to CALAIS with conducting party of one N.C.O. & 17 men to bring remounts from N°5 Base Remount Depot, CALAIS for 23rd Division.	
			Leave allotment 2 per day.	
	"2nd"	—	Railhead RENINGHELST SIDING. Supplies drawn by lorries & dumped near respective Company Camps.	
ZEVECOTEN	"3rd"	—	Train Headquarters moved from MILLEKRUISSE to ZEVECOTEN G.35.c.6.6 (Sheet 28).	
	"4th"	—	190 Company moved from SCHAEXKEN, R.35.a.5.0 Sheet 27 to A.Kendix I G.35.a.9.4 Sheet 28 (ZEVECOTEN – OUDERDOM Rd.)	
			192 Company moved from MILLEKRUISSE N.2.c.2.2 Sheet 28 to A.Kendix II STEENVOORDE AREA, K.13.c.9.2 Sheet 27.	
			Visit of H.M. The King to this Area. All available men of 191, 192 & 193 Corps were informally gathered along road Appendix II LA CLYTTE – MILLEKRUISSE & cheered the King as he passed.	
			T.L.I. S.K. WALENN inoculated on leave	

Army Form C. 2118.

WAR DIARY
or
INTELLIGENCE SUMMARY.
(Erase heading not required.)

Place	Date	Hour	Summary of Events and Information	Remarks and references to Appendices
ZEVECOTEN	July 5th	—	T/Lt. C. BRIDGES. returned with remounts which were distributed to units of 23rd Division.	
	5th	9 a.m.	23rd Division transferred to II Corps (V.Army).	Appendix IV
		—	191 & 193 Coys. Q.S.C. moved from MILLEKRUISSE, N2.C.22 to ZEVECOTEN, G.35.d.8.5 (Sheet 28)	
	6th	—	Transport 6 G.S. wagons for Divisional work.	
		—	Major. H.P. BARUGH, proceeded on leave.	
	7th	—	Transport 16 G.S. wagons for Divisional work.	
		—	Extract from London Gazette dated 6-7-17. — T/Lt R.V. HOLGATE to be T. Captain 7-7-17.	
	8th	—	Transport 16 G.S. wagons for Divisional work.	
		—	T/Lt. R.A. KEENE joined the train from B. & T.D. HAYRE & is posted to 193 Coy. ASC.	Authority D.D.O.75/5/7. Second Army No 2229 dated 4-7-17
		—	T. Lt. W.H. BROWN, is struck off the strength of the Train.	
	9th	—	Lt Col. A. NORTHEN, proceeded on leave.	
		—	Transport 20 G.S. wagons for Divisional work.	

Army Form C. 2118.

WAR DIARY
or
INTELLIGENCE SUMMARY.
(Erase heading not required.)

Place	Date	Hour	Summary of Events and Information	Remarks and references to Appendices
ZEVECOTEN	July 10th	—	T. Major T.H. Montgomery returned from leave. T/040675 Dr A.D. Dick, 192 Coy. A.S.C. attached to 69th Brigade Headquarters, awarded the Military Medal.	
		11½	Transport 28 G.S. wagons for Divisional work.	
		12½	Transport 23 G.S. wagons for Divisional work. 193 Company moved from ZEVECOTEN G.35.d Central to STEENVOORDE Area K.13.c.9.2 Sheet 27. 192 Company moved from STEENVOORDE Area K.13.c.9.2 Sheet 24 to ZEVECOTEN G.35.d Central Sheet 28. All companies of Train drew supplies in detail from Railhead.	
		13½	Transport 21 G.S. wagons for Divisional work. Capt. A. St. G. Adams, proceeded on leave.	
		14½	Transport 29 G.S. wagons for Divisional work. Transport 30 G.S. wagons for Divisional work.	

WAR DIARY
or
INTELLIGENCE SUMMARY.

(Erase heading not required.)

Army Form C. 2118.

Place	Date	Hour	Summary of Events and Information	Remarks and references to Appendices
ZEVECOTEN	July 15th	--	Lt. Col. A. NORTHEN & T.L.T. S.K. WALENN returned from leave. Transport 25 G.S. wagons for Divisional work.	
	16th	--	Transport 28 G.S. wagons for Divisional work. T/Capt. H.P. BARGH returned from leave	
	17th	--	Transport 28 G.S. wagons for Divisional work. T/Lt. W.G. LACEY proceeded on leave.	
	18th	--	163 Coy. moved from STEENVOORDE Area K13c92 Sheet 27 to METEREN Area X & S.6. Supplies conveyed by lorry to Refilling Point at 193 Coy Camp. Transport 25 G.S. wagons for Divisional work.	Appendix V
	19th	--	Lt. Col. A. NORTHEN. Proceeded on a T.C.M. at ZEVECOTEN. Transport 19 G.S. wagons for Divisional work.	
	20th	--	Transport 18 G.S. wagons for Divisional work.	
	21st	--	191 Coy. moved from ZEVECOTEN G35a Central Sheet 28 to THIESHOEK Area, Q34 & 84 Sheet 27 Refilling - Divt Troops (less D.H.Q. Mnt'd) arms & supplies	Appendix VI

Army Form C. 2118.

WAR DIARY
or
INTELLIGENCE SUMMARY.
(Erase heading not required.)

Place	Date	Hour	Summary of Events and Information	Remarks and references to Appendices
ZEVECOTEN	July 22nd	—	In bulk from RENINGHELST Siding from 24th Div. Pack & refill at camp of 190 Coy. at G.35.a.9.4. Sheet 28. Railhead for Division BAILLEUL:- Supplies for 68th Bde. conveyed by lorry to Rytilling Point at THIEUSHOEK area, W.6.a. Sheet 27. Supplies for 69th Bde. (including D.H.Q. units) conveyed to Rytilling Point at 192 Coys. Camp. G.35.d. central Sheet 28. 70th Brigade draw supplies in bulk by Horse transport from Railhead & refill at 193 Coys. Camp. Lyndhurst Camp Allotment 3 per day. Transport 11 G.S. wagons per Divisional work. Lt. Col. A. NORTHEN, Member of a General Court Martial.	
METEREN	23rd	—	Headquarters train moved from ZEVECOTEN, G.35.d.6.6 (Sheet 28) to METEREN, X.15.d.6.6. (Sheet 27) 192 Coy. A.S.C. moved from G.35.d. central, ZEVECOTEN, to ROUKLOSHILLS Area, R.32.d.9.5. (Sheet 27).	"

Army Form C. 2118.

WAR DIARY
or
INTELLIGENCE SUMMARY.
(Erase heading not required.)

Instructions regarding War Diaries and Intelligence Summaries are contained in F. S. Regs., Part II. and the Staff Manual respectively. Title pages will be prepared in manuscript.

Place	Date	Hour	Summary of Events and Information	Remarks and references to Appendices
METEREN	July 23rd Cont.		23rd Division transferred to XI Corps (II Army). T/Capt. A.S.G. Adams, returned from leave. T/3/027287 Driver T. AMESBURY, 191 Coy. A.S.C. awarded Military Medal.	July II Corps 192/HR/23/7 4/23-7-17
	"24/7"		Leave allotment 3 his days & every third day.	
	"25/7"		192 Coy. proceeded en route from ROUKLOSHILLE Area (R32d.9.5 Sheet 27) to BOISDINGHEM Area, halting for night near EBBLINGHEM (U19c4.8 Sheet 27A.S.) T. 2/Lt. H.T. GILCHRIST, proceeded on leave.	
	"26/7"		192 Coy. A.S.C., moved from EBBLINGHEM to BOISDINGHEM Area Q.25c9 + Sheet 27A. Supplies for 69th Brigade conveyed by lorry to refilling point at BOISDINGHEM. T. Capt. R.V. HOLMES, proceeded on leave.	
	"27/7"		T. 2/Lt. H. CROFT, joined his train from B.H.T.D. HAVRE & is posted to 190 Coy. A.S.C. for duty	Monthly 2353 A.25/343 27-7-17

Army Form C. 2118.

WAR DIARY
or
INTELLIGENCE SUMMARY.
(Erase heading not required.)

Place	Date	Hour	Summary of Events and Information	Remarks and references to Appendices
METEREN	July 29th	—	Transport, Six pairs of H.D. horses attached to X Corps Roads Officer for work in the forward area. 69th Brigade draw supplies in bulk by Horse Transport from ST OMER.	
			191 Company proceeded en route to WIZERNES, halting Appendix VII	
	30th	—	for night near EBBLINGHEM (U19c 4.8 Sheet 27J).	
			191 Company moved from EBBLINGHEM to Billets at Cross Roads between WIZERNES & LONGPONS WINS.	
	31st	—	191 Company draw supplies in bulk by Horse Transport from ST OMER.	

3st August 1917.

A. Norton
Lt. Col.
OOM G. 23rd DIVISIONAL TRAIN A.S.C.

****
S E C R E T.
****

<u>TO ALL RECIPIENTS OF 23RD DIVISIONAL ORDER NO:132.</u>

Para. 12.   For METEREN read MERRIS.

[signature]

Lieutenant-Colonel,
General Staff.

<u>23rd Division.</u>
<u>20th July, 1917.</u>

Ack Appendix I

SECRET. COPY NO. 18

23RD DIVISION OPERATION ORDER NO.125.

Reference: Sheets 27 and 28, Scale 1/40,000.

1. The 23rd Divisional Artillery will relieve the 24th Divisional Artillery on 3rd/4th and 4th/5th.
All details of relief will be arranged by C.R.As. concerned.

2. C.R.A., 23rd Division takes over command from C.R.A., 24th Division at ZEVECOTEN at 10 a.m. on 5th July.

3. ACKNOWLEDGE.

A C Richardson,
General Staff.

1st July, 1917.

Issued at 8-30 p.m.

Copies to :-

No.	
1	C.R.A.
2	C.R.E.
3	68th Infantry Brigade.
4	69th Infantry Brigade.
5	70th Infantry Brigade.
6	Signals.
7	194th Machine Gun Coy.
8	A.&.Q.
9	A.D.M.S.
10	X Corps.
11	X Corps.
12	30th Division.
13	47th Division.
14	C.R.A., 24th Division.
15	File.
16	Diary.
17	Diary.
18	Train.

Appendix II Ack. July 3

SECRET.   Copy No. 9

DIVISIONAL ADMINISTRATIVE INSTRUCTIONS No. 125.
----

1. – Reference para 7 of Division Operation Order 126 dated 1st July.

   The 69th Infantry Brigade (dismounted personnel only) will, after concentration in the area N.1.a., entrain as follows :-

   OUDERDOM Station   arrive   GODEWAERSVELDE.

   Train No. 1   13 hrs.   13-45 hrs.
   "   "   2   16 "   16-45 hrs.

   Accommodation on each train:- 1,600.

   Entraining Officers and parties will report to R.T.O., OUDERDOM Station 1 hour before entrainment.

2. – All transport and mounted personnel will proceed by march route under arrangements to be made by G.O.C., 69th Inf Brigade. Route – RENINGHELST – ABEELE – STEENVOORDE. Starting Point: N.1.a.7.8. 8-30 a.m.
   No transport to be on ZEVECOTEN – LA CLYTTE Road between 8-30 and 9-30 a.m.

3. – No. 3 Coy, Divl. Train will proceed to the new area under arrangements to be made by O.C., Divisional Train with G.O.C., 69th Inf Bde.
   Railhead: no change.

4. – Advance parties will proceed by 2 lorries from 69th Infantry Bde Transport Lines N.1.a.7.8. at 5 a.m. under the command of the Brigade Billeting Officer.
   Some bicycles will be taken.
   6 lorries will report at N.1.a.7.8. at 5 a.m. for surplus kit.

5. – The Billeting area allotted to 69th Inf Bde is as follows :-
   STEENVOORDE – ST. LAURENT Area. Map, Sheet 27, 1/40,000.
   Details to be obtained direct by Bde Billeting Officer from Area Commandant, STEENVOORDE.

6. – ACKNOWLEDGE.

                              E.F. Falkner.

                              Lieut-Colonel,
3rd July, 1917.   A.A.& Q.M.G. 23rd Division.

Copies 1 to 5 69th I. Bde.   No. 12 A.D.M.S.
Copy No. 6   Signals.   13 D.A.D.O.S.
         7   "G"   14 D.A.D.V.S.
         8   "A" & "Q".   15 S. Chaplain.
         9   O.C. Train.   16 N.C.O! 1/c Posts.
        10   O.C. No. 3 Coy Train.   17 File.
        11   A.P.M.   18 Diary.

SECRET
and
URGENT.

Appendix III
Ack

Xth Corps No.25.

- VISIT OF H.M. THE KING -
- Wednesday, 4th July, 1917 -

1. His Majesty The KING will pass through Xth Corps Area on Wednesday, 4th July, in accordance with the following time table and routes :-

OUTWARD.

Pass ABEELE .... 8.45 a.m.
   ABEELE - RENINGHELST Road.
Pass RENINGHELST .... 9.0 a.m.
   RENINGHELST - LA CLYTTE Road.
Pass LA CLYTTE .... 9.15 a.m.
   HALLEBAST CORNER - VIERSTRAAT Road.
Arrive VIERSTRAAT .... 9.30 a.m.

HOMEWARD.

CANADA CORNER - LA CLYTTE Road.
Arrive LA CLYTTE .... 3.30 p.m.
   Visit Xth Corps Counter Battery Office.
Pass along LA CLYTTE - RENINGHELST Road .... 3.45 p.m.
   RENINGHELST - HEKSKEN - ABEELE Road.
Arrive ABEELE .... 4.15 p.m.
   Meet representatives of Xth Corps in CONVENT YARD, (Corps Headquarters Offices.)

2. Troops are not to be paraded, nor roads lined, but as many troops as possible should be given the opportunity of seeing His Majesty.
   Troops in the neighbourhood of the route should be informed of the time His Majesty will pass on both the outward and homeward journeys, and should be collected informally by the roadside to cheer The KING, particularly in the morning.

3. B.G.,H.A. will arrange for his Staff to be present at The King's visit to the Counter Battery Office at 3.30 p.m.

4. 23rd and 47th Divisions and B.G.,H.A. will report to Headquarters, Xth Corps, by noon on 2nd July the names and map location of Units under their Command on The King's outward and homeward routes.

5. All troops on the move on The King's route will be warned to clear the road and cheer, as His Majesty passes them.

6. As many officers of Xth Corps of and above the rank of Brigadier General as are available, an Officer of G.S., Xth Corps, and the D.D.M.S., Xth Corps, will parade in the Convent Yard, ABEELE, at 4 p.m. to be presented to His Majesty. 24th, 41st and 47th Divisions will report to Headquarters, Xth Corps by noon on 2nd July, the names of Officers attending.

7. His Majesty The KING will present the C.M.G. to the following Officers at Second Army Headquarters, CASSEL, at 6 p.m. :-

   Brig-General R.McDOUALL, C.M.G.,D.S.O., Comdg., 141st Inf. Bde.
   Brig-General W.F.CLEMSON, C.M.G.,D.S.O., Comdg., 124th Inf. Bde.
   *Brig-General F.W.TOWSEY, C.M.G., Comdg., 122nd Inf. Bde.

   *(Unless he attended an Investiture whilst on leave.)

/The Army

- 2 -

The Army Commander hopes that these Officers will come to tea at his house at 5 p.m.

8. 24th Division will detail a Guard of Honour of 100 rank and file, with a band limited to 25 performers, under the Command of a Captain with 2 Subalterns, to be in position at Army Headquarters, CASSEL, at 5.40 p.m. for the presentation parade. 24th Division will inform Headquarters, Xth Corps, by noon 2nd July, at what time and place buses are required to convey the Guard of Honour and Band to CASSEL.

9. The following Officers representing Xth Corps (additional to those mentioned in para. 7) will attend the presentation parade at 6 p.m.:-

        B.G., R.A., Xth Corps.
        D.A. & Q.M.G., "
        G.S.O. 2, "

2 General Officers from each of 24th, 41st and 47th Divisions.

10. Acknowledge

W.K. Legge
Brig-General,
D.A. & Q.M.G.,
Xth Corps.

H.Q., Xth Corps.
1st July, 1917.

Distribution :-

    23rd Division.
    24th Division.-(With copy of orders for O.C., Guard of Honour).
    41st Division.
    47th Division.
    B.G., H.A., Xth Corps.
    G.O.C.R.A., "
    G.S., "
    C.E., "
    D.D.M.S., "
    A.P.M., "
    A.D.A.S., "
    A.D.C., "
    French Mission, "
    Belgian Mission, "
    Captain HAYWOOD, Headquarters, Second Army.

SECRET.   COPY NO: 21

23RD DIVISIONAL ORDER NO. 126.

Reference: Sheet 28, Scale 1/40,000.

1. The 23rd Division will be transferred to the II Corps from 9 a.m. on 4th instant and the present Right Brigade Sector will be handed over to the 47th Division on night 3rd/4th. Relief to be completed by 9 a.m. on 4th instant.

2. After transfer of the Division to the II Corps, the Southern boundary of the 23rd Division, which will also be the boundary, between the II and X Corps, will be as follows:-

From I.36.a.86.42 (KLEIN ZILLEBEKE) - Railway at I.29.c.8.0 to junction of GRAND FLEET STREET with the old British front line - to point where stream crosses SUNKEN ROAD at I.28.c.72.08 thence to CHESTER FARM (exclusive to 23rd Division) to I.32.d.3.3. thence by FRENCH TRENCH and CONVENT LANE TRENCH (both inclusive to 47th Division) to road junction at H.36.c.7.7. to WILTSHIRE FARM (inclusive to 47th Division) thence along light railway to CROSS COUNTRY TRACK at N.5.a.3.8., thence by track to the DICKEBUSCH - LA CLYTTE ROAD at H.33.c.0.6. (Tracks and light railway inclusive to X Corps). thence along S. edge of roads DICKEBUSCH - MILLEKRUISSE - OUDERDOM and thence as at present.

23rd and 47th Divisions will both have users right over roads and tramways serving their sectors.

3. The 69th Infantry Brigade at present holding the Right Sector, less Machine Gun Company, will be relieved on the night 3rd/4th July by the 141st Infantry Brigade (less Machine Gun Company) of the 47th Division.

4. The relief of the 69th Machine Gun Company by the 141st Machine Gun Company will be carried out on the night 4th/5th July, 1917.

5. All details of relief will be arranged direct between Brigadiers concerned.

6. Reconnoitring parties and observers of the 141st Infantry Brigade will be attached to the 69th Infantry Brigade on the night 2nd/3rd instant.

General Officer Commanding 69th Infantry Brigade will give every facility for these parties to learn the line.

7. The area to which the 69th Infantry Brigade will withdraw after relief will be notified later.

8. All Aeroplane photographs, and copies of Intelligence Summaries and Patrol reports, programmes of work in hand and trench stores, etc., will be handed over and receipts taken.

9. The C.R.E. will make arrangements for the accommodation of the R.E. and Pioneers in the new Divisional Area.

All details of the relief of R.E. and Pioneers will be arranged direct between C.R.Es. concerned.

10. Alterations in medical arrangements will be made direct between A.D.M.S. concerned.

P.T.O.

(2).

11. General Officer Commanding 47th Division will take over command of the present Right Brigade Sector at 9 a.m. on 4th instant.

12. 23rd Divisional Head Quarters will remain at ZEVECOTEN.

13. Completion of reliefs will be wired in code to Divisional Head Quarters.

14. Artillery reliefs will be notified later.

15. ACKNOWLEDGE.

A.C. Richardson Capt.
General Staff.

1st July, 1917.

Issued at 8.30 p.m.

Copies to :-

No.	
1	R.A.
2	R.E.
3	68th Infantry Brigade.
4	69th Infantry Brigade.
5	70th Infantry Brigade.
6	Signals.
7	A.&Q.
8	A.D.M.S.
9	X Corps.
10	X Corps.
11	II Corps.
12	24th Division.
13	30th Division.
14	41st Division.
15	47th Division.
16	C.R.A., 24th Division.
17	194th Machine Gun Coy.
18	File.
19	Diary.
20	Diary.
21	Train.
22	A.P.M.
23	D.A.D.O.S.
24	A.D.V.S.
25	Camp Comdt.

Appendix V

SECRET.

23rd. Division
No. S.G. 471/7/9.

70th. Inf. Bde.
"Q"
Signals.
D.M.G.O.
A.D.M.S.
11 Corps.) For information.
X. Corps.)   "   ".

      The 70th. Infantry Brigade (Less Machine Gun Company) will move by march route to-morrow to METEREN billeting area under orders of G.O.C., 70th. Inf.Bde.

      The movement will be made via. STEENVOORDE, but no troops will enter that place before 12.noon and must be clear of it by 6.p.m.

      "Q" will issue the necessary billeting and administrative orders.

      Completion of move will be reported by telegram to Divisional Head Quarters.

23rd. Division.
17.7.1917.

(SD) C. EVANS. Lieut.Col.,
General Staff.

O.C.
193 Coy notified.

Appendix VI

S E C R E T.

COPY NO: 20.

23RD DIVISIONAL ORDER NO. 132.

REFERENCE: Sheets 27 and 28, Scale 1/40,000.

1. The 23rd Division (less Artillery, one Field Company R.E. and Pioneer Battalion) will be relieved in the Right Sector of II Corps Front by the 24th Division.
    The relief will commence on the night of 21st/22nd July and will be carried out in accordance with Table "A" attached.

2. Details of Machine Gun relief are given in Table "B" attached. One man will be left by each gun detachment relieved who will remain with the incoming gun detachment until daylight the following morning.

3. Guides will be provided on relief nights by 69th Infantry Brigade for infantry and machine gun companies and by C.R.E. on night of 21st/22nd for 104th Field Company, R.E.
    Other details will be arranged direct by commanders concerned.

4. Observers of 72nd Infantry Brigade will report at 69th Infantry Brigade Head-Quarters, LARCH WOOD by 10 a.m. 22nd and will be attached to 69th Infantry Brigade Observers during that day.

5. All maps of the area, aeroplane photos and trench stores will be handed over by 69th Infantry Brigade and receipts taken.

6. 71st Field Ambulance from RENINGHELST will move so as to reach WESTOUTRE at 10 a.m. 21st where it will join 68th Brigade column.
    72nd Field Ambulance from DICKEBUSCH will move under orders of G.O.C. 69th Infantry Brigade.

7. Nos. 2 and 3 Companies, Divisional Train, will accompany 68th and 69th Infantry Brigades respectively.
    The head of the former will reach LA CLYTTE at 9 a.m. 21st where it will join 68th Brigade column.
    69th Infantry Brigade will issue orders for the move of No. 3 Company.

8. The Mobile Veterinary Section will accompany No. 3 Company Divisional Train.

9. 68th Infantry Brigade will come under orders of X Corps from 9 a.m. 21st July.

10. An interval of 200 yards between Companies and 400 yards between Battalions and other units will be maintained during the above movements.

11. "Q" will issue instructions as to accommodation in the BERTHEN Billeting Area.

(2).

12. Divisional Head-Quarters will close at ZEVECOTEN at 10 a.m. 23rd and re-open at METEREN at the same hour, from which hour it will be under X Corps orders.

13. ACKNOWLEDGE.

Evans.

Lieutenant-Colonel,
General Staff.

19th July, 1917.

Issued at 1.30 p.m.

Copies to :-

Nos.	
1	Royal Artillery.
2	Royal Engineers.
3	68th Infantry Brigade.
4	69th Infantry Brigade.
5	70th Infantry Brigade.
6	72nd Infantry Brigade.
7	Signals.
8	"A" & "Q".
9	A.D.M.S.
10	X Corps.
11	X Corps.
12	II Corps.
13	24th Division.
14	47th Division.
15	18th Division.
16	D.M.G.O.
19	194th Machine Gun Coy.
20	Divisional Train.
21	Right Double Group Commander.
22	D.A.D.V.S.
23	D.A.D.O.S.
24	A.P.M.
25	Camp Commandant.
26	9th South Staffords R.
27	File.
28	Diary.
29	Diary.

TABLE "A".

MARCH TABLE TO ACCOMPANY 23RD DIVISIONAL ORDER NO: 132.

DATE.	UNIT.	FROM.	TO.	ROUTE.	REMARKS.
21st.	72nd Inf. Bde. (24th Division).	RENINGHELST Staging C.	MICMAC.	March.	To be clear of RENINGHELST by 9 a.m.
	68th Inf. Bde.	MICMAC.	THIEUSHOEK AREA.	"	Via LA CLYTTE – WESTOUTRE and BERTHEN. To be clear of LA CLYTTE by 9 a.m.
21/22.	4 Coys. 72nd Inf. Bde.	MICMAC.	Support R. Divn.	"	On relief by 4 Coys. 72nd Bde.
	4 Coys. 69th Inf. Bde.	Support R. Divn.	MICMAC.	"	Pack transport to be used.
	72nd M.E.Coy.	MICMAC.	Right Division.	"	
	69th & 70th M.G. Coys. (10 guns).	Right Division.	MICMAC.	"	On relief by 72nd M.G.Coy.
	6 Secs. R.E. & attd. Infantry. 102nd & 128th Field Coys.	LARCH WOOD.	CAMP.	"	On relief by 104th Field Coy.
	4 Secs. 104th Fd.Coy. and att. Infantry.	CAMP.	LARCH WOOD.	"	

P. T. O.

TABLE "A". (Continued).

DATE.	UNIT.	FROM.	TO.	ROUTE.	REMARKS.
2nd.	2 Fd. Coy. R.E.	CAMP.	BERTHEN BILLETING AREA.	March.	Via LA CLYTTE – WESTOUTRE – BERTHEN. Under orders of C.R.E.
/25.	73 M.G.Coy. 6 guns. 17 M.G.Coy. 4 guns. 191 M.G.Coy. 10 " 69th Inf. Bde. 66 & 69 M.G.Coys(16 guns).	MICMAC. MICMAC. Right Division. "	Right Division. Right Division. MICMAC. "	" " " "	On relief by 72nd Inf.Bde. On relief.
23rd.	69th Inf. Bde.	MICMAC.	ROCKLOSHILLE AREA.	"	Via LA CLYTTE – WESTOUTRE and BERTHEN on relief by 17th Bde. To be clear of LA CLYTTE by 7.30 p.m.
	194 M.G.Coy. 70 M.G.Coy.	" "	" "	" "	} Under orders of G.O.C. 69th } Infantry Brigade.
	17th Inf. Bde.	RENINGHELST Staging C.	MICMAC.	"	

****
S E C R E T.
****

TO ALL RECIPIENTS OF 23rd DIVISIONAL
　　　ORDER NO: 132.
_____

The following amendment will be made to Table "A" :-

Column 2.　For 68 & 70 M.G.Cos.(16 guns).

　　　　　　　　read

　　　　　　69 & 70 M.G.Cos.(16 guns).

23rd Division.
19th July, 1917.

　　　　　　　　　　Lieutenant-Colonel,
　　　　　　　　　　　General Staff.

Appendix VII

23rd Div. G.104/1/4.

68th Infantry Brigade.
Divisional Train.
A.D.M.S.
"Q"
X Corps (for information).

---

1. 68th Infantry Brigade will move to QUELMES on 29th and 30th July; transport on 29th, dismounted personnel on 30th.

2. Transport will move by such route and at such hour as G.O.C. 68th Infantry Brigade may decide.

3. A company of the Divisional Train will march with the Transport of units.

4. G.O.C. 68th Infantry Brigade will appoint a commander of the transport Column and issue necessary orders for its march.

5. A.D.M.S. will issue necessary orders regarding medical arrangements for the move and on arrival.

6. "Q" will issue orders regarding rations and train arrangements.

Chaus.

23rd Division.   Lieutenant-Colonel,
27th July, 1917.   General Staff.

23 Divnl Train
A.S.C.

Army Form C. 2118.

WAR DIARY
or
INTELLIGENCE SUMMARY.
(Erase heading not required.)

Vol 24

Place	Date	Hour	Summary of Events and Information	Remarks and references to Appendices
METEREN	August 1st	—	Railhead for 70th Brigade Group, BAILLEUL. 68th & 69th Bdes Groups St OMER. Div: Troops administered by 24th Division. Leave allotment for the train four per day.	
	3rd	—	7 cat/R. H. NORTHEN, proceeded on leave	
	4th	—	Leave suspended. Establishment of train reduced by twelve riders. (C.Q.M Ss, & Farriers) 190 Coy A.S.C. moved to HOOGRAAF (G 32 a 8.8 Sheet 28).	Auth: Q.G. letter 609 (Q.P.1) of 23-7-17
	5th	—	Leave re-opens.	
	6th	—	2/Lt H.T. GILCHRIST, returned from leave. 193 Coy A.S.C. proceeded en route from STEENVOORDE Area Appendix I K13c 9.2 Sheet 27 to BULLESCAMPS, halted for night 6½/7½ at ARQUES. T. cat/E. R.V. HOLMES A.S.C. returned from leave.	
GORDARDENNE	7th	—	Railhead St OMER. Supplies for 70th Bde Group conveyed by lorry to R.P. at RENESCURE	

WAR DIARY
or
INTELLIGENCE SUMMARY.
(Erase heading not required.)

Army Form C. 2118.

Place	Date	Hour	Summary of Events and Information	Remarks and references to Appendices
GORDARDENNE	Aug 7th	-	Train Headquarters Moved to WIZERNES (GORDARDENNE) F.11 a.3.9. Sheet 36D N.E.	Appendix II
			193 Coy. A.S.C. Moved to BULLESCAMPS (main ST OMER - CALAIS Rd)	Appendix I
EPERLECQUES	9th	-	Train Headquarters Moved to EPERLECQUES, K.35.4.2.3. Sheet 27a N.E.	
			191 Coy. A.S.C. moved to HOULLE, Q.11 a.2.5. Sheet 27a N.E.	Appendix III
			192 Coy. A.S.C. moved to HOULLE, Q.	
			23rd Division (less Artillery) transferred to V Corps, Fifth Army.	
			T/Capt. H. NORTHEN, returned from leave.	
	10th	-	193 Coy. A.S.C. Proceeded en route to ST JANSTER BIEZEN Area, halted for night 10th/11th at WORMHOUDT.	
	11th	-	193 Coy. A.S.C. moved to F.28.B.4.2. Sheet 27. 70th Inf. Brigade, administered by 51st Division, with Railhead at PROVEN.	Appendix IV
			154 Inf Bde. (51st Division) administered by 23rd Division supplies	

WAR DIARY
or
INTELLIGENCE SUMMARY.

Army Form C. 2118.

Place	Date	Hour	Summary of Events and Information	Remarks and references to Appendices
EPERLECQUES	11th Cont^d		Supplies for this Brigade conveyed by lorry to Rylling Point at BAYENGHEM	
	12th	-	190 Coy A.S.C. moved to M.3.C. Sheet 28 (KENORA Camp?) 191 Coy A.S.C. moved to SALPERWICK R.21.C.7.1. Sheet 27.A. S.E.	
	13th	-	Transport, 5 G.S. Wagons for Divisional work. T/Lt. D.D. Bulger A.S.C. joined from B.H.T.D. & HAVRE & is taken on the strength of the train	Authy. D.R.Q.M.G. Fifth Army V/8/388/17 dd/10.7.17
	14th	-	Transport 4 G.S. Wagons for Divisional work T/Lt A.W.R. Miller A.S.C. proceeded on leave	
	15th	-	Transport 4 G.S. Wagons for Divisional work 190 Coy A.S.C. moved to F.27.b.7.6 Sheet 27 (near Proven)	
	16th	-	Transport four G.S. wagons for Divisional work T/Capt. J.A. Francis, proceeded on leave.	
	17th	-	T/Lt. C.C. de Wilton, proceeded on leave	

Army Form C. 2118.

WAR DIARY
or
INTELLIGENCE SUMMARY.
(Erase heading not required.)

Instructions regarding War Diaries and Intelligence Summaries are contained in F.S. Regs., Part II. and the Staff Manual respectively. Title pages will be prepared in manuscript.

Place	Date	Hour	Summary of Events and Information	Remarks and references to Appendices
EPERLECQUES	Aug 19th	cont.	Extract from London Gazette dy/16-8-17:- Army Service Corps. C.Q.M.S. R.A. KEENE from London Regt. T.F. to be Lieut. (23.6.17).	
	20th		T/Capt. E.H. MITCHELL proceeded on leave. Trade allotment, two ten days. Transport 8 G.S. wagons for Divisional work.	
	21st		190 Coy. move to G3c3.9 Sheet 28. (near POPERINGHE) Transport 5 G.S. wagons for Divisional work.	
	23rd		191 Coy A.S.C. proceeded en route to RENINGHELST Area, halting for night 23rd/24th at NOORDPEENE (near CASSEL) 192 Coy. A.S.C. proceeded en route to WIPPENHOEK Area, halting for night 23rd/24th at NOORDPEENE (near CASSEL).	Appendix V
	24th		193 Coy. moved to G.22.D.2.4 Sheet 28 (near RENINGHELST) 191 Coy. A.S.C. moved to G.22.D.2.1 Sheet 28 (near RENINGHELST) 192 Coy. A.S.C. moved to L.35.a.8.8 Sheet 27 (near WIPPENHOEK)	

Army Form C. 2118.

WAR DIARY
or
INTELLIGENCE SUMMARY.
(Erase heading not required.)

Instructions regarding War Diaries and Intelligence Summaries are contained in F. S. Regs., Part II. and the Staff Manual respectively. Title pages will be prepared in manuscript.

Place	Date	Hour	Summary of Events and Information	Remarks and references to Appendices
ESQUELBECQ	August 24th	—	70th Brigade administered by 23rd Division. 23rd Division (less Artillery) transferred to II Corps.	Appendix V
	" 10 a.m.	—	Train Headquarters moved to G.22.D.4. Sheet 28 (Ruen RENINGHELST)	
RENINGHELST	" 25th	—	RAILHEAD RENINGHELST.	
			Supplies drawn in bulk by Horse Transport from Railhead & conveyed to Refilling Points at respective Coy. Camps. Transport 4 G.S. wagons for Divisional work.	
DICKEBUSCH	26th	—	Train Headquarters move to H.27.D.9.8 Sheet 28 (DICKEBUSCH)	Appendix VI
			193 Coy. A.S.C. move to DICKEBUSCH, H.27.D.2.0 Sheet 28.	
			192 Coy. A.S.C. move to DICKEBUSCH, H.27.D.3.0 Sheet 28.	
			T. Capt. J.A. FRANCIS returned from leave.	
			Transport, 7 G.S. wagons for Divisional work.	
	27th	—	Railhead DICKEBUSCH.	
			Brigade Groups draw supplies in detail by Horse Transport from Railhead.	
			T. 2/Lt. C.C. du WILTON returned from leave.	

Army Form C. 2118.

WAR DIARY
or
INTELLIGENCE SUMMARY.
(Erase heading not required.)

Instructions regarding War Diaries and Intelligence Summaries are contained in F. S. Regs., Part II. and the Staff Manual respectively. Title pages will be prepared in manuscript.

Place	Date	Hour	Summary of Events and Information	Remarks and references to Appendices
DICKEBUSCH	August 27th	-	Cont'd Transport 13 G.S. wagons for Divisional work.	
	28th	-	Transport 17 G.S. wagons for Divisional work.	
	29th	-	T./Lt. A.W. HOOLEY & Lt. H.T. GILCHRIST, with 24 pack animals proceeded to ECOLE, YPRES, for duty temporarily as carrying party.	
			T./Lt. A.W.R. MILLER returned from leave.	
			191 Coy. A.S.C. moved to DICKEBUSCH. H.27.D.22. (Ref: Appendix VII)	
	30th	-	Transport 16 G.S. wagons for Divisional work	
			T./Lt. A.W. TURNER, A.S.C. joined the train from B.H.T.D, & taken in taken on the strength of the train.	
			193 Coy A.S.C. moved to WIPPENHOEK Area, L.29.C.5.1. Sheet 27.	
	3/38	-	T./Lt. D.D. BULGER & T.2/Lt. C. BRIDGES proceeded on leave.	
	1-9-17			

A. Miller Lt.Col.
COM'G. 2nd DIVISIONAL TRAIN A.S.C.

Appendix I

SECRET.

COPY NO: 12

23rd DIVISIONAL ORDER NO: 134.

REFERENCE: Map Sheet HAZEBROUCK 5.a Scale 1/100,000.

1. The 70th Infantry Brigade Group, 194 Machine Gun Company and Mobile Vet. Section will move to the Second Army Area tomorrow 6th instant in accordance with the attached march table.
 The dismounted portion will entrain at CAESTRE for ARQUES whence they will march to billets in the RENNESCURE Area for the night 6th/7th, and will march to the BOUVELINGHEM Area on the following day. Head of column should enter CAESTRE at 12.30 p.m.

2. Transport and mounted portion will march to RENNESCURE tomorrow under the Brigade Transport Officer. They will rejoin their units in billets the same evening. Transport will march with units on 7th instant.

3. Transport of 194 Machine Gun Company and the Mobile Vet. Section will march with transport of 70th Brigade Group. G.O.C. 70th Infantry Brigade will issue necessary orders.

4. Details of 68th Infantry Brigade and 70th Infantry Brigade which have been employed with X Corps will, after relief tomorrow, rejoin their units at RENNESCURE in accordance with arrangements made by 23rd Div. "Q".

5. The two Companies of the 70th Infantry Brigade employed at X Corps School will rejoin their Brigade in the BOUVELINGHEM Area on 7th instant. G.O.C. 70th Infantry Brigade will inform Commandant X Corps School where these Companies should be sent.

6. The Divisional Gas School will remain at METEREN until the completion of present course on evening of 6th instant, when it will move to WIZERNES. "Q" will arrange for the return of the class to their units.

7. The A.D.M.S. will issue orders to Medical Units.

8. Administrative instruction will be issued by "Q".

9. ACKNOWLEDGE.

ACPickendon Capt
for Lieut-Colonel,
General Staff.

5th August, 1917.

Issued at 10 p.m.

Distribution overleaf.

2.

Copies to :-

Nos.
1. R.A.
2. R.E.
3. 68th Inf. Bde.
4. 69th Inf. Bde.
5. 70th Inf. Bde.
6. Signals.
7. A.&.Q.
8. A.D.M.S.
9. X Corps.
10. X Corps.
11. 194 Machine Gun Coy.
12. Div. Train.
13. D.A.D.O.S.
14. D.A.D.V.S.
15. A.P.M.
16. Camp Comdt.
17. D.G.O.
18. 9th S/Staffs.
19. File.
20. Diary.
21. Diary.
22. Mobile Vet. Section.

Appendix I.a

MARCH TIME TABLE TO ACCOMPANY 23rd DIVISION ORDER 134.

UNIT.	DATE	MOVE. FROM.	MOVE. TO.	ROUTE.	REPORT FOR BILLETS TO	SUPPLY RAILHEAD.	REMARKS.
70th Bde. Group 194th M.G.Coy. (dismounted portion).	Aug. 6th.	X Corps Area.	RENNESCURE Area.	By train from CAESTRE to ARQUES.	Area Commdt. RENNESCURE in advance.		
Mounted portion of above and Mob. Vet. Section.	"	--ditto--	--ditto--	EECKE -ST. SYLVESTRE CAPPEL KOORTEN LOOP (Sheet 27 - P.27.d)	--ditto--	Bde. Group will draw at ST. OMER for first time on 7th Aug.	Mounted portion must be west of ST. SYLVESTRE CAPPEL by 10 a.m. on 6th Aug.
The whole.	Aug. 7th.	RENNESCURE Area.	LUMBRES Area.	TATINGHEM, QUELMES.	Area. Commdt. LUMBRES in Advance.		

Appendix II

SECRET.

COPY NO: 12

23rd DIVISIONAL ORDER NO. 133.

REFERENCE: Map Sheet HAZEBROUCK 5.a Scale 1/100,000.

1. In accordance with instructions from X Corps, Divisional Head-Quarters will move to WIZERNES on 6th instant.

2. 68th Infantry Brigade Head-Quarters will move from WIZERNES to ESQUERDES on 6th instant.

3. The Divisional Gas School will remain at METEREN.

4. Divisional Head-Quarters will close at MERRIS at 10 a.m. and will open at the same time at WIZERNES.

5. Administrative instructions concerning the move will be issued by "Q"

6. Acknowledge.

A.C. Richardson Cpt.
for. Lieutenant-Colonel,
General Staff.

5th August, 1917.
Issued at 9 a.m.

Copies to :-

Nos.						
1	R.A.	6	Signals.	11	194th M.G.Coy.
2	R.E.	7	A.&Q.	12	Div. Train.
3	68th Inf. Bde.	8	A.D.M.S.	13	D.A.D.O.S.
4	69th Inf. Bde.	9	X Corps.	14	D.A.D.O.S.
5	70th Inf. Bde.	10	X Corps.	15	A.P.M.
				16	Camp Commdt.

17 9th S.Staffs R.
18 File
19 Diary.
20 Diary.

Appendix III

SECRET.

COPY NO: 12

23RD DIVISIONAL ORDER NO: 135.

REFERENCE: Map Sheet HAZEBROUCK 5.a., Scale 1/100,000.

1. The Division will move on 9th instant to EPERLECQUES Area.

2. 68th Infantry Brigade Group will march to SERQUES Area and will use any roads East of the line drawn through 1st S of SETQUES - Q of QUELMES - M of MOULLE.
   70th Infantry Brigade Group will march to EPERLECQUES Area and will use any roads West of line B of BAYENGHEM - Cross Roads ½ mile W. of B of BOISDINGHEM - H of HOULLE.
   69th Infantry Brigade will march to the MOULLE Area and will use any roads between the above lines.
   Brigades wishing to use roads outside the above lines must make mutual arrangement with the Brigade concerned.

3. 194th Machine Gun Company and 35th Mobile Veterinary Section will march with 70th Infantry Brigade Group.

4. Administrative instructions and billeting areas will be issued by "Q".

5. The A.D.M.S. will issue orders for moves of Medical Units.

6. The Field Companies R.E. will move to-day under orders of C.R.E.

7. ACKNOWLEDGE.

A.C. Richardson Capt
for. Lieutenant-Colonel,
General Staff.

8th August, 1917.

Issued at 1 P.M.

Copies to :-

Nos.		Nos.	
1	R.A.	13	194 Machine Gun Coy.
2	R.E.	14	Divl. Train.
3	68th Inf.Bde.	15	D.A.D.O.S.
4	69th Inf.Bde.	16	D.A.D.V.S.
5	70th Inf.Bde.	17	A.P.M.
6	Signals.	18	Camp Comdt.
7	A.&Q.	19	D.G.O.
8	A.D.M.S.	20	9th S/Staffs.
9	V Corps.	21	File.
10	X Corps.	22	Diary.
11	X Corps.	23	Diary.
12	XVIII Corps.	24	Mobile Vet. Section.

Appendix IV

SECRET.   COPY NO: 17

23RD DIVISIONAL ORDER NO: 136.

REFERENCE: Map Sheet HAZEBROUCK 5.a., Scale 1/100,000.

1. The 70th Infantry Brigade will move tomorrow August 10th to TUNNELLING CAMP, ST. JAN TER BIEZEN, exchanging with 154th Infantry Brigade of 51st Division which will come into the GANSPETTE Area.
   Moves will take place in accordance with the following Table :-

UNIT.	DATE.	FROM.	TO.	REMARKS.
70th Inf.Bde. (Dismounted portion).	AUGUST 10th	WATTEN.	PROVEN.	By train. March to ST. JAN TER BIEZEN.
70th Inf.Bde. (Mounted portion).	10th	GANSPETTE AREA.	Staging Area. VIII Corps.	Further orders will be issued by "Q".
- do -	11th	Staging Area VIII Corps.	ST. JAN TER BIEZEN.	

   Details of Train will be issued by "Q". *Medical arrangements will be made by A.D.M.S.*

2. The 70th Infantry Brigade will continue to be administered and trained by the 23rd Division and the 154th Infantry Brigade by the 51st Division.
   70th Infantry Brigade will be rationed by 51st Division and 154th Infantry Brigade by 23rd Division.

3. Completion of moves to be reported to Divisional Head-Quarters by wire.

4. ACKNOWLEDGE.

                                                         A C Richardson Capt.
                                                         for Lieutenant-Colonel,
                                                             General Staff.

9th August, 1917.

Issued at 2-30 p.m.

Copies to :-

Nos.		Nos.	
1	70th Inf.Bde.	11	194 Machine Gun Coy.
2	68th Inf.Bde.	12	Divisional Train.
3	69th Inf.Bde.	13	D.A.D.O.S.
4	R.E.	14	A.P.M.
5	Signals.	15	File.
6	A.&Q.	16	Diary.
7	A.D.M.S.	17	Diary.
8	V Corps.		
9	VIII Corps.		
10	XVIII Corps.		

Appendix V

COPY NO: 9

SECRET

23RD DIVISIONAL ORDER NO: 138.

1. The 23rd Division (less Artillery) is to be transferred to II Corps with effect from 10 a.m. 24th August.

2. Moves will be carried out in accordance with the attached March Table.

3. The following intervals will be maintained on the march in II Corps Area.

   (a) E. of RENINGHELST - POPERINGHE Road 200 yards between Companies.

   (b) W. of above road 500 yards between Battalions.

4. Divisional Supply Column will move by road under arrangements to be made by "Q" II Corps.

5. Mounted portions of the Division halting for the night at NOORDPEENE will report in advance to Area Commandant, NOORDPEENE for details as to accommodation.

6. Transport of 194th Machine Gun Coy., Divisional Signal Company and Mobile Veterinary Section will be attached to 69th Brigade Group for the march.

7. Commanders of Mounted Columns will be appointed by 68th and 69th Infantry Brigades.

8. "Q" will issue orders as regards train movements, supply and other administrative arrangements.

9. ACKNOWLEDGE.

A.C. Richardson Cpt.
Lieutenant-Colonel,
General Staff.

22nd August, 1917.

Issued at 2.30 p.m.

Copies to :-

No. 1 C.R.A.
2 C.R.E.
3 68th Inf. Bde.
4 69th Inf. Bde.
5 70th Inf. Bde.
6 Signals.
7 "Q"
8 A.D.M.S.
9 Train.
10 D.A.D.O.S.

No. 11 D.A.D.V.S.
12 S.S.O.
13 A.P.M.
14 Camp Comdt.
15 II Corps.
16 V Corps.
17 XVIII Corps.
18 D.M.G.O.
19 Area Comdt., NOORDPEENE.
20 File.
21 War Diary.
22 War Diary.

MARCH TABLE TO ACCOMPANY 23RD DIVISIONAL ORDER NO:138. (CONTINUED).

SERIAL NO:	DATE.	UNIT.	FROM.	TO.	UNDER ORDERS OF.	REMARKS.
6.	26th	3 Field Companies, R.E. Pioneer Battalion.	XVIII Corps Area.	1 Fd.Co. BUSSEBOOM. 1 Fd.Co. WIPPENHOEK AREA. 1 Fd.Co. OUDERDOM AREA. Pioneer Battalion WIPPENHOEK AREA.	II Corps.	Via VLAMERTINGHE-OUDERDOM Rd. To arrive at destination by 10 a.m. Orders for move to be issued by C.R.E.

MARCH TABLE TO ACCOMPANY 23RD DIVISIONAL ORDER No. 158.

SERIAL NO:	DATE.	UNIT.	FROM.	TO.	UNDER ORDERS OF.	REMARKS.
1	23rd	70th Infantry Bde. Group.	XVIII Corps Area.	DOMINION AREA. (G.23.b.).	II Corps.	Via POPERINGHE-N.SWITCH Rd.-POPERINGHE VLAMERTINGHE Rd. as far as G.5.c.9.3.-G.17.c.6.9. Head of Column enter POPERINGHE-VLAMERTINGHE Rd. at 9.30 a.m.
2	23rd	Mounted Portion 68th Bde. Group.	EPERLECQUES AREA.	NOORDPEENE AREA.	V Corps.	via SERQUES-ST. MOMELIN AND LEDERZEELE. To be clear of SERQUES by 9 a.m.
3	23rd	Mounted Portion 69th Bde. Group.	EPERLECQUES AREA.	NOORDPEENE AREA.	V Corps.	To follow 58th Bde.Group at 1 mile distance.
4	24th	Dismounted Portion 23rd Divn.	EPERLECQUES AREA.	D.H.Q. RENINGHELST. 68th Bde. OUDERDOM AREA. 69th Bde. WIPPENHOEK AREA.	II Corps.	By train. Details to be issued by "Q" 23rd Division.
5.	24th	Mounted Portion 68th & 69th Bdes.	NOORDPEENE AREA	68th Bde. OUDERDOM. 69th Bde. WIPPENHOEK.	II Corps.	Via HARDIFORT-OUDEZEELE-STEENVOORDE-ABEELE-RENINGHELST. Head of Column to enter STEENVOORDE at 9 a.m. Order of March as in Serial No. 2 and 3.

P. T. O.

SECRET. *Appendix VI* COPY NO: 9

23RD DIVISIONAL ORDER NO: 139.

REFERENCE: Sheet 28. Scale, 1/40,000.

1. The 23rd Division (less Artillery) will relieve the 14th Division (less Artillery) in the Centre Sector of the Corps front, which extends from about point J.19.b.7.7. to J.8.c.65.20.

2. The 70th Infantry Brigade will take over this front to-night. Details of the relief will be arranged direct between G.Os.C. Brigades concerned. Completion of the relief will be reported in code to 14th Divisional Headquarters.

3. Two battalions 70th Infantry Brigade will move by lorry to CAFE BELGE at 11.30 a.m. and thence march to CHAU SEGARD, the remainder of the Brigade moving in a similar manner and to the same place at 3.30 p.m.
    Transport, except cookers, will not move till the afternoon under orders to be issued later.

4. Special precautions will be taken to gain and maintain touch with Brigades on the flanks; and for the defence of the strong point at J.14.a.3.2.

5. The 73rd Brigade, 24th Division, will be on the right of 70th Infantry Brigade. Head-Quarters LARCH WOOD.
    The 142nd Infantry Brigade, 47th Division, will be on the left of 70th Infantry Brigade. Head-Quarters BIRR CROSS ROADS.

6. The 69th Infantry Brigade and 194th Machine Gun Company will move by lorry this afternoon from WIPPENHOEK AREA to CHAU SEGARD and DICKEBUSCH. Separate orders for this move will be issued later.

7. G.O.C. 23rd Division will assume command of the front at 10 a.m. on 26th, at which hour the office of the Division will open at H.27.b.7.7.

8. ACKNOWLEDGE.

Evans
Lieutenant-Colonel,
General Staff.

25th August, 1917.

Issued at 10.45 a.m.

Copies to :-

No. 1.	C.R.A.	No. 10.	S.S.O.
2.	C.R.E.	11.	A.P.M.
3.	68th Inf.Bde.	12.	II Corps.
4.	69th Inf.Bde.	13.	14th Division.
5.	70th Inf.Bde.	14.	24th Division.
6.	Signals.	15.	47th Division.
7.	"A" & "Q".	16.	D.M.G.O.
8.	A.D.M.S.	17.	File.
9.	Train.	18.	War Diary.

No. 19. War Diary.

Appendix VI a

SECRET

23rd Divn.No.S.G.116/7/4.

C.R.A.
C.R.E.
68th Infantry Brigade.
69th Infantry Brigade.
70th Infantry Brigade.
Signals.
"A" & "Q".
A.D.M.S.
Train.

S.S.O.
A.P.M.
II Corps.
14th Division.
24th Division.
47th Division.
D.M.G.O.

Para. 2 of Divisional Order No. 139 is cancelled and the following will be substituted :-

"G.O.C. 41st Infantry Brigade will command this front.

Two battalions 70th Infantry Brigade and 70th Machine Gun Company will be placed at his disposal from 4 pm. to-day; remainder of 70th Infantry Brigade will be at CHAU SEGARD from 8 p.m."

ACKNOWLEDGE.

23rd Division.
25th August, 1917.

Lieutenant-Colonel,
General Staff.

Appendix VII

SECRET　　　　　　　　　　　　　　　　　　　　Copy No. 12

23rd DIVISION ORDER NO. 141.

Map Reference — Map 1/20,000, Sheet 28 N.W.

1. The 68th Infantry Brigade will move from the OUDERDOM area to the DICKEBUSCH area (vacated by 41st Infantry Brigade) on 29th instant.

2. The Brigade will not move before 5.30 p.m. and move will be completed by 8.30 p.m.

3. Transport will move under Brigade arrangements.

4. ACKNOWLEDGE.

A.C. Richardson, Capt
Lieut.-Colonel,
General Staff.

29th August, 1917.

Issued at 11.30 a/m

Copies to :—

No.	
1	C.R.E.
2	Signals.
3	68th Inf. Bde.
4	69th Inf. Bde.
5	70th Inf. Bde.
6	D.M.G.O.
7	A.&.Q.
8	A.D.M.S.
9	D.A.D.O.S.
10	D.A.D.V.S.
11	A.P.M.
12	Train.
13	S.S.O.
14	Camp Commdt.
15	II Corps "G"
17	II Corps "Q"
18	War Diary
19	War Diary.
20	File.

Army Form C. 2118.

23 D Train
96 25

WAR DIARY
or
INTELLIGENCE SUMMARY.
(Erase heading not required.)

Instructions regarding War Diaries and Intelligence Summaries are contained in F. S. Regs., Part II. and the Staff Manual respectively. Title pages will be prepared in manuscript.

Place	Date	Hour	Summary of Events and Information	Remarks and references to Appendices
DICKEBUSCH	Sept 1st 1917		Railhead DICKEBUSCH Siding	
			68th and 69th Bde Groups drawn in whole from railhead. 70th Bde Group by D.S.C.	
			R.P. at WIPPENHOEK. R.A. and No.1 Co Train attacks by enemy raiders at	
			DESELHOEK. Train by D.S.C. to R.P. at POPERINGHE - VLAMERTINGE road.	
			No T3/025010 Dr. O. BRADLEY 192 Co. HQ killed by shell fire on 31st ult.	
			Leave allotment two per day.	
DICKEBUSCH 2nd			Train H.Q. moved to STEENWOORDE	
			192 Co. A.F.C. moved to STEENWOORDE area	
			Supplies for 69th Bde Group by D.S.C. to R.P. in STEENWOORDE area	
STEENWOORDE 3rd			Railhead WIPPENHOEK. Supplies by D.S.C. to A.S.C. Coy from lorries an incoming	APPENDIX Vol 1r, 16
			191 Co. A.F.C. moved to STEENWOORDE area	
			192 " " " LEDERZEELE "	
			19.3 " " " OOSTHOEK NOORDPEENE "	
STEENWOORDE 4th			Train H.R. moved to LEDERZEELE. Supply arrangements as on 3rd	s - No 2
			O.C. Train issued new rolls of Div Train lifting to each Supt. Lowest Ranks	DRO 2408 2411-9-17
			193 Co. A.F.C. moved to OOSTHOUCK area.	

Army Form C. 2118.

WAR DIARY
or
INTELLIGENCE SUMMARY.
(Erase heading not required.)

Instructions regarding War Diaries and Intelligence Summaries are contained in F. S. Regs., Part II. and the Staff Manual respectively. Title pages will be prepared in manuscript.

Place	Date	Hour	Summary of Events and Information	Remarks and references to Appendices
LEDERSEELE	Sept 5th		Rallies ST. OMER - Supplies drawn from Detail Issue Stores by DSC to RD Coys	
			ASC Conference Camp.	
			191 C DSC moved to ARNEKE area	
	6th		7 Lieut LEWBURG processed to England on 2nd leave for attachment to infantry	[notes]
			Following of W.O. Cl 1 proceeded to C.I, J. BLYTH, A.J. DRAPER, A.T. EMBLETON, J. MONTGOMERY. Acting MC. ASC Sec. P.O/3472/1154 of 29-8-17	
			7 Lt RASELIOT and T2LT (a/L) WALACY proceed to England for attachment to Infantry	[notes]
			T2Lt. CC de WILTON left on 14 days of Autumn Leave - temporarily from Lt. W.B. LACEY MC.	
			Inspected Motor Transport by FD ASC Govt with DADVS.	
			Thank DD BUGER relieved of leave	
	7th		191 C ASC moved to BRAKE Camp - WESTOUTRE	
			Capt H. MORTHEN proceed on 14 days leave to England, and 2 Lt RAKESME on 10 days leave	
			Lieut D GREEN attacks to Train for instruction	
			Inspected 1st Line Transport 71st & 74 Brit Group with DADVS	

WAR DIARY
or
INTELLIGENCE SUMMARY.
(Erase heading not required.)

Army Form C. 2118.

Place	Date	Hour	Summary of Events and Information	Remarks and references to Appendices
LE DERZEELE	Sept 8		Inspected 1st Aux Transports 66 Coy Bn Group both DADsS	
			Reported following casualties in 4th Army from 1st to 6th Sept: Killed OR 2, Died of wounds OR 1, Wounded OR 8	
	9		Rallens FB Group Bakery Supplies by DSC Lt RP on the 1st Coy Camp	
			Following transferred to II Army Packer (Pard) in 2Lt AWR MILKER, OR 3 and One Motor car	
			Authority AMG 61/74 (QAI) of 16-6-17	
	10		Inspected 1st Line Tr. of 3 Fields Ambulance, 9th Sc Shopp. & 3 Co R.E. and DADsS	
	11		102nd F.C. R.E. 43 Co. 9th S. Shafford's found 245 Divnn O/10 E new supplies	Appendix No 3
			from 24 F Div this day	
	12		193 C ACC moved to ZUYTPEENE area	Appendix No 4 - 4a, 4b
	13		191 C. ACC moved to STEENWORDE Town area. 192 C ACC to STEENWORDE WEST	
			193 C ACC to STEENWORDE EAST	
			Supply arrangements made for R.P.s on ASC Coys in Corps Camp	
			Capt. LLOYD DAVIS proceeded on 10 days leave to England	
			Capt. A St G. ADAMS transferred to RFC on 12 Aug Authority ASC 17246 Dy g-2-17	

WAR DIARY or INTELLIGENCE SUMMARY.

Army Form C. 2118.

Place	Date	Hour	Summary of Events and Information	Remarks and references to Appendices
LEDERSEELE	Sept. 14.		TRAIN H.Q. moved to ZEVECOTEN area REMINGHELST	
			RAILHEAD OUDERDOM. Supplies by D.S.C. to A.S.C. Corporal's Camps for 3 Brigade Groups	
			and by H.T. to R.P. at LA CLYTTE for H.Q. Group	
			192 Coy. A.S.C. moved to WESTOUTRE area – see Appx 37	Appendix 5
			191 & 193 Coys. to town area ZEVECOTEN (G.35.d central)	
			2 Lt A.W. TURNER admitted to 140 F.A. and subsequently to No. 2 Stationary Hospital, Rouen	
ZEVECOTEN	15.		All supplies drawn by H.T. from OUDERDOM	
			Train H.Q. moved to G.31.d central.	
			Purchase of all supplies in Belgium forbidden X Copy R.O. 1397	
			Transport 6 G.S. wagons for Divisional work	
	16.		192 Coy A.S.C. moved to MIC MAC Camp. BARRAGE ration issued to R.A. & 66th 13th Bde Groups Appendix	5&7
			Capt APPLEYARD attached to Train for instruction	
	17.		Transport 6 G.S. wagons on Divisional work	
			BARRAGE rations issued to 69th & 70th 13th Bde. Groups	
			Bivouac Park rations issued to H.Q. and 66th 13th Bde Groups	ditto

Army Form C. 2118.

WAR DIARY
or
INTELLIGENCE SUMMARY.
(Erase heading not required.)

Instructions regarding War Diaries and Intelligence Summaries are contained in F. S. Regs., Part II. and the Staff Manual respectively. Title pages will be prepared in manuscript.

Place	Date	Hour	Summary of Events and Information	Remarks and references to Appendices
ZEVECOTEN	Sept. 18th		Received Pack saddles issued to 6g.F. & 70.F. Bde groups	Appendix 5 and 7.
			Transport 17 G.S. wagons on Divisional work	
	19th		Clipping of all horses to be completed by 15th Nov. G.R.O. 2624 of 15-9-17. R/Lieut. E.A. MICHIE joined from Base 4th Depot. Auth'y DDS-7 A/S6079 No. 2229	
			2/Lt CROFT detailed as Off. in "a" sup[ply] at 112 Tank YOURMEZEELE for convey.	Appendix No 8.
			Handed over field line east of ST pont	
			2nd Lt LODGE detailed for duty as O.C. 6 G.S. wagons at Boot Show	
			Transport 19 G.S. wagons for Divisional work	
	20th		Transport 13 G.S. wagons for Divisional work	
	21st		Casualties 191 Co. A.S.C. Killed O.R. 1 Wounded O.R. 1 by shell fire	R/Lt Huston
			192 Co. Killed O.R. 4 Died of wounds O.R. 2 Wounded O.R. 5 all by shell.	No. 9
			193 Co. Died of wounds O.R. 1 by shell. Rounds filled 8, wounds received 5.	
			Wounded 5 -	
	22nd		Transport 18 G.S. wagons on Divisional work.	

Army Form C. 2118.

WAR DIARY
or
INTELLIGENCE SUMMARY.
(Erase heading not required.)

Instructions regarding War Diaries and Intelligence Summaries are contained in F. S. Regs., Part II. and the Staff Manual respectively. Title pages will be prepared in manuscript.

Place	Date	Hour	Summary of Events and Information	Remarks and references to Appendices
ZEPECOTEN	Sept 23		Special order of the day	Appendix No. 10
			Lieut BULGER and 7 NCOs went to STOMER to draw removals	
			Capt H NORTHEN grants exlension of leave from 13th each to 7th Oct.	
			Transport 6 P.S. wagons	
	24	6—	191 G. Arr. moved to CONQUEROR Camp HERKEN	Appendix
"		"	193 G " " " Camp 37 on RENINGHELST—LOCRE road	11-11a-11b
			Supplies for 6F & 6Bde Group conveyed by DSR to CONQUEROR Camp	
			SSM. g/ LCSSM N McDonell promoted LCQMS from 2.9.19	
			Railhead RENINGHELST siding. Supplies drawn by HT to RPs on Train Coy lorries	
"	25		HD Train moved to WESTOUTRE	
			192 G. ARR moved to Camp at MIC 36, on RENINGHELST—LOCRE road	
			Capt AC PERRYMAN to England on 10 days leave	
			1A HD removals arrived from STOMER with Lieut BULGER	
WESTOUTRE	26—		FGCM on Dr GIBBARD 192 G. Arr. accused in acquitted.	Appendix
	27		69 and 70 LH of Bde moved to forward area, Train Coys was did not move	12

Army Form C. 2118.

WAR DIARY
or
INTELLIGENCE SUMMARY.
(Erase heading not required.)

Instructions regarding War Diaries and Intelligence Summaries are contained in F.S. Regs., Part II. and the Staff Manual respectively. Title pages will be prepared in manuscript.

Place	Date	Hour	Summary of Events and Information	Remarks and references to Appendices
WESTOUTRE	Sept 28		H.Q. Train moved to LA CLYTTE Camp	App. 9xx
			191 Co. A.S.C. reported to M.L.O 27 in Lt HERISON-HOGARTH (in)	App. 3
			192 Co. A.S.C. ditto	
			Train Park Company under Lt HOOLEY 2nd & 2Lt GILCHRIST, 33 NCOs rank and file	
			20 animals. proceeded to H.29 Central - Dar Road Show for duty	
			Transport to form a Personnel work.	
LA CLYTTE	29		Reinforcements. 2 Sergts & 2 Cpls & 6 Drivers from Base H.T. Depot	
			Capt. R.V. HOLMES took over duties of Adjutant temporarily from 2Lt CLARKSON	
			Transport 24 hours on Dei work.	
			Train Park Company moves to Nod Central	
	30		Railhead BAILLEUL. Supplies by D.S.C. "C" R.P.3 in Train Composite hrs	

October 1st 1917

A. Nesbitt
Lt.Col.
Comg 23rd D.S. Train

Appendix No 1

SECRET.   Copy No. 9

23rd DIVISION ORDER No. 143.

Reference Map: HAZEBROUCK 5A, 1/100,000.

(1) Moves as shewn in the attached March Table will take place on Monday 3rd inst.

(2) Divisional H.Q. will remain at STEENVOORDE.

(3) ACKNOWLEDGE.

A C Richardson Capt
for
Lieut-Colonel,
General Staff.

23rd Division.
2nd September, 1917.

Issued at 6 pm

Copies to :-

No. 1 C.R.E.
    2 C.R.A.
    3 68th Inf Brigade.
    4 69th Inf Brigade.
    5 70th Inf Brigade.
    6 A. & Q.
    7 A.D.M.S.
    8 D.A.D.V.S.
    9 Train.
   10 S.S.O.
   11 Signals.
   12 Xth Corps "G"
   13 Xth Corps "Q"
   14 II Corps.
   15 War Diary.
   16 War Diary.
   17 File.
   18 Area Comndr, STEENVOORDE
   19   "   "   NOORDPEENE
   20   "   "   LEDERZEELE

Appendix No 1a

MARCH TABLE ISSUED WITH 23rd DIVISION ORDER NO. 143.

Serial No.	Unit.	Date.	From	To	Route	To report for billets to	Remarks.
1	68th Inf Bde Group less 1 Bn (in STEENVOORDE Area)	Sept 3rd.	DICKEBUSCH Area and WIPPENHOEK	STEENVOORDE E. Area.	RENINGHELST ABEELE.	Area Commandant STEENVOORDE.	Head of Column to enter RENINGHELST at 2 p.m.
2	69th Inf Bde Group	3rd.	STEENVOORDE.	LEDERZEELE Area.	RAVINCOVE.	Area Commandant LEDERZEELE.	Not to enter LEDERZEELE Area before 2 pm.
3	70th Inf Bde Group	3rd.	WIPPENHOEK Area.	NOORDPEENE Area.	do.	Area Commandant NOORDPEENE.	To follow 69th Bde Head of column to enter STEENVOORDE at 9-30 a.m.
4	70th Inf Bde Group	4th.	NOORDPEENE Area.	LEDERZEELE Area.	Any	Area Commandant LEDERZEELE.	

All movement E. of RENINGHELST - POPERINGHE Road to be by Companys at 200 yards distance.
All movement W. of above line to be by Battns at 500 yards distance.
Transport will march with units.

RE and Pioneers are not included in Bde Groups.

SECRET

Appendix No. 1 C.

23rd DIVISIONAL ADMINISTRATIVE INSTRUCTIONS No.133 issued with reference to DIVISIONAL ORDER No.143, 2nd September 1917.
───

Reference Map: HAZEBROUCK.5.a., 1/100,000.

1. SUPPLY. Railhead. No change for 3rd.
   71st Field Ambulance will accompany 68th Inf. Bde. on 3rd September.
   70th Field Ambulance (less detachment and 1 Tent Sub-Division) will accompany 70th Inf. Bde. on 3rd September.
   69th Field Ambulance and Tent Sub-Division of 70th Field Ambulance will join 69th and 70th Inf.Bdes. respectively on 4th. Grouping for Supplies will be arranged accordingly by O.C. Divisional Train.

   Refilling Points on 3rd.

         68th Brigade. RENINGHELST. (Train Coy. to march full).
         69th Brigade. LEDERZEELE Area.
         70th Brigade. NOORDPEENE Area.

   Under arrangements to be made by O.C. Divisional Train.

   R.E. Units and Pioneers will be supplied direct by lorry under arrangements to be made by O.C. Train.

2. ORDNANCE. D.A.D.O.S. will move to LEDERZEELE on 3rd inst. Location of Ordnance Stores will be notified later.

3. LAUNDRY. The Laundry Personnel under Lieut. HORNE will remain in charge of the RENINGHELST Laundry until further orders. Application for clean clothing will be made to Divisional Headquarters.

4. GAS SCHOOL. The Gas School will move to LEDERZEELE on 3rd inst.

5. Lorries for Advance Parties and spare kit will be provided as follows :-
       69th & 70th Inf.Bdes.   9 each.
       68th Inf.Bde.   7.
       D.A.D.O.S.   3. (For Gas School.)

E. F. Falkner.
Lieut-Colonel,
A.A. & Q.M.G., 23rd Division.

2nd Sept. 1917.

Copies issued at 8.0 p.m. to :-

68th Inf.Bde.	Train.	D.A.D.O.S.
69th Inf.Bde.	S.S.O.	Posts.
70th Inf.Bde.	A.D.M.S.	Divl. Gas Officer.
C.R.E.	D.A.D.V.S.	G., AQ, Diary, File.

SECRET.   Copy No. 9

23rd DIVISION ORDER No. 144.

Reference Map:- HAZEBROUCK 5A, 1/100,000

1. Divisional Head-Quarters will move tomorrow to LEDERZEELE. The offices will close at STEENVOORDE at 10 a.m. and will open at LEDERZEELE at the same hour.

2. The 68th Infantry Brigade will move from STEENVOORDE Area into the NOORDPEENE Area on the 5th instant under instructions to be issued later.

3. The 70th Infantry Brigade will concentrate in the OOSTHOUCK - BROXEELE Area tomorrow 4th instant. Details regarding accommodation can be obtained from Area Commandant, OOSTHOUCK.

4. ACKNOWLEDGE.

for Lieut-Colonel, Capt
General Staff.

3rd September, 1917.

Issued at 6.30. p.m.

Copies to :-

No. 1   C.R.E.
2   C.R.A.
3   68th Inf. Brigade.
4   69th Inf. Brigade.
5   70th Inf. Brigade.
6   A & Q.
7   A.D.M.S.
8   D.A.D.V.S.
9   Train.
10   S.S.O.
11   Signals.
12   X Corps "G".
13   X Corps "Q".
14   War Diary.
15   War Diary.
16   File.
17   Area Commdt. STEENVOORDE.
18   Area Commdt. NOORDPEENE.
19   Area Commdt. LEDERZEELE.
20   " " OOSTHOUCK

Appendix 3

SECRET   COPY No. 10

23rd DIVISIONAL ENGINEERS.
OPERATION ORDER No.31

1. The 102nd Field Coy. R.E. and 3 Coys. 9th Sth. Staffs.
    will proceed to the 24th Division area on the 10th instant to
    work under the orders of the C.R.E. 24th Division on preparation
    for the coming offensive.

2. Location of Billets will be as follows:-

    102nd Field Coy. R.E.   - H.33.d.8.4.

    2 Coys. 9th Sth. Staffs. - RAILWAY DUGOUTS (104th Field Co.
                                R.E. 24th Div. at Rly. Dugouts will point
                                out billets).

    1 Coy. 9th Sth. Staffs. - RIDGE WOOD Huts. N.6.central.

                                (129th Field Co. R.E. 24th Division at
                                H.33.d.8.2. will point out billets).

    Horse lines H.33.d.8.2.

3. Units will move under their own arrangements, sending an
    officer to H.Q.R.E. 24th Division (ZEVECOTEN) in advance on
    the 10th instant to receive instructions as to work to be
    carried out commencing on the 11th instant.

4. Work must be pushed on as rapidly as possible.

5. Completion of move to be wired to Hd. Qrs. R.E. 23rd & 24th
    Divisions.

6. ACKNOWLEDGE.

                                            [signature]
                                            Lieut: Colonel R.E.
9.9.17.   C.R.E. 23rd Division.

Issued at 10.30.a.m.

Copy No. 1 to 23rd Division "G"
        2   "   "   "   "Q"
        3   C.R.E. 24th Division.
        4   O.C. 101st Field Coy. A.E.
        5   "   102nd   "   "   "
        6   "   128th   "   "   "
        7   "   104th   "   "   "   24th Division.
        8   "   129th   "   "   "   "   "
        9   "   9th Sth. Staffs.
       10   "   23rd Divisional Train.
       11-12   War Diary.
       13-14   File.

SECRET.   Copy No. 9

23rd DIVISION ORDER No. 145.

1.   The 23rd Division will move in accordance with the attached table.

2.   Half a mile will be maintained between battalions and one mile between brigades.

3.   The C.R.E. will arrange with C.R.E. 24th Division for the relief of Field Companies and Pioneer Battalion of 24th Division on 14th instant.

4.   The A.D.M.S. will arrange with A.D.M.S. 24th Division for the relief of Field Ambulances.

5.   "Q" will arrange for billets or bivouacs for 70th Infantry Brigade on night 12th/13th.

6.   Brigades will detail 100 N.C.Os. and men each for attachment to Field Companies. At least two officers will be detailed to accompany each party. They will join Field Companies on 15th by mid-day. C.R.E. will inform brigades direct where these parties should report.

7.   The attached map shows the division of the Forward Area into nine Brigade areas. Bde, Q, adms, ATM only

8.   Divisional Head-Quarters will move to BURGOMASTER'S FARM, H.54.central, on 14th September.

9.   ACKNOWLEDGE.

                                                    Covans
                                                    Lieutenant-Colonel,
11th September, 1917.   General Staff.

Issued at 11 a.m.

Copies to :-
	No. 1	C.R.A.	No. 11	Signals.
	2	C.R.E.	12	X Corps "G"
	3	68th Bde.	13	X Corps "Q"
	4	69th Bde.	14	24th Div.
	5	70th Bde.	15	41st Div.
	6	A.& Q.	16	War Diary.
	7	A.D.M.S.	17	War Diary.
	8	D.A.D.V.S.	18	File.
	9	Train	19	Area Commdt. STEENVOORDE.
	10	S.S.O.	20	Area Commdt. LEDERZEELE.

AFTER ORDER. Mob. Vety. Section and Mounted Portion of D.H.Q. will be attached to and march with 39th Brigade.

Appendix
4a

SERIAL NO:	UNIT.	DATE.	FROM.	TO.	STARTING PT:	HOUR TO PASS.	REMARKS.
1.	70th Infantry Bde. 194th M.G.Coy. 69th Fd. Amb.	12.	Billets.	ZUYTPEENE Area.	-	-	Under orders of G.O.C. 70th Infantry Brigade.
2.	70th Infantry Bde. 194th M.G.Coy. 69th Fd. Amb.	13.	ZUYTPEENE Area.	STEENVOORDE EAST.	Road Junction. O.16.c.	11.30 a.m.	via BAVINCHOVE.
3.	38th Infantry Bde. 70th Fd. Amb.	13.	NOORDPEENE Area.	STEENVOORDE TOWN AREA	Road Junction. ZUYTPEENE	1.0 p.m.	via BAVINCHOVE.
4.	39th Infantry Bde. 71st Fd. Amb.	13.	OOSTHOUCK AREA.	STEENVOORDE WEST.	Cross Roads. H.32.b.	1.30 p.m.	via BAVINCHOVE.
5.	70th Bde. Group.	14.	STEENVOORDE EAST.	No. 1. (DICKEBUSCH) AREA.	Road Junction. K.35.d.	6.30 a.m.	via ABEELE-RENINGHELST & OUDERDOM. To be clear of ABEELE-BOESCHEPE Rd. by 1 p.m.
6.	68th Bde. Group.	14.	STEENVOORDE TOWN AREA	No. 5. (MURRUMBIDGE) AREA	Road Junction. K.35.d.	8.30 a.m.	via ABEELE & RENINGHELST. To be clear of ABEELE-BOESCHEPE Rd. by 1 p.m.
7.	69th Bde. Group.	14.	STEENVOORDE WEST.	No. 8. (WESTOUTRE) AREA N.W.	Road Junction. K.32.d.	9.45 a.m.	via ABEELE. To be clear of ABEELE-BOESCHEPE Rd. by 2 p.m.
8.	68th Bde. Group.	16.	No. 5. Area.	No. 4. Area.	-	-	Time of move to be notified later.
9.	69th Bde. Group.	18.	No. 8. Area.	No. 1. Area.	-	-	Time of move to be notified later.

SECRET.

Appendix 4 b

23rd DIVISIONAL ADMINISTRATIVE INSTRUCTIONS No. 134 issued with reference to DIVISIONAL ORDER No. 145 dated 11th September, 1917.

Reference : Map mentioned in para 7 of above quoted Order.

1. **BILLETING PARTIES**: Advance parties will report to Area Commandants under arrangements to be made by Brigade Groups concerned vide Billeting Area Table attached.

2. **MOVES**:

    193 Coy A.S.C. will move with 70th Brigade Group.
    192 Coy A.S.C. will move with 69th Brigade Group.
    191 Coy A.S.C. will move with 68th Brigade Group.

    71st Field Amb. will be attached to 68th Brigade Group for rations in addition to 70th Field Ambl. from 12th inst. and on 13th inst. will rejoin 69th Brigade Group vide serial No. 4 of Divisional Order No. 145.

3. **THE DIVISIONAL TRAIN** (less H.Q. Coy) will march under orders of Brigade Commanders.

4. **REFILLING POINTS** will be selected by O.C., Train who will notify all concerned later.

5. **RAILHEADS**:   ST. OMER on 13th inclusive.
               OUDERDOM on 14th onwards.

6. **BAGGAGE** Wagons will march with Units.

7. **ORDNANCE STORES** will be moved to new area under arrangements to be made by D.A.D.O.S.

8. **LORRIES** for advance parties and spare kits will be provided as follows :-

    70th Brigade   11 lorries for 12th.

    70th Brigade   )
    69th Brigade   ) For 13th.
    68th Brigade   ) To be notified
    D.A.D.O.S. (for Gas School)) later.

9. **ACKNOWLEDGE.**

E. F Falkiner.

Lieut-Colonel,

11/9/1917.
Issued at 11 45 p.m.   A.A.& Q.M.G. 23rd Division.

Copies to: All recipients of Div. Order 145 and N.C.O. i/c Posts.

P. T. O.

BILLETING AREAS.

	12th	13th	14th	16th
D. H. Q.			LA CLYTTE CAMP 28/N.6.d.5.8.	
Adv. D.H.Q.			BURGOMASTERS FM. 28/N.34.Central.	
68th Bde Group.		STEENVOORDE TOWN AREA.	No. 5 MURRUMBIDGEE AREA.	No. 4 AREA.
69th Bde Group.		STEENVOORDE WEST.	No. 8 WESTOUTRE AREA N.W.	No. 1 AREA.
70th Bde Group.	ZUYTPEENE AREA.	STEENVOORDE EAST.	No. 1 DICKEBUSCH AREA.	

On arrival of 69th Bde Group the Mobile Vet. Section will proceed to Rear D.H.Q. LA CLYTTE CAMP.

SECRET *Isin* 23rd Div.S.G.104/18/28.

Appendix 5

To all recipients of 23rd Divisional Order No. 145.

In confirmation of telegram G.S.385 to 68th, 69th Brigades, X Corps and 23rd Division "Q" and with reference to 23rd Divisional Order No. 145 of 11th September, 1917:

1. 68th Infantry Brigade will move on 16th instant from No. 5 Area to No. 4 Area via LA CLYTTE, to be clear of that place by 10 a.m.

2. 69th Infantry Brigade will move on 16th instant from No. 9 Area to No. 4 Area via RENINGHELST and OUDERDOM, to be clear of RENINGHELST by 10 a.m.

3. Companies will move at 200 yards distance.

4. Serial Nos. 8 and 9 of March Table issued with above quoted order to be amended accordingly.

5. 68th and 69th Infantry Brigades to acknowledge.

A.C.Richardson Capt
for Lieutenant-Colonel,
General Staff.

23rd Division.
15th Sept.1917.

Appendix 6

S/1211.

S E C R E T.

X Corps.

Supply Arrangements for Operations.

In conformity with Second Army letter S.Q. 964 of 5/9/17, following instructions as regards supply arrangements during forthcoming operations are forwarded for information and guidance.

Kindly circulate to Formations concerned.

Normal System of consumption.
1. The present system by which Divisional Supply Columns are empty and one complete fresh ration remains in hands of Divisional Trains over-night, will be maintained during operations. Supplies, therefore, arriving at Railhead on any given day will be <u>consumed by Units</u> on day after following day.

Method of Evacuation of Supply Trains.
2. Corps will arrange for the evacuation of Trains in bulk from Railheads by horse drawn vehicles to Divisional Refilling Points, and thence to Units as desired.

Reserve Rations other than normal, which may be held in front of Railheads.
3. In addition to the one Day's supply in hands of Trains afforded by para. 1., the following Reserve Rations may be held by Corps in Front of Railheads.

(a) Preserved Meat and Biscuit for men in Supporting Points. Number of days supply varies as sanctioned by A.H.Q.
(b) One days Iron Rations for Troops in the front line system on a scale of 1 per man of proposed garrison, to be held in reserve in addition to the iron rations on the man. To be used in the event of any occurence preventing the normal delivery of rations, or in the event of an advance, should it be considered necessary to carry 2 days iron rations on the man.
(c) One days rations, preserved meat and biscuit with tea sugar and jam for all troops inside a possible enemy barrage.

Method of receipt of and adjustment for "Barrage Rations".
4. Rations required to be drawn under "C" will be demanded by S.S.O's. on a separate A.F. W.3317. Corps will kindly indicate their approximate requirements under "C", and date desired at railhead, at least 3 days in advance. Earliest possible notice of date of intended consumption of these rations should be given to this Office, in order that packs may be adjusted to meet underdrawals.

Proportion of fresh meat and bread or Pres.meat & biscuit desired at railheads during offensive.
5. As Corps may wish to modify the proportion of fresh meat and bread arriving at railhead for certain of their Formations on or about zero day, necessary instructions will be given to Base, on receipt in this Office, of proportions required, three clear days in advance.

Supply of Heavy and Siege Artillery.

6.   A copy of the instructions of the D.A. & Q.M.G., Second Army, for supply administration of Heavy and Siege Artillery during Messines Operations is attached, and will be adhered to, also, during forthcoming operations.

The system of actual delivery to Batteries will be arranged by Corps as desired either by the Formation of a Heavy Artillery Train Company or similar expedient as the situation and conditions of each may demand.

Chewing Gum and Solidified Alcohol.

7.   Chewing gum for use during actual operations will be available on demand from R.S.O's. Solidified alcohol for some time past has been delivered to Corps on a weekly scale of 5,000 ounces per Division, and stored or distributed. A Corps reserve has thus been formed which, together with the weekly consignments, will be distributed to Divisions in the line at the discretions of Corps.

In case of emergency an Army Reserve both of chewing gum and solidified alcohol is held at No. 2 Field Supply Depot, CAESTRE. Applications for issues from this Reserve should be made to A.H.Q. by wire.

Changes of Formations drawing at Railheads.

8.   As much notice as possible of desired changes of Railhead of Divisions, Divisional Artillery, Army Field Artillery Brigades, or other units, should be given by wire to this Office by Corps concerned, to facilitate the necessary adjustment in Packs and Feeding Strengths.

Railhead Reserves.

9.   To meet inevitable unforeseen moves of small formations, a reserve of not less than 6,000 rations will be maintained at Railheads serving Formations taking part in operations. A suitable reserve of Forage, Petrol and Oils will also be maintained.

Issues of Oxo and Pea Soup.

10.   During the inclement weather, the Army Commander has approved of the daily issue of 2 ounces Pea Soup or 2 Oxo Cubes or other available substitute, such as Cocoa and milk, to men in Trenches, and men of Heavy Artillery during special operations. This will be continued until further notice.

Whale Oil. Oxford Grease. Oxford Powder.

11.   Will be available at No.2 Field Supply Depot, CAESTRE, on demand through R.S.O's. in the usual manner.

Medical Comforts, etc., etc..

12.   Medical Comforts and special supply requirements of Casualty Clearing Stations, preparatory to and during operations, are available at No. 2 Field Supply Depot, CAESTRE. As much notice as possible of exceptional requirements should be given to this office.

Headquarters,

SECOND ARMY.
8th September 1917.

(Sgd) A. PHELPS,
Colonel,
D.D.S. & T.,
SECOND ARMY.

Appendix 4

APPENDIX B.

SUPPLIES.

The following shows detailed Supply arrangements :-

DAY.	SERIAL No.	METHOD OF SUPPLY.	REMARKS.
Attack Day -4.	1 ∅ 2	Train deliver for Attack Day +1. Train deliver for Attack Day -3.	Barrage. From Railhead.
Attack Day -3.	2 3	Consumed. Train deliver for Attack Day -2.	From Railhead.
Attack Day -2.	3 4 5 ∅	Consumed. Train deliver for Attack Day -1. Train Deliver for ATTACK DAY.	From Railhead. From Train Res.
Attack Day -1.	4 -	Consumed. Train deliver - NIL.	
ATTACK DAY.	5 -	Consumed. Train deliver - NIL.	Train Reserve.
Attack Day +1.	1 6	Consumed. Train deliver for Attack Day +2.	Barrage Ration. From Railhead.
Attack Day +2.	6	Normal.	

∅ To be dumped forward under Brigade arrangements.

The above for 68th, 69th, & 70th Inf.Bdes. complete, also Batteries, Fld. Companies R.E., and Fld. Ambulances.

TRANSPORT.

An Advanced Transport Aid Post is established at H.30.d.35.23. (KRUISSTRAATHOEK).

When any vehicle, M.T. or horse-drawn, breaks down or is ditched, notice is to be sent at once to the Advanced Transport Aid Post, in order that the vehicle may be removed and the road cleared without delay.

Tractors and Lorries labelled "FIRST AID" have right of way over any road in either direction.

If any vehicle has to be towed back, the A.T.A.P. will bring it back to its post, and notify the unit concerned, who will fetch it away from the A.T.A.Post.

Emergency lorries are held ready as under to repair without delay shell holes or other damage to roads :-

At ELZENWALLE in charge of P.M.R.E. for roads NORTH of the CANAL, and EAST of the LILLE Road.
At MILLEKRUISSE in charge of No.319 Road Construction Coy. for roads SOUTH of the CANAL, and from the LILLE ROAD inclusive, WESTWARDS.

Emergency Road Lorries are so labelled, and have right of way over all roads in either direction.

Appendix 8

APPENDIX "E".

WATER.

1. Supplementary arrangements issued on 17th inst. are cancelled.

   (i) BATTALION DUMPS.

RIGHT BRIGADE.	JAM DUMP.	J.19.a.5.5.	80 galls.
" "	JEFFERY DUMP.	J.19.c.5.9.	80 "
LEFT BRIGADE.	STIRLING CASTLE DUMP.	J.13.d.1½.3.	80 "
" "	CLAPHAM DUMP.	J.13.d.9.8.	80 "

   (ii) BRIGADE DUMPS.

RIGHT BRIGADE.	OBSERVATORY DUMP.	I.24.d.1.4.	600 "
LEFT BRIGADE.	JACKDAW DUMP.	I.24.b.9.9.	200 "
" "	DORMY HOUSE.	I.23.a.5.5.	400 "

   To ensure water being fresh it should be used and replenished daily under arrangements to be made by Brigades.
   Stoppers to replace those destroyed by shell fire will be drawn from Divnl Bomb Officer, N.1.Central, under Brigade arrangements.

   (iii) CORPS WATER TANKS are allotted to Brigades as follows :-

RIGHT BRIGADE.	TORR TOP.	1000 galls daily. ɸ
LEFT BRIGADE.	STIRLING CASTLE.	1000 galls daily.
		Commencing 20th or 21st.
RESERVE BRIGADE.	I.23.c.6.6.	2300 galls daily.

   ɸ This is additional to the Canadian Tunnellers' Tank which is also at disposal of **Brigades of this Division**, if required.
   Brigades concerned **will be responsible** for posting guards over the above tanks **to ensure** they are not fouled or mis-used in any way.

   (iv) In addition, Tanks capable of producing 1000 galls daily are situated as follows :-

   HEDGE STREET - I.30.b.3.8.   MOUNT SORREL - I.30.c.7.9.
   and HILL 60. - I.29.c.4.5.

Also	TANK No. 60.	H.32.a.2.1.	PUMP HOUSE at H.34.b.1.2.
"	" 13.	H.28.d.2.2.	" " H.35.a.2.9.
"	" 111.	I.21.c.2.8.	" " I.21.b.4.1.
"	" 116.	I.23.d.8.9.	" " I.21.d.8.9.

   Although certain Water Tanks have been allotted to Brigades for the purpose of furnishing guards it must be clearly understood that water parties of every unit must be made acquainted with the location of all water points and given access to same.

   NOTE. As the Tank at STIRLING CASTLE will probably not be ready until the 21st inst. LEFT BRIGADE will have access to the two Tanks at TORR TOP by arrangement with RIGHT BRIGADE.

   In the event of any CORPS TANKS being destroyed by shell fire, priority wire will be sent, addressed C.E., X Corps repeated 23rd Division "Q".

2. (i) O.C. Train will dump 2000 filled Petrol Tins at Tank No. 103 (I.31.d.4.4. - VOORMEZEELE) commencing immediately.

   (ii) Two trucks will be placed at VERD SIDING (I.31.d.1.6.) at 6 p.m. 19th inst., and daily at 6 a.m. and 6 p.m. commencing 20th inst. These two trucks can take up to 1000 filled Petrol Tins.

   The WATER TRAIN will leave VERD SIDING for about I.24.a.Central at 8 a.m. and 8 p.m. daily.

   O.C., No.9. Tramway Coy is arranging for a guide to report at VERD SIDING at 6 p.m. tomorrow to accompany the Water Train and see that the petrol tins are off loaded at I.24.a.Central or any suitable point EAST of where the ZILLEBEKE track crosses the C.4. line about I.24.a.2.5.

   Any change of destination desired will be notified immediately to 23rd Division "Q" by priority wire.

- 2 -

3. Cont. The party of 1 N.C.O. and 10 men already detailed by
(III). 70th Inf.Bde will immediately move to Tank No. 103 for
the purpose of guarding refilling and loading. This party
will be in charge of 2/Lt.CROFT 191 Train Coy. A.S.C.
and will be rationed by their own Brigade, as before, and
accommodated at a point to be selected by 2/Lt.CROFT by
arrangement with 41st Division, in close proximity to No.
103 Tank where they will remain until further orders.

The A.D.L.R. is arranging for a party to off load the
petrol tins at I.24.a.central, and load up empty petrol tins
there.

(IV). This party will be supplemented by 1 N.C.O. and 2 Men
from each of the 68th and 69th. Brigades and will be posted
at I.24.a.central by 8 p.m. 19th inst, where they will remain
until further orders. They will report to Guide provided by
O.C. No 9 Tramway Coy on his arrival. Their duties will be to
assist in off-loading train immediately on arrival, guard and
issue water tins and watch interest of all troops in forward
Divisional Area; COLLECT and assist in reloading the train
with empty tins - full tins only to be exchanged for empties.
It is therefore, essential that all empty tins be sent to
I.24.a.central by 8.p.m. 19th inst.

3. (1). In the event of the Light Railway breaking down O.C. Train
will order 6 G.S. Wagons to stand to from 6 p.m. 19th inst,
ready to report to 2/Lt.CROFT at 103 Tank.

These Wagons will be loaded and sent to VALLEY COTTAGES
I.23.c.8.8. and hand over filled tins to N.C.O. in charge of
tank at this point bringing back as many empty tins as
possible - 180. 2 gall. petrol tins being the correct load for
a G.S. Wagon.

4. A.P.M. will issue necessary instructions to ensure that
all vehicles conveying water, or wagons returning with
empty petrol tins, have a right of way over all roads in
either direction, whatever Division they belong to.

E. F. Falkner.

Lieut.Colonel,
19. 9.17.   A.A. & Q.M.G., 23rd Division.

Copies to :- All recipients of 23rd Divisional
Administrative Arrangements No Q.S. 146.

List of Casualties 21st Sept 1917.   Appendix 9

Corps No	Rank	Names	Coy	Nature of Casualty	Remarks
T4.036790	Sergt	Dyson J.	191	Died of Wounds	By Shellfire
T4.036144	"	Hayes A.	191	Wounded	"
T2.14505	Cpl	Deighton W.T.	192	Killed	By Bomb from aeroplane
T3.02484/	a Cpl	Woodhouse G.V.	192	do	"
T3.029621	Dvr	Nelson J.	192	do	"
T4.216752	Pte	Sykes S.H.	192	do	"
T4.036864	Dvr	Casey C.	192	Died of Wounds	"
T4.216760	Pte	Paul W.	192	do	"
T4.040730	Dvr	Geddes W.J.	190	do	"
S4.158693	Pte	Bennett F.W.	192	Wounded	"
T 35418	Dvr	Bray R.W.	192	do	"
S.4.035659	Pte	Buckley H.	192	do	"
T4.040713	Dvr	Dickey A.	192	do	"
T 33565	"	Gorman J.	192	do	"

Appendix 10

Special Order of The Day
September 23rd 1917.

The following is published for information from Head Qrs Second Army to G.O.C. 23rd Division

The Army Commander directs me to convey to all ranks of the A.S.C. (M.T. H.T. & Supply) in the Second Army, his great appreciation of the excellent work performed by all ranks and which has materially assisted towards the success of the recent operations.

Please ensure that all ranks under your Command are informed of the above.

Signed A Phelpes Colonel.
D.D of S & T Second Army.

H.Qrs Second Army.
21.9.1917.

To O.C. Train.

For Communication to all ranks under your Command Please.

The G.O.C. would also like to add his own appreciation of the excellent work performed by all ranks of the Divisional Train, which has materially assisted towards the success of the task allotted to the Division during the recent operations.

Signed E.F. Falkner.
A.A. & Q.M.G
23rd Division

```
* * * * * *
  SECRET                                      Copy No. 12
* * * * * *
```

23rd DIVISION ORDER No. 151.

Reference: Map Sheets 27 and 28, Scale 1/40,000.

1. The 33rd Division will relieve the 23rd Division between J.21.b.45.15 and the southern edge of POLYGON WOOD (MOLENHOEK – CLAPHAM JUNCTION ROAD inclusive) on the night 24th/25th September.

2. The 39th Division will take over that portion of the front which is south of point J.21.b.45.15 (50 yards north of the MENIN ROAD) on the same night.

3. The boundary between 33rd and 39th Divisions will be J.21.b.45.15 – J.20.b.0.1 – J.19.b.7.0., thence as at present.

4. (a). On relief, 23rd Division will withdraw to areas 4., 6. and 8. in accordance with attached march table, and subsequently to the BERTHEN Area.

   (b). The general allotment of areas will be as follows :–

   (i)   No. 8. area – 68th Infantry Brigade.
   (ii) No. 6. area – 69th Infantry Brigade.
   (iii) No. 4. area – 70th Infantry Brigade.

   Head-Quarters 68th Infantry Brigade will move to No. 8 area on 23rd when relieved by a brigade of 33rd Division.

5. The 70th Machine Gun Company (less 2 sections) will be attached to the 33rd Division to reinforce their machine gun barrage.

6. The 194th Machine Gun Company will move to No. 6 area under orders of 69th Infantry Brigade when that brigade is relieved in the line. Guns in barrage positions may be withdrawn on 24th.

7. The 100th Infantry Brigade will take over the Right Sector now held by 70th Infantry Brigade.
   The 98th Infantry Brigade will take over the Left Sector held by 69th Infantry Brigade.
   These two brigades will move into bivouacs about BEDFORD HOUSE and KRUISSTRAATHOEK on 23rd and will relieve two supporting battalions of 70th and 69th Infantry Brigades respectively during the day of 24th under arrangements to be made direct by G.Os. C. concerned.
   69th and 70th Infantry Brigades will provide guides to ensure that all posts are relieved during the following night.

8. R.E. and Pioneers will be relieved by R.E. and Pioneers of 33rd Division on 24th under arrangements to be made by C.R.Es. concerned.
   R.E. and Pioneers (23rd Division) will be at the disposal of C.E., X Corps, from 25th instant.

9. A.D.M.S. will arrange medical details direct with A.D.M.S. 33rd Division.

10. G.O.C. 33rd Division will assume command of the front at 7 a.m. 25th instant.

11. Acknowledge.

22nd September, 1917.
Issued at 4.50 a.m.

Lieutenant-Colonel,
General Staff.

Distribution overleaf.

Copies to :-

1	R.A.
2	R.E.
3	68th Inf. Bde.
4	69th Inf. Bde.
5	70th Inf. Bde.
6	Signals.
7	"A" & "Q".
8	A.D.M.S.
9	D.A.D.O.S.
10	D.A.D.V.S.
11	D.M.G.O.
12	Train.
13	A.P.M.
14	Camp Comdt.
15	X Corps "G".
16	X Corps "Q".
17	33rd Division.
18	41st Division.
19	1st Aust. Division.
20	5th Aust. Division.
21	File.
22	Diary.
23	Diary.

MARCH TABLE TO ACCOMPANY 23RD DIVISIONAL ORDER NO: 151.

NO:	UNIT.	DATE.	FROM.	TO.	ROUTE.	REMARKS.
1.	1 Bn. 68th Bde.	23.	BEDFORD HOUSE.	No. 8 Area.	OUDERDOM & RENINGHELST.	To No 6 A 24th
2.	1 Bn. 69th Bde.	23.	RAILWAY DUGOUTS.	No. 6 Area.	Ditto.	
3.	1 Bn. 68th Bde.	23.	TORR TOP.	No. 1 Area. H.28.d.3.5.	VALLEY COTTAGE TRACK.	As detailed by G.O.C. 70th Infantry Brigade.
4.	1 Bn. 69th Bde.	24.	FRONT AREA.	No. 1 Area. H.28.d.6.5.	ZILLEBEKE TRACK.	As detailed by G.O.C. 69th Infantry Brigade.
5.	1 Bn. 69th Bde.	24.	Ditto.	No. 1 Area. N.2.b.8.6.	Ditto.	Ditto. This Bn. will move to No. 6 Area during afternoon.
6.	1 Bn. 68th Bde.	24.	Ditto.	No. 1 Area. H.33.c.5.6.	VALLEY COTTAGE TRACK.	As detailed by G.O.C. 70th Infantry Brigade.
7.	1 Bn. 68th Bde.	24.	Ditto.	No. 1 Area. H.33.c.5.6.	Ditto.	Ditto.
8.	Serial No. 3.	24.	NO: 1 AREA.	No. 8 Area.	OUDERDOM.	Not Issued. No 8 before
9.	3 Bns. 70th Bde.	24/25th.	FRONT AREA.	No. 4 Area.	—	As detailed by G.O.C. 70th Infantry Brigade.
10.	1 Bn. 70th Bde.	24/25th.	Ditto.	No. 4 Area.	—	As detailed by G.O.C. 69th Infantry Brigade. Camp to be allotted by 70th Brigade.
11.	1 Bn. 69th Bde.	24/25th.	Ditto.	No. 1 Area. N.2.b.8.6.	ZILLEBEKE TRACK.	Move to No. 6 Area on afternoon of 25th.
12.	Serial No. 4.	25.	No. 1 Area.	No. 6 Area.	OUDERDOM & RENINGHELST.	Not to pass HALLEBAST CORNER before 10 a.m.
13.	Serial No. 6 & 7.	25.	No. 1 Area.	No. 8 Area.	Ditto.	To clear HALLEBAST CORNER by 10 a.m.

Cottopps

69 P Box C - 37 Cony
No 6 Ave
No. 6
Ontario

68 P Box No 8 Ave
Congress Ave
M & E 8 F

70 Rose
No - 33 Traini
Rue L Clyde
West —

719 Waterlu
Sarce
69 5 — 6 ave
70 5 — No 5

SECRET.

23rd DIVISIONAL ADMINISTRATIVE INSTRUCTIONS No. 135 issued with reference to DIVISIONAL ORDER No. 151 dated 22nd September, 1917.

1. BILLETING PARTIES: Advance Parties will report to Area Commandants under arrangements to be made by Brigade Groups concerned.

2. MOVES: D.H.Q. will move to WESTOUTRE, 25th inst., under arrangements to be made by Camp Commandant. Camps to be clear by 7 a.m.

   69th Field Ambce. will move to 69th Bde. Area,
   70th Field Ambce. will move to 70th Bde. Area,
   71st Field Ambce. will remain at WESTOUTRE,
   under arrangements to be made by A.D.M.S.

   The Mobile Vet. Section will move to M.16.a.5.6. on 25th under arrangements to be made by D.A.D.V.S. with D.A.D.V.S. 33rd Div.

3. SUPPLIES: Railhead on 25th inclusive – RENINGHELST.
   Refilling Points will be selected by O.C. Train, who will notify all concerned later.

   The following Camps are allotted to Nos. 2, 3, and 4 Coys.:-

   M.5.c.1.9. – M.5.c.2.8. – M.2.d.9.2.

   23rd Div: Train will ration R.A. and attached units up to, and for consumption on the 25th inst. The 33rd Division rations these Units for consumption on the 26th.

4. ORDNANCE STORES: Will be moved to new area under arrangements to be made by D.A.D.O.S. with D.A.D.O.S. 33rd Division.

5. LORRIES for spare kits will be provided on usual scale. Time and rendezvous required to reach this office not later than 12 noon, 24th inst.

6. The Bomb Store and Baths will be handed over to 39th and 33rd Divisions respectively to-day. The personnel will return to 223rd Employment Coy on relief.

7. The CAMBRIDGE A.R.P. will be handed over by 23rd Div: R.A. to 39th Div: R.A. on 25th, the former reporting completion to 23rd Division "Q".

8. ACKNOWLEDGE.

                                         E. F. Faulkner.
                                              Lieut-Colonel,
23/9/17.
Issued at 4 p.m.   A.A. & Q.M.G., 23rd Division.

-2-

```
Copies to :-    No. 1. C.R.A.           No. 13. D.A.D.O.S.
                    2. C.R.E.               14. D.A.D.V.S.
                    3. 68th Inf. Bde.       15. A.P.M.
                    4. 69th Inf. Bde.       16. S.C.F. C/E.
                    5. 70th Inf. Bde.       17. S.C.F. Non C/E.
                    6. 9th S. Staffs.       18. 223 Employment Coy.
                    7. Signals.             19. N.C.O. 1/c Posts.
                    8. O.C. Train.          20. A.Q. 33rd Div.
                    9. Camp Commdt.         21. A.Q. 39th Div.
                   10. A.D.C.               22. A.Q. 23rd Div.
                   11. "G".                 23. War Diary.
                   12. A.D.M.S.             24. File.
```

SECRET.　　　　　　　　　　　　　　　　　　　Copy No. 12

Appendix 12

23rd DIVISION ORDER No. 152.

Reference: Map Sheets 27 and 28, Scale 1/40,000.

1. The 23rd Division will relieve the 33rd Division in the line on the night 27th/28th with 69th and 70th Infantry Brigades.

2. Busses to convey two Battalions of 70th Infantry Brigade will be at LA CLYTTE at 9 a.m., and for two Battalions 69th Infantry Brigade at G.34.d.0.5. at the same hour.
   These Battalions will debuss as near RIDGE WOOD and SCOTTISH WOOD as possible.
   Busses to convey remaining Battalions of 69th Infantry Brigade will be at G.34.d.0.5. at 2 p.m. Remaining Battalions of 70th Infantry Brigade will march to RIDGE WOOD.

3. Each Brigade will move two Battalions forward during the afternoon to the general line STIRLING CASTLE - CLAPHAM JUNCTION, in readiness to relieve the front line as soon as it is dark.
   BEDFORD HOUSE and RAILWAY DUGOUTS will be at the disposal of 70th and 69th Infantry Brigades respectively for a support battalion.

4. G.O.C. 100th Infantry Brigade commands the present Right Brigade front and G.O.C. 98th Infantry Brigade the Left Brigade front.

5. Dividing line between Brigades will be Road Junction J.15.d.2.7. - J.14.c.0.3. - JAM AVENUE (inclusive to 70th Infantry Brigade).

6. R.E. and Pioneers 33rd Division will be attached to 23rd Division for work.

7. G.Os.C. will assume command when relief is reported complete.

8. G.O.C. 23rd Division will assume command of the front at 9 a.m. on 28th instant.

9. Two Sections 194 Machine Gun Company will be attached to 70th Infantry Brigade.
   Two Machine Gun Companies 33rd Division will be attached temporarily to 23rd Division.

10. ACKNOWLEDGE.

Evans
Lieut-Colonel,
General Staff.

27th September, 1917.
Issued at 12.30 a.m.

Distribution overleaf.

Copies to:-

1	R.A.
2	R.E.
3	68th Infantry Brigade.
4	69th Infantry Brigade.
5	70th Infantry Brigade.
6	Signals.
7	A.&.Q.
8	A.D.M.S.
9	D.A.D.O.S.
10	D.A.D.V.S.
11	D.M.G.O.
12	Train.
13	A.P.M.
14	Camp Commandant.
15	X Corps "G".
16	X Corps "Q".
17	33rd Division.
18	5th Australian Division.
19	File.
20	Diary.
21	Diary.

Appendix 12 A

```
❋⋯❋⋯❋⋯❋⋯❋
  S E C R E T.                                23rd Divn. S.G.104/20/11.
❋⋯❋⋯❋⋯❋⋯❋
```

To all recipients of 23rd Div. Order No. 152.

Divisional Headquarters will move tomorrow to BURGOMASTER FARM and LA CLYTTE.

Evans

23rd Division.
27th Sept.1917.

Lieut-Colonel,
General Staff.

WAR DIARY
or
INTELLIGENCE SUMMARY.
(Erase heading not required.)

Army Form C. 2118.

Place	Date	Hour	Summary of Events and Information	Remarks and references to Appendices
LA CLYTTE	1917 Oct 1st		Railhead BAILLEUL. Supplies drawn by D.S.Col. & Repacking Pends as follows:	
			68 & 13th to METEREN, 69 & 70 & D.W. Tmps to Train Conference Lines	Appendices
			191 Co. moved from HERZEELE to FONTAINE-HOUCK	April 1/A
			Lt. MOLEY & 2nd Lt. GILCHRIST with Div Pack Co. rejoined Train	13-1C
	2nd		Train H.Q. moved to METEREN. 191 Co. to THIEUSHOEK area. 192 Co. to HERZEELE	
			area. to METEREN area. 193 Co. from REMINGHELST area to FONTAINE HOUCK area	
			R.Ps on Train Conference Lines.	
			T/4/257226 S.S.M. EDMUNDS C. joined Train from 5 A. 190 Co	
			33 (Reserve) arrived at BAILLEUL for Divison, collected & distributed by Train	
METEREN	3rd		Thud E. A. NICHOLS transferred from 192 Co to 191 Co. T/4 D. BULGER from 192 C.L.	
			192 Co. T/4 A. CROFT from 191 to 192 Co.	
			69 & 70, 6 Bde's Groups drawn from Railhead by H.T. (reinforced by D.S.Col	
			Baggage & supply wagons of 6 in Battalion 69 6 Bde detached to N. ZEALAND	
			Div Train	
	4th		4pm Conference at Staff Captains. A.T.P. Train allotted.	

WAR DIARY
or
INTELLIGENCE SUMMARY.
(Erase heading not required.)

Army Form C. 2118.

Place	Date	Hour	Summary of Events and Information	Remarks and references to Appendices
METEREN	Oct 6		T/Major W. THOMAS and 2/Lt. MACKIE joined Team from France, also 3 Other ranks	Authority DDSVT II Army No
"	7		2/Lt DE WILTON disappears from 193 C. to 192 C.	2229 dd 3-10-17
"	8		192 C. moved to another Camp in WESTOUTRE area	do.
"	9		2/Lt. LOCKIE to Corduroy Packhorse (Bases) in relief of 2/Lt A.W. MILLER	Appendices 2.
"	10		192 and 193 Companies moved to REMINGHELST and Supplies for all Groups drawn by D.S. Col B.T.Ps on Team Corduroy lines	Authority QMG 820 16.10.15
"			Lt. A.W. HOLLEY to England on Leave to Infantry	
"			Capt. EASTHOPE proceeded on 10 days leave on 9.	RR 193 9/10/15
"			S.S. MOORE to England for Cook School for Off. Cookman	DHS 8-10-17
"	11		Team HQ moved to CHATEAU SEGARD DICKEBUSCH area	
"			2/Lt A.W. MILLER rejoined Team from Corduroy Packhorse Bases	
DICKEBUSCH	12		Capt. EASTHOPE disappeared from 192 C. B 193 C. Capt. A.C. BERRYMAN from 193	
			C. to 192 C.	
	13		Capt R.V. HOLMES appointed Adjutant of Team from 29-9-19 17	Authority H.Off. A.L. 29/39 of 10-10-17
			Railhead OUDERDOM B Siding. Supplies drawn by H.T.	
			Divisional Troops transport supplies to 1st Division	

WAR DIARY
or
INTELLIGENCE SUMMARY

Army Form C. 2118.

Place	Date	Hour	Summary of Events and Information	Remarks and references to Appendices
DICKEBUSCH	Oct 13		2nd Lt. A.N. TURNER evacuated to England returned off strength	S.M.& A.& E 1774/23 B/ 7-10-17
	14th		Dvr. Clifford shot himself. 12 men from Train sent. 1 man admitted to hospital wounded.	
	15th		Bombs dropped by enemy aircraft on camp of 191 Coy. killing 11 H.D. 1 L.D. 4 riders & wounding 9 H.D. 1 L.D. 2 Riders. One man slightly wounded, remained at duty.	
	16th		Court of Inquiry on Pte. Kemp O (Buckingham's C.) of Train who died on 13th.	
			15 Reinforcements arrived UPPER HOEK for Divnl. Mtr. Transport collected & distributed by Train	
	19		193 Coy. moved into No. 70 Bn. (Cavalry) to EECKE and Court of Inquiry on Cpl. NIXON 193 Coy. evacuated on 14 inst.	Appendix 3 - 3.D
			Lt. DD BURGER proceeded on 10 days Special leave to England	
			191 Coy. received 18 recruits from No.2 Advanced Remount Station	
	20th		Lt. Col. MORTIMER President of Court of Inquiry on above	
			193 C. moved to ESQUERDES. Supplies for 70 S/Bge. group by D.S.C.T	No 1
	21st		191 Coy. moved into "Chien Tête" & Corporals Mess of Co. Lt. EECKE	3 E
			Supplies for 70 S/Bge. group from D.I.S. STAVER	

WAR DIARY
or
INTELLIGENCE SUMMARY.

(Erase heading not required.)

Army Form C. 2118.

Place	Date	Hour	Summary of Events and Information	Remarks and references to Appendices
DICKEBUSCH	22nd		191 Coy. moved to LONGUENESSE, 192 Coy. to EECKE with 1st Class Transport	Appendices 3, 4, 5.
			4. 69.S. (Cooper.s.) Report	
			Railhead 69.S. & H.Q. Coy. ORDERED up by H.T., 68.S. & 70.S. Coy. by D.S. Coy.	
			From D.I.S. STOMER	
			H.Q. Team moved to WIZERNES, 192 G.L. QUERCAMP	
	23rd		Railhead STOMER R.P.S. 68.S. LONGUENESSE Church. 69.S. 192.G. Camp QUERCAMP	
			70.S. ESQUERDES Church	
WIZERNES	24 D		Lt. Col. A NORTHEN to England on 10 days leave. Major T.H. MONTGOMERY Ltd ass.	
			Command of Team	
			6 Other Ranks R. & H.Q. clerks joined from BHQE	
	26th		Capt. H NORTHEN Transferred to 93rd Div. Team	D.D.S.T. II Army 2229 - 15-10-17
			Capt. E.R. SOUTHEE took over duties of S.O.1	
			193 G. moved to WIZERNES (BOMBARDEEN)	
			Capt. H.P. BARVAN employed on 11 days leave	
	29		Capt. E. SOUTHEE left with Advance Party for NEW AREA	D.D.S.T II Army
			Major H.N. HOARE joined Team as S.S.O. vice Major W.T.H.M.A.D to 36th Div. Team	T.T. No. 63 28.10.17

Army Form C. 2118.

WAR DIARY
or
INTELLIGENCE SUMMARY.
(Erase heading not required.)

Place	Date	Hour	Summary of Events and Information	Remarks and references to Appendices
WIZERNES	Oct 29		Lt. Col. A NORTHEN rejoined from leave - cancelled.	
"	30		O.C. Col. left for NEW AREA	
"	31		2nd Lt. M. LOCK, IS rejoined Train from Cadet Punchion Board	
			2-11-1917	
			A Northen	
			Lt Col	
			Comdg. 23rd Divl. Train	

SECRET.   Copy No. 12

23rd Division Order No. 153.

Reference – Map Sheets 27 and 28, Scale 1/40,000.

1. The 23rd Division, less R.A., R.E. and Pioneers, will be relieved by the 5th Division and will move to the BERTHEN area in accordance with the attached table.
   Details of relief will be arranged by Brigade Commanders concerned. Maps, aeroplane photos, etc., in possession will be handed over to incoming brigades.

2. Machine Gun Companies will be relieved with their Brigades but will leave two men per gun in action until the following morning.

3. After the relief on night 1st/2nd has been completed, 69th Infantry Brigade H.Q. will move to RIDGE WOOD, proceeding to BERTHEN area on the afternoon of 2nd.
   70th Infantry Brigade H.Q. will move to a.4.d.2.1. after relief of that Brigade is completed on night 2nd/3rd.

4. Completion of relief on 1st/2nd October will be notified by 69th Infantry Bde. to Divisional H.Q. by code words "NOT REQUIRED".

5. The A.D.M.S. will arrange with A.D.M.S.5th Division for relief of Field Ambulances and also for necessary detachments to accompany battalions on the march.

6. The two companies 10th Northumberland Fusiliers now employed under C.E. X Corps and C.R.E.23rd Division will march to No. 8. Area on October 2nd and rejoin their battalion the following day.
   Billets to be obtained from the Area Commandant, WESTOUTRE for night 2nd/3rd October.

7. 23rd Division "Q" will issue orders as to the billets to be occupied in the BERTHEN area and for any moves which may be necessary to concentrate brigades in their own areas.

8. No mention of the relief is to be made over the telephone.

9. G.O.C.23rd Division will hand over command of the front to G.O.C.5th Division at 10 a.m. 2nd October.
   Divisional H.Q. will then move to BERTHEN.

10. Acknowledge.

                                                Lieut-Colonel,
30th September, 1917.   General Staff.

Issued at 8 p.m.   Distribution overleaf.

Appendix 1A

March Table to accompany 23rd Div. Order No. 153.

Serial No.	Unit.	From.	To.	Date.	How.	Remarks.
1	A & B Bns. 13th Bde.	BERTHEN Area.	No. 3 Area.(RIDGE WOOD).	1st.	Bus.)	Busses bring two Bns. &
2	A & B Bns. 95th Bde.	BERTHEN Area.	----ditto----	1st.	Bus.)	return for remaining two.
3	23th Bde. 194 M.G.Co. attached.	No. 3 and 8 Areas.	BERTHEN Area.	1st.	March.	
4	Serial No. 1.	No. 3 Area.	Support. R. Bde.	1st.	March.)	Guides from 69th & 70th
5	Serial No. 2.	No. 3 Area.	Support. L. Bde.	1st.	March.)	Bdes. to be at N.5.b.2.3. for 1 Bn. each at 9 a.m. and 2 p.m.
6	C. Bn. 70th Bde.	Support.	No. 3 Area.	1st.	March.	Camp to be notified by Q.
7	D. Bn. 70th Bde.	BEDFORD HO.	No. 3 Area.	1st.	March.	Camp to be notified by Q.
8	C. Bn. 69th Bde.	Support.	No. 3 Area.	1st.	March.	Camp in RIDGE WOOD. N.
9	D. Bn. 69th Bde.	CANAL BANK	No. 3 Area.	1st.	March.	Camp in RIDGE WOOD. S.
10	Serial No. 5.	Support.	Front Line.	1st/2nd.		
11	A. Bn. 69th Bde.	Front Line.	Support.	do.		
12	B. Bn. 69th Bde.	Front Line.	CANAL BANK.	do.		
13	C & D. Bns.13th Bde.	BERTHEN Area.	(Support. R. Bde. (BEDFORD HOUSE.	2nd. 2nd.	March. March.	Guides for Bns. going up to Support to be at N.5.b.2.3. at 9 a.m.
14	C & D. Bns.95th Bde.	BERTHEN Area.	(Support. L. Bde. (CANAL BANK.	2nd. 2nd.	March. March.	----ditto----

P. T. O.

S E C R E T.   Copy No.

Appendix 1B

23rd DIVISIONAL ADMINISTRATIVE INSTRUCTIONS No. 136
ISSUED WITH REFERENCE TO DIVISIONAL ORDER No. 153
              dated 30th September, 1917.
----

1. ADVANCE PARTIES will be sent forward on cycles under Brigade arrangements for billeting purposes.
   Advance parties must in every case be sent forward to take over all tents, camp equipment, etc. the day before vacation of Units to be relieved.

2. MOVES: Divisional Train Companies move to BERTHEN Area under arrangements to be made by O.C., Train in consultation with Brigades.

   Mobile Veterinary Section will move under arrangements to be made by D.A.D.V.S.

   The Div. Employment Coy will move to BERTHEN Area on 2nd.

3. SUPPLIES: Railhead = BAILLEUL.
   Refilling Points to be selected in Brigade Areas by O.C. Div. Train and the locations reported to Div. H.Q. (Q) for approval.
   The Divisional Supply Column will be used from Railhead to Refilling Points.

4. ORDNANCE: Stores will be moved to METEREN under arrangements to be made by D.A.D.O.S.

5. LORRIES: for spare kits will be provided on the usual scale if available.
   Time and rendezvous required should reach D.H.Q. (Q) by 12 noon the day before the lorries are required.

6. TRENCH STORES & MUNITIONS: List of these stores should be sent to D.H.Q. (Q) by 6 p.m. 2nd October.

7. BILLETS: The following are the areas allotted to Brigades in the BERTHEN Area :-

68th Inf. Bde. & 194 M.G. Coy.	THIEUSHOUK AREA.
68th Inf. Bde. H.Q.	THIEUSHOUK
A Battn.	Q.34. & 35.
B Battn.	Q.36.a.b. & c. - 30.c.& d. - R.25.b.c. & d. - R.31.a. & b.
C Battn.	Q.36.d. - R.31.c. & d - X.1.a & b.
D Battn.	X.1.c & d.
Bde Troops.	Q.29 - X.30.a.& b.

         Now occupied by 15th Inf. Bde.

69th Inf. Bde.	NOCTE BOOM Area.
H.Q.	X.4.a.5.9. & R.34.c.5.1.
A Battn.	X.2.c. & d.
B Battn.	R.33.a. & B.
C Battn.	R.27.a. (less PIEBROUCK) R.27.b.& d.
D Battn.	R.28.a.b.c. & d.

         Now occupied by 13th Inf. Brigade.

P. T. O

```
70th Inf. Brigade.           METEREN AREA.
    H.Q.                     METEREN.
    A, B, C & D Bns.)        X.3, X.4, X.8, X.9, X.10, X.15
    Brigade Troops  )        X.16.
```

Now occupied by 95th Inf. Brigade.

Advance parties must report to Area Commandant, BERTHEN.

69th and 70th Inf. Brigades will detail a permanent billeting party in No. 3 Area.

68th Inf. Brigade will detail a permanent billeting party in No. 8 Area.

These parties will be in charge of camps in their respective areas and allot to units as they arrive on 1st, 2nd and 3rd.

They will return to their Units on 3rd inst. under Brigade arrangements.

Inf. Brigades will occupy areas in BERTHEN Area in accordance with attached Table.

E. F. Falkner.

30/9/1917.   Lieut-Colonel,
    Issued at 10-30 p.m.   A.A.& Q.M.G. 23rd Division.

```
        Copy No.  1  C.R.A.              13  D.A.D.O.S.
                 2  C.R.E.              14  D.A.D.V.S.
                 3  68th Inf. Bde.      15  A.P.M.
                 4  69th Inf. Bde.      16  S.C.F. C/E.
                 5  70th Inf. Bde.      17     "   Non c/E.
                 6  9th S. Staff. R.    18  223 Emp. Coy.
                 7  Signals.            19  Posts.
                 8  O.C. Train.         20  AQ 5th Division.
                 9  Camp Commandant.    21  AQ 23rd Division.
                10  A.D.C.              22  War Diary.
                11  "G"                 23  File.
                12  A.D.M.S.
```

SUPPLY ARRANGEMENTS

Appendix 1C

Date	Location of a.c. Companies 191	192	193	For Consumption	68th Bde Group plus 194 M G Co	69 Bde Group	70 Bde Group	Div Troops	D H Q Units	Fd Ambl 69	70	71
	METEREN	M 2 B 5. d	M 5. C 3. 8	2nd	2 Coy 10 NF already rationed Remainder issued by Supply wagon in METEREN area	Issued to Units by Supply wagons	Issued to Units by supply wagons	Issued to Units by Supply wagons	already drawn on 30th	Issued in forward area	Issued in forward area	Issued in forward area
				3rd	To Coy Camp at METEREN by lorry includes rations for 2 Coy NF	To Coy lines by lorry (less 69 Fd Amb) plus D H Q Units	To Coy lines by lorry includes 70 + 71 F.A. + 70 M G Co	To Coy lines (less 70 M G Co plus 69 F.A.	By lorry to 192 Coy (Units draw in afternoon	Dumped with D.T.	Dumped with 70th	Dumped with 70
2nd	THIEUSHOEK	METEREN AREA	METEREN AREA	3rd	2 Coy 10 NF by lorry to WESTOUTRE Remainder to Units in THIEUSHOEK by Supply wagon	2 Batt by Supply wagons to No 3 AREA Remainder Supply wagons to METEREN AREA	2 Bns by supply wagon to METEREN AREA Remainder to FORWARD AREA	Issued to Units by supply wagons	already drawn on afternoon of 1st	Issued by DT	with 70th	Issued in METEREN AREA
				4th	By lorry to Camp in THIEUSHOEK	By lorry to Camp in METEREN AREA	By lorry to Camp in METEREN AREA	By lorry to Coy lines	By lorry with 69 Group	with DT	with DT	with 70th
3rd	Do	Do	Do	4th	Normal	2 Bns by lorry to No 8 AREA Remainder Supply wagons to Units in METEREN AREA	2 Bns by lorry to No 3 AREA Remainder by Supply wagons to Units in METEREN AREA	Normal	with 69 Bde Group	Do	Do	Do
				5th	Normal	By lorry to METEREN AREA	By lorry to METEREN AREA	Normal	with 69	Do	Do	Do
4	Do	Do	Do	5th	Normal	By supply wagons to all units in METEREN AREA	2 Bns by lorry to No 8 AREA Remainder by supply wagons to units in METEREN AREA	Normal	with 69th	Do	Do	Do
				6th	Normal	Normal	Normal	Normal	Normal	Do	Do	Do
5				6	Do	Do	Do	Do	Do	Do	Do	Do

A. Noble [illegible] Lt Col [illegible]

Appendix 2

S E C R E T.

Copy No. 12

23rd DIVISION ORDER No. 154.

Reference - Map Sheets 27 and 28, Scale 1/40,000.

1. The 23rd Division will relieve the 7th Division on the front REUTELBEEK (J.10.d.8.0) to J.5.b.5.1. commencing on night 10th/11th October. Relief will be completed on night 11th/12th October.

2. 68th Infantry Brigade will hold the Right sub-sector from the REUTELBEEK to JUDGE COTTAGE (inclusive). The 70th Infantry Brigade from the latter point to J.5.b.5.1.
The dividing line between brigades will run from J.12.a.2.2 - J.11.a.9.5. - J.10.b.1.4. - J.13.a.6.3.
Head-Quarters of both brigades will be at HOOGE.

3. The 14th Division will be on the right of the Division and 5th Australian Division on the left.

4. Details of the relief will be arranged by G.Os.C. 68th and 70th Infantry Brigades with G.O.C. 20th Infantry Brigade.
Each brigade should arrange to have three battalions east of HOOGE. The reserve battalion of 70th Infantry Brigade will be in ZILLEBEKE BUND and of the 68th Infantry Brigade in RAILWAY DUG-OUTS.

5. Battalions of 68th and 69th Infantry Brigades in No. 6.Area will move to No. 1 Area tomorrow but will not reach that area before 2 p.m.
The battalion of 68th Infantry Brigade will move at 1 p.m. and those of 69th Infantry Brigade at intervals of one hour under mutual arrangements.

6. 12th Durham Light Infantry, now at SCOTTISH WOOD, will rejoin its brigade from 11th inclusive.

7. 69th Infantry Brigade Head-Quarters and remainder of that brigade in BERTHEN Area will move to No. 6 Area tomorrow afternoon under orders of G.O.C.69th Infantry Brigade.

8. 70th Infantry Brigade Head-Quarters will move to CHATEAU SEGARD tomorrow afternoon.

9. 194th Machine-Gun Company will move tomorrow afternoon to No. 6 Area.

10. A.D.M.S. will make necessary medical arrangements with A.D.M.S.7th Division.

11. The three Field Companies will return to the Division on 11th instant.
The Pioneer Battalion will remain out of the line until its reorganization is complete.
Such part of the 7th Division Pioneers as is working in 7th Division area will remain under orders of 23rd Division.

12. Divisional Head-Quarters and Mobile Veterinary Section will move to vicinity of CHATEAU SEGARD on morning of 12th October.
Command of the front will pass at 10 a.m. on 12th October.

13. Acknowledge.

Lieutenant-Colonel,
General Staff.

9th October, 1917.
Issued at 8 p.m.

Distribution overleaf.

Copies to :-

1. R.A. 23rd Division.
2. R.E. 23rd Division.
3. 68th Infantry Brigade.
4. 69th Infantry Brigade.
5. 70th Infantry Brigade.
6. Signals.
7. A. & Q.
8. A.D.M.S.
9. D.A.D.O.S.
10. D.A.D.V.S.
11. 194 M.G. Coy.
12. Train.
13. A.P.M.
14. Camp Commandant.
15. Xth Corps G.
16. Xth Corps Q.
17. R.E. Xth Corps.
18. 5th Division.
19. 5th Australian Division.
20. 7th Division.
21. 14th Division.
22. File.
23. Diary.
24. Diary.

SECRET. Copy No. 12

Appendix 3

23rd DIVISION ORDER No. 156.

Reference:
Sheets 27 and 28, Scale 1/40,000.

1. The attached tables show the proposed method of relief of the 23rd by 21st Division.
It is based on the assumption that the two mixed brigades at present in the line will be entrained at YPRES on 22nd and 23rd October.

2. The 64th Infantry Brigade (21st Division) will relieve 68th Infantry Brigade on night 21st/22nd and 62nd Infantry Brigade (21st Division) the 69th Infantry Brigade on night 22nd/23rd. Details of relief will be arranged by G.Os. C. concerned. Machine Gun Companies will be relieved on 21st and 22nd October.

3. In order to make room on 21st October for relieving battalions of 64th Infantry Brigade about ZILLEBEKE, it will be necessary to move back a battalion of 69th Infantry Brigade from ZILLEBEKE BUND on that day.

4. Head-Quarters of 68th and 69th Infantry Brigades will occupy the Head-Quarters near Divisional Head-Quarters in turn, the rear echelon of both being accommodated at the Detail Camp west of DICKEBUSCH LAKE.

5. Details will join their battalions previous to marching off to entrain under arrangements to be made by brigades.

6. The 70th Infantry Brigade Head-Quarters will issue any necessary orders to units in No. 6 Area.

7. "Q" will issue orders as regards the movement by road of the Mobile Veterinary Section and of all transport and for the entrainment of units.

8. Separate instructions will be issued as regards Divisional Artillery, R.E. and Pioneers.

9. The A.D.M.S. will arrange for the relief of Field Ambulances.

10. Divisional Head-Quarters will move to BLARINGHEM on 23rd Oct.

11. Command of the Divisional front will pass at 11 a.m. on 23rd October.

12. Acknowledge.

Lieutenant-Colonel,
General Staff.

18th October, 1917.

Issued at 8.p.m.

Distribution overleaf.

Copies to :-

1. R.A. 23rd Division.
2. R.E. 23rd Division.
3. 68th Infantry Brigade.
4. 69th Infantry Brigade.
5. 70th Infantry Brigade.
6. Signals.
7. A.&Q.
8. A.D.M.S.
9. D.A.D.O.S.
10. D.A.D.V.S.
11. D.H.G.O.
12. Train.
13. A.P.M.
14. Camp Commandant.
15. X Corps "G".
16. X Corps "Q".
17. 5th Australian Division.
18. 14th Division.
19. 21st Division.
20. File.
21. Diary.
22. Diary.
23. 7th Div. Arty. Group.

MARCH TABLE TO ACCOMPANY 23rd DIVISION ORDER No. 158.
20th September.

UNIT.	FROM.	TO.	
H.Q. 70th Bde.	CHATEAU SEGARD Bde. H.Q.	No. 6 Area.	Starting point HALLEBAST Cross Roads. To pass starting point at 9 a.m.
Battalion	HALLEBAST CAMP	" "	--do-- at 9.30.
Battalion	BREWERY CAMP	" "	--do-- at 10 a.m.
Battalion	'C' CAMP	" "	--do-- at 10.30.
Battalion	'B' CAMP	" "	--do-- at 11 a.m.
70th M.G.Coy.	Camp	" "	--do-- at 11.15 a.m.
68th M.G.Coy.	Camp	" "	--do-- at 11.30 a.m.
70th T.M.Bty.	Camp	'C' CAMP	March at 10.30 a.m.
Bn. 68th Bde. Group.	RAILWAY DUGOUTS	HALLEBAST CAMP	--do-- 11 a.m.
Bn. 69th Bde. Group.	ZILLEBEKE BUND	RLY. DUGOUTS ZILLEBEKE BUND	To relieve Right Sector front line battalions on 21st/22nd.
Battalion } 64th Bde. Battalion }		BREWERY CAMP 'B' CAMP	To relieve Right Support Bn. 21st/22nd.
Battalion } Battalion }			

21st September.

UNIT.	FROM.	TO.	
1 Battalion } 64th Bde.	BREWERY CAMP	ZILLEBEKE South	To reach ZILLEBEKE South 11.0 a.m.
1 Battalion }	'B' CAMP	RIGHT Support	Bivouac at ZILLEBEKE for dinners.
1 Battalion, 69th Bdo.	ZILLEBEKE South.	BREWERY CAMP	To leave ZILLEBEKE South 11.0 a.m.
194 M.G.Coy.	Front Line	Transport Lines	On relief.

21st/22nd September.

1 Bn. 68th Bdo.Group.	RIGHT Front	RAILWAY DUGOUTS	On relief.
1 Bn. " " "	LEFT Front	ZILLEBEKE BUND	"
1 Bn. " " "	Support	CAMP 'B'	"
H.Q. 68th Bdo.	HOOGE	CHATEAU SEGARD Bde.H.Q.	"

22nd September.

1 Battalion } 62nd Bde.	ZILLEBEKE BUND	RAILWAY DUGOUTS	
1 Battalion }			
1 Battalion } 62nd Bde.		CAMP 'B'	When vacated by battalions of 58th Bdo.
1 Battalion }		CAMP 'C'	Group, dependent on time of entraining.
69th M.G.Coy.	Front Line	Transport Lines	On relief.

22nd/23rd September.

UNIT.	FROM.	TO.	
1 Battalion ⎱ 32nd Bde.	ZILLEBEKE BUND	RIGHT Front, LEFT Bde.	
1 Battalion ⎰	RAILWAY DUGOUTS	L. Front, LEFT Bde.	
1 Bn. ⎱	RIGHT FRONT	ZILLEBEKE BUND	On relief.
1 Bn. ⎰ 69th Bde.Group.	LEFT FRONT	RAILWAY DUGOUTS	" " "
H.Q. 39th Bde.	HOOGE	CHATEAU SEGARD, Bde.H.Q.	" " "

23rd September.

1 Battalion ⎱ 62nd Bde.	CAMP 'B'	ZILLEBEKE BUND	When vacated by battalions of 69th Bde.Group, dependent on time of entraining.
1 Battalion ⎰	CAMP 'C'	RAILWAY DUGOUTS	

TRANSPORT MARCH TABLE.
++++++++++++++++++++

70th COMPOSITE BRIGADE.

UNIT.	DATE.	FROM	TO	DATE.	FROM	TO	REMARKS.
70th Bde. H.Q. 68th M.G.C.(less 2 Secs. plus 1 Sec. 194 M.G.C. and 2 Secs. 70th M.G.C.) 8th Yorks.(less 2 Coys.) 2 Coys. 10th N.F. 8th K.O.Y.L.I. 9th Yorks. No.4 Coy. Divl Train.	19th	Present Area	EECKE Area.	20th	EECKE Area.	WIZERNES Area.	Advance parties report to Area Commdt. EECKE for billets in EECKE Area.

DETAIL OF TRANSPORT TO PROCEED BY ROAD.

No.4 Coy. Divisional Train.
Field Ambulance (less 4 limbered G.S. Wagons by train.).
Each Inf.Bn. 4 Ammunition Limbers, all chargers and pack animals.
Signal Section.
M.G.Coy. (less 5 limbered G.S. Wagons by train.).

TRANSPORT MARCH TABLE.
++++++++++++++++++++

68th COMPOSITE BRIGADE.

UNIT.	DATE.	FROM.	TO	DATE	FROM	TO	REMARKS.
68th Inf.Bde.H.Q. 12th D.L.I. 13th D.L.I. 10th N.F.(less 2 Coys) plus 2 Coys 8/Yorks. 10th W.Riding R. 194 M.G.Coy. No.2 Coy. Divl Train.	21st Oct.	Present Area.	EECKE Area.	22nd Oct.	EECKE Area.	WIZERNES Area.	Advance parties report to Area Comdt.,EECKE, for billets in EECKE Area.

DETAIL OF TRANSPORT TO PROCEED BY ROAD.

No.2 Coy. Divisional Train.
Ammunition, Lewis Gun, and Tool Limbers for each Battalion.
Signal Section.
Machine Gun Coy.(less 5 L.G.S. Wagons and 2 Carts by train.).

TRANSPORT MARCH TABLE.
++++++++++++++++++++++

69th COMPOSITE BRIGADE.

UNIT.	DATE.	FROM	TO	DATE.	FROM	TO	REMARKS.
D.H.Q., & Mob.Vet.Sec. 69th Inf.Bde.H.f. 8th York & Lancs.R. 9th York & Lancs.R. 11th West Yorks.R. 11th Sherwood For. 69th M.G.Coy.	22nd Oct.	Present Area.	EECKE Area.	23rd Oct.	EECKE Area.	WIZERNES Area.	Advance parties report to Area Commdt., EECKE, for billets in EECKE Area.

DETAIL OF TRANSPORT TO PROCEED BY ROAD.

No.3 Coy. Divisional Train.
Field Ambulance (less 4 Limbered G.S. Wagons by train.).
Each Inf.Bn. 4 Ammunition Limbers, all chargers and pack animals.
Signal Section.
M.G.Coy. (less 5 Limbered G.S. Wagons and 2 Carts by train.).

www.ingramcontent.com/pod-product-compliance
Lightning Source LLC
Chambersburg PA
CBHW081424300426
44108CB00016BA/2298